'Legally, I can't even say "Groom Lake",' Ben Rich, former head of the Lockheed Skunk Works, told Phil Patton, but the U-2 and the SR-71 Blackbird spy planes were tested there, as was the F-117 Stealth fighter and captured Russian MiGs and who knows what other craft. Some say those other craft include flying saucers supplied by alien beings. Part of Dreamland, known as Area 51, is alleged to be where alien flying craft are stored, but for years the US government would not admit that Area 51 even existed. Dreamland is not marked on Government maps and US satellite photos of the area are not sold. Private aircraft are not allowed in its airspace. In 1994 the open-skies policy revealed one of the longest runways in the world. Faced with court action in 1995 the US Government admitted it had 'facilities' at Groom Dry Lake. As Phil Patton says: 'I have stood on the ridge above the dry lake and seen the base there and walked as close as the law allows to its perimeter, marked with weird silver balls on poles – high-tech sensors. "Use of lethal force authorised", the signs say . . .'

PHIL PATTON is the author of *Made in the USA: The Secret History of the Things that Made America*, *Open Road* and *Voyager*, an account of the first round-the-world unrefuelled airplane flight. He is a contributing editor of *Esquire*, *Wired* and *i-D* magazines and writes the 'Public Eye' column for the *New York Times*.

Travels in Dreamland

THE SECRET HISTORY OF AREA 51

Phil Patton

MILLENNIUM

Orion Paperbacks
A Millennium Book
First published in Great Britain by Orion Media in 1997
This paperback edition published in 1998 by Millennium,
a division of Orion Books Ltd,
Orion House, 5 Upper St Martin's Lane,
London WC2H 9EA

A CIP catalogue record for this book
is available from the British Library.

ISBN: 0 75281 608 X

Typeset by Selwood Systems, Midsomer Norton
Printed and bound in Great Britain by
Clays Ltd, St Ives plc

Contents

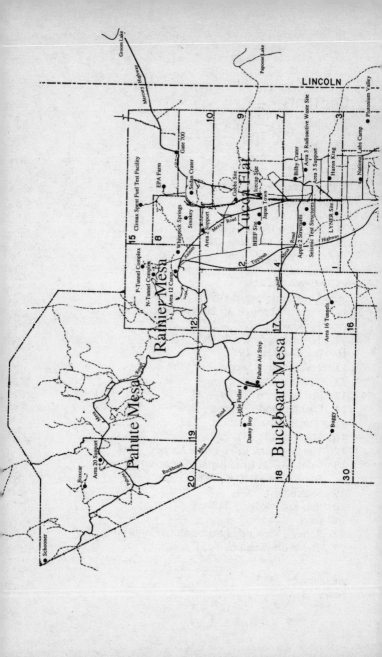

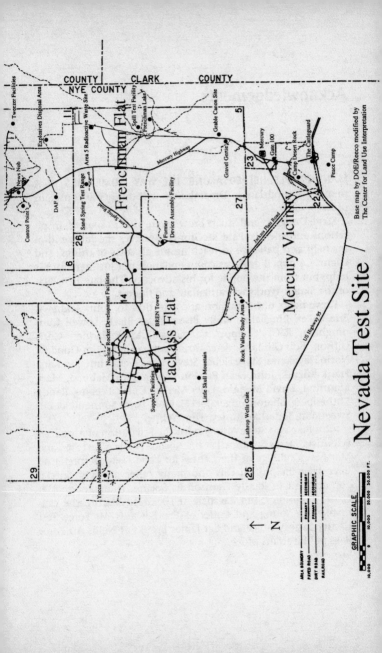

Acknowledgements

MANY PEOPLE HELPED ALONG THE WAY, SOMETIMES IN A manner appropriate to Dreamland – without being conscious of it.

Steve Douglass and Stuart Brown were vital as sources, inspirations and friends. Paul McGinniss deserves special mention for help and patience in teaching me all sorts of things, and Glenn Campbell deserves commendation not just here for his help, but from the public for his advocacy. The late Ben Rich of the Skunk Works was articulate and honest.

I owe debts of instruction and direction to: John Andrews, Eric Baker, Jim Balos, Wally Bison, Peter Black, Lowell Cunningham, R. C. 'Chappy' Czapiewski, Mark Farmer, Chris Gibson, Bob Gilliland, Peter Goin, Joshua Good, Jim Goodall, Norio Hayakawa, Steve Heller, Steve Hofer, Gene Huff, Jon Katz, Frank Kuznik, John Lear, Preston Lerner, Tom Mahood, Mary Manning, David Menard, Peter Merlin, Curtis Peebles, Randy Rothenberg, Sharon Singer, Joel Slayton, Barry Sonnenfeld, Bill Sweetman, Jonathan Turley, Tim Weiner.

John Pike and Steve Aftergood at the Federation of American Scientists, Derek Scammell at the Nevada Nuclear Test Site, and Matthew Coolidge at the Center for Land Use Interpretation have been helpful in this and many other projects. Special appreciation to Randy Harrison at Boeing, Doug Fouquet at General Atomics, Jim Ragsdale at Lockheed Martin, the estimable Drs Young and Puffer at the Edwards Air Force Test Center history office and Sgt James Brooks at Nellis Air Force Base public affairs office.

At the Boneyard

'YOU DIDN'T SEE THAT,' THE OFFICER SAID.

We were walking amid aircraft in the desert in Arizona. It was a boneyard, like the one in the famous scene in the film *The Best Years of Our Lives*, where planes await the day they will either fly again – perhaps for some Third World air patrol – or be crushed in great machines and melted down into pure aluminium.

Hundreds of acres of aircraft shimmered silver in the desert sun south of Tucson – an elephants' graveyard of planes.

Military police in blue berets, shiny black boots and shiny blue pickup trucks patrolled the perimeters. German shepherd dogs rode with them.

It was not a big career builder, this command, and the commander of the facility talked too much – about how important the job was they did here, that it was like a blood bank for aircraft parts, not a graveyard. He hated the word 'graveyard'. I suspected he had been given this job because he talked too much.

We walked down the long aisles of Vietnam era F-105s, their canopies bandaged white like eye surgery patients, the tiger teeth painted on their noses dulled, the red stars counting downed MiGs chipped and peeling. Wherever exposed, the Plexiglas of windows and canopies was scratched, dulled, cataracted. The sun had blistered and flaked the colourful unit symbols, faded the elaborate delicate green and brown mottling of camouflage, and smeared the standard issue military stencils – 'No Step' and 'Rescue'.

We passed round green oxygen tanks stacked in pyramids like cannon balls, ejector seats lined up in a phantom theatre, white radomes piled like dinosaur eggs, and the black cubes of old altimeters.

There were planes I knew only from putting together models of them in my childhood. Hellcat, Avenger, Hustler, Starfighter, Voodoo, Thunderchief. Aggressive names a kid would like.

In an area they called the 'back forty' sat acres of B-52s, their backs broken open to reveal green innards. A clown chorus of bulb-nosed helicopters laughed at us as we walked by. Grass and sagebrush had grown knee-high among flattened tyres. Birds nest behind ailerons and flaps, jack rabbits live in jet intakes.

Even in broad daylight, the back forty is a ghostly place. It's the noise, the creaking of old metal, the writhing rustle in the wind of dangling metal and spaghetti wire, the low whistle of an occasional breeze.

I met a man who had worked in the boneyard for thirty years. He was from Waco, Texas, and his skin had been cured to a leathery red-brown by grease and dust and sun. He paused from his work and said, 'I always make sure to slap the side of a plane with a wrench or something to scare out the rattlers and bullsnakes and Gila monsters before I get too close.'

He was removing an engine. 'Some days,' he said, 'it gets so hot out we have to keep the tools in buckets of cold water just so we can pick them up.

'This whole field used to be covered with '36s,' he said – B-36s, the huge bombers that flew over my house when I was a child, growing up during the Cold War, under the aegis of the Strategic Air Command and the eagle vision of Curtis E. LeMay.

The man went on: 'Had to bring smelters right out here in the field to sweat 'em down. They were too big to move. For days there were columns of black smoke.'

Other craft are dragged to the edge of the field, then chopped by guillotine into parts small enough for the smelter, a huge piece of machinery. At its base, the oven emits a liquid as bright as mercury, as thin as water, coursing thinner than you expect metal ever to flow. 'Molten' is too thick and stolid a word for it, which quickly cools in ingots that are shipped off to be turned into auto parts, pots and pans, folding backyard lawn chairs.

I spent a whole day at the boneyard. Near the end of it, I caught sight of something different in the corner of my vision, a black shape, like a big engine with vestigial wings, with no windows or canopy – no face – no wheels, its shape biological, even aquatic. It seemed greedy and insensate like a deep ocean dwelling creature, with the hungry mouth of a ram jet front, as sinister and mysterious as if from another world altogether.

'You didn't see that,' the base commander and tour guide said evenly. We paused and looked for a while, then moved on.

I did not know it yet, but I had seen my first piece of Dreamland.

1

The View from the Ridge

BEYOND THE JUMBLED HILLS, IN THE WIDE EMIGRANT Valley of southern Nevada, bracketed by the Timpahute and Pahranagat Ranges, lies Groom Lake, just one of many dry lakes that dot the desert reaches of Nevada and California, an expanse of white, hard alkaline soil – caliche, *'ka lee chay'*. Rocky mountain sheep and wild burros wander on its surface and for years the bare horned skull of a sheep sat here, a Western cliché as accent mark.

Relentless winds lift small pebbles and drive them across the surface. Once or twice a year, a couple of inches of rain come and leave a thin liquid layer, a mock lake, shimmering and wavey, whose evaporation rapidly smoothes the surface once more to a polish.

Groom Lake would sit like this for centuries before asphalt and metal buildings, wooden barracks and hangars would arrive, turning it into the Shangri-la, the Forbidden Temple of 'black', or secret, aircraft.

It is set inside 4742 square miles of restricted air space, and nearly four million acres of bomb range – a space as big as a Benelux nation.

It would come to be called by many names: Groom Lake, Watertown, Paradise Ranch, the Remote Location, the Box, Area 51. But the name for the airspace above the lake and the secret test facility and base that would grow there was called, irresistibly, 'Dreamland'. And it was the airspace that made it special, where strange craft appeared and disappeared like whims and suspicions, where speculations glowed and hovered, then zipped off into the distance.

For years it had remained virtually unknown to the public who paid for it, its very existence denied by the government agencies and military contractors that ran it.

It was illegal for those who worked inside to speak of it. Fighter pilots, flying out of Nellis Air Force Base, were forbidden to cross into the Dreamland airspace. They called it 'The Box' and if they strayed into it they were interrogated and grounded.

The most famous planes known to have flown at Dreamland were those created by the legendary Lockheed Skunk Works. But the head of the Skunk Works, Ben Rich, would tell me shortly before his death, 'I can't even say "Groom Lake"'. To those in the know it was simply the 'Ranch' or 'the remote location'.

A child of the Cold War, growing up fascinated with the mystique of aircraft, I knew the legend already: here was where the U-2 first flew, and the SR-71 Blackbird spy plane and the F-117 Stealth fighter – all in secret.

For years only a few grainy pictures of the place – taken surreptitiously from distant ridges or by satellites – served to prove its existence. In theory, it was illegal to photograph – or quaintly, even to sketch, it.

There on the ridge above Dreamland, I would find I was not alone. My fascination was shared by many others. Some were aircraft buffs, Skunkers, Stealth chasers, Interceptors, like my friend Steve from Texas, like the journalist called the Minister of Words, guys with self-bequeathed codenames like Agent X, Zero, Bat, Fox, and others. They were gathered here, trying to find out about rumoured, occasionally sighted, and sometimes only speculated on, planes called Aurora, Black Manta, Goldie and 'the mothership'.

But here, too, I encountered another group, the UFO buffs, the 'youfers' I would call them. Ever since a man named Bob Lazar emerged from the base in the late Eighties claiming to have seen captured flying saucers and worked 'reverse engineering' on the alien craft, black planes took on a new meaning. Area 51 became the world's leading UFO shrine.

To some it was here, on this battlefield, that that strange war we called Cold had been won, an anti-war fought with anti-weapons: spy planes. The U-2 that saved us in Cuba in October of 1962, the Blackbird that defused the superpower confrontation in 1973 in the Middle East.

To a veteran, perhaps cynical, observer of the Pentagon, it was the symbol of a black world run amok, a cult of secrecy grown obsessive, a 'secret city', 'the last great preserve of Cold Warriors, a symbol for that wonderful secret world, a testament to how much fun it was to build hugely expensive planes and save the world'.

To another watcher, who was obsessed by strange craft in the air, whatever their source, it was a site where 'we are flight-testing vehicles that defy description, things so far beyond comprehension as to be really alien to our way of thinking'.

And to still others, this literally meant craft from beyond our planet, recovered in secrecy from desert crash sites or bequeathed in secret treaties with extraterrestrials – craft we were trying to learn how to fly ourselves.

The aliens had lent us stealth technology, one school held, and now they were teaching us about anti-matter reactors.

For the most extreme conspiracists, looking down on the base from the Ridge, it was a place itself controlled by aliens: there had been a shoot-out, the darkest of the stories held, and the aliens who once dined side by side with earthlings in the base cafeteria were now in total control.

Or it was, a final school argued, a place of the grandest deception, a shadow box of saucer stories playing out a Punch and Judy show designed to make us accept a final earthly tyranny.

Most of the 'flying saucers' or mysterious lights were simply flares used to decoy missiles or illuminate targets at night, the military argued, and it was plain that some were also landing lights seen through the distance of the rippling desert air.

'Yeah, they are unidentified and they fly,' one sceptic would tell me, 'and they are sent by a mysterious alien civilization – the Pentagon.'

But it was also clear that those watching for secret planes and those watching for alien craft appeared alike in their fascination and their procedures, in their careful accumulation of bits of knowledge, their descriptions of sightings, and above all, their elusive dreams of a clear view, a clear video image, a clear photograph.

This was the most striking finding of a report on black – or secret – aircraft produced by an organization called the Federation of American Scientists. The FAS had been established in the late Forties by Manhattan Project scientists concerned about the misuses of atomic weapons. In the years since, the FAS had tracked down abuses of military research, Pentagon fiscal waste and excessive government secrecy. Now, with *Mystery Aircraft*, it crossed into a new realm, one of philosophy and cultural analysis, to note that: 'It is useful to consider mystery aircraft not simply as an engineering product, but also as a sociological and epistemological phenomenon.'

What had happened to Dreamland was a parable about knowledge and secrecy, about assembling facts and bits of information into a pattern, about learning and speculation. It was about what the watcher known as Psychospy rather pretentiously called 'the nature of truth', but was perhaps closer to the opposite: the absence of certain truth and the abundance of uncertain lore, legend and just plain 'rumint', as the watchers on the Ridge liked to call it (their version of the military intelligence terms of 'photint', for photographic, 'elint' for electronic and 'humint' for human forms of intelligence).

'The signal-to-noise ratio is very low here,' one Stealth chaser told me. Or as Steve, the master Interceptor, put it in his Texas Panhandle locution, 'It's awful tough to pick the pepper out of the shit.'

It was about mystery engendering fantasy, blank oceans on charts inspiring sea monsters, or the empty spaces in continents which medieval cartographers supplied with elephants.

Now, the curtain was about to go down completely. Freedom Ridge was due to be closed. In a mixture of protest and curiosity, two dozen Stealth chasers, monitors, and UFO buffs climbed to the top of Freedom Ridge for a final glimpse before the shades came down. I had joined them to catch a last look, but I would find it to be only my first.

I had driven up from Las Vegas past the F-15s, F-16s and B-1Bs landing and taking off at Nellis Air Force Base. An ad for the upcoming air show here, sponsored by a large casino, promised 'An American Dream Come True'. The desert seemed like low-resolution detail on a flight simulator game: RISC landscape.

I passed through sudden brief showers. Clumps of cumulus

clouds dragged their own dark shadows across the plains and flung up parodic rainbows from mesa to mesa.

Along the way, the handful of convenience stores at rare intervals boast a remarkable variety of beef jerkies – spice, barbecue and jalapeno.

The only green area on the way up to the base through the desert – lined for miles with tilted slabs of stone, great scarps striated, I thought, like nicely cooked bacon, tans and browns and blacks – was a shock, a sudden interruption, like a stage set, in the middle of a desert drive. The Pahranagat Valley looked like a dark Gothic 1840s vision of heaven, one born of the sensibility of funeral urns and weeping willows, Protestant hymns and early deaths from typhoid.

This strange valley oasis of Pahranagat, its shallow lakes dotted with birds, offered the richest land for hundreds of miles around. In the nineteenth century, horse rustlers used it to fatten animals stolen in Nevada, California, Utah and even Arizona. At one point, some 350 different brands were reported to have been identified among the herds grazing there.

Occasionally, I had read, local vigilantes would attempt to control the rustlers, arresting them and summarily executing them. One culprit was standing with the noose literally around his neck when a crony with a double barrelled shotgun showed up and forced his release.

Past the valley, I came to the little town of Alamo, where someone wanted to sell a down-at-heel cafe, then feeling the engine strain, I climbed up a long, looping stretch of road that crested in a high pass called Hancock Summit, where the road begins to descend and the view opens ahead.

It seems to have taken its name from a murderer named Hancock, a man who passed through the area with his wife and child in the late 1800s. A 1908 map marks the murder site. Hancock was apparently befriended by two local men named Billy Edmonson and Doc Engstrom, whom he promptly murdered, and browsing through their effects for useful items, headed off to California with his little family.

A decade later, Hancock was convicted of other crimes in California, and his wife, feeling guilty but likely intimidated for all those years, told authorities of the Nevada murders. After he had served ten years in a California prison, he was extradited to Lincoln County and tried for the killings of Edmonson and Engstrom. When the verdict came down, he is reported to have politely said, 'I thank you, gentlemen of the jury.'

'You are entirely welcome,' the foreman graciously replied.

Cresting Hancock, with sharp cuts holding the road close on either side, I caught my breath as suddenly, around a theatrical bend in the road, the curtain came up on a vast open view west across a rising plain and a dusty white stick appeared pointing straight up in the air. At least that was my momentary impression; a second later I recognized it as a gravel road, running so straight, so far and so directly up a slope miles away that it only seemed in the perspective like a pole of swirling dust, no longer attached to the land but rising from it like a tightly spun dust devil.

This, I realized, was Groom Road, and cars were running on it, sending up dust streamers – roostertails that hung like contrails – as they moved steadily down then up the slung valley, visible mile after mile, but barely seeming to make any progress. It was the road that ran up over the Jumbled Hills to Dreamland.

We assembled at the trailhead in full view of the 'deadly force authorized' signs, beside the motor home that Psychospy had made his base. Psychospy, the self-appointed watchdog, gadfly, omsbudsman and tour guide of the base, had warned us all: this might be the last chance to see Dreamland.

Psychospy was Glenn Campbell, author of the *Area 51 Viewer's Guide*, organizer of the Whitesides Defense Committee, and publisher of the *Desert Rat Newsletter*. He had discovered the closest and most accessible viewpoint and named it 'Freedom Ridge'. He was delighted when he heard the local guards using that name on their radios. Dreamland was growing.

Once it was possible to walk almost up to the base. But after too many curious citizens, including Greenpeace demonstrators protesting against testing at the adjoining nuclear test site, had disturbed their privacy, in 1984 the Air Force went to the Bureau of Land Management (BLM), then to Congress and had large tracts of previously public land around the base declared part of the Nellis Air Force Base Bomb and Gunnery Range. But two high points that allow a glimpse of the base to intrepid hikers had remained accessible. By the late Eighties, the place began to draw crowds like the apparition of a saint. And it began to draw camera crews and even whole television shows. It began to turn into a legend.

Now, in October, 1993, the Air Force was applying to take over the viewpoints at Freedom Ridge and Whitesides Mountain too.

That was why we were heading for Freedom Ridge: for a last chance to look into Dreamland.

Hiking up to Freedom Ridge, dodging the brambly and fragrant sage and the fuzzy, Muppet-like Joshua trees, we crossed rocks that seem inscribed with some alien cuneiform. We walked a few feet from the perimeter of the base, marked by orange signposts running across the high desert: 'Use of deadly force authorized.' On the other side of this barrier were strange-looking silver balls the size of basketballs on poles. The lore held that they were motion detectors or other sensors. Some claimed they could sniff the difference between a human and a wandering cow or rocky mountain sheep thanks to ammonia sensors. In any case, the exclusion of the public has made Dreamland a *de facto* wildlife preserve.

I had learned about the video cameras and road sensors, triggered by the weight of a passing vehicle. In these still early days on the perimeter, at sunrise, helicopters would sweep along the border to pick up anyone who had spent the night, and sometimes 'sandblast' them with downwash from the rotors.

I had heard of the men on the other side of the barrier, in their camouflage uniforms and white Jeep Cherokees, known locally as 'camou dudes', who keep an eye on intruders and call the local sheriff if need be.

So I kept my eye on the edge, marked with those strange silver balls, until the path bent behind a slope and rose more steeply until, surprisingly soon, we reached the top.

And there it was: I thought of Jules Verne's *Twenty Thousand Leagues Under the Sea*, when Captain Nemo's men crest the top of the atoll and suddenly see dozens of toiling figures down in the circular harbour.

It was all in sharper detail than I had anticipated.

We saw a Jeep come up a road far in the distance. A bus

glittered. The base unfolded beneath us as we reached the crest – the long dry white lake, a line of buildings, fuel tanks, an old bus, the big radar dish, a seven-mile runway – and the white horizontal of the dry lake itself. The vehicle turned around after a while and left.

The hangar larger than the rest is said to house 'the mother ship' and is jokingly known as Hangar 18, after the one at Wright Patterson Airbase, where, according to youfer lore, crashed saucers and recovered alien bodies are stored. But some who come here don't take the hangar designation as a joke – such is the logic of Dreamland, where the deadly serious changes quickly into the absurd, and back again.

I kept finding myself looking back in the other direction, over the valley to the east where the long dirt road puffed up in dust as an occasional car passed.

The only black birds we saw that day were ravens – perhaps a dozen hovering near sunset in the thermals at the edge of the rocks, spiralling in formation.

The ridge at the top was narrow, with a back like a whale, scattered with rocks and tufts of grass and the dead stalks of Joshua trees.

I worked to wedge my sleeping bag in between the rocks before dark made it impossible to move. The images that came instantly to mind were Matthew Brady's photographs of dead sharpshooters on Little Round Top at Gettysburg. I sorted my gear: my flashlight still bore masking tape that had identified it at summer camp as my daughter's. My rations were Yuppie MREs (Meals Ready to Eat) – Power Bars and trail mix, with a self-indulgent Hershey bar thrown in.

I stood gazing quietly down at the base. 'If there are extra-terrestrials,' the heavy man beside me said, 'it would be the greatest discovery in human history. It would be an intellectual crime not to investigate.' He was stern, almost lecturing. He had that chip on his shoulder of conspiracy buffs and rightwingers. 'Please let me finish,' he would say too quickly when someone interjected with an objection or comment.

His sternness implied disrespect, as if we had been children snickering in church. He wore a klutzy pocket knife in a leather holster attached to his belt. We had all agreed not to carry cameras to the ridge, but now he pulled out his camera and began taking pictures.

Since the law also forbade 'sketching or drawing' the site, the notebook and pen I carried would at least in theory make me as liable to arrest as a Nikon.

Other photographers, and film and video crews had been here many times and given *de facto* confessions of their law-breaking by broadcasting the results to millions of people. Our nation's major television networks have broadcast taped views of the secret base, in open and obvious defiance of the law. Yet they have never been charged.

'People get nervous when you mention it,' the heavy man went on. The discovery of extraterrestrial life, he said, would shake people's assumptions too deeply. They couldn't deal with it. It would demolish the conceit that we were the be-all and end-all of creation.

But it occurred to me, the question was not how we would explain the existence of other life forms to ourselves, but how would we explain ourselves to them? How would they deal with us? How would we sum up life here, give a capsule summary of our situation now and the events of even just the last half century?

It was a firmly established part of the youfer lore that one motive for alien visits was to deal with human possession of deadly weapons – the potential for destroying ourselves – perhaps other civilizations in the universe. That was the theme of such films as *The Day the Earth Stood Still* (1951). It was offered as an explanation of why UFOs appeared near Roswell, Sandia, and other weapon storage sites.

The very possibility – and the prospect of Dreamland stretched out before us – suggested that the exercise of account-ing for ourselves was a useful one: what would we say to them?

How would we explain the atomic bomb and the stand-off of two major world powers and near destruction of the planet? Or, even stranger, the end of that war, and the deprivation many felt from its lack, the need for an enemy to define ourselves against?

Dreamland seemed the perfect place to do that. I came to believe that its legend and lore, that the language and para-doxes about it were a kind of weird time capsule encompassing half a century of Cold War and black secrecy, of a unique era in history.

Here, the cultures of nuclear power and airpower merged with the folklores of extraterrestrials and earthly conspiracies; their interference patterns define a *moiré* of the weird.

It was a place perhaps to see our own planet afresh, with the eyes of an outsider.

What you called the place revealed what you thought about what was flying there, told who you were too, in a sense, just as whether you called a group of islands the Malvinas or the Falklands, and whether you said 'West Bank' or 'Judea' or 'Samaria' told who you were. People from the Skunk Works called it 'the Ranch' or 'the remote location'. At Nellis Air Force Base, it was 'the Box', or 'Red Square'.

And to hear someone refer to it as 'Area 51', the name given by the Atomic Energy Commission, now meant that their interest was in flying saucers.

Beneath all these names, the place offered glimpses into the overlapping cultures of UFO lore, of Stealth craft, of nuclear energy and espionage – into a world whose common ground was secrecy.

Before I went, I talked to buffs on the phone late at night. I studied images and descriptions like a traveller anticipating his trip to say, Rome, saving up for months in advance; those months proving in retrospect and on balance the most pleasurable part of the process, and in memory the city he imagined in anticipation came to replace the actual memory of being there after a time. But then too, there was the process of shock and realization as the map took shape in the real world, came alive in 3D with the real sensation of space and distance.

I imagined it quite abstractly, as you necessarily do any unknown land. But it was also, metaphorically, a Black Box, in computer science, a 'unit whose internal structure is unknown but whose function is documented,' according to an encyclopedia definition. Both hardware and software designers use this term to refer to circuits or to a program code that performs a certain function. The internal mechanics of the function don't matter to a designer who uses a black box to obtain that function.

That was important: forget internal mechanics – the viewer was the designer, 'reverse engineering' what was in there, hypothesizing to meet the observed output. Reverse engineering like Lazar's described saucer engineers. It flies ten thousand miles an hour, turns on a dime, now how does it work?

I wanted to reverse engineer a design for the place.

Or as a black body – a perfectly stealthy shape: 'black body', in theoretical physics, is 'an idealized object that absorbs all the radiation that strikes its surface, without reflecting any of the radiation or emitting any of its own'.

But in nature there is no perfect black body. And there is something else about black bodies: 'In theory, a black body is therefore also a perfect emitter of radiation, and at any specific temperature it would emit the maximum amount of energy available from a radiating body, at any wavelength, through temperature alone.'

I was looking for some kind of radiation.

The radiation came from the black world, the world of secret programmes. The black budget. These black or Special Access Required programmes are required by law to be known only to four people in the entire U.S. Congress.

'It's true,' Trader would tell me, 'refer to Title 10, United States Code, Section 119'.

You can read *Aviation Week*, say, absorbing the coolest specifications and programme descriptions of new planes or other weapons, full of ideas about performance envelopes and flyaway costs and then all of a sudden the bottom drops out and you get a sentence such as: 'The other projects, however, remain firmly concealed in the black world.' As if you had sailed to the edge of the pre-Columbian map, and discovered the message 'here lie dragons'.

I had just encountered the New Age term 'portal' – a gateway to spiritual energies, through which UFOs might ride in as on a ramp, as in Sedona or Gulf Breeze – and above which they are said to hover, like fishing boats above a promising spot in the lake. It was easy to snicker at 'portal' but it was a useful metaphor. I came to think of Dreamland as a gateway in another sense – to the troubled dreams of the American soul, assuming you believed in such a thing.

Dreams were the corny core of American commercial mythology. The American dream, dream houses, dream cars, dream girls. Dreamcatchers – the ostensibly native American nets, like miniature snowshoes, that had become a staple of Southwest kitsch.

Dreamland was a state of mind, of course, as much as a place, a locus of information, misinformation and disinformation.

In the age of information Dreamland is an information desert, dotted with bright pebbles and short-lived flowers.

But to call a landscape a desert is like calling a people or tribe primitive – it smacks of ignorance and condescension.

It was a landscape into which much could be read, but it also opened up to another beyond, a figurative, cultural one, of shifting perspectives, of hills even more darkly shadowed. It was a virtual place, a theoretical landscape, like the bomb project called the Manhattan Engineering District, which was in fact a vast geography of installations, at Los Alamos, at Oak Ridge, and at Hanford.

Dreamland, sprung from the forehead of the nuclear test site was like this: the special access programmes for which it was created were the offspring of the granddaddy of all special access programmes, the one that gave us the atomic bomb.

It was a think tank for Cold War engineering, where smart scientists saved the world, as in a science fiction film, the Manhattan Project made permanent. But at the end of the Cold War – a war which produced its own victims of shell shock and battle fatigue, despite never having actually been fought – Dreamland was the centre of a great network, in ruins now.

Dreamland is the tabloid edge of technology, aptly sited near Las Vegas: it is to technology what Las Vegas is to normal economy. They are looking for 'silver bullets' in Dreamland, aiming to striking it rich with superplanes, to hit the jackpot of invincibility.

The players are the quiet important ones in the military industrial complex: Bechtel, E-Systems, TRW, Hughes, Lockheed, SAIC, and perhaps the least known of all, EG&G.

Standing on the ridge, listening to the discussions, picking up lore, I learned about this company called Edgerton, Germeshausen & Grier (EG&G), which did all sorts of things at the test site, from photography to security, and elsewhere had tested radars, measured radiation and run an airline. The 'Edgerton' is from Harold Edgerton, the MIT physicist and photo whiz, the man best known for his stroboscopic photos of bullets passing through apples. He used this technique to photograph atomic explosions for the military and soon his company had expanded to provide a variety of services to the Air Force, CIA and then Atomic Energy Commission. EG&G has a building at McCarran Airport in Las Vegas from which it operates the so-called 'Janet' Airline of 727s that fly to Groom Lake. The planes ferry workers – perhaps a thousand, perhaps 2000 – to and from the base. Buses with blacked-out windows carry others from Crystal Springs or Alamo, mere wide spots in the road closer by.

On the ridge, black plane buffs, true believing youfers, agnostics and sceptics, radio scanners and heavy optic fans, mingle in the democracy of curiosity. Even old test pilots come up here and look at the runway from which they had once taken off.

Standing on the Ridge, I realized that its value grew not out of how much you could see, but how little: how great the opportunity it created to see, to imagine, fantasize, dream. 'It can be whatever you want it to be,' one of the youfers had said. I came to imagine the ridge imperfectly, dividing what is seen from what is imagined, what is known from what is secret.

The irony was that they were spying on spies, peeking in on remote locations at people and machines whose job was to peek in on remote locations. They wore the same camou as the camou dudes that guarded the place, listened on the same scanners, watched the watchers with the same nightscopes. Their spying was made possible by the Pentagon: by the Internet it had created and the computers its money had developed. In effect, they were self-made spies spying on real spies. And, I would find, others were spying on the spies spying on spies. It was *MAD* magazine made real. And Dreamland too – 'the remote location' as it was euphemized in hundreds of contractor references – took on qualities of other, even more remote locations: Kapstan Yar, Tyuratum, Lop Nor. Conceived as a place to facilitate the 'penetration of denied areas', it ended up itself a denied area.

For a time, I thought of Dreamland as resembling the prints of Hiroshige, such as his *Twenty-four Views of Edo* in which large things in the foreground get in the way – or in which the deep backgrounds are really only there to accent that foreground. In that floating world, the image of Mount Fuji is always there, but off in a corner somewhere – the real subject is the stuff in the foreground.

'The problem', the watcher known as the Minister would tell me in a phrase I couldn't forget, 'is that the place has no *edges*.'

No edges, but a perimeter. Video cameras, sensors, guards, signs, vehicles, choppers. *Laws*.

'Use of deadly force authorized' the signs famously said, citing the Internal Security Act of 1950 – also known, notoriously so – as the McCarran Act. It was named, as is the airport in Las Vegas from which the Janet flights bring workers to Dreamland, after Nevada Senator Pat McCarran but it was promoted and written mostly by then Congressman Richard Nixon and Karl Mundt. It struck me as appropriate to think of Richard Nixon writing the warnings on the perimeter.

The law's language includes one of the clearest and most specific statements of the outlook and assumptions of the Cold War Warrior. It declared: 'There exists a world Communist movement which in its origins, its development, and its present practice, is a worldwide revolutionary movement whose purpose it is, by treachery, deceit, infiltration into other groups (governmental and otherwise), espionage, sabotage, terrorism and any other means deemed necessary, to establish a Communist totalitarian dictatorship in the countries throughout the world through the medium of a world-wide Communist organization.'

Many of these weightier thoughts, conceived in advance, of course vanished on the scene, but not all. This was a military base, at heart, and therefore a temple of routine and tedium, of the grittiest sort of reality.

*

The light began to fade, the warm sun to soften as it sank. The cold wind flickered around our limbs. We all got together and built a privy, in a wedge of rocks, draped with a blue tarpaulin for privacy.

Two teens spoke in a controlled tone, curious, not fanatic, but credulous too. 'Lazar spoke the other day. My friend went. Said he was very open, friendly. Answered questions.'

They talked about Dulce, in New Mexico, where there were said to be dozens of aliens living underground. By one account they had massacred their guards and were in control of the complex. There was also the Anthill, near Tehachipi, and Helendale, other underground bases.

There was talk of things flying in and out of apertures in the concrete at night. 'Say there are dozens of aliens underground there too,' one teen said, keeping all astonishment, all indications of belief or suspicion from his voice. 'Say they are in full control.'

Of course I wanted to know what was down there, what was inside Dreamland. But more interesting was what was *thought and dreamed* to be there.

Everyone seemed to be selling a different version of Dreamland, representing their own views, agenting their own image. You had to make your own way, blaze your own trail, trace your own thread through the data. It was like Vannevar Bush's view of information in his 1947 – that year again! essay – *As We May Think*: the scientist claimed to have been the head of the mysterious MJ12 and had laid out a vision of information through which the individual blazed his own trail, but left markers for others. What he was describing was very much like threads on the Net.

As the sun went down, we built a fire, collecting stubs of Joshua trees which looked like soft, oversized pieces of coral but burned with surprising surges of flame and then a fitful glow.

The UFO types talked about Lazar. A fat girl talked about wanting to see something strange – not UFOs themselves, but weird UFO types.

*

'This,' Glenn Campbell (Psychospy) said around the campfire that night, 'is about the nature of truth.' Thank you, Pilate! But he was right. It was about truth, knowing and seeing. Especially it was about seeing – about epistemology and phenomenology, if you wanted to get fancy. Campbell did – he listed himself as philosopher and psychologist. That was right, he thought, even if it meant distancing the 'content' of the lore.

I could handle epistemology – the science of knowing – but there was unknowing here too. This was the ridge between believing and inventing, I concluded, between information and disinformation, where more ideas hung in the air than parachute flares or hovering saucers.

From here I would learn how weirdly the paradoxical worlds of real planes kept secret and imagined aircraft made public paralleled each other.

But mostly it was about not knowing, about cupping mystery in your hands like a match in the wind on the ridge, a precious flame of uncertainty.

I found myself drawn back again and again to the perimeter. I would use whatever opportunities took me to Las Vegas for some dreary convention or to Los Angeles to divert to the area. Eventually, I had to acknowledge my growing fascination: I began to plan, more or less systematically, travels to circumnavigate the area. I spent too much time on-line delving into the lore of the area, too much time in libraries. I appointed myself a kind of investigator of the place. One of the odd effects of visiting the ridge seemed to be that it made visitors feel this impulse to investigate, in a vigilante way. So I came to fantasize: I saw myself as a mock version of one of those explorers charged by Congress and the Corps of Engineers with delving into distant reaches of the West, the guys like John Wesley Powell or Clarence King. The idea of a travel account of a place you couldn't physically visit was irresistible.

But I got a surprise: the place seemed to spin me away from it so I could find out more about it. And I would become more fascinated with the watchers than with watching: my self-assigned travels turned into a kind of shaggy dog story, where the tail wagged the enormous invisible beast.

There is an Indian petroglyph, a spiral, that is thought to

represent language. This was my spiral: out and then in.

The camou dudes grew to near mythological stature. Reports tended to overstate their aggressiveness wildly: visitors were warned to avoid letting the sun glint off binocular or camera lenses, as if such a flash of a light would draw M-16 fire. In fact, the fundamental condition of their jobs, as of those of most rentacops, was tedium. Intruders were irritants and incidents meant paperwork. In the old days, they had ranged freely on public land, working on the principle of deterring the curious before they got near the perimeter.

The camou dudes follow, lurk and watch. Cameras and audio listening devices hung on poles or from their vehicles. Video cameras had been set up around the perimeter, and there were sensors on the roads that detected any passing vehicle, fairly crude battery-powered devices packaged in old ammunition cases, buried by the edge of the road. When disturbed by passing magnetism they emitted a radio signal, indicating their location. Some were set up on public land, in the area administered by the BLM.

At first they were called the Wackendudes, when Wackenhut was handling security on the perimeter. Then, when it became clear that most of them were from another agency, and deputized as part of the Lincoln County Sheriff's office, they became just the 'camou dudes', or the 'dudes'.

Wackenhut, which also ran the security force at the Nuclear Test Site, had risen to the top of the rent-a-cop business. Like Bechtel or RAND or Mitre, it was one of the specialist organizations that grew up in the Cold War. George Wackenhut, an ambitious former FBI agent, joined with three other ex-agents in 1954 to form the private security agency. He was politically well-connected and enjoyed close friendships with Florida Senator George Smathers, a carousing pal of JFK, and later Governor Claude Kirk, who did most of his carousing alone, to obtain government contracts. An 1893 law, passed in resentment at the use of Pinkerton detectives to break strikes and protests, forbade the Federal government to employ private detectives, but Wackenhut's lawyers found a loophole and began to obtain government contracts as guards. Wackhenhut managed in this way to grab contracts for the Titan missile silos and Cape Canaveral. Soon Wackenhut guards were working, not just for NASA, but also for other agencies, guarding embassies around the world, and sometimes handling jobs for the CIA and other parts of the government who wanted to keep their fingerprints off, say, moving armaments.

I had met Wackenhut men at the Nuclear Test Site and they looked like they spent more time working out than reading, for example. Dressed in temperate zone camou, neither did they seem to be students of the natural world around them. Now that Wackenhut had shifted to an emphasis on more promising business strategies, such as operating prisons under contract for governments eager to 'privatize', EG&G found itself in the security business too, with guards and even SWAT teams at the NASA and DOE facilities where it had contracts. But the camou dudes seemed to be a mixture of private and Air Force guards. Psychospy managed to discover – after one of the dudes flashed a Lincoln County deputy sheriff's ID while hassling him – that many of the 'dudes' were deputized. Their deputizations were on public record. Psychospy got the records and published many of their names. The notary involved was a man who had an office right on Paradise (!) Road in Las Vegas.

I went up to the notary's office in the middle of a business day and found it closed. There was no name on the door.

As night fell, the lights came on in the base below, where personnel were probably watching television amid the inevitable military tedium that attends even the most exotic of projects, more intently than they watched the few people, high above Dreamland, watching them.

I fell asleep at last. The camp sites were scattered, miscellaneous, like the social dynamic. I woke to hear the fat girl groping her way down the ridge in the middle of the night, sleepless and grumbling.

2

The Black Mailbox

THE NEXT MORNING, AFTER DESCENDING THE MOUNTAIN, WE paid the obligatory visit to the Black Mailbox. It is found near milepost 29.5 of Highway 375, about twenty-five feet west of the pavement: a large round-topped mail box painted black. Lazar used this mailbox as a convenient landmark to direct viewers to watch for the appearance of the craft he said flew from Dreamland.

But from a mere landmark, the Black Mailbox quickly became a monument, a symbol and icon as hundreds of watchers flocked to the area hoping to catch a glimpse of saucers rising above the mountains from the Groom Lake base.

Could any symbol be handier than a mailbox? A key trope of the information age, a repository for missives – some official, some personal, some commercial – love letters and junk mail, the believable and the exaggerated.

The box belonged to rancher Steve Medlin, whose cattle had the right to cross into Dreamland – and did. They also lurked by the side of the highway, looking positively eager to be mutilated by aliens, and loped across the road to endanger rental cars driven by UFO tourists – black cattle against black pavement at night. 'Stealth steers,' someone called them.

In the lore, the Black Mailbox was the very epitome of the Groom Box itself, of secrecy, of the mystery that is a curiosity and fascination, compelling us to fill it with our own messages.

It was the iconic relative of the Black Chamber, the Manhattan office in which Herbert Yardley famously broke codes until 1929, when an outraged WASP Secretary of State, Henry Stimson, declared 'gentlemen don't open each other's mail'.

The relative too, of Kelly Johnson's personal mail box in Encino to which government cheques came directly – rather than through Lockheed – to preserve secrecy in a time of handshake deals and lean and mean development at the Skunk Works, then building the U-2.

And perhaps, too, of the black lacquered box in which the British, desperate for help in the Battle of Britain, carried the breakthrough they had made in radar – along with the atomic bomb, the most revolutionary weapon of that war, to the United States, to trade for military help.

It was the perfect symbol of Dreamland itself! Of Area 51! Of the whole black world, the black budget! Of the Cosmic Cover-up, the Grand Deception! It spoke of blackmail and Men in Black and black helicopters.

What you could see from the Black Mailbox 'was better than having sex for the first time', Gene Huff would say '– not for the second time, but the first'. It was that exciting, seeing the lights, the discs, appear over the Jumbled Hills when Bob Lazar took him out there.

These were the first sightings, the ones that kept people coming out, that gave Dreamland its appeal.

I thought as I stood at the Black Mailbox – as everyone did who stood there – about the original sightings, those of the people Bob Lazar took out to the road, one Wednesday night in March, 1989.

Arriving from Las Vegas in an RV, they pulled up on the Groom Road and soon saw a bright light rise above the mountains, jumping and dancing around in the sky, then coming to a dead stop, hovering, before slowly sinking back down behind the Jumbled Hills.

Huff recalled that the light was so sudden and bright they instinctively moved behind the open boot of the car, to shield themselves. The next Wednesday night, they returned and the disc staged an even more breathtaking performance, blinking – and with each blink seeming to jump toward them.

And this was the remarkable thing, the lynchpin of Lazar's credibility: he could tell when the saucers would come. After the reports began to appear, more and more people made the pilgrimage to the Black Mailbox to enjoy the same thrill.

And thrill they did. They saw everything from red darters to orange orbs, green glows to discs that turned on the proverbial dime and shot away at incredible speed. They thrilled to 'objects that glow with an amber light and flitted like fireflies', to dots that 'performed zig zag movement incomprehensible in terms of conventional aerodynamics'. They talked of HPACs – 'human piloted alien craft' captured or donated saucers, flown by humans.

Their accounts appeared on the Internet, full of a sense of menace – more in anticipation of the camou dudes than from their actual behaviour. They all had the same sense of being among the first ever to see. And as a rule, the farther the distance they had travelled to get there, the more they saw.

Was it just that they had come all the way from Norway that worked one group into a lather of twenty or thirty sightings one night, none of which were recorded, for some reason, on their videotapes? The group posted a verbose account of their visit to the Mailbox on the Internet. The account tells of dozens of saucers and a sky filled with 'lazars'. I nearly jumped – was this a spell checker error or simply imperfect English? The 'lazars', the report said, crisscrossed and danced across the sky in all colours – laser beams. They thought they saw fake clouds, generated by machinery, that hid the saucers from view – lenticular clouds produced by weather manipulation technology. But only the actual words of the viewers can capture their intensity:

> ... the first sightings were lights bouncing ... We watched flickers, flashes, and sparks – also tremendous rapid 'streaks' of light from base to cloud. ... Now for the following time until 2:30am we were having continual sightings. Up to six ships at a time, appeared ... All in all, we had at least 40 sightings ... We grew accustomed to the ships in such a short minimal period of time. After an hour and a half, we were 'used' to them ... There was no 'threat' no nothing, just playful, curious encounters – goes to show HOW fast we humans can grow accoustomed (sic) to things. ...
>
> I turn and there's a beautiful 'green' ship hovering ... Then another one came in to the right, an orange one. We sat watching, enjoying and agreed upon turning the car around and get closer to the green object, more Pleiadian shaped than the others we had seen ...

... At the bottom of it, two bright lights in motion, but connected to the wholer ship, all in orange colors ... It vibrated and was as if it were ... alive ... there was definitely a feeling of life & intelligence ... for several minutes we were paralysed in joy and disbelief...

This particular sighting was the longest one of them all, and gave us real time to 'tune in' to it, and become 'acquainted' with it's presence ... We were feeling so relaxed about it all, didn't seem at all strange that we were there with UFO's, and the next thing we thought was like: '... so, now what?'

Yet the locals, the citizens of Rachel and Lincoln County, themselves rarely saw anything at all out of the ordinary. Of course the ordinary included all the craft flying from Nellis, dozens of planes from Nellis' Red Flag, Green Flag and other exercises roaring over the area east of the forbidden box. Helicopters, flares, lights.

To Sean David Morton, self-proclaimed 'world's foremost UFO authority', and erstwhile astrologer, predictor of earthquakes and channeller from Hermosa Beach, California, it was the only place in the world where you could see flying saucers on a regular schedule and therefore the only place to which he could lead people for good money. This was their landscape, the visiting youfers felt. One of them, Gary Schultz, proclaimed himself the world's authority on Area 51, and established a tourist-like outfit he called 'Secret Saucer Base Expeditions' and had the temerity to rename one of the mountains nearby after his girlfriend, Pearl. No one else called Whitesides 'Pearl's Peak'.

But was it not odd, the Interceptors noted, that the schedule corresponded to that of flights from McCarran to Groom Lake? That Old Faithful – the UFO that appeared each Thursday morning so predictably that Morton could be sure his customers would not be disappointed – coincided with the schedule of the early Janet airline flight bringing workers from Las Vegas? Didn't a lot of the green lights suggest magnesium flares dropped by fighters to decoy heat-seeking missiles or illuminate ground targets?

For the black plane buffs, the sightings tended to be more widely dispersed, as far away as Beale Air Force base, and

Mojave. Supersonic planes after all could take the width of a good-sized Western state just to make a turn. Agent X spotted a bat-winged aircraft over the town of Alamo, just up the road from Rachel, but so did Steve, in Texas.

For the black plane watchers, Dreamland was simply the end of a corridor that ran back to the aerospace centre on the Antelope Valley, to Edwards AFB and Palmdale's factories. They were the suburbia of aerospace, to which the contractors moved from their original urban factories in Long Beach, Culver City, Burbank, and Santa Monica. Dreamland was the vacation house, the country place, where the serious hunting and fishing went on.

For a time, *Aviation Week* would report in great detail such sightings under headlines such as 'Possible Black Aircraft Seen Flying in Formation with F-117s, KC 135s,' and the details would make hearts beat faster. Some of the hearts were in the medal-encrusted chests of Air Force generals, who expressed displeasure to the editors. In any case, when correspondent Bill Scott was shifted from Southern California to the magazine's Washington bureau, such articles became fewer and notably less speculative.

Some pointed to contrails – the 'donuts on a rope' said to be characteristic of the new high-tech 'pulse detonation engine' – a real enough technology, but of unclear technical maturity.

There were sounds as well as sights: the 'Aurora roar' or the 'pulser sound' 'like the sky ripping', 'a very very low rumble, like air rushing through a big tube'.

The black plane watchers and the youfers were two very different groups, but they would find themselves standing side by side looking at the same sky, seeing different things and uttering a common cry: 'did you see that?'

Driving back down to Las Vegas I passed through rain, and saw a double rainbow, arched from mountain to mountain. I wouldn't have believed it had I not seen it myself, as the sighting reports say.

At home much later, when I listened to my tape recorder, what came through from my time on the ridge was the noise of the wind, hissing, flickering, licking. Much noise, little signal. Or was the noise itself the signal?

3

'They're Here!'

THE BOTTOM BEGAN TO GLOW BLUE AND HISS SOFTLY AND THE silver saucer rose about twenty-five feet and stopped, hovering, Bob Lazar recalled. It was the one he called 'the sports model', your basic sci-fi flying saucer, but with square windows, one of the saucers he claimed the US government was flying and 'back engineering', they called it, in a corner of Dreamland known as S-4. The saucers were hidden inside a cliff behind Papoose Dry Lake, just to the south of Groom, behind sliding doors camouflaged so they were invisible to distant viewers and to satellites.

This was the tale that emerged in the spring of 1989 when Lazar showed up on a TV show in Las Vegas, his face disguised and his name changed to 'Dennis'. It was the tale elaborated – and firmly installed into the Lore – that autumn in a nine-part series created by newsman George Knapp on Las Vegas' Channel 8, KLAS, the local CBS affiliate. He would appear again and again on radio shows the rest of that year, and be featured on Nippon TV. His story soon became a basic book added to the bible of UFO lore.

Lazar's story went on like this:

I saw flying saucers in Dreamland. I worked on flying saucers owned by our government in an area called S-4, at Papoose Lake, south of Groom Lake. I thought I was going to work at Area 51 but was taken in a bus with blacked-out windows to a place where I saw the saucers.

I learned of antimatter reactors used to bend gravity waves fuelled by element 115, a reddish orange substance, of which we have about 500 pounds and which comes in discs the shape of half dollars. I had one but the government stole it back.

I saw golf balls bounced off the gravity wave the reactor from the saucer generated. I was allowed to read strange documents – autopsy images of aliens, and a history of the earth as viewed from Zeta Reticuli where the aliens came from.

I saw my fellow workers wearing security badges with one light blue diagonal stripe and one dark blue and the letters MJ. My supervisor had one that read 'Majestic'.

I saw little chairs in the saucers that suggested little creatures – aliens.

Once I walked by hangars and caught glimpses of – I think – a little alien. But I'm not sure. It could have been a million things. But I think I saw one.

For me, the weirdest part of the story was not the saucers or the aliens, however. It was the poster that Lazar said he saw in the offices at S-4, the one with the picture of a saucer hovering above the desert and the words, 'They're here!' It looked, he said, as if it had come from K-Mart.

It began with a chance encounter with Edward Teller, the father of the H-bomb and godfather of Star Wars. Lazar had been working at Los Alamos, for a contractor to the physics lab there called Kirk-Mayer. His job involved particle detection equipment – Geiger counter stuff. He was linked to the Meson or Positive Proton Lab. Locals remembered him as intelligent, kind but a bit of a con man, trying to rustle tools and funds for another project.

In his spare time Lazar had designed a 'jet car', a weird mating of a Honda CRX and a jet engine. The local paper, the *Los Alamos Monitor*, had done a story about Lazar and his car, right there on the front page, and on 23 June 1982, the day after the story appeared, Lazar went to a lecture Teller was giving in town. Before the lecture, he spotted Teller reading the *Monitor*. 'That's me you're reading about,' Lazar told him, and chatted to him.

Several years later, after his marriage had dissolved and his finances gone to rack and ruin, after he had been let go by the contractor in Los Alamos for using government equipment to work on the jet car, after he had moved to Las Vegas he would write to Teller, seeking work. And Teller would direct him to the people who hired him as what Agent X would later call 'the Mr Goodwrench of flying saucers'.

That autumn of 1988, Teller called back, saying he didn't have any jobs for physicists – which is what Lazar presented himself as – but knew someone who might. Fifteen minutes later his phone rang again. It was the folks at EG&G, inviting him for an interview that led to the job at S-4.

At the interview, Lazar would brag, he had 'dazzled' them. Who were they? EG&G at first, but his final employer he said was listed as the Office of Naval Intelligence. Lazar was able to produce a W-2 form that totalled his earnings as $977.11.

In December, 1988, Lazar would say, he began work at S-4. He described being flown to Area 51 and waiting in a cafeteria for a bus with blacked-out windows that then carried him to S-4, ten or twelve miles away.

Lazar had come to Las Vegas in April 1986, broke, his first marriage in ruins, trying to start over again. On 19 April 1986 he was married at the We've Only Just Begun wedding chapel of the Imperial Hotel to a woman named Tracy Anne Murk.

Two days later his first wife – from whom he was never formally divorced – committed suicide, inhaling carbon dioxide in the garage of the Las Vegas home the two jointly owned.

In October, he declared bankruptcy, and married Murk again – only this time she called herself 'Jackie Evans'.

With the bankruptcy and new marriage, Lazar had begun to put the past behind him, to put his life together again – and his self image.

Bob Lazar liked to feature himself as a physicist, as in his most widely circulated photograph, chalk in hand, in front of a blackboard covered with abstruse equations, like Oppenheimer or Teller. He claimed attendance at MIT and Cal Tech and said he had two masters degrees. But all that was documented was that he had attended Pierce Community College and had a mail order degree from a place called Pacifica University.

He talked of 'getting back into physics', as if he had been a major lab scientist and referred to the great Edward Teller as

'Ed'. But he wasn't a physicist in any professional sense. He had made his living as a technician and later as the owner and operator of a fast photo processing outlet.

Gene Huff first knew him as 'Bob, the photo guy'. Huff was a real estate appraiser in Las Vegas who, like many in his business, used Lazar's photo shop to develop pictures of houses. Lazar's shop would deliver developed pictures to the real estate agents. Usually, his wife Tracy made the deliveries but sometimes Lazar did himself, driving his Honda CRX jet car – using its regular motor only. It was on these occasions that Gene Huff got to know Lazar, talking with him about science and technology. They were both interested in explosives and were part of a group that went into the desert to set off big explosions. Huff once saw Lazar mix up some nitroglycerine at his kitchen table. Lazar was also fascinated by rockets.

Lazar liked fast cars even better than big booms. He once drove a 1978 Trans Am powered by hydrogen, owned a Corvette – until it was repossessed – and a sporty Honda CRX, and he showed up at the Ultimate UFO Conference in Rachel in a Corvette with a matching female in the passenger seat. He built the jet car – the one that was featured in the *Los Alamos Monitor* that Edward Teller read, a Honda Civic with a jet engine in the back and the licence plate JETUBET. Later, he would borrow $2000 to build a jet-powered dragster, a 32-foot long conglomeration of steel pipe with a surplus Westinghouse J-34 jet engine from a Navy Banshee fighter. Its top speed is over 400 mph.

Tom Mahood, the most relentless archivist among the Interceptors, travelled to Los Alamos and Las Vegas to document Lazar's life. Lazar had been born in Coral Gables, Florida, adopted, and attended high school in Long Island. There was no record he had attended Cal Tech or MIT as claimed. But on 27 June 1982 the *Los Alamos Monitor* referred to him as a physicist at the Los Alamos Meson Physics Facility, or as he called it, the Polarized Proton section. His aptitude seemed to be for particle sensing equipment – he was at work on an improved Geiger counter type of machine that could identify the particles detected as well as signal their presence.

A geeky-looking character with large glasses – your classic nerd – Lazar described his work at S-4 as a different speciality entirely: trying to figure out the propulsion system of the saucers. There were nine different kinds of saucers, he reported, and he gave them nicknames: the sports model, the one he saw fly – it resembled the silver discs photographed by Billy Meier in Switzerland – the jelly mould, the top hat.

The saucers travelled by means of a gravity wave generator, involving a reactor of some sort, and an amplifier that directed the waves. Lazar took credit for identifying the fuel on which the reactor ran as 'element 115', a heavy rust-coloured substance with an atomic weight far greater than that of lead. He had surreptitiously pocketed some of the supply of element 115. He called it his way of proving his story, but it had been stolen from his house.

But – and here he assumes his role as 'physicist' – Lazar expressed shock at the crude state of the research at S-4 and the low qualifications of those doing it. They tried to make a saucer run on plutonium instead of 115, he claimed, and it had been a disaster. (But one that subtly tied in with other elements of youfer lore, such as the Cash-Landrum sighting, in which two women who saw a saucer suffered radiation sickness.) And they had foolishly cut open a reactor while it was operating, Lazar said. It was the resulting deaths, in 1987, that had opened up a job slot for him. In Lazar's account, he did that job very well: it was he who, in only a few days, dealing with 'materials, that were – pardon the pun – totally alien,' he said, and he who had figured out the principle of the thing. He was a big time physicist at last, working on a project even bigger than Edward Teller's.

If anything proved Lazar's story, it was that he knew when the saucers were due to be tested – they flew on Wednesday nights – and would appear over the Jumbled Hills between the Groom Lake road and S-4.

He took Huff, John Lear and others up to see the saucers fly. On 15 March, using Lear's RV, Lazar, Huff, Lazar's wife and sister drove up to Groom, turned out the headlights and headed down the long sloping dirt road that runs up into the mountains and eventually to the Groom Lake perimeter, sweeping through a bowl of a valley for fifteen miles or so.

Lazar, looking through a telescope, soon reported an elliptical light rising above the mountains which were between them and S-4. The light began jumping and dancing around, doing step moves in the sky. Then it would come to a dead stop and hover. But after just a few minutes, the light slowly sank back down behind the mountains.

The next trip was more dramatic. On Wednesday, 22 March 1989, Huff recalls, 'we arrived right at dusk, turned our lights off, and went in about 5 miles on the Groom Lake road.' On this trip were Lazar and his wife, and a guy named Jim Tagliani drove up.

The next Wednesday, 29 March 1989, Lazar, his wife Tracy, Tagliani, and Huff rented a Lincoln Town Car 'to make the trip a little more comfortable'. They all owned compact cars and the round trip out to Groom Lake was a rough one: 'We arrived, turned our lights off, and went in about 5 miles on the Groom Lake road. We pulled off on a side road and unloaded our video camera, telescope, binoculars, etc. out of the trunk and we left the trunk lid open.'

The disc came up around the same place but, this time, it staged a breathtaking performance. It repeated moves similar to the week before, but this time it came down the mountain range toward them. At first it seemed far away, then they would blink and it would seem a lot closer, then they'd blink again and it would seem much closer. There was no sense of continual movement; the disc simply 'jumped'.

The object was also incredibly bright, Huff recalled, so bright they moved behind the open boot of the car, to shield themselves, reflexively seeking protection as if from an explosion.

Lazar told them this quality of motion was due to the method of propulsion and the way it distorts space/time and light. He also explained that the bright glow of the disc was due to the way it was energized. 'The fact is that an explosion was the only thing, other than the sun, that we had ever seen that was as bright,' Huff would recall. They took a videotape, and the camera recorded the sighting at around 8:30.

It, too, eventually sank down behind the mountains and they left. Never, Huff would record, had he seen or heard of anything comparable to this in the sky in central Nevada.

The next Wednesday, 5 April 1989, the party consisted of Lazar, Tracy Lazar and her sister, Huff and Lear. They arrived shortly before dusk. On the drive out, Lazar told them he had been called to go into work the next day. Huff recorded, 'Numerous security vehicles were sweeping the roads that the cattle ranchers use to round-up their cattle after open range grazing. It seemed that this night, more than the previous Wednesday nights, they wanted to make sure no one was outside of Area 51.

'We tried to sneak in using our usual "stealth" mode,' Huff would recall, 'but security saw our brake lights and began to chase us. We tried to beat them out to the highway, but they came from all directions and ultimately we had to stop. We told them we were simply out there star gazing, which they didn't believe for one moment. They agreed that they couldn't chase us off of public land, but simply said they would "prefer" that we retreat back up to the highway. They issued us a copy of a written warning that said we were approaching a military installation and cited the relevant statutes, including the penalties for taking pictures of the base.'

Then the group returned to the highway, but didn't leave. A short time later a Lincoln County deputy named LaMoreaux pulled them over, and asked for identification. He took their IDs and radioed the security base station. It was obvious, Huff felt, that the guards and the sherriff's office worked together. But the deputy finally let them go.

The next day, Lazar got a phone call. His supervisor at S-4, Dennis Mariani, had learned of the last expedition to the Black Mailbox. He was to report for debriefing. 'When we told you this was a secret,' Lazar recalled Mariani saying acidly, 'we didn't mean you should bring your family and friends to watch.'

On 7 December, Friday, Mariani drove him up the forty-odd miles from Las Vegas to the old air field at Indian Springs. There, Lazar was grilled. They told him the test scheduled for the night he was caught had been cancelled. But this was the odd thing: according to Lazar, they neither fired him nor revoked his security clearance! He simply never went back to work.

*

He had been warned about Security from the beginning with a gun to his head. Security people visited his house again and again and dropped in on his friends. The disc of element 115 he had secreted disappeared.

When Huff and Lazar talked at Huff's home, they were sure they were being overheard by listening devices, so they passed notes when they were together; Huff burned them afterwards. They referred to each other as Bufon and Gufon, a joking reference to the UFO organization MUFON (Mutual UFO Network).

Once, someone shot out a rear tyre on his car while he was heading for the airport. The Indian Springs meeting was another warning.

But still, in Lazar's tale, it was not these indiscretions that led to his job's termination – indeed, in his tale he was never really fired – but the discovery that his wife was having an affair. At the time he says he worked at S-4, Tracy/Jackie was taking flying lessons of her own. And soon she was having an affair with her flying instructor. This made Lazar possibly unstable – and a potential security leak. All her phone calls had been recorded and transcribed. By May the couple would be separated.

It was then that Lazar decided to go public. He had already recorded a video interview with newsman George Knapp and in May he agreed to appear on camera, but in disguise, to tell his story again.

The contact was John Lear, who had met Lazar sometime in 1988, when Huff was appraising Lear's house. Lazar was a sceptic about UFOs then, Huff would recall, and he wanted him to listen to Lear. The show in which he took Dennis Mariani's first name as his own alias ran in May.

But it was not until 10 November, when new coverage identified Lazar by name and showed his face that the story had a major impact. On 21 November, Knapp and Lazar together appeared on the *Bill Goodman Happening*, a powerful AM radio show on KVEG AM, with a huge audience. On 25 November, KLAS ran a two-hour compilation of the Lazar interviews and other clips under the title *UFOs: The Best Evidence*. On 20 December he was back on the Goodman show. Lazar was hardly keeping a low profile and now the story was getting international coverage.

Lazar increasingly relied on Huff as his confidant and his handler in dealings with the Press.

Lazar wanted someone else to get a confirming look at Dennis Mariani, his supervisor, so he set up a meeting with him at one of the casinos in Las Vegas. Without telling Mariani, he brought Gene Huff along.

Huff had been told what to look for: a bulky ex-Marine type, with a little blond moustache. In what Huff called a 'stealth' strategy, they got there early. Finally Huff picked him out. Mariani was sitting at the blackjack table between two large-breasted women and behaving oddly – that is, he was not looking at them at all! In Las Vegas, it seemed to Huff, this was highly aberrant behaviour. But even worse, Mariani wouldn't pay any attention to Lazar. He pretended not to recognize him and the meeting never came off. Mariani had noticed Huff, perhaps, and Huff caught sight of someone who looked like a security man with him.

The next spring, Norio Hayakawa, the UFO researcher who had seen the KLAS TV broadcasts, brought Lazar to the attention of Nippon TV. In February 1990 he took the Japanese crew to Las Vegas. They interviewed Lazar at what was described as his house there. It all felt strange, Hayakawa thought. There wasn't much furniture, it didn't look lived in. A man introduced only as 'a friend' sat beside Lazar all the time and even followed him when he went to the bathroom. The man had some kind of a beeper on his belt.

Lazar suggested a time and place the crew could watch the saucers fly, film them and confirm his story. He sent them to the Black Mailbox. At 6:45 one morning they saw a bright light over the Groom Mountains. At 8:15 there was a brilliant orange orb, jumping erratically.

Lazar agreed to appear live on Japanese television. He was scheduled to fly to Tokyo to appear on the show. He had even accepted tickets for himself and Gene Huff. But Hayakawa waited for him in vain in the terminal at LAX. He never showed. When Hayakawa telephoned, Lazar told him that he could not come; his life was in danger. His tyre had been shot out when he was on the way to the airport. But significant money had changed hands, as well as the plane tickets, so to save face, the network set up a telephone link: that way, Lazar could at least answer phone-in questions live during the show. In Japan some 30 million viewers saw the programme.

Then something even weirder happened. In April 1990, not long after the Japanese show, Lazar was arrested for 'pandering', an obscure charge, akin to living off immoral earnings, in Nevada. On 18 June he was convicted.

Lazar had long boasted about a legal brothel he had planned to start when he was still in Los Alamos. He planned to call it the Honeysuckle Ranch and there is some evidence he filed the necessary legal papers and even had T-shirts made up. But whether the brothel idea was simply a running joke, a fantasy, or a half-realized business effort remains unclear.

The Las Vegas episode had begun when, after his separation, in Huff's wonderful phrase, Lazar 'took comfort with a hooker'. He became friendly with the girls and, according to the charges, had ended up working with a prostitute named Toni Bulloch and helped set up a computer data base – hadn't the Mayflower Madam used such high-tech methods? – for a brothel in the Newport Cover apartments, a Spanish-style complex with little red tiled roofs near the airport.

Sentenced to community service, Lazar helped install computer systems for worthy organizations and showed up at a Las Vegas children's museum to give courses in computing. But those researching his probation report found that all government records about Lazar's past had been sealed away under a Federal 'need to know' restriction, intriguing the believers. Was it a further part of a plot to silence Lazar, to make him disappear? Had he been set up for the whole charge? Or was the government just protecting its own?

This mystery made Lazar's story irresistible. His manner had the same effect: a combination of bright highlights and dull spots. To John Andrews, his appeal lay in the fact that he was one of the rare UFO witnesses to say 'I don't know'. He refused to speculate on the source of the saucers, for instance. A secret treaty, perhaps? Recovery? He wasn't sure.

There were problems with his story, of course. The Social Security number on the W-2 form did not belong to a man named Robert Lazar. The CV Tom Mahood had shown did not jibe with reality.

There were many objections to the way Lazar described the saucer programme. He was shown more than was believable. Special access programmes were famously 'compartmentalized'. The engine people were not allowed to see what the wing people were doing, and so on. At Groom Lake, for instance, the SR-71 ground crews never knew the destination of the planes. But in Lazar's accounts he was offered glimpses – and sometimes he said he thought he was allowed these glimpses as tests of his loyalty – of all sorts of aspects of the programme.

Lazar took two polygraph (lie detector) tests, but both were inconclusive. At best, the tester said, Lazar believed what he was saying, but he might have been relaying information given to him by someone else.

And Tom Mahood's researches into Lazar's background revealed deception: however much power 'they' had to erase his past, it is inconceivable that they could have altered all copies of MIT or Cal Tech year books and directories to make Lazar's attendance vanish.

In his essay 'Lazar as fictional character', Psychospy got to the core of Lazar's appeal: that willingness to admit the limits of his knowledge, the restraint in his speculation and the almost eerie consistency of his tale through interviews over years. It was perhaps like a witness who tells too good a story in court. Yes, there were a few places that didn't gel. Once Lazar said that one of the saucers, 'looked like it was hit with some sort of a projectile. It had a large hole in the bottom and a large hole in the top with the metal bent out like some sort of, you know, large caliber 4 or 5 inch (shell) had gone through it.' But in most interviews he said, 'None of the discs looked damaged to me.'

Still, it was remarkable how steady Lazar was in his telling and Psychospy praised the 'impressive coherence and integrity of the story itself'.

It is: 'far superior to most science fiction in creating a world that could be true.

'His is the sort of story I could believe because it is subtle, detailed and restrained, involves only a very limited government conspiracy and does not digress into any kind of speculation.'

It was just these qualities about the tale, the watcher known as the Rat noted, that explain why it '... appeals to engineers, computer programmers and other techie types'. It is 'heavy on plausible technical details and free of the emotional overtones' that characterize some other shrill UFO accounts.

'If Lazar's story is fiction, it's great fiction, filled with a richness of plausible details and complex philosophical dilemmas that you can't find in most popular novels these days.'

And yet it was exactly this similarity to the tone of a fictional character's tale – sometimes detailed, sometimes vague, highly subjective, with even at times an hallucinatory quality; the sense of imperfect memory washed out by mind control or other means, that made me think of Lazar as different kind of fictional character.

His descriptions include odd details, like worlds melting into one another. Sometimes his mind seemed like a teenager's room, with its posters on the wall and designations like 'sports model' – a Frisbee brand name – and 'variety pack' as he called the nine different saucer designs he had seen.

The more I studied his tale, the more Lazar reminded me of the hero – or anti-hero – of a science fiction novel by Philip K. Dick. Many of Dick's heroes are dweebish, sometimes seedy, average guys who get caught up in matters of planetary import. They live in crass commercial worlds while dealing with important philosophical questions. And they face realities that fade in and out of each other, raising questions – are there sinister influences at work or only demented solipsism? Is it in my head or is something very wrong with this universe? They often feel they are in a carefully-crafted illusion, but that some of the works have spoiled the effect by leaving empty sandwich wrappers and soda bottles around.

Their lives have the quality of half-waking dreams – time and space are warped as well as by any gravity wave amplifier from the sports model. Lazar's tale, too, has the same quality of a dream. Levels of reality drift in and out of each other in a weird way. Details of the quotidian world blend with those of the Lore.

He noticed that the security badges bore blue and white stripes and the legend Majic – 'it made me crack a smile' – because it is straight out of the Lore: MJ12, the famed secret committee, Majestic. (MJ is said to be a security clearance '38 levels above Q' the demarcation of so many levels is a frequent feature of youfer lore.)

'I don't know whether it was a kind of nostalgia thing,' he commented. 'I began to wonder is this really the Majestic everyone talks about, or was it something done almost for nostalgia reasons . . . Assuming the Majestic 12 documents were false, did these guys just use this insignia for the hell of it, kind of as a joke?'

And the flip side of Lazar's unwillingness to speculate is that the big issues of the more tendentious lore are ignored: do the aliens run the base? How did we get the saucers? Was there really a link to MJ12? The implication of these questions lies heavily over the Lazar story – it is part of the intriguing quality of it – but it could also be designed that way: to stir up and latch on to the implications of the rest of the Lore.

Another dreamy effect was the strange alien book Lazar says he saw. He was allowed to read the book, which combined a history of the Earth and a history of Reticulum 4. The book had pages that were translucent, like an encyclopedia with a series of acetate layers, but all in one sheet, so you could see into a house, x-ray style, from brickwork to chimney insides.

In the book, Lazar said, human beings are referred to as 'containers' – for souls or for genes or whatever is unclear.

It detailed some 65 'genetic interventions' beginning at the time when men were still apes – a tweaking of DNA. These interventions appeared to be designed to make the human being a breeding species for the aliens – a kind of grafting stock for a race that had lost its ability to reproduce.

This was one of the finer details of the story: it implicitly helped answer the sceptics who would say, out of all the planets in all the stars in the universe, how come the ones that came here happened to share this same weird shape of our human bodies with only minor variants of size and proportion?

But – to consider Lazar's account simply as a story for a moment – introducing information in this way is a clumsy plot device, worthy only of a computer adventure game, like Myst, say, or a wavy transition from an opening book to real action in a film. The book serves as a device to introduce a lot more information than would otherwise have come to Lazar's attention, than he could have seen directly.

This dreamy quality, the hazy aura of Lazar's whole story was part of its overall appeal.

Unlike many UFO sources, he didn't claim to know every detail, or fill in the gaps with the 'it is thought' or 'it has been observed' sort of qualifications common in the Lore. He had begun as a sceptic; he had gone on record as deriding the youfers.

Another convincing detail, in shaping his own image and character, is Lazar's statement that when he first caught sight of the saucers, he thought they were terrestrial military craft. 'Well, there's the explanation for UFOs', he thought. 'We must have made them, our military.'

But when he learned they were not from Earth, he had a strange reaction. That night, he said, he lay in bed, unable to sleep – giggling.

What charms in Lazar's accounts is his reluctance to overstate. 'I hate to mention this,' he would say. 'I don't want to get too deeply into that,' he would say in answer to a question, lending more mystery, or 'I don't like to talk about this'.

He was almost coyly casual about his one sighting of an actual alien. It could have been a mannequin, he says, or a mock-up. 'It could have been a million things.'

But Lazar's story has the useful feature, too, of leaving edges – like the round sides of jigsaw pieces – that invite associations with the rest of the Lore. The very vagueness and limits of his knowledge inspire the listener to make other links. He's not sure where the saucers he saw came from – could it have been Roswell, or the storage site at Hangar 18 at Wright-Pat? He hears rumours of the shoot-out with aliens – perhaps it was at S-4, or Area 51, or at Dulce, as the Lore tends to have it?

*

In the spring of 1989, when he went public, Lazar must have felt that his past troubles were repeating themselves. The new life he had built in Las Vegas and his second marriage were falling apart. When he took his wife out to see the saucers, there was already tension between them. He knew about her affair.

A recurrent theme in Lazar's story was his sense that they – his employers at S-4 – were 'trying to make him disappear' by removing records. This happened even before he left the job. In fact, he claimed that it was this sense that he was being made invisible that led him to go public. He couldn't find records of his own life, he said: 'They're trying to make me look nonexistent,' or elsewhere, in a weirdly dislocated locution, he felt 'that someone was going to disappear'.

Was this the driving force, or was it in another sense that he saw himself disappearing – that he saw his life collapsing around him – again? Only two years after regaining his feet economically and remarrying, his second marriage was in trouble. He had learned that his wife had been having an affair – a fact the security people knew about before he did. That affair made him a security risk. Was he cracking up?

Worse, he was forgetting things. Had they done something to his mind? Had he been given something to drink, as the Lore held they often did? It was supposed to have a smell like disinfectant, like Pinesol.

His memories were disappearing too. By September of 1990 he was complaining he had forgotten the name of the two modes of travel of the saucers – one low speed, the other high, intergalactic speed – and resorted to calling them alpha and beta. Nor could he any longer remember an important coefficient for one of the processes, he said, or certain frequencies of the gravity wave and other details he was convinced he had once known. 'I've developed a mental block,' he said. 'It really bugs me.' Lazar went to a hynotherapist, one Layne Keck, to help him remember, but it was not very successful.

Lear noticed too, that Lazar at some point began to forget things. 'Don't you remember that night you came over to my house all excited?' Lear asked him. But Lazar had completely forgotten it. It was a night in January, 1989, (or perhaps 6 December 1988), Lear recalls, when Lazar came by his house in a state of high excitement. Lear was writing out cheques, paying bills. 'It was bitterly cold, but we talked outside because it made him more comfortable. He was in shirt sleeves. He told me about seeing the alien. He was very excited. Now, he can't remember it.'

'I saw a disc,' Lazar told him, in Lear's account.

'Ours or theirs?'

'Theirs.'

'I just got back from the test site.'

'Oh, my God. What are you doing here? You should continue to work up there for a while. Don't jeopardize your security clearance.'

'But John,' Lazar replied, 'you've taken so much flak about this stuff that I'm going to tell you.'

'And for the next three hours and 47 minutes he proceeded to tell me all of it. He told me we did have secret bases on the Moon and Mars. He told me things, some of which were so unbelievable, had I not known Bob, I would have been very suspicious.'

Once Lazar was asked 'Don't you feel – no pun intended – alienated? In fact aren't you kind of connected with them, and removed from the rest of society that doesn't accept them?'

'Absolutely, I feel like I really know what's going on, and everyone's an idiot. I really feel that way. Alienated is the perfect word for it.'

He was, you might say, a classically alienated type. But the S-4 experience had given order to his life.

The saucers phenomenon, he said, was 'the only thing that makes sense: it takes a lot of the confusion out of things. A lot more knits together ...'

So Psychospy was spot on in his essay 'Lazar as fictional character' – take the account as fiction, he says. The implication is that if Lazar did not exist the youfers would find it necessary to invent him. That they *may* have invented him, or that AFOSI or some other government organization may have invented him or that he invented himself are possibilities that hang in the air like the lights over Dreamland. But who would invent Lazar, and why? Or did someone else make Lazar up? Was he a government disinformation agent? But again why?

As cover for secret programmes: to make sure that people believe the lights they see moving above the Jumbled Hills are flying saucers instead of manned terrestrial aircraft or more likely UAVs (Unmanned Aerial Vehicles)? The Stealth fighter was revealed in the autumn of 1988, just as Lazar went to work at S-4. Was there a connection? Other craft to hide? But Lazar's story would only draw more curious viewers to the perimeter, where they might see real aircraft while looking for Lazar's saucers. (Indeed, the first images of the Stealth fighter, heavily airbrushed, were released about the time Lazar surfaced.) To make the Interceptors appear indistinguishable from the youfers? Or to muddy the water in general? Some of Lazar's lore seems to dovetail too neatly with the MJ12 papers' disinformation.

Did Lazar invent himself? For money, or for fame?

There was a film deal, although the amount of Lazar's income from the rights was unclear. The film languished in production. Originally due in 1994, it went through many scripts and suffered from the troubles of the production company, New Line. And he had been paid to serve as consultant for a plastic kit of the 'sports model UFO'. Packed with each kit was a poster, just as Lazar had described, bearing the words, 'They're here!'

Did he do it for fame? Or maybe just to become a legend in his own mind, to feel comfortable and real there in front of the blackboard in the Teller/Oppenheimer pose, to become at last a real authority, someone to be listened to, an expert?

Ironically, had Lazar really had the education to go work with Teller and his kind on bombs he might never have delved into the saucers – whether they were real or not.

His story hovers on the Ridge. Studied and restudied, chewed over, tugged at, poked, prodded and twisted it quickly became a modern legend of its own, obsessing viewers who came to the Black Mailbox to see if they could see Lazar's saucers.

4

Aurora

IN THE 1890s, STRANGE REPORTS BEGAN TO SURFACE OF
airships drifting over the Midwest and West. There were tales
of mysterious airships in Appleton, Wisconsin and Harrisburg,
Arkansas, but Texas had the largest number of reports.

Some of the crews talked to those on the ground. One group
asked for food. Another was said to have sung *Nearer My God
To Thee*. There was even a cattle mutilation report: a steer had
been lassoed, pulled into the airship, roasted and eaten, and
only the skin and bones dropped back overboard.

The height of the craze came in April 1897. One report, on
19 April, came from the small town of Aurora, Texas. Appearing
in the *Dallas Morning Times*, it told of a craft crashing into a
windmill, of wreckage and a pilot's log being found. There was
even word of one of the crewmen – and speculation held they
were from Mars – being killed in the crash and buried in the
small town.

The reports resembled those of the post World War II flying
saucer era, except that the speeds cited were in the tens or
hundreds of miles per hour, rather than thousands, and the
materials cited were no more exotic than aluminium.

The mid-1890s were a period of economic depression, political instability and general cultural unease. The first diri-
gibles – 'air ships' – had flown in Europe and Samuel Langley
of the Smithsonian Institution flew his crude aircraft from a
houseboat on the Potomac River in May 1896, an event that
was given widespread publicity. The invention of the plane
seemed imminent. Aurora was a dusty little town, bypassed by
this sort of progress and prosperity as it was bypassed by the
railroad. Having an airship sighting meant being up to date;
an account of another sighting in Denton, Texas suggested that
the event proved Denton 'was not behind' other towns.

But the report from Aurora was one of the most dramatic, and quite startling in its claims:

About 6 o'clock this morning the early risers of Aurora were astonished at the sudden appearance of the airship which has been sailing throughout the country. It was travelling [. . .] due north, and much nearer the earth than before. Evidently some of the machinery was out of order, for it was making a speed of only ten or twelve miles an hour, and gradually settling toward the earth. It sailed over the public square and when it reached the north part of town [it] collided with the tower of judge Proctor's wind-mill and went to pieces with a terrific explosion, scattering debris over several acres of ground, wrecking the windmill and water tank and destroying the judge's flower garden. The pilot of the ship is supposed to have been the only one aboard, and while his remains are badly disfigured, enough of the original has been picked up to show that he was not an inhabitant of this world.

Mr T. J. Weems, the U.S. [Army] Signal Service officer at this place and an authority on astronomy, gives it as his opinion that he [the pilot] was a native of the planet Mars. Papers found on his person – evidently the records of his travels – are written in some unknown hieroglyphics, and cannot be deciphered. This ship was too badly wrecked to form any conclusion as to its construction or motive power. It was built of an unknown metal, resembling somewhat a mixture of aluminium and silver, and it must have weighed several tons. The town today is full of people who are viewing the wreckage and gathering specimens of strange metal from the debris. The pilot's funeral will take place at noon tomorrow. Signed: E. E. Haydon.

This report was different from most: it involved a crash and artefacts of the airship. But none of the strange metal ever showed up; the 'papers' were not shown. No one at the Dallas paper or anywhere else picked up on the dramatic suggestions of the report. And no one, apparently, inquired about the pilot's grave.

But it was a foreshadowing of a Roswell style crash – the hieroglyphics, the widely scattered debris, the strange materials and the recovered body were all standard elements of future saucer crashes.

And no one in 1897 felt compelled to inquire. Not until 1967 did a British UFO publication take up the story again, in an account by Jacques Vallée and Donald B. Hanlon called *Airships Over Texas*. After that story appeared, a UFO investigator visited Aurora. He found that the Proctor farm where the crash had been reported to have occurred was now a filling station, run by one Brawley Oates. Oates referred the investigator to another man, Oscar Lowry, who had been eleven at the time of the original incident.

Lowry and interviews with other surviving citizens who were children at the time strongly suggested that the whole thing had been a hoax. There was no Army Signal officer in the town – T. J. Weems was the town blacksmith. And Proctor's farm didn't even have a windmill.

The man who wrote the story, a stringer for the Dallas paper, was the local cotton buyer, who had noted the decline of Aurora, once the largest town in Wise County, since a new railroad had bypassed it. It was almost certainly a prank, in the spirit of Rachel's efforts to cash in on the UFOs with the ET Highway.

In 1973, with the country sitting through the Watergate hearings and – perhaps not incidentally – finding itself in the grips of one of its periodic waves of UFO sightings, reporters from UPI picked up on the old Aurora tale. A report that appeared in many newspapers on 24 May 1973, quoted Hayden Hewes, director of an organization called the International UFO Bureau who had been in Aurora to investigate. Hewes claimed to have discovered the spaceman's grave and threatened to go to court to have it opened.

Hewes found a strange rock, marked with an arrow and three circles, in the cemetery, under which the spaceman was reported to have been buried.

Reuters and the AP joined the chase. The AP reported that samples of strange metal had been found near the filling station. Later, they were analyzed and turned out to be mundanely terrestrial. And Reuters interviewed a ninety-one year old woman who had been in town at the time of the incident. She, too, claimed to recall that the pilot had been buried in the cemetery, which was run by the local Masonic order and an organization called the Aurora Cemetery Association. But the map the group kept of the plots in the cemetery revealed no sign of the spaceman's grave, or of any unidentified graves.

The cemetery group blocked attempts to dig up the place and the strange rock disappeared as mysteriously as it had arrived on the night of 14 June 1973.

Was it the name that lent the fascination, so romantic and mythological, stuck there in the Pentagon document, a jewel on the head of a toad? Aurora, Goddess of the dawn, with evocations of the drifting, luminous northern lights – the Aurora Borealis – that sometimes so enraptured pilots they would fly toward them to their deaths.

In any case, the Aurora of the 1980s set off a phenomenon not unlike the airship sightings of the 1890s. The name became near-mythical when it entered the lore of black aircraft, popping up in a P-1 or procurement budget document, near line items for the U-2 and the SR-71, and attached to the phrase 'air breathing reconnaissance'.

Its inclusion appeared to be a mistake. But the stealthies and Skunkers noticed it. And they noticed when the size of the requested appropriation for Aurora rose from $8 million to $2.3 billion in the financial year 1986–7. The next year the item vanished completely. They assumed it was a successor to the Blackbird and the U-2, the legendary craft that flew above Dreamland. The Skunk Works must be at it again. Soon, they began to see Aurora everywhere.

What the Lazar story was for UFO watchers, Aurora was for black plane buffs. Aurora became the centre of speculation among the watchers during the late Eighties and early Nineties – the pin-up goddess of the Interceptors.

First reports came in the aviation press, of rumours and sightings. In 1988 the *New York Times* ran a story on the plane, which claimed that it could fly as fast as Mach 6.

In 1989 an oil-drilling engineer named Chris Gibson spotted what he identified as Aurora refuelling with two F-111s. It seemed likely that the craft could be flying in and out of Machranish, the Scottish special forces base that had also hosted the SR-71.

Gibson, perhaps a bit too conveniently, sceptics noted, was a member of the Royal Observer Corps, an organization trained in recognizing aircraft. In August 1989, Gibson was working on a rig called the 'Galveston Key' in the Indefatigable Oil Field. He was below decks when his friend, co-worker and old university chum, Graeme Winton, came down and said, 'Have a look at this.' They both went up and took a look: flying overhead, not too high, and not particularly fast, was a large plane, two smaller ones – and a triangle that amazed Gibson.

He was trained in instant recognition, but this triangle had him stopped dead. His first thought was that it was another F-111, but on second thought it didn't look like one.

It was too long and lacked the 'gaps' of the F-111. His next thought was that it was an F-117, which had just been made public. Again the triangle was too long and had no gaps. After considering and rejecting a Mirage IV, he was totally out of ideas.

Gibson's friend noticed his hesitation and asked what was going on.

'The big one is a KC-135 Stratotanker,' Gibson said, 'the two on the left are F-111s and I don't know what the fourth is.'

'I thought you were an expert?'

'I am,' Gibson said.

'Some expert.'

The two watched the formation for a minute or two and went back inside. At the time Gibson was writing an aircraft recognition manual. He had in his briefcase what he considered the best aircraft recognition book ever produced: the Danish Luftmelderkorpset *Flykendingsbog*. He looked through it, but nothing matched.

Then he sketched what he had seen. That autumn he sent it to journalist Bill Sweetman, who in December, 1992, reported the sighting in *Jane's*, the aviation publication, as one of the lynchpins of his pro-Aurora argument.

In 1990, after a ceremonial flight over the Skunk Works, which the ailing Kelly Johnson viewed from his car, the SR-71 was retired, lending strength to the Aurora stories. The Air Force or CIA wouldn't have retired the Blackbird, the reasoning went, if they didn't have something else ready to replace it with.

The question was asked, why had the Air Force not fought harder to keep the SR-71? And yet there were complex politics, with the Blackbird lacking powerful patrons within the Pentagon, even though its legend attracted many in Congress: they had previously put the Blackbird back in the budget after the Air Force had left it out.

Logically, Aurora seemed the next thing for the Skunk Works to do, a continuation of what it had always done – build a plane that flew higher and faster than anything known and keep it under wraps as long as possible.

But the Soviets had always known about the SR-71 and tried to shoot it down more than a thousand times, by Kelly Johnson's own account. Better surface-to-air missiles may have made it vulnerable.

The story soon came to include the idea that Aurora was powered by methane, a technology involving cryogenics, such as the Skunk Works had explored as early as 1957, when it nearly built the hydrogen powered CL-400 or Suntan. But Kelly Johnson had killed the project at the last minute when he realized the prohibitive cost of setting up an infrastructure for handling liquid hydrogen at bases around the world, and refuelling in flight.

It would be a reconnaissance plane but might also be useful to drop a wickedly heavy projectile on a hardened command post with an uppity dictator inside it. Kelly Johnson had advocated such a system years ago, using the SR-71. Flying at such speeds, a heavy hardened steel projectile is like an A-bomb – each thousand miles of velocity is worth a pound of TNT.

In 1991 a series of 'skyquakes', as the local media liked to call them – long rumbling sounds that sounded like atomic bombs – rolled over Los Angeles. To seismologist Jim Mori these suggested a sonic boom and the possibility of a craft returning from high altitude, say 100,000 feet, or even from space, descending over LA to land in Dreamland.

Sightings around the same time in the Palmdale and the Antelope valleys proliferated. Many of the reports depicted a long triangular craft, with wings swept back about 70 degrees. Others suggested an XB-70 like craft, or 'mothership'.

A TV writer named Glenn Emery had a sighting near Atlanta, hardly black plane country, in May 1992. In August 1992 there

were more reports of delta shapes. The sound was described –
in several reports including one near Mojave – as a 'low-pitched
rumble'. That month, a viewer near Helendale, the location of
Lockheed's radar cross section test facility, described a craft
crossing the road at less than 200 feet. It may have landed at
Helendale, the reports said, because the Groom and Nellis areas
were suffering from severe thunderstorms.

There were reports of shrouded shapes being loaded onto
cargo planes at the Skunk Works in Burbank and of airliners in
near misses with strange triangular craft.

But as the FAS study, published in August 1992, noted, there
were more sightings than planes. It was an epistemological
problem: too much information, too many possible planes.

But Aurora flew on, at least on the covers of aviation and
popular science magazines. Aurora flew with all the fidelity
that skilled air-brushing and gouache could convey. The paintings and models made the mythical craft seem as real as a Piper
Cub – or rather, more real. Amphibian, feline, ray-like shapes,
delicately modelled, seen against orange sunsets and blue
depths of sky: if they did not exist, they should have.

In 1993, John Andrews' Testors model of Aurora appeared.
The mothership bore the name 'SR 75 Penetrator' – macho
enough – and on its back rode the 'XR-7 Thunderdart', like a
larger, manned D-21. The Thunderdart was supposed to fly at
Mach 7 and boasted the pulse detonation wave engines that
emitted the already famed 'donut on a rope' contrail.

The model made the idea of Aurora more tangible. It made
the plane an inescapable idea, just as the 'F-19' model had.
Somehow, the fact that a person like Andrews would contemplate the concept of Aurora right down to vent and rivet,
made it seem real. And putting the model together, gave the
notional aircraft a reality. As painted for the model box or
imagined on the covers of magazines or in home-made ren-
derings posted on the Internet, Aurora seemed no harder to
believe in than, say, brontosauruses romping across a com-
puter-generated savannah after your fourth or fifth viewing of
Jurassic Park. They embodied the faith in Aurora and other craft
and seemed to make its existence tangible.

In August, 1992, John Pike and the FAS published their
Mystery Aircraft report, which was, at best, agnostic about it.

The FAS study pointed out the epistemological problems: there were too many sightings, too much information, too many possible planes – and yet not enough evidence. And despite the budget document listings, the FAS report pointed out, no money had ever actually been appropriated for the Aurora before it was removed.

As usual, the signal-to-noise ratio was invoked. Based on the report, in January 1993, the *New York Times* came out with a story that denied Aurora's existence.

But Jim Goodall was convinced. Goodall believed that about $15 billion had been spent on the thing, that it was there to sniff out Third World nukes, a joint project of the US and the Russians.

And even Bob Lazar claimed to have seen what he thought was Aurora, inside Dreamland.

Speculation over Aurora brought all sorts of proposed hypersonic craft designs out of the closet as stealthies rushed to find corroboration for a real plane. These were dream wings, paper planes. Aircraft companies and engineers are constantly dreaming up possible planes. Sometimes they are simply fantasies, aeronautical engineers' wet dreams, and sometimes they are teasers, like concept vehicles shown at car shows, intended to whet the public's appetite for the future. And of course the generals and the Pentagon have appetites that can also be whetted.

So there was Scarlet II, a navy waverider proposal, and Lockheed drawings, and Boeing. All these were rendered in a delicate airbrush sensitive to light along the flanks and wings of the craft, sometimes with cartoony speedlines, and always with a romantic distant landscape in the background.

By the autumn of 1993 there was a whole book on the plane by Bill Sweetman, consisting mostly of citations of all sorts of earlier hypersonic aircraft proposals, going back to the early supersonic X planes. There was Lockheed's hypersonic glide vehicle, which could have reached Mach 18.

Another story held that work began in 1983 to create a successor to the SR-71. It was called 'Q', *Aerotech News* reported, but it had become too expensive and was cancelled.

In Rachel, Chuck Clark said, he saw Aurora one bitterly cold night for about thirty seconds. The hangar doors rolled open and it came out and almost at once the lights went out. But often, he added, he saw the purple flame of a methane engine.

It would cost, say, a billion a year. What aircraft didn't cost that much?

Trader believed at first that Aurora was a programme code-named Senior Citizen. But he tracked that one down and concluded it was a stealthy transport – a short take-off and landing craft for sneaking troops behind enemy lines. Later, the programme he finally decided was the real Aurora was what he knew only as 0603223F.

Perhaps Aurora was not hidden at all, but was the dark shadow of Ronald Reagan's Orient Express, a supersonic dream plane that would fly from New York to Tokyo in a couple of hours. No one could figure out how this aircraft, called the National Aerospace Plane, made any economic sense as a passenger craft, but perhaps it was all cover for the black version.

John Pike speculated on this theory. Aurora might be hiding in plain sight as the NASP, 'a purloined letter' of an aircraft. And Sweetman noticed too that the NASP planners were confidently counting on building the Orient Express of a titanium alloy that had never been used in any publicly known aircraft before.

Or was Aurora not a manned plane at all, but a robot, the UAV, unmanned aerial vehicle that was rumoured to be called Q or Tier III? Perhaps the romance of the name was elusive as well: a *Glossary of Aerospace Terms and Abbreviations*, a supplement to the aerospace magazine *Air International*, claimed that Aurora was an acronym for 'Automatic Retrieval Of Remotely-piloted Aircraft'.

So was Aurora a UAV? Was it an updated D-21 drone like those I had seen at the Boneyard?

One theory held that the plane had been cancelled in 1986 because it was too expensive or didn't work. Later, it was said it had suffered catastrophic failure on the eve of the Gulf War.

Another claimed it had been pushed ahead because of the Air Force's desperation for a space plane, something it had always wanted – a real take-off from a runway and land on a runway aircraft – in the wake of the Challenger disaster in

January 1986, and the failure of two Titan booster rockets carrying spy satellites shortly thereafter. But the dates did not gel with the budget document.

The B-2 had been given the go-ahead in 1981, and did not fly until 1989. How long would it take even the Skunk Works to bring an Aurora to fruition?

In July 1994, the Senate Appropriations Committee reported that, 'The system which some hoped would be developed and procured as a follow-on to the SR-71 has not materialized.'

Throughout the process, some military and contractor denials suggested that the Stealthies should be looking elsewhere: the craft they were after could be unmanned and subsonic.

Rarely did project names get chosen with deeper secret meanings. Gusto, Suntan and Aquatone did not suggest anything about the project itself. True, irony had intruded before, as when the Blackbirds had been developed under the name 'Oxcart' and the first name for early stealth research had been 'Harvey', after Jimmy Stewart's invisible rabbit friend. But Aurora seemed right.

After Sweetman's report in *Jane's*, which the *Wall Street Journal* and *Washington Post* picked up, the government responded. Donald Rice, the Secretary of the Air Force, issued a categorical denial in a letter to the *Post* in December 1992. He wrote:

Let me reiterate what I have said publicly for months. The Air Force has no such program either known as 'Aurora' or by any other name. And if such a program existed elsewhere, I'd know about it – and I don't. Furthermore, the Air Force has neither created nor released cover stories to protect any program like 'Aurora'. I can't be more unambiguous than that. When the latest spate of 'Aurora' stories appeared, I once again had my staff look into each alleged 'sighting' to see what could be fueling the fire. Some reported 'sightings' will probably never be explained simply because there isn't enough information to investigate. Other accounts, such as of sonic booms over California, the near collision with a commercial airliner and strange shapes loaded into Air Force aircraft are easily explained and we have done so numerous times on the record. I have never hedged a denial over any issue related to the so-called 'Aurora'. The Air Force has no aircraft or aircraft program remotely similar to the capabilities being attributed to the 'Aurora'. While I know this letter will not stop the speculation, I feel that I must set the record straight.

The Air Force commissioned an independent testing lab to show that the 'skyquakes' in Los Angeles were nothing more than booms from offshore Navy fighters.

Whether it was Rice's denial or the arrival of a new Administration, scepticism in the Press began to grow. In January 1993 the *New York Times* published a story denying the existence of Aurora.

But in Amarillo, Interceptor Steve Douglass had scanned a revealing conversation from an Air Force aircraft phone. The transmission took place on the 'Mystic Star' network used by aircraft transporting heads-of-state, military VIPs and even Air Force One. The transmission was made on 10 December 1992, when a general placed a phone-patch from SAM (Special Air Mission) 204 through Andrews AFB to 'AF public relations'.

Aurora was discussed. The general quoted the article in the *Washington Post* as well as the previous article in *Jane's*. He said:

It's almost laughable the number of hokey inputs they had. It's kind of similar to the UFO flap. We need to develop a release in response to inquiries. The guts of this should be that we've looked at the technical aspects of the sightings and what the logical answers for them are. You can quote Dr Mori and cite the Lincoln Lab physics and the FAA's efforts to debunk other incidents. Go through three or four of the sightings, take each one on and conclude with a paragraph that says the fantasy of Aurora doesn't exist.

They went on to discuss the sighting in the North Sea from an oil drilling platform. 'Someone saw something accompanied by three F-111s. The secretary wants us to talk with McMann and say it was an F-117.'

To Steve, it was clear there was a cover-up underway.

*

Aurora vanished from the next budget documents and later Ben Rich would report that Aurora was the codename for the funding of the B-2 competition between Lockheed and Northrop. Others in the industry made fun of the legend.

A stealth expert at Northrop once asked me, 'Have you heard the news about Aurora?' He waited the requisite two beats then said, 'It's an Oldsmobile.'

And true enough, Oldsmobile had come out with a dramatic-looking new car of that name – the designer credited looking at F-15s for part of the body's shape – that was supposed to help bring the company's laggard sales back. In the ads, they even referred to the plane: You can't see the Air Force's, but you can buy ours.

In 1985, a movie loosely based on the Aurora, Texas, airship story appeared. It featured a childlike, elfin ET who wore jewelled, almost medieval, clothing and piloted a Victorian flying saucer, all set in an ambiance left over from a cheap Western. The spaceship, its rivets exposed like Captain Nemo's submarine in *Twenty Thousand Leagues Under the Sea*, seems something that would have impressed audiences in the 1890s as high tech at the time.

'It was a squatty shape with wings,' the colourful old coot who makes patent elixir in the movie says, 'but the strangest thing was the little feller driving it.'

The film spins out the original story: the landing is real, and a newspaper editor capitalizes on the landing to save her ailing publication and bring the town fame.

At the time of the great airship wave, William Randolph Hearst himself denounced the reports of the sightings in the same tones that future newspaper editors would use for castigating tabloid newspapers.

In an editorial of 5 December 1896, in the *San Francisco Examiner* Hearst intoned:

Fake journalism has a good deal to answer for, but we do not recall a more discernible exploit in that line than the persistent attempt to make the public believe that the air in this vicinity is populated with airships. It has been manifest for weeks that the whole airship story is pure myth.

*

It was a shrill tone to take for a man who, two years later,
would be largely credited with puffing up tensions in Cuba
into the Spanish American War. 'You provide the headlines, I'll
provide the war,' he famously told his correspondent.

Was the latter day Aurora a headline without a war? Or could
Aurora have been as mythical as the airships over Aurora,
Texas? A craft full of hot air, a shape compounded of dis-
information? That was one theory.

Even Aurora as an imaginary aircraft could have had some
of the effects of the real plane: have made potential enemies
aware that they could be observed at any moment, and not just
when satellites, which one general lamented 'were scheduled at
the mercy of God and Kepler', flew overhead.

Could it even be that whoever named the craft Aurora knew
about the Texas town and its tale? Was this an inside joke?

By the mid-nineties a flock of new high-speed aircraft came
into the open. One was called LoFlyte, a so-called waverider, a
triangular-shaped aircraft that surfs on the shock wave
produced when it pushes beyond the speed of sound. And
when Lockheed Martin received a contract to build the X-33,
the hypersonic suborbital aircraft, Skunkers became suspicious.
The promised delivery date and comparatively low bid suggested that Lockheed had technology from somewhere else –
possibly Aurora – to give it a head start. Was the X-33 simply
the 'white' version of Aurora?

And if there was no Aurora, or nothing like it, why were
buildings going up so fast at Area 51, why were Lockheed's car
parks full, what was it that needed a six-mile runway across
Groom Lake, in Dreamland?

5

Maps

THE SIGN THAT WARNED 'NEXT GAS, 110 MILES', WAS A GOOD
enough reason to stop in Rachel, Nevada, up the road from the
Black Mailbox, I thought. But Joe Travis and his wife Pat didn't
sell gas. So when they took the place over in 1989 they packed
the Little A-Le-Inn with pictures of planes and UFOs, patches
of military units and portraits of aliens, UFO models and
knicknacks. On a small shelf across from the bar they established a lending library of UFO- and stealth-related books and
videos. And as a result they jammed the space between pool
table and counter, between video poker game and sticky-topped
tables with the new tourists that Dreamland was luring. Aurora
and Lazar were the lures.

In the back of the inn were trailers with rooms to rent, done
in a style that could be called generic crime scene. The only
thing missing was the chalk outline on the floor.

What I would always remember about the Inn, in a Proustian
sort of way, was the taste of the coffee. The bitter taste of
coffeemakers years between descalings, of rubbery buildup
from overheated warming pads.

When I first showed up there after visiting Freedom Ridge, a
pro football game on television competed with a right-wing
phone-in-show on the radio.

At one end of the room, each time I visited, sat a bucktoothed
homely woman scribbling in a notebook. This sort of fervid
writing was not unfamiliar to me, but the only place I had seen
it before was among would-be poets in Greenwich Village cafés.

Most days, too, Chuck Clark was there. 'Chuckie', the Interceptors called him derisively, saw his first UFO in August 1957,
near his home, just six miles from the Skunk Works in Burbank.
There were a flock of them, actually, he told me, and he recounts
how F-89s were scrambled to chase the shapes. A crowd gath-

ered to watch. He had often seen the characteristic blue flame of methane down behind the big hangar at the base which the watchers called Hangar 18.

He came to Rachel to pursue his study of astronomy in the clear air, he said, and his interest in secret planes and flying saucers was just a side line. He had seen Aurora, he said, one cold winter night, and he talked of how the aliens might come from 'another dimensional reality' or be 'time travellers'. He was calm about these possibilities, including them, it seemed, just to be fair. It was unfortunate, however, that when he grinned he turned into howdy doody, a grin like he must have had as child, fine then on a freckled boy of six, but disturbing on a man of fifty and irresistibly suggesting – it wasn't a charitable thought but it was inevitable – an arresting of development.

And this, I suspect, is why the appellation Chuckie managed to stick, with the barb of cruel truth.

Rachel's ground plan was compounded of triangles, according to the map in the phone book, although its street plan was not readily discernible from the first view of the trailers beside the desert, like a cove full of boats.

One side of a triangle was Groom Road, the back entrance to the base. The Little A-Le-Inn anchored the north side, the rival Quik Pik the south. And at the centre of the town is a kind of monument: a radiation recording station, to measure possible fall-out from the nuclear test site to the south-west, set up on a little plot the way the statue of a Confederate soldier might be in a small (but never this small) town in South Carolina. Every component is labelled: there's a mini refrigerator for one sensor, amid a sculpture of other mysterious boxes.

Once the town was on its way to 'site'. That is the Nevada map euphemism for ruin. (Ghost town generally indicates a 'site' brought up to tourist ruin standards.) Then in 1973 Union Carbide began mining tungsten, and the town, once called Sand Springs, was reconstituted, like a dried shrimp in a science kit, and renamed after the first child born under its new economy. But young Rachel Jones would die just three years later, after her family had moved on – a victim of the Mount St Helen's eruption, and not the drifting dust or radiation of the town named after her. Her place of death was recorded as Moses Lake, Washington State, which was the site of another secret test area, used by Boeing.

The Inn was renamed too, in 1990, after the Lazar craze began to bring UFO tourists to the town. 'A-Le-Inn' was Joe and Pat's initial marketing inspiration. The rest flowed from that: the coy 'Earthlings Welcome', the collections of alien masks and UFO snapshots, the menu with 'alien burgers'. Joe let it be known that he had once worked at the base, and did not discourage the impression that the place was the prime watering hole for workers at Groom Lake. And Pat told the eager tourists and Press – at first, the *Weekly World News* and later the *Wall Street Journal* – that she believed the place was guarded by an alien named Archibald. Behind where Joe Travis stands at the bar and beside the sign that says 'Thank you for holding your breath while I smoke' is another, 'We don't have a town idiot. We all take turns.'

In February, 1993, when electricity rates were raised in the Rachel area, Joe and Pat decided to hold a conclave of UFO buffs they boldly entitled 'The Ultimate UFO Conference'. Bob Lazar himself arrived, with female companion, in a Corvette, and Gary Schultz spoke. Norio Hayakawa, creator of the *Secrets of Dreamland* video tape, played country and western music in the corner. It was cold and windy but the crowd became so large that it outgrew the Inn itself. Joe mysteriously procured a large tent which was set up outside and when he was asked where he got it he said, 'The boys at the base lent it to me.'

At the other end of the little town of Rachel was Psychospy's trailer. Glenn Campbell was Psychospy and was also known as the Desert Rat. Glenn was in his activist mode that week, decrying secrecy and waste. His circulars opposing the takeover of Whitesides and Freedom Ridge called the base a 'sacred temple to waste inefficiency incompetence mismanagement and maybe even fraud'. It was absurd to pretend that a huge base didn't exist when in fact anyone with breath enough to make it up the mountain could see it. You can't say about a whole base, 'you didn't see that' and have credibility. It was breeding mistrust in government; the government was alienating its own citizenry.

'The stories of alien spacecraft at Area 51 cannot help but thrive,' Campbell argued.

The Little A-Le-Inn did good business in maps – bought from the government and significantly marked up in price. But they did not show the base over the ridge.

The fascination Dreamland radiated began with the fact that for years it did not officially exist. I bought a map at the Bureau of Land Management office in Las Vegas, where I browsed beside an old prospector type – beard, Confederate forage cap – but that map did not show it. The 1:100,000 metric scale, 30 × 60 minute map from 1985 claimed to show 'highways, roads and other manmade structures' but bore no signs of runways, hangars, or buildings to house hundreds of workers and engineers at the base. Perhaps, they were not made by men, the youfer would suggest. But why should it be on the map, one might ask in a more elevated mode: it was, after all, not a real but an imagined place, a virtual landscape, a 'notional' land, and its map was to be found drawn on the mind.

Still, I studied the mint and mocha shades of the Coast and Geodetic Survey maps and looked at the official tourist map of Nevada, with its upbeat registration of ghost towns. I put my hands on maps from the Defense Mapping Agency, and the Federal Aviation Administration aerial charts, with a landscape of ochres and burnt yellow hatched with the purple edges of restricted military operations areas, like blackberry juice stains, or old, fading bruises and the VORs for guidance rendered as gear-toothed compass wheels.

One afternoon I stopped by the state museum in Las Vegas. There was a display on the original native Americans, the Shoshone tribes, with such names as Tainti, Tsaidika, Pahian, Mahaknhaditka, and Kniyahitkani scattered across the area. Beside a panoramic photograph of Tonopah in the heyday of the silver boom – a collection of mines, shacks and a hotel bearing a Bull Durham ad – hung a map promoting the Tonopah and Tidewater railroad, the brainchild of 'Borax' Smith. In the map's legend, the twin T's of the railroad name were cleverly eye-punned into twin T-rails and across its expanse my eye was shocked to find no boundaries – no dotted perimeters, no shaded restricted areas, no overlapping colours. So used had I become to maps of restricted spaces.

Oddly, too, the landscape as depicted nearly a hundred years ago looked more inhabited and detailed, packed with mines, claims and crisscrossing railroads.

I looked at every map I could find. I even 'flew' over the lake and the mountains on a computerized map, stored on CD-ROM, that could show in three dimensions any part of the landscape of the whole country. I flew over the mountains from the area of the Black Mailbox, moved up the Groom Road, then over the hills and zoomed along the runway and past the hangars – neither of which was marked – and turned to cross over Bald Mountain with a sickening crash. I turned on the terrain-following feature – and nosing down, saw it all dissolve as proximity overwhelmed the program's resolution and individual pixels grew into angular coloured shapes, into facets like those of a stealth plane. Finally, the screen turned as blank as the maps were in the beginning.

Maps show how Dreamland has grown from an aerial gunnery range in the 1940s and a desert airstrip for flight tests in the 1950s, to a huge test facility, with one of the longest runways in the world. The land and airspace restricted around it has also been expanded by stages, from its original six-by-ten mile box. Irked by intruders and watchers, including Greenpeace protestors seeking a back way to the Nuclear Test Site in 1984, the government had seized additional acres around the base, including the towering 9200-foot extinct volcano called Bald Mountain, justifying its move on the usual national security grounds.

It is said to be the home of AFFTC 'Detachment 3' – of the Air Force Flight Test Center at Edwards Air Force Base – 'Det 3', and of the Air Development Command's 'Det 1', a detachment of the main development group based at Wright-Patterson, in Dayton, Ohio.

But it is also run by private contractors: Reynolds Electric (REECO), EG&G, Lockheed-Martin, Hughes. Others involved over the years are SAIC, the nation's leading war gaming contractor, as well as the writer of environmental impact statements – and, of course, Wackenhut Security.

*

The Atomic Energy Commission took control of the area just to the south and west of the dry lake in 1950. Airspace here was limited at the beginning in 1955, and the area formally shifted from the public lands of the Nellis range to the control of the Atomic Energy Commission.

In January 1962, the Federal Aviation Administration issued an order delimiting the Military Operating Area, airspace number R4808E. On thousands of bulletin boards in large airports and tiny control towers across the country, a NOTAM – 'Notice To Airmen' – apprised pilots of the new boundary.

Nellis Air Force Base had greater needs too, and by 1959, all the grazing and most of the mineral rights within the range were purchased by the Air Force.

Beginning in 1956, 369,280 acres of the Nellis range to the northwest of the lake were lent to AEC as the Tonopah test range for ballistic missiles. In 1958 the Public Land Order 1662, signed by one Roger Ernst, Assistant Secretary of the Interior, withdrew from the public lands 38,400 acres (60 square miles) for use '... by the Atomic Energy Commission in connection with the Nevada Test Site'. The area was the first formal survey of the six-by-ten mile 'box' around the base.

On 11 August 1961, with tensions rising in Berlin and bad news from Laos, the FAA established a new restricted airspace, designated R-4808 covering the Test Site and Groom Lake. Use is restricted from the surface to FL600, including the five-by-nine mile box around Groom Lake.

In mid-January 1962, the air space was expanded to 22-by-20 nautical miles in response to a request by the Department of the Air Force citing an immediate and urgent need due to a classified project.

And in the early '60s, military maps began to show their controllers' name for the newly restricted air space over and around the base. Bordering air spaces known as Coyote, Caliente, and Alamo it was 'Dreamland'.

Beginning in about 1978 'in the interest of public safety and national defense,' the Air Force began – and here the authors of the 1985 Environmental Impact Statement become gloriously politic and delicate with the words: 'actively discouraging, and at times preventing, public or private entry to the Groom Mountain Range.' They also put up fences on the east side of the range.

The next seizure under Public Law 98–485, in October 1984, included Bald Mountain, the 9000-foot former volcano. Deputy Assistant Secretary of the Air Force, James Boatright, in a letter dated 6 July 1984, assured rancher Steve Medlin – the owner of the Black Mailbox – of his continuing water and grazing rights. These are measured out by the BLM in 'Animal Unit Months' (AUMs). The Bald Mountain Allotment contains some 5811 AUMs, which translates as an allowance of 480 head of cattle and five horses. But the Sheahans, heading for their mine, one day found the way blocked by blue-bereted Air Force police. There were thirteen of them, Pat Sheahan noted.

Exactly forty years after the survey was made, environmentalists visited the area again, to support the Air Force's effort to withdraw the land – your tax dollars at work. They found, that spring of 1985, that wildlife was flourishing. Jackrabbits and cottontails were abundant, coyotes sighted frequently, badger and kit foxes common. Two mountains lions were recorded. Naturalists defined several plant and animal communities in the area, ranging from saltbush to mixed Mojave, blackbrush and sagebrush to pinyon-Juniper and mountain mahogany. There is a tiny spot of white fir community at the top of Bald Mountain, the Air Force commissioned report noted; soon it would be interrupted by a new high-tech emplacement of antennae and helipads. Thanks to the land closures, the law required archaeological investigation, which showed the area dotted with a number of petroglyphic sites, even a well-preserved nineteenth-century wooden wickiup (an Indian shelter).

All in all, Dreamland was one of the most carefully documented areas in the United States, thanks to required environmental impact studies.

The military had to be sure no endangered species were affected. It makes me feel good about my country that tanks and nuclear tests are dependent on the co-operation of desert species: at Fort Irwin, not far away, major military manoeuvres are required to stop if they encounter the endangered desert tortoise. The NTS, the mother block of the Box, was equally carefully monitored by both naturalists and archaeologists. The land annexation in 1984 (the process began in 1978) also required an environmental impact statement. Both the Nellis Range and the Nuclear Test Site must have their withdrawal from the public lands regularly renewed, which resulted in an environmental impact statement prepared in 1995–6 for the whole Test Site. It ran to five fat, purple spiral-bound volumes.

Since then, it has touched or overlapped several wildlife preserves and because it prohibited human hunters, Dreamland was itself, *de facto*, a nature reserve. This was also true of large portions of the Nuclear Test Site. And animals could move back and forth between the two in a way humans could not. There were tales – rumint strictly – among the Interceptors that the sensors on the perimeter could tell the difference between a human being and, say, a wild burro by sniffing ammonia in its perspiration. This seemed doubtful.

But the government, for all its secrecy in other matters, certified that the area around Groom Lake was home to six kinds of rattlesnakes as well as the furruginous hawk, Swainson's hawk, mountain plover, western snowy plover and long-billed curlew. It also shelters the desert tortoise, the spadefoot toad and the western whiptailed lizard along with four bats, ranging from the big brown bat to the little brown myotis, Townsend's big-eared to the Brazilian free-tailed.

The maps showed that Dreamland is a place where things overlap. Mojave Desert meets Great Basin and quartzite over-shoots Cambrian limestone, where Nevada Nuclear Test Site overlaps the Nellis Air Force gunnery and bombing range – which in turn are overlapped by the National Desert Wildlife Range, created in 1936 by FDR to save the big horned sheep.

The area is both part of the Nellis Range and part of the Nevada Nuclear Test site. The signs warning of use of deadly force on Dreamland's perimeter are authorized by the USAF/DOE liason office in Las Vegas, for which they provide a post box number. From the best accounts, the Air Force and Department of Energy jointly administer the area, under a 'Memo of Understanding'.

On some maps, the overprinting and cross-hatching indicating these various territories grow dark and obscure, almost black, where they lie thickly layered over Groom Lake. The maps suggest an illustration in a maths book on set theory.

What is illustrated, what is written on the physical, as well as the cultural, map was the fact that Dreamland had grown from the restless explorations of two cultures, two faiths: air power and atomic power, and above their twin secrecies, like the *moiré* produced by interacting grids, rose shimmering myth.

Once, the map was blank. Once, it was a real place. 'One of the most desolate regions upon the face of the earth,' First Lt George Montague Wheeler called it after leading Army Corps of Engineers expeditions through the area in 1869 and 1871 – the latter in company with ninety mules along with thirty men, including a geologist, a meteorologist, two collectors in natural history and a photographer. It was tough territory, and Wheeler reminded his readers, in the report he submitted after his return, that his expedition took place, 'amid the scenes of disaster of those early emigrant trains who are accredited with having perished in "death valley".' He was referring to notorious reports dating from 1849, when part of the Death Valley Party decided to take a short cut, en route from Utah to California and camped near Groom and Papoose Lakes. Only the intervention of the friendly Paiutes saved them from dying of thirst and starvation.

On the earlier foray, in 1869, Wheeler had camped nearby, at a place he called Summit Springs, between Pahranagat and the Jumbled Hills. It was not far from the heights from which the Interceptors would later survey Dreamland. His maps showed a great deal of white space in the area he traversed; he tried to fill it. His map of the area on a scale of 1:12 miles marked an 'Indian rancheria' near Tickaboo Spring, and named another spring 'Disappointment'. It also referred to the big conical mountain – an old volcano – that is now called Bald Mountain as Timpahute, a name now reserved for the whole range.

Unlike earlier expeditions dedicated to science, such as Clarence King's landmark exploration of the 40th Parallel a few years earlier, the mandate of Wheeler's 'reconnaissance' was to map the area, survey minerals and mines and help guide 'the selection of such sites as may be of use for future military operations and occupation' – a note neatly foreshadowing the later uses of the land.

In 1871, Wheeler, escorted by a detachment of the Third US Cavalry, encountered the Paiutes, whom he described as 'friendly and quite intelligent', 'raising corn, melons and squashes', and harvesting wild grapes. Of this people, who saved emigrant parties that had run out of food and water while trying to take a short cut across the Emigrant Valley, he added, 'Virtue is almost unknown among them and syphilitic diseases very common'.

The photographer, called 'the Shadowcatcher' by the Paiutes, was the great Timothy O'Sullivan, who not only left us with the first, lasting images of such wonders of the West as Canyon de Chelly but as one of Matthew Brady's photographers he had recorded dead sharpshooters at Gettysburg, General Grant holding a staff meeting in a churchyard with pews for seating, and the carnage of Antictam, Petersburg and the Wilderness.

The images O'Sullivan left of Wheeler's party show men who look even harder than those Civil War soldiers. Hard-bitten, resigned, they were as used to fear in this landscape as in battle. Their faces are darkened by the sun above full beards.

On 23 July 1871, Wheeler's men and the mules he described as 'cantankerous', camped at a spot near Groom Lake they called Naquinta Springs. Wheeler's geologist, a friend of O'Sullivan's named G.K. Gilbert, visited Groom Mine and the party's report described it as 'one vast deposit of galena' a low grade version of the ore, mostly lead containing some silver, zinc and copper. An advance party had been sent ahead to the west, toward Death Valley proper, but that very night their guide disappeared – apparently having deserted them, and they very nearly died: the men were down to their last mouthfuls of water before coming upon a green spot they immediately named Last Chance Springs. A second guide would vanish on the trip also: Wheeler wrote, 'his fate, so far, is uncertain; that of anyone to have followed him in the particular direction he was taking when last seen would have been CERTAIN death'.

After leaving the campsite at Naquinta, Wheeler headed west, trying to link up with the side party. The hills gradually opened up a prospect of Death Valley that, Wheeler wrote, 'met our eyes in strange and gloomy vibrations through the superheated atmosphere'.

The same foreboding sense of the landscape – more desert hallucination and nightmare of thirst than American dream – emerged in the maps Wheeler's expedition produced and also in O'Sullivan's photos.

Before Wheeler, maps showed the interior of Nevada as a great blank space. His cartographer, Louis Nell, filled it with the caterpillared hatchings of hills and lava flats, the warts of peaks and scars of passes. It is hostile, rough, forbidding. The geology of the time emphasized calamitous events – a history of battles instead of cultures – volcanoes, earthquakes: displacements of the sediments of ordinary routine. The feeling of Nell's map is of a hostile and tortured land, with boils and pits, like a great acned face, having fought its way through some geological adolescence but not yet repaired and softened into maturity. Fuzzy hatchings – whisker lines – mark the dry lakes.

Groom and other mining districts appear as neat boxes overlaying the scarred landscape; the Black Metal Mine, a mile south of Groom, is also shown, along with the road to Indian Springs, now closed off, and another back to the east and Hiko. Like bandages on the tortured face, the upright lines of these squares of the mining districts – the only political markings on the map save roads and tiny towns – reveal a civilian settlement that is no more than a stopgap.

O'Sullivan's photographs show a similarly forbidding landscape: stark, even terrifying. His Nevada was far from the majestic, dreamy land of Ansel Adams, who would make even Death Valley look cool. O'Sullivan's work, like the whole expedition, was produced under the most onerous conditions. He was still using glass plate negatives and a huge camera. His darkroom was a converted army ambulance. Mules rubbed the packs bearing his photographic plates against rocks and the ambulance was bounced over hard rock and dragged across lava flats. Often, he posed it in front of dry lakes or towers of tufa stone to lend a sense of scale to the land. He scrupulously photographed many of the mines, but not Groom.

When Wheeler directed the party up the Colorado River, O'Sullivan commanded one of the boats, which he named 'The

Picture'. When The Picture capsized, some of his photographs were lost; others survived that ordeal only to go astray on a train bound for San Francisco. In the lost images may well have been a vision of Dreamland as primeval wasteland, full of terror to the white man's eyes, a landscape as strange and alien as the surface of Mars.

Today, the sense of of foreboding, terror, comes across as stark beauty. Photography critics would later note how, in their function as government-financed visual documentation and in the deadpan views of alien landscapes they presented, these photographs resemble those of lunar or Mars landing probes.

Wheeler noted that while there was wood and water in abundance, Groom Mine was not being worked. In September 1872, claims were filed by J. B. Osborne and partners in the White Lake and Conception Lode, and British capital was invested so production could begin.

The area was not called Groom until after World War II when a geologist named Fred Humphrey surveyed it for the Nevada State Bureau of Mines. Before it had variously borne such names as Naquinta Mountains, or the Tequima Range. He found the whole area 'imperfectly mapped', and took the range's name from the Groom Mine, itself named after a man called Bob Groom who was on his way to Oregon when he came across a promising chunk of ore one day in 1864. He never got rich from the claim, and never mined it commercially, but lent it – and eventually the mountains and the lake nearby – his name.

Not until a family named Sheahan took ownership in the 1880s did any successful production begin; the Sheahans would keep the mine open through war and thin times, to the present day. Silver was the first goal of the miners, but lead would later been the predominant mineral brought out of the mine. More silver was found in the nearby Pahranagat district, inspiring the 1866 Nevada legislature to create Lincoln County. Silver had driven the creation of the State of Nevada, and would fuel its subsequent booms. And at Dreamland the goal would be to find 'silver bullet' weapons.

Conducting his survey, in the fall of 1944, geologist Fred Humphrey's photos show a quiet desert landscape, the lake smooth and empty (except for shells from the wartime gunnery activity). Humphrey traced and mapped the faults, the graben, in geological terms, that contained concentrated lead and silver. What had happened, I understand, was that two huge masses of different rocks had pressed together, struggled, over-lapped. Limestone had battled shale. The result was like Dream-land itself: an area where substances came concentrated from out of the conflict.

6

'The Great Atomic Power'

DREAMLAND, LIKE GODZILLA AND A HUNDRED OTHER SCIENCE
fiction monsters, was the incidental product of nuclear
testing, a mutation of Cold War thinking – an offshoot of
the Nevada Nuclear Test Site. That is why it was also called
Area 51. Like Paris with its arrondissements or Chicago with
its political wards, the Nevada Nuclear Test Site is divided
into numbered areas. But the numbers seem scattered at
random on the map of the mostly rectilinear areas. From
one perspective, the outline of the test site looks like a
squared-off bird, a wren, say, with its beak at the northwest
formed by Pahute Mesa, Area 20 and its stubby tail, to the
southeast, and the site's company town, Mercury. Area 51,
not marked on the map, would unfold as a wing to the
northeast. On maybe, a chip on its shoulder.

I was trying to make sense of the map of the Test Site, as I
planned my trip there, conscious that soon I would be sitting
in the most powerful seat of the century, the big Naugahyde
chair from which an entire nuclear arsenal had been detonated:
in the Command Post of the Nuclear Test Site.

I had driven this way before, part of my circumnavigation of
the whole Site and the Nellis Range of which Dreamland was
the centre, the nucleus, or as I often thought of it, the critical
core of the bomb.

I stopped at Indian Springs, the little air field from which B-
29s and B-50s had taken off to drop the first test bombs in the
early Fifties.

I had passed the legal whorehouses of Nye County, lonely
trailers surrounded by pickup trucks, gas pumps with red lights
out by the highway – big red dome lights visible from a couple

of miles down the road, the sort you might see atop a fire engine.

'It's the only place in the world where you can fill your tank, change your oil and get a blow job all in one stop,' Derek joked.

Derek was the man who took me through the test site. He worked for the Department of Energy and did this for a living, spending whole days driving across Jackass Flats and Yucca Lake and Paiute Mesa.

Derek and I drove up from Las Vegas in one of the earliest snowfalls on record. Eighteen wheelers had slid off the road and a pickup truck had turned over not far from a billboard offering tax-free cigarette sales on the Indian reservation. 'I've never seen it like this,' Derek said as the snow swirled thicker.

We turned off at the entrance to the test site, and what you see first is 'the Pen' – the chain link fenced yard that had regularly been used to hold anti-nuke protesters, women on one side of a divide, men on the other.

The sign above the main gate that reads 'Welcome to the Nevada Test Site and Environmental Research Park' invariably elicits snickers. But I kept a straight face and clutched my map in my lap as Derek drove. It marked the various territories of the nuclear death's head, the varieties of nuclear obsession, fantasy and fear. Here was the site where the bizarre nuclear ramjet was tested, here weapons were tested, and waste spills happened, codenamed Broken Spear and Bent Arrow. Here 'Grable', the nuclear cannon, was fired. There JFK visited the nuclear rocket Nerva, on which once rode our hope for trips to the planets – JFK with entourage, in sunglasses in the bright sun, dark suit, narrow tie, looking up at the torturous pipes of the test stand. At the top of the map was the amazingly named Climax Spent Fuel Facility; to the left, and west, the Yucca Mountain project, for planned storage of nuclear wastes into the next several millennia.

Derek, I learned in the miles intervening between tour spots, was a Brit, and a child of the Blitz. He had been evacuated from London into the country when the Germans began the first exhibition of the idea of airpower as terror. His father had been in North Africa with Monty, he said, and during six-hour ceasefires he and his fellows had played soccer with the Germans, then gone back to trying to kill each other.

Later, he flew helicopters in Vietnam. He had 'taken two armour piercings in the stomach' and swore the Viet Cong paid their troops a $25 bonus for every chopper pilot they took out. Before he came to Las Vegas and the Test Site, he had worked for the DOE in Colorado, where he became a big Denver Bronco fan. Discussion of John Elway was one of the few things that brought a smile to Derek's face.

The basecamp at Mercury, the little company town of the site, aka Area 23, provided an inventory of government architecture, from Nissen huts to pastel breezeblock apartments. A sign in the cafeteria advertised an upcoming bowling tournament.

The road through the site runs straight from the turn off from the highway at Mercury and if you could cross the ridge, on to S-4 – Papoose Lake, putative site of the saucer base. Along the road were old signs warning in boldly painted letters about security and safety, their stridency muted by the wear and tear of wind and sun.

At Frenchman Flat, to the south end of the site, I stood on ground zero – on many ground zeroes, actually. Most of the first blasts were set off in the air or from towers and balloons in Jackass Flats. But nothing was hot any longer, the radiation had long since faded and some of the top layer of soil in places had been removed.

We pulled up to the test structures set up at Frenchman Flat for the 1957 explosion called Priscilla. It was a virtual sculpture garden of shapes: an underground garage entrance, built to test using garages as fallout shelters. Concrete dome shelters, like spheres with just their bald tops protruding from the earth. The twisted forms of aircraft hangars, reddened with rust, like an Anthony Caro sculpture executed in fast rusting Cor-ten steel. A series of concrete boxes used to test blast resistance and known as the 'motel' or the 'sugar loaves', suggest a Donald Judd sculpture.

We paused at the Sedan Crater, in Area 10, recently added to the National Register of Historic Places, a great empty cone in the ground. A few tumbleweeds had gathered in its bottom like dust bunnies in an ill-kept apartment.

The crater is 325 feet deep and 1280 feet wide and was created by a hydrogen blast on 6 July 1962, the part of Edward Teller's

Plowshare programme aimed at devising peaceful uses for nuclear explosives. Say a Third World dictator whose country owns a major canal balks at renewing the treaty lease. Well, Teller figured, you just light up a few nukes and dig a new one, in the country next door. Sedan lifted some eleven million tons of earth into the air in a blossoming explosion whose dust took on the shape of a great shrub above the desert. It jolted the ground with the force of an earthquake of 4.7 on the Richter scale. From the air, the crater appears lunar and Apollo astronauts used it for training.

In Area 1, we stopped by Doomtown, where a couple of identical houses still stood from the 1955 Apple II blast: little bits of Levittown in the desert, still stocked with mannequins from J.C. Penny and typical canned and frozen foods flown in from Chicago the night before the blast. This was not the Doomtown of the famous film clips where light and heat roar through similar houses; that was Annie, in 1953, and those houses had been completely destroyed, but the images came back nonetheless.

To the north is another little village of test structures: Japan Town, realistic Japanese structures exposed to fallout in order to compare the results with Hiroshima and Nagasaki.

From a long way off, behind the Control Point, I could see the Device Assembly Facility, the DAF, which had been built for assembling nukes just before testing stopped – at a cost of $100 million. The DAF looks like a huge long bunker, or a giant submarine surfacing. Inside are special rooms slung on wire cables so the roof would collapse and trap blast and radiation in case of an accidental explosion. But the DAF also had huge wired fences around it, video cameras and high-tech radar sensors on poles and two watchtowers, each forty feet high, posting up at its ends. It cried out to be included in a movie – it occurred to me we taxpayers ought to have a chance to recover our expenditures by renting it out to Hollywood.

We passed 'News Nob' where, in the early 1950s, any reporter worth his typewriter, any broadcaster worth his mike, had to make an appearance at the test site and see an A-bomb for himself. The high spot was named by a construction worker when Operation Big Shot became the first blast to be televised and thereafter served as the Press section. Congressmen, aides and top government officials were brought here as well. For the St Pat's blast of 1953, the revelry was at its peak, and the Test Site brought a group of journalists who produced upbeat stories in publications from the *New York Times* to *National Geographic*.

The EPA had set up a research farm at the distant edge of the site, and sometimes visitors laughed at the big sign at its entrance that read 'An Environmental Research Park'. Derek said that in the area were coyotes and deer who had been so far from human contact for so long they would come right up to you. 'They have no fear at all,' he said. 'It's as if time had stopped there.'

We stopped at the blockhouse control centre, the command post, with guards in camou who appeared to spend a good deal of time working out. They opened the doors and flipped on the lights for us. It was cold and quiet inside. No explosions had been set off for a year and a half and it had the slightly musty smell of a vacation house left vacant for a long time. Inside the control room itself the big thick wooden tables and consoles turned out to be Formica, and chipped at that. I sat at last in the chair from which the big booms were set off. It seemed cheap – the surface absurdly artificial, the size pitifully pompous, like the chair of a minor county functionary, full of his own importance.

Everything in the room seemed a few years out of date, more like the furnishings of a government health clinic than like the powerful sort of high-tech centre one imagined from NASA launchings or such films as *Failsafe* and *Dr Strangelove*. It was slightly seedy. The TV monitors were less than the latest and sharpest. The telephones looked old-fashioned with Lucite cube buttons. But by one of them I saw the designation 'dremland' (sic). I surreptitiously jotted the number down. It was clearly to co-ordinate test operations with the tower at Groom. I imagined calling it from all sorts of places around the world, and hanging up, staying in touch with the tower in Dreamland. Later I did call it, hoping foolishly for the several seconds I had to wait that I would not get the inevitable 'not in service' recording.

*

We stopped for lunch back at Mercury. In the afternoon, we returned to the northern part of the Test Site and the talk turned to the other side of the ridge, and the parts of the site we could not visit. 'Area 51?' Derek had said. 'I'm probably the only one out here who knows what they are really doing over there.'

Derek looked at me to gauge my reaction. I didn't dare to ask: 'Well, what then?' Because the answer was obvious: a serious: 'Well, of course I can't tell you.' Or the facetious, the cliché: 'Well, I could tell you but then I would have to kill you.'

I looked over toward Gate 700 and it occurred to me that this might be the closest I would get to the heart of Dreamland, Groom Lake, and certainly, in physical distance, to its mysterious sibling Papoose Lake.

I just let the question, as Henry James would say, 'hang in the air'.

Beyond Gate 700

Not long afterward I drove through a quiet suburb of Las Vegas. At midday it was empty and silent, neat little houses on neat little lots. Modified ranch with a slight Mexican accent. Stucco. Lots of iron work. Pastels. Neatly clipped lawns.

There, sitting on his porch was a man named Joe Bacco.

Joe Bacco had helped build the road I saw running off through Gate 700, connecting the Test Site to Dreamland. For years, he had worked as a maintenance man, fixing roads and other facilities at the nuclear test site and in Area 51. He wore on his identification the number '8' that allowed him to cross the border into Area 51.

We talked in the dining room, under the eyes of a Madonna on the wall.

Joe Bacco sweats constantly now. There is a perpetual thin sheen over his body, as if he were in a New Orleans August instead of the dry Nevada desert. His eyes, always partly closed, as if swollen, glisten like his body. Bacco takes showers regularly every few hours.

I met Bacco at a hearing on the future of the nuclear test site. After the high-pitched Greenpeacers and the Shoshone nation reps and the man who said he had worked with plutonium daily with no ill effects had spoken, Bacco got his turn.

He takes the showers because in 1970 an underground explosion called Baneberry leaked, sending a towering cloud, almost mushroom in shape and size, above the flats, cracking the ground like an earthquake, leaving a fissure in some places two or three feet wide – and making the roads into Area 12, site of the blast, impassable.

The camp at Area 12, where some nine hundred workers lived in trailers and sometimes tents, was swept with fallout. Three hundred were found to be contaminated with radiation.

The NTS authorities panicked. The radiation release was a PR nightmare and they suspected sabotage. They immediately sent Bacco and a crew of other workers to patch the road. The members of his crew are almost all dead now, he tells me.

'It was hotter than a motherfucker,' he said, referring to the radiation.

'The foreman was Herschel Baker, and there was Charlie Archulet, who's dead now.' He lists the names of his other crewmates. 'We had to put chains on the four by four.'

That day, it was snowing heavily, and Bacco wore long johns. Sparks flew from them he said. It was so hot, their safety badges were quickly overwhelmed with radiation.

'There was electricity all over my body,' he told me, 'red and green sparks.'

It took four or five months to repair and clean up the area.

'Later I was paralyzed and I was passing blood for six or seven months.'

It was an account full of primal fear, as much as from what he had seen as experienced. Baneberry was not the only leak he had seen.

He talked of men who had fallen asleep in trailers before a blast and been killed. He had hauled out bodies, he said. The workers had burned dead cattle and drums of waste, burned badges that recorded how much radiation the workers had received beside the baseball diamond in Mercury – 'to hide the evidence'.

One of the men contaminated by Baneberry, the supervisor Harley Roberts, fought the AEC and later DOE, and helped win rights and recognition for the workers. Baker and others in the crew developed leukemia within two years after Bane-berry. In 1972 Roberts and another worker named William Nunamaker filed a suit for some $8 million against the Test Site, charging negligence. The case lingered on for ten years as the court kept postponing judgment. But by 1974, Harley Roberts was dead.

Bacco, too, felt he had been ill-treated by the Energy department and his old employer REECO, Reynolds Electric, the largest contractor at the site. His requests for benefits had been denied: the two organizations each claimed they had no record of his employment even though he had his work identification card. He felt he had been exploited. 'They thought, this is a sucker, we will use him,' Bacco said. 'I was a guinea pig.'

At the hearing I could tell he appeared regularly in any public venue where he could tell his story.

'The lawyer offered me twenty thousand. I told him a big bad word. What I wanted was my job back.

'I talked to the doctor. All I said was, do me a favour, when I die give my body to research.'

'Well, Joe,' the doctor said, 'you ought to feel lucky you're still living. Just keep taking those showers.'

The lady from the DOE shook her head sadly about Joe Bacco. This sort of thing was all supposed to be in the past for the Department. Yes, mistakes had been made, but a new page had been turned.

The test site tours themselves were at once part of the new attitude and a revival of a Fifties tradition of proudly bringing Press and public here – the tradition of News Nob, where Walter Cronkite, Bob Considine, Dave Garroway, John Cameron Swayze, and others were courted as they reported on the Bomb. The DOE was trumpeting its new openness, making available old records, pledging not to repeat the exposure of soldiers and civilians to downwind radiation.

Derek and I did not discuss the way that the bombs exploded at the test site had affected Dreamland.

Among the newly opened records were documents showing that Dreamland itself had been a victim of fallout and of nuclear blasts, even after U-2 testing began there. Work on the U-2, and later the Blackbirds, would be put at the mercy of the needs of nuclear testing. Even the crews and pilots at Water-town were in danger. Kelly Johnson had been concerned from the beginning about the dangers of fallout from the test site. Now, the staff at Watertown would frequently be interrupted with warnings of evacuations when testing took place at the test site. And the authorities debated among themselves what tests at Groom Lake, if any, would justify delaying a nuclear test.

The first part of Operation Plumbob was called Project 57, a programme conceived to make sure that a nuclear weapon damaged in an accident, dropped or otherwise broken open would not detonate – even if some of its conventional activating explosives went off.

The test took place just seven miles from the main base at Groom, in the Groom Lake Valley, near the mine. A ten-by-sixteen-mile block of land surrounding the planned location was added to the Test Site and designated Area 13.

No one involved with Project 57 seems to have had much of a contingency plan in case the bomb went nuclear – wiping out the U-2 programme already underway at the lake, not to mention the mine and its operators, among other incidental effects.

Later it occurred to the people in charge that with Groom growing, this was not a good thing. So in the 1980s the Government spent $21 million to have the land scraped and the toxic portions removed, a process clearly visible in spy satellite shots.

Training for the U-2 was moved in June to Texas, probably because of these tests.

Soon afterwards, on 5 July, a huge blast called Hood, designed by the University of California Radiation Laboratory, was detonated from a balloon 1,500 feet over Area 9 in the test site, about 14 miles southwest of the dry lake. At 74 kilotons it the most powerful airburst ever detonated within the continental United States. It was also a hydrogen bomb – the first to be set off at the test site. There was no public announcement, but fallout fell on the base at Groom Lake, shattering windows in the mess hall and a barracks and buckling the doors of two metal Butler buildings.

During the tests, the crews at the new base were regularly warned and evacuated. They were unaware that they were part of a long tradition and that other neighbours of the Test Site had not been so lucky.

'Dirty Harry'

In the early 1950s a man named Bob Sheahan assembled a unique photo album. The mushroom clouds rising from the spots I had visited at Frenchman Flat and Yucca Flat were visible from where he lived, at Groom Mine, on a ridge about forty miles from ground zero. He took dozens of pictures of the blasts, a whole catalogue of mushrooms – twenty, thirty Hiroshimas, seen from over the ridge, looking over the shoulder of the men setting them off, from the edge of what was to become Dreamland.

Bob Sheahan had grown up around Groom Mine, with its cluster of mining works buildings and adjacent cabins. The mine had been in his family since 1885 and now his father Dan ran it. Bob Sheahan was 31, a former engineering student at the University of Nevada, when one day in early 1951 a polite, well-dressed man from the Atomic Energy Commission came calling. There would be atomic blasts, he warned them, at the new proving ground about thirty miles to the southwest, and some radioactive fallout might drift over the mountains. He gave them a Geiger counter and taught them how to use it. He left flat sticky plates to catch fallout for later testing and set up a radio.

The fallout would head northeast toward them, over the Groom Range to Coyote Gap, near what would become the town of Rachel, with its little monitoring site on the town square. The Groom mine was part of the proving ground, whether officially or not.

Dan Sheahan had the AEC boys sign his guest book. 'We're all family,' he said.

The first shot, on 2 February 1951, broke the Sheahan's front door and cracked several windows. Others quickly followed in the 'Buster-Jangle' series.

With the Korean War turning ugly, research into tactical nuclear weapons was pushing ahead hard. Their use seemed a very probable prospect.

Soon the Sheahans began to see signs of the fallout. Bits of metal big enough to pick up with a magnet fell out of the sky, all that was left of the steel towers on which the bombs were sometimes placed, vaporized by the explosions. These were hot when tested with the Geiger counter.

Strange white spots about the size of a silver dollar began to appear on the backs of cattle and horses. These, the AEC man would tell them, were called beta burns.

One day Sheahan saw an object on the ground and when he got up to it found it was a dead deer, marked with the same white spots as the cattle. He noticed something else strange: there were very few rabbits. Usually, the desert was full of them, you would turn a bend of a hill or mount a rise and startle one, but now he realized he wasn't coming upon them much any more.

The first series of shots came in rapid succession. They were part of the series called Upshot Knothole. But the ones for Operation Buster Jangle were worse. These were run mostly by the Army.

Preparing for tactical nuclear warfare, the Army set up a whole tent town at the proving ground called Camp Desert Rock and exposed tanks and troops to the edges of the blast, and all sorts of equipment. In one especially weird test, the Army tried to determine the effects of an atomic blast on uniforms at varying distances from ground zero. So miniature uniforms were made complete with zippers, snaps and toggles to custom fit pigs – 111 white Chester hogs. The pig was chosen because, flattering to our species or not, it is the animal whose muscle and fat distribution most nearly resembles that of a human being.

Most of the pigs, each in its specially tailored little pig uniform, ended up barbecued alive; there must have been a smell of roasting pork that might not have been entirely repulsive. It was jokingly called The Charge of the Swine Brigade. But the troops too were being exposed, far more than many knew, to radiation.

On 5 May 1952 soldiers came to warn the Sheahans of an impending very 'dirty shot' and suggested evacuation.

Dan and Bob Sheahan stayed; the rest of the family went to

Las Vegas. The next day, a blast went off, breaking windows and tearing sheet metal off the buildings.

The worst of all was the ninth shot in the series codenamed Harry, which took place on 24 March 1953. It irradiated some 4000 sheep just over the Groom Range from the mountains. They were being herded through Coyote Pass, near Rachel, toward Bald Mountain. Within a few days they would all die.

The fallout from the Harry blast travelled as far as St George, Utah, with deadly effect. It would become the subject of lawsuits years later, and the trail of cancers and other effects it left behind would crystallize the common cause of the Downwinders.

Closer to the Sheahans, after 'Dirty Harry', cattle drinking from Papoose Lake died. The Sheahans still felt the AEC was taking care of them. A special research team from UCLA came to the mine and set out cages of rabbits for tests. But the Army was running more of the tests now.

The Sheahans once made a trip to the office at the test site. An officer forthrightly explained to them that the shots were set off when the winds blew toward Groom for an important reason. They sent them that way, he said, because the wind conditions most to be avoided were those that would send the fallout toward Las Vegas.

And once soldiers came to check the Sheahans' water hole. They took samples and the sergeant assured them it was fine. Then one of the enlisted men asked if he could have a cup of water. 'Can't you wait until we get back to camp, soldier?' his commander gruffly interrupted. When the men realized the implications of what they had said, both became silent and embarrassed.

During all this time, Dan and Bob Sheahan had to keep interrupting operations at the mine, sometimes for two weeks at a time, because of the tests. Nor was the mine safe from conventional weapons. It was still part of the gunnery and bombing range and in 1954, an over-eager trainee strafed the mine buildings, presumably mistaking them for one of the target buildings on the range.

And finally Dan Sheahan discovered that his wife had cancer. He would eventually sue the AEC, but both of them would die from it. But the Sheahans held on to their land and mine, passing it to the next generation, Pat and Bob, and worked out an uneasy truce with the Air Force. But Bob never showed off his photographs and into the Nineties he was fearful to talk at all about the mine lest the Air Force make his life difficult. After the guards showed up at the mine in 1984, the Sheahans began to fall silent. At least some of the family were given security clearances. Earlier, Martha Sheahan had wondered how the military could say they were defending freedom at the base while trampling on the freedoms of those on its edge. Now one family member said, 'They take care of us,' and refused to talk about the Air Force, and even then didn't want to be identified.

The dirty blasts of the early fifties baptized Groom and Papoose Lakes with radiation. And the base that would grow up there, like a gigantic mutant in a science fiction film, would share the ethos of emergency, justifying the pollution of the 'unpopulated' areas around it.

In its own irrepressible way, Las Vegas seized on the proximity of the test site in a more festive manner. The mushroom cloud became another party theme, like themes of the Old West, the Middle East, Ancient Rome – another of those exotic locales invoked as keynotes for decor at the Sands, or Caesar's Palace.

The Flamingo served an Atomic Cocktail – vodka, brandy, schnapps and touch of sherry, and Gigi, its top hairdresser, arranged bits of wire to produce an Atomic Hairdo. In May 1957, the Sands held a Miss Atomic Bomb contest in which the competing beauties appeared with the iconic mushroom cloud rendered in cottonwool on their silvery swimsuits.

Vegas grew up with the A-bomb and with airpower. And its boomerangs and bubbles of neon arrived just about the same time as the flying saucer. In honour of the destruction of Doomtown, the suburban town built for the Apple II explosion in 1955, one hotel filled its swimming pool with 2000 mush-rooms. Parties assembled to watch the blasts from convenient high spots. There were picnics on Mount Charlestown, half way up to Mercury, a future site of Interceptor expeditions. Even weddings were scheduled to coincide with nuclear tests: honeymoon in Las Vegas! Did the earth move for you too, dear? Doomtown was a mere sideshow to Boomtown.

*

Las Vegas was hardly typical of the rest of the United States, but for a time the whole country shared in the eagerness to embrace the atom. Historian Paul Boyer calls it the search for the silver lining of the mushroom cloud. There was an effort to diminish the effects of fallout and blast – a good wide-brimmed hat could offer a lot of protection, and all sorts of civil defence drills for schools became legendary parts of the childhoods of those growing up in the shadow of the bomb. The stylized logo of the atom, with its zippy futuristic orbiting electrons was soon joined by the three triangles on yellow of the fallout shelter icon. Disney published a children's book called *Our Friend the Atom*. The Boy Scouts added an atomic energy merit badge to their sashes.

But beneath the cheery atom culture – so well documented in the film *Atomic Café* (1982) – was a deeper, and often denied, fear. The atomic bomb shook heartland America to the core.

Country and Western music struggled with the mixed messages of the bomb. As I drove around the fringes of Dreamland, I often played tapes of music of the Fifties and one song in particular seemed to me to sum up – poignantly and weirdly – middle America's effort to deal with the shadow of the mushroom cloud: 'The Great Atomic Power', by Ira and Charlie Louvin, a mid-Fifties document of the bomb's impact on mid America:

Do you fear this man's invention that they call atomic power?
Are we all in great confusion?
Do we know the time or hour?
When a terrible explosion may rain down upon our land
Leaving horrible destruction,
Blotting out the works of man.

Are you ready for that great atomic power
will you rise and meet your savior in the air
will you shout or will you cry
when the fire rains from on high
are you ready for that great atomic power?

While Las Vegas was dancing to 'The Atomic Bounce', and other upbeat songs, the Louvins were echoing the darker fears of the heartland. Their song took off from 'Atomic Bomb', penned by Fred Kirby the night after the first bomb went off, 7 August 1945, when he was unable to sleep. Recorded by many groups, 'Atomic Bomb', along with 'The Hell Bomb', 'Jesus Hits Like an Atom Bomb', by Lowell Blanchard and the Valley Trio, and similar songs, were big hits in the late Forties and early Fifties.

Like others in the genre, 'The Great Atomic Power' was a conflation of Bible and Cold War, a rendition of the apocalypse as nuclear holocaust. It was a high harmonic expression of the fevered reaction of rural America to the Bomb.

The bomb's coming was the second coming and you'd better be ready, better turn to Jesus for salvation. 'Jesus will be your sword and shield', the lyrics ran, like SAC itself, the fire raining from on high, Bob Dylan's hard rain anticipated in the mode of Protestant hymns and backwoods bluegrass.

It was as if the bomb had gone off in Omaha itself, the heart and headquarters of SAC, jolting Jacksonian white trash, mobile home living, pickup truck driving America out of complacency – a desperate, even heroic, effort to graft the impact of the bomb's existence onto fundamentalist Christian theology, to force the terrible new knowledge into the net of traditional teaching. And that net grotesquely deformed, almost but not quite, bursting, the old myth incorporating the new.

Here it was, Jesus as the ultimate version of SAC – 'He will be your shield and sword,' that was right off the logos painted on the noses of B-36s and B-47s.

'When the mushroom of destruction falls in all its fury great, God will surely save his children from that awful, awful fate.' But Curt LeMay wasn't waiting for God to do the saving; his plan was to hit the Russians with everything he had before they could light up the skies over New York and Washington, over Dallas and Houston, over Memphis or Nashville, over Omaha, home of SAC.

7

'Victory Through Air Power'

EAST OF THE NUCLEAR TEST SITE, WRAPPING IT IN THE shadow of its bomb ranges, and north of Las Vegas, the ideology of Air Power lived on, beyond the Cold War, beyond the Strategic Air Command, at Nellis Air Force Base.

'Global Power for America', 'JP 7' read the words on the huge bright tank of jet fuel at Nellis Air Force Base in Las Vegas. Emblazoned with the shield and sword of the Air Combat Command, the tank shimmers in the heat just up the road from the pawn shops and watering holes – 'SNAFU Lounge' – that have sprung on the verges of the base, as they do around any military base.

Dreamland is part of Nellis' vast bombing ranges, but Nellis is best known as the home of the Air Force's Red Flag training games, the equivalent of the Navy's famed Top Gun school.

Today, Green Flag – for electronic warfare – has joined Red Flag, but the result is the same: the sky for hundreds of miles around the base is filled with aircraft – 22,000 sorties a year. I stopped by one afternoon during a Red Flag to watch the planes returning. There was already a crowd, half a dozen or so cars and trucks, with people lounging in the driver's seats, or sitting lazily on the bonnets. Their expressions of face and body bore the patient, purposeless air of fishermen.

First at intervals, then close together, F-15s and F-16s came home in pairs, each touching down with a little puff of smoke as its tyres hit the runway. A big AWACS or other electronics plane, a huge hump of antenna on its back, came in and then over our heads, a helicopter drifted overhead, creating a little crater of dust in the air.

For Red Flag, the planners at Nellis are constantly creating 'notional countries', imagined allies and aggressor nations that play out the scenarios of conflict, reinventing the area around Dreamland.

For Nellis, Dreamland is always 'the Box'. Military Operating Areas, restricted to civilian air traffic, show up on aviation maps. They are given names like Talon and Cheyenne and acronymized as MOAs – an unintentional irony, since the moa, the bird from New Zealand, is flightless.

Pilots take the Box very seriously – because their commanders do. It is more than a MOA: it is off-limits even to the military pilots, at all altitudes and all times.

At the beginning of every Red Flag session, crews spend several hours, and one 2-hour sortie, becoming orientated to the various Nellis ranges, memorizing landmarks so that in the 'heat of battle' they do not stray into the Box. Even crossing buffer zones around R-4808 (air spaces R-4807, R-4806, and R-4809) results in the crews being given a slap on the wrist, but it frequently happens.

A former Red Flag player explained to me that, 'If a pilot accidentally strayed into the area, the day's exercises would immediately terminate and the offending aircraft would be ordered to land at an isolated area on the east side of Nellis AFB. Intelligence officers would confiscate the radar film, detain the crew, search everything in the cockpit, and then conduct a lengthy interview to determine why there was an overflight. Overflying R-4808 is cause for very heavy penalties, including an automatic Article 15 (administrative reprimand, which for officers is the "kiss of death"), demotion, and loss of pay. If the overflight was intentional, one could expect a court-martial, a dishonourable discharge, and imprisonment.'

Dreamland and the Box figure as a recurrent reference – part factual, part fictional – in techno-thrillers such as Tom Clancy's or Dale Brown's. Clancy even refers to the saucer lore as 'the frisbees of Dreamland'.

Brown, who flew in Red Flags during his Air Force days, refers frequently to the place. He describes a fictional High Technology Aerospace Weapons Center – HAWC is the acronym – at Groom Lake in his novels *Sky Masters* and *Flight of the Old Dog*: 'a secret US Air Force research facility in Dreamland that conducts flight-test experiments on new and modified aircraft and new weapon systems.'

Skymasters – dedicated to Curtis LeMay, the 'Iron Eagle' – describes the testing of fuel air bombs: a real technology in which a huge cloud of gasoline vapour is ignited producing a shock wave that crushes troops on the ground and deprives them of breath – a miniature Tokyo firestorm in a single bomb.

Nellis was created as part of the network of bases in the vast Western build-up during World War II, at first as the Las Vegas Army Air Corps Gunnery School, established in January, 1941. By June, it was graduating four thousand students every five or six weeks. A number of auxiliary runways were built in the huge expanse of the range, including two 5000-foot runways in a cross tilted to the northwest on the edge of Groom Lake. Soon the lakebed was littered with .30 and .50 calibre shells.

After the war, Nellis served as a major mustering point for airmen and soldiers. It was closed down in 1947, then reactivated two years later, in time to become the main training centre for Korean War fighter pilots and, in time, the temple of fighter tactics and morale. It would become the home of the Thunderbirds, the Air Force's performing aerobatic team.

Today, in the dry cleaners and pizza joints of the area surrounding Nellis, their numbers and the intensity of display declining with distance like collateral damage, proud entrepreneurs display signed Thunderbird photos, Thunderbird banners, Thunderbird plaques.

The Air Force aerobatics team figures around Nellis here something like the football team in other cities. There are weekly tours of the Thunderbird hangar, led by their perky bubbly disarming PR guy. One day during a tour, the crowd largely of oldsters, gathered. First you see the shrine, the trophy room – wood panelled – packed with plaques and certificates, and a round table at which you can envision Sean Connery as King Arthur sitting, in a fancy flying suit. The T-birds are said to meet around that table.

'Aren't they handsome?' said one woman looking at the photographs on the wall.

Across the hall, an auditorium in which, before you enter the white-floored hangar, Thunderbird history and glory is outlined in slides and narrative. They make goodwill tours like those of Teddy Roosevelt's great white fleet. They cannot blink during manoeuvres. They watch their leader and nothing else. At the end, questions are entertained.

Immediately comes the impertinent inquiry, from a retiree at the back of the room: 'Do you have anything to do with this Area 51?' There is a faint scattered laugh among the knowing minority in the full room.

'That's where we get our pilots,' says the PR man, quick-witted.

'No, seriously, that's a good one. I wish I knew.'

On another ridge, some fifty years before I stood on Freedom Ridge, a loose gaggle of men stood wrapped in long coats and scarves, shivering in front of small fires. In the hour just before dawn on 8 January 1944, some two dozen engineers and workers of the original Lockheed Skunk Works awaited the first flight of the jet fighter they had produced in only 68 days, the XP-80. The ridge stood above the dry lake called Muroc, 100 miles north of Los Angeles.

Among them was a man named Wally Bison who had worked in the Skunk Works from the beginning.

'It was cold, colder than a well,' Bison told me years later. 'All of a sudden somebody said, "here he comes!", and the airplane passed by a couple of hundred feet off the deck in dead silence. Then the jet blast came, a sound we'd never heard before, I was goose pimples from the top of my head to the bottom of my feet.'

The plane was called Lulu Belle, but the guys around the shop had wanted to call it the Fartin' Fury of Forty Four. These were men who worked on a relentless schedule, with big legends above the girlie calendars that gloomily read 'Our Days Are Numbered'.

The formal name of the facilities around Rogers Dry Lake, a huge expanse of white cracked mud, was the Muroc Bombing and Gunnery Range. As early as 1933 the Air Corps had established a gunnery range on the lake bed not far from a small settlement established by Clifford and Eve Corum in 1910. When the Corums had applied to set up a sub post office under their name in the store for the convenience of customers, the authorities replied that the name was already taken by another office. So they reversed the letters in their name and 'Muroc' it became.

With the coming of the war, more and more military projects ended up using the vast spaces of the lake, which afforded plenty of room for bombing and strafing training and testing, and a huge runway for landing experimental planes in an emergency. Within months after Pearl Harbor there were thousands of men and hundreds of bombers and fighters here and at many other new bases springing up throughout the west, safely inland and isolated.

The military arrived in force at Muroc and other dry lakes – China Lake, El Mirage – and chased off the hotrodders and cyclists. The Navy built a wooden mockup of a Japanese cruiser, a grey looming practice target, with only the dry lake for waves. They named it the Muroc Maru and for years it floated on the liquid of mirage as if on the Pacific.

The plane that flew that day in January, 1944, was the second 'black' aircraft, built wholly in secret, as carefully concealed as the Manhattan Project – Top Secret, 'need to know' only and the first product of the Lockheed Skunk Works. Bell Aviation had built the first, the XP-59, and flown it here in 1943, although it had flown more slowly than the top prop fighters of the day. But the XP-59, optimistically named the 'Aircomet', turned out to be little better than the best conventional planes of the day – a lesson from the beginning that black projects could turn out turkeys as well as eagles.

But the project had already taken on some of the strange qualities of black projects to come, the combination of secret society and odd practical jokes. The Bell crew took the derby hat as their symbol and would fly wearing derbies and gorilla masks. Forbidden to acknowledge their work openly, they sported insignia from which the propellers had been removed. The strange new experimental planes – flying wings and stubby rocket planes, bastard double fuselages and push-me-pull-you configurations – were assigned to a special area, called North Base.

Already, too, the little signs of camaraderie and conspiratorial clannishness were emerging, in part a compensation for the isolation and secrecy of black projects.

This aircraft was 'Special Secret', and when in January, 1943, heavy rains flooded the dry lake at Muroc they moved to a field near Victorville called Hawes, which would later become George Air Force base. For the trip, they covered the jet engine inlets and exhausts with fabric and rigged up a mock four blade prop.

When they went out to Juanita's in Rosamond, and Pancho Barnes' soon-to-be-famous bar closer to the base, they wore their black derbies with fake moustaches from a Hollywood costume store.

But once the Lockheed jet flew, the Bell project was doomed. By February 1944, Bell's work at North Base was dismantled and closed up.

Lockheed's XP-80 would be a durable design, quickly improved with a more powerful engine, it became the YP-80A, the 'Gray Ghost'. Eventually some 6000 aircraft to be based on the type would be produced – a whole family of jets, including the P-80 and F-80 military fighter, the Shooting Star and the T-33 trainer.

That day, the head of the Skunk Works, Kelly Johnson, stood impatiently by the plane in a long overcoat and knitted watch cap. Johnson, then just 33 years old and already the designer of the Lockheed Electra, the P-38 Lightning fighter and – for Howard Hughes – the lovely tri-tailed Constellation airliner, had flown to Wright Field in Dayton just the summer before. At 1:30 on the afternoon of 8 June 1943, he had been handed a signed contract to build the aircraft that was now complete.

Wally Bison, Skunk Works veteran, recalled something else. The old man had a hard time recalling names, and he kept apologizing for it. But the cold he remembered and the lunch – afterwards, Bison remembered that Johnson took the whole gang to a restaurant for lunch – and paid for it. Used to bringing his lunch in a brown bag to work at the makeshift quarters of the Skunk Works in Burbank, Bison saw the restaurant lunch as an act of unprecedented largesse on the part of the penny-pinching Johnson. Things were that tight around the Skunk Works and Kelly Johnson was that cheap.

The lunch, for Bison, overshadowed even the beer party that followed that evening, accompanied by armwrestling contests. Johnson loved arm wrestling because his arms were strong – a reminder of his blue collar beginnings. He had worked building walls of lath and plaster, and he could go onto the shop floor and build anything he asked his workers to build.

When the jet contract arrived, Johnson had to build his own secret team. The aircraft company founded by the brothers Lockheed had suffered lean years during the early Thirties, nearly going under several times, but with the coming of war its offices and factories on the edge of the Burbank Airport were busy.

All of Lockheed's production capacity, all of its engineers and workers were hard pressed just to meet normal war-time contracts for the P-38, for B-17 bombers for the US Army Air Corps, sub hunters for the Navy and Hudson Bombers for the British, that Johnson had to scrounge a staff of 23 engineers and about twice as many mechanics, fabricators and clerical workers.

Johnson's work, and washing dishes, had got him through the University of Michigan. He had been at Lockheed since 1933, when he was hired at a salary of just $33 a week. His first achievement was pointing out a serious aerodynamic flaw in the prototype Model 10 Electra on which the firm's entire fortunes rode, and then figuring out how to fix it.

Kelly Johnson was already one of the top aircraft designers in the world. He had been born the seventh of nine children to a poor Swedish-American family in Michigan, and baptised Clarence, taking the name Kelly when his classmates deemed him more Irish than Swedish due to his pugnacious – and sometimes violent – streak. It was a foretaste of the temper that would become legendary around the Skunk Works.

Johnson grew up reading Tom Swift and the Rover Boys in the local Carnegie library in Ishpeming, Michigan, a mining town that sent its ore to Carnegie's mills. He built dozens of model planes and by the time he was twelve he knew he wanted to be an aircraft designer.

At Lockheed, he quickly emerged as the young star. He met Amelia Earhart and prepared the Electra for her record flights and for her last, fatal journey. He had worked for Howard Hughes, on the tri-tailed Constellation that had flown for the first time almost exactly a year before, as the C-69, and already gone into service for the military, wearing olive drab.

During work on the Constellation, Johnson often met Howard Hughes, huddling with the billionaire in one of his stealthy bungalows, more frequently used to stash would-be starlets. Hughes himself was a pilot, his fame grown from his 1930s round-the-world flight that kept him in the headlines, his fortune grown from film and aviation – Trans World Airlines, Republic Pictures – and he tested the plane himself.

Once, when he took the wheel of the prototype Connie, Johnson and others in the craft were overcome with terror as he attempted to stall the plane to test its stability. When the airspeed indicator read dead zero, this terror finally superseded deference to their client and Johnson forced Hughes away from the controls.

In a secret room that was a forerunner of the Skunk Works he designed the P-38 fighter and when its wings began to come off in a dive, due to something then called compression, Johnson found himself anticipating the attack on the sound barrier and its shock waves as he worked to fix the plane.

His methods were instinctive and highly practical. Johnson demanded that every part possible be bought or adapted rather than designed for the purpose and he administered by emotional economy as well: by temper and fear. Like a tough football coach he could exhibit flashes of kindness, too.

Bison recalled that, 'Johnson could be intimidating and brutal, but yet at our parties he was delightful. When I had to go to Kelly's office I was in fear but in the end I was always amazed at his knowledge of the most detailed things.'

The key to the Skunk Works speed was cutting out administration. 'The main thing was that Johnson cut the paperwork. He drew things upstairs, then walked down and told the mechanic, "build the damn thing" and then you helped him do it.'

Johnson and his staff had already been looking ahead to jet aircraft. They had proposed a design called the L-133, a stainless steel vision of the future, with a jet engine of Lockheed's own design, a long fuselage and canards promising a top speed of 650 miles per hour. On 17 May 1943, when Johnson was on a visit to Eglin Air Force Base, (where a dozen years later I would be living my first few years) a general took him aside and told him of the P-59A, that hapless Bell jet, kept secret at Muroc with a fake propeller on its nose. He wanted Johnson to do something better. On the airliner home – his ulcer working overtime – he jotted down the ideas for a jet fighter he thought he could build in six months. This could be a war winner.

The open spaces where the engineers set up their drawing boards and the shops downstairs were cobbled together around a machine shop beside Lockheed's windtunnel, in a leaky extension built from the old wooden crates in which Wright engines had been shipped, the roof from a rented circus tent. Right next door was a chemical factory that continuously emitted noxious fumes.

Working ten-hour days, six days a week, beneath the calendars that read 'Our Days Are Numbered', the group would beat the deadline: they put the jet in the air in just 143 days after the formal signing of the contract.

The tale was already famous, as was the name of the company, although they got it by accident: no one had told them how to answer the phone, there in the crude buildings where the smell of chemicals seeped in from a factory next door, and an engineer named Irv Culver picked it up one day and spoke the immortal words, 'Skunk Works'. It was inspired by Al Capp's Little Abner, the comic strip where a character named Injun Joe brewed up a foul moonshine called Kickapoo Joy Juice, and the question Culver and the others kept being asked but could not answer, 'What's Kelly brewing up in there?'

Above all, the name was born of secrecy. There was no name, nothing to answer the phone with, so those inside had to dream one up.

Johnson would continue to call the base where the XP-80 flew from Muroc Skunk Works for years after the name was officially changed to Edwards Air Force Base (after Glen Edwards, a test pilot killed in a crash of the 'flying wing' bomber in 1954). He would test many other aircraft here. But by 1955, when the Skunk Works was looking for a place to test the U-2, Edwards AFB was no longer private enough. Like some wild species that needed lots of range or whose environment was changed by the advance of suburbia, the engineers who built secret aircraft had to flee further and further into the wilderness.

The Skunk Works would create the planes that made Dreamland necessary, and its legend grew up along with the secret base. It would enjoy a following as intense as any flying saucer site or prophet of interglactic visitors ever did.

One day I drove to Burbank to visit the original site of the Skunk Works. My guide was a local man named C. R. 'Chappy' Czapiewski. Chappy was proof of the power of the legend: he had never worked at the Skunk Works, never served in the branches of the military that flew its planes, but was simply a local citizen who appreciated its achievements and was caught up in a sense of the history and lore of the place.

We met in downtown Burbank, which for all Johnny Carson's jokes struck me as pleasant: an inoffensive mall, a new media centre, and elegant Moderne-style public buildings. The city hall, in particular, was a WPA era fantasy, worthy of the service as film set it had often performed. Its soaring lobby was painted with romantic murals of Thirties aircraft and heroic movie cameras – icons of the leading local industries.

A querulous man with an edge of outrage in his voice, Chappy was simply a Skunk Works fan, one of that wide loose network of its buffs. Retired now, he was an active citizen and it appeared something of pain in the ass to the local councillor types. I had to like him right away.

Over a Japanese lunch Chappy agreed to take me on a tour. He gave me a yellow-green badge that said 'SOS save our Skunk Works'.

He was trying to muster the citizenry of Burbank to save the original Skunk Works buildings from destruction, he explained, and make at least one of them a museum, dedicated to the aircraft designed here, from the P-38 to the Stealth fighter.

The organization most opposed to this plan, he told me, was Lockheed itself. The local airport authority coveted the land on which the hangars stood for a planned expansion, and Lockheed had agreed to sell it.

The company had become involved in nasty lawsuits, and the Skunk Works had ironically lived up to its name, pumping foul juices – PCBs and other pollutants – into the surrounding aquifer. Lockheed had recently settled for about $130 million with a group of local residents who lived near the first Skunk Works facility, the locale of the famed packing crates where the jet project was assembled, and that building had already been taken down. Huge pipes called a vapour extraction system would pump steam into the ground and pump the toxins out.

The company apparently feared bearing the costs of other environmental actions, from other facilities.

'This was historic,' Chappy lamented, 'and now it's being forgotten. It was secret, but we – all of us living here – knew what was happening. The U-2, the Blackbird, the Stealth – they won the Cold War. Kids today don't remember the Cold War,' he said. 'They think U-2 is a rock band.'

And Lockheed itself was the worst: they acted as if blind to their own history. Chappy drove me out to the airport and the original works.

'We all know what happened here,' Chappy said. 'It was super secret but now we all know.'

We scrambled up a steep hill with a water tank at the top to take pictures across the valley. Chappy loaned me his wide angle; it was hard to deal with the fences and power lines.

We wandered among the hangars. Myrtle trees at wide intervals dotted the avenue in front of them, their pink and green the only touch of colour across expanses of grey pavement, grey chainlink.

For painting the hangars, Lockheed favoured a soft yellow, the yellow of creme brulée, or the yellow rose of Texas. They had chosen the same colour out at Helendale in the secret RCS complex.

Chappy pointed out the landmarks and recounted the legends as we drove among them.

'Here's building 82,' Chappy would say, 'the engine test facility.' Or, 'There is where Kelly supposedly had his office.'

We could see building number 360 with its complex system of window panels, like an abstract painting. I tried to count the panels and make sense of the system: four modules of four rows of three.

This, Chappy would point out, is where they did the F-104 – 'the Starfighter', 'the missile with a man in it', developed to counter the superiority of the MIG-15s that the US pilots encountered in Korea. Stubby-winged, with a downward firing ejection seat, it would be a hot rod, but also a widowmaker, with no more glide in it than a bathtub pushed off a roof.

Here, Kelly and his boys created the U-2, and turned back

over to the US government – your tax dollars at work again – two of the $26 million he had agreed to take and tossed in half a dozen extra planes to boot.

There, they built the Blackbirds, the A-12 and YF-12, then the SR-71, for first the CIA and then the Strategic Air Command, pioneering whole new technologies such as extruding titanium to create a plane that is still – and will be through the millennium – the fastest and highest flying ever, at temperatures requiring a whole list of new products, oils and lubricants, paints and wires, gaskets and pipes and tyres.

Now, the huge yellow hangar was used to film movies and TV scenes – a big convenient studio.

'Beside those hangars,' Chappy said, 'is where they set up the first stealth prototype between two tractor trailer trucks with camou net covering the ends and fired up the engine.'

In that hangar, the Stealth fighter grew from a mere footnote in a translation of a Soviet scientific journal, and became the seed that crystallized into a black-faceted body that from the front looked like an angular flying saucer. Looking hacked, chopped, with every corner cut, the shape of the stealth was the very embodiment of the Skunk Works philosophy of cutting away of excess. 'KISS' was their motto – 'Keep It Simple Stupid'. 'Simplificate and add lightness.'

At the end of the flightline was the big hangar, where stealth watchers had seen shadowy tarpaulin-covered payloads moving into huge cargo lanes, and noted odd shipments.

'They were flying something on a big C5A out of here in 1991 and 1992,' Chappy said. On one wall was a sort of bay window allowing a full view of the runways at the airport. An observer could be sure the coast was clear on the commercial field before anything came out of the Lockheed building.

'They would shut the airport down when sensitive cargo was being loaded,' Chappy recalled. 'They stopped all airport traffic at eleven thirty on Friday for it.'

They could only have done all this in secrecy. The Skunk Works was the best argument for black projects. Only by keeping the number of people in the know small had Johnson worked so fast. But it was always a gamble. There had been failures: the Saturn commercial transport, the F-90 fighter, the weird tail-landing XFV-1 Salmon (named after Herm 'Fish' Salmon, the test pilot and only man crazy enough ever to fly the damn thing). The D-21 I had seen in Arizona – a failure and a secret for decades. Suntan, the liquid hydrogen-powered super plane of the late fifties that cost $2 billion before someone stopped to think of the expense of building bases with cryogenic facilities to keep it fuelled.

And even the successes were close enough to failures, like the A-12, the Blackbird that by rights should never have worked, to serve as a reminder that this was a high-risk gamble.

But as I rode around with Chappy, I found the sense of the legend I had arrived with beginning to wilt. I wondered if now perhaps the darkness was too great and the gambles no longer paying off.

I kept thinking about a talk I had had with Ben Rich, the last head of the Skunk Works to preside over the Burbank facility, and I kept remembering his tone. He had written a book, but two chapters had been rejected by the CIA and the DIA when he submitted it, as required for review. It irked him.

He was less interested in talking about the legendary achievements of his outfit than in bitching about the onerousness of secrecy. Why, they had even made him lock up his coffee mug, he told me. The mug, you see, read 'Mach 3 plus' and showed a picture of the SR-71. But that speed had never been officially released to the public and therefore the information was still classified. So each evening the mug went into a safe, and each morning it came out again before Rich could sip his brew.

He told how he had invented a heater for pilots at high altitude in the Fifties. The heater was required to enable them to urinate; otherwise, the drain tube froze and backed up. But the invention was still secret.

Only one other group of people irked Rich as much as the security people: the EPA. They threatened to shut his programme down if it didn't comply with regulations. And in the equivalence of irritation Rich felt, I thought I saw an equation. It was as if the concern for leaks of information and leaks of chemicals into the watertable were somehow equivalent. But I wondered if Rich didn't have it upside down, if secrecy itself hadn't become something like a toxic chemical, extremely powerful and useful in small controlled amounts, but treacherous and poisonous if misused and over-used.

We drove out of the hangar area past a range of dumpsters. Suddenly, a big plastic bag caught a gust of wind and flew up in front of the car. 'UFO!' Chappy cried.

At last we stopped in the airport lobby; you could imagine Cary Grant in *North by Northwest* striding through it. Inside are displays dedicated to the history of the place. Amelia Earhart and other aviation pioneers of the Thirties flew out of here.

But the war made it boom. There was a menu from the old Sky Room restaurant that offered a secretary's special small chicken salad for 55 cents.

After a Japanese sub surfaced off the coast of California in 1941, Lockheed put in a desperate call to the Disney studios in Burbank. Their best artists came in to hide the factory under camouflage. Using all of Hollywood's techniques and skills they created an artificial, subscale village on top of the factory buildings and airport terminal. It was a fool-the-eye model of the very American way of life they were designing and building aircraft to save, the American dream of magazine ads and radio serials, erected over the factories. Workers inside turned out P-38 fighters and B-17 bombers, then went home to little bungalows like those simulated above their heads.

From the air, even from the mountains, you couldn't tell where the roof stopped and real houses started. It was like little Monopoly houses dropped into a particularly thick layer of cobwebs. Huge poles held up the netting and camouflage, done in chicken feathers, and the real buildings beneath were painted in similar mottled vegetable shades. 'Someone who worked here,' Chappy said, 'told me that when it rained the chicken feathers stank to high heaven.'

Finally we drove to the original site of the Skunk Works, which now lay flat and bare, loosely covered with rubble like a site ready for construction. Across the street, bougainvillea climbed concrete walls, behind which lay houses into whose yards pollution had seeped from the site. Now the object of massive litigation, the Skunk Works joke having turned sourly true, even deadly, as PCBs and other substances leached into the land, travelling toward the sturdy little bungalows around it. The area was a wasteland.

At last we stood in front of the level rubble-textured field that had been the original plant and the first Skunk Works. It lay fenced, barbed wire at the top.

'They should have known,' Chappy said. 'They had the best engineering and science talent you could buy.' Chappy had taught junior high school science. 'My eighth graders,' he said 'would know'.

The legend of the noble engineers as Cold War Warriors suffered a blow, and there was a cruel irony: the original name Skunk Works had referred humorously to a sort of prototype toxic waste dump, the site where Al Capp's character Injun Joe distilled his Kickapoo Joy Juice. Now, the exotic vapour system was a kind of grotesque distillery, pumping toxic PCBs and heavy metals out of the ground the Skunk Works buffs held sacred.

But the Skunk Works had moved out, headed to Palmdale, a more remote location, fleeing closer to their desert test base. What was left was wreckage. There was something dark and sinister about it, as if secrecy itself had grown liquid and seeped into the ground.

I drove away from the dark and gory ground of the original Skunk Works, as it now seemed to me, hopped on the freeway and headed out, thoughtful. I passed the Disney complex, now sporting playful pastel cones and boxes, post modernist architecture. Disney was hiring all the best architects to do its buildings now.

While Disney sent his artists down the boulevard to create *trompe l'oeil* buildings atop the Lockheed factory, he was putting others to work for the war effort. Some were creating unit patches and insignia – Goofy and Thumper were going to war. And a few doors down, others were creating one of the great myths that was to create Dreamland – air power.

They were working on the film *Victory Through Air Power*, one of the most powerful pieces of propaganda of the war. Disney did the film at his own cost, so enamoured was he with its source: the book *Victory Through Air Power* by Count Alexander P. de Seversky.

Filming began only after ten at night, because of the sound during the day of new P-38s, Hudson bombers and the B-17s

Lockheed made for Boeing noisily taking off from Burbank airport.

Seversky was a White Russian émigré who had distinguished himself as a naval aviator in World War I, losing a leg in the process. He came to the United States because of the Revolution and Russia pulling out of the war. He allied himself with Billy Mitchell, the maverick general who pushed for bombing against conservative admirals and generals, and after Mitchell died in 1936 he ranked as the leading exponent of the faith that strategic bombing would be the dominant force in all modern wars.

Seversky became head of Republic Aviation and his book, a collection of articles that had appeared in journals as diverse as *Saturday Evening Post* and *Town and Country*, was a huge bestseller and Book of the Month Club selection. It warned Americans that they could no longer rely on oceans for safety. They were no longer safe from war in Kansas City or Chicago. But, Seversky held out a promise – if Americans built a massive force of bombers and destroyed the distant cities of our enemies first, we could return to our comfortable isolation.

Walt Disney was enraptured by it: it offered a neat, ideological solution to the muddles of war – technology to keep the distant enemies at bay. He decided to bring the Count's message to the public.

Seversky, nicknamed 'Sasha', narrated with his exotic and authoritative Russian accent. The film blended newsreels of Bill Mitchell, his mentor, and his famous demonstration of how to bomb battleships, along with cartoon-style explanations of the development of military aviation – how pilots learned to fire machine guns through synchronized propellers in World War I. Animated maps explained the present situation, using shields and arrows that turned into aircraft and eagles.

It showed six engine pusher prop bombers, foreshadowing the B-36s, with streamlines running off their edges, and in the end air power became personified as an eagle, fighting the Japanese octopus, destroying its head as the tentacles slowly released their hold.

It was an appropriate conjunction: Hollywood was already enamoured of air warfare. *Dawn Patrol* won the very first

Academy award. In 1937, the Army Air Forces had lent all of its new B-17 bombers to Hollywood for the production of *Test Pilot*, with Clark Gable and Spencer Tracy. The war itself quickly brought such films as *Thirty Seconds Over Tokyo*, and *Air Force*, with the likes of John Garfield.

But Disney especially liked air power, Richard Schickel argued, in his history of the Disney studios, because it was efficient, clean warfare, in which the corpses are never seen. No one seems to suffer any more than in a cartoon.

Schickel says shrewdly that strategic bombing appeals to the right-wingers, because of their tendency to see people as masses. (The same could be said of the left, of course.) And air power especially seemed to have held great appeal to the Midwestern – like Disney, like Curt LeMay of Ohio or Dwight Eisenhower of Abilene. To those areas that once felt themselves at the greatest remove from foreign influences, air power was in an odd way the flip side of the area's traditional isolationism. And it seemed cheap too – in lives and in dollars – a feature that would make it especially attractive in the post war years.

I found a copy of Seversky's book, in its original Book of the Month Club jacket. This was the ideology that would send my father and thousands of other young men from small American towns and farms to war, over the Himalayas, over Saigon and Rangoon, over Osaka and Tokyo. Its cover showed a lowering grey cloud in a blue sky: a dark anticipation of SAC's iconography. Here the rationale was laid out that would lead to the A-bomb. Soon, poet Randall Jarrell, who served in the Air Corps, would write, 'In bombers named after girls we bombed cities we had learned about in school.'

James Agee, then film critic for *Time*, found the film a skilful piece of propaganda, but noted that it never showed the target. And he was disturbed about the total absence of images of the victims on the ground. It was full, he wrote, of 'gay dreams of holocaust'.

It was not long before Seversky and Disney's dreams of holocaust would be realized. The B-29, the long-range bomber, was being developed in top secrecy at Boeing in Seattle even as the film was being made. It was a black project too: the level of secrecy was comparable to the Manhattan Project. When test pilot Eddie Allen flew a prototype with an engine on fire into a packing plant practically over downtown Seattle, an alert bus driver snapped pictures. Shortly afterwards government agents confiscated every single copy of the issue of the *City Transit News* in which his photos had appeared.

And Curtis LeMay, then training at Muroc, would follow the B-29 to Asia. First the bomber would have to make its torturous way through technical teething problems – engines that were constantly catching fire, for instance – and logistical ones. It moved from bases in India to runways in China, supplied by flights over the Himalayas, levelled out by hundreds of coolies pulling giant stone rollers, each taller than a man. The next stop was Okinawa, then the Marianas, from which at last the bombers could effectively reach Japan; Disney's eagle attack on the octopus.

When the first raids – aimed at precision – failed due to bad weather and bad bombing to strike their intended targets effectively, LeMay was put in command.

Invariably referred to as 'cigar chomping', LeMay had been a navigator on one of the crucial demonstration flights in which bombers took on Navy battleships and won the day for the theory of air power. The episode also shaped LeMay's thinking about the enemy forever: the Navy had cheated during the tests, and LeMay became a brutal practitioner of interservice rivalry, cutting down the competition first on behalf of the Air Force, then on behalf of SAC.

The B-29 was a complement to the A-bomb programme. Already when LeMay took over, crews were training for the A-bomb mission in a godforsaken corner of Utah, near Wendover. But it had been ineffective in carrying out the high altitude precision bombing for which it was designed and which was the key tenet of LeMay's air power theory.

So he tried something new – gambling the lives of his crews. He turned to terror bombing: firebombing whole cities. Now his target problem was simpler: find the areas of cities that were the oldest, with the largest proportion of wooden buildings. The first target was Tokyo's largely wood Shitamchi district.

Stripping the bombers of most of their guns and sending them in low, at night, on 9 March 1945, LeMay dispatched 334 of the bombers from bases in the Marianas Islands, each carrying about seven tons of incendiary bombs. Because he knew of such secrets as the A-bomb project, LeMay himself was not allowed to fly on the Tokyo raid.

He paced the floor of his office on Guam while his long-time second-in-command, Tommy Powers, led the raid. (Powers, LeMay would later say, was a bit of a 'sadist'. He would succeed LeMay as head of SAC.)

The lead bombers marked an X in fire on the area: the bombs burned more than the sixteen square miles targeted, killing between 80,000 and 100,000 people. The raid created the most devastating firestorm of the war, a fire so powerful it sent updraughts that tossed the bombers about as their crews breathed the sickening smoke of burning houses and human flesh.

To those on the ground, the bombs seemed to flow down like silver rain, a liquid rather than a series of objects.

The fires on the ground moved in waves and then columns of flame. Women fleeing, carrying babies on their backs, would continue to walk, not knowing that the bundles on their backs had burst into flame. Bodies assumed the twisted, pumice quality of Pompeiian victims. Those who dropped into canals or pools seeking refuge were boiled to death.

The fires died down fairly quickly and processions of silent refugees began to move out of the area, walking under moonlight amid the burning ruins. One man paused to light a cigar at a still-burning telephone pole.

Time magazine called the raid 'a dream come true'. It showed that 'properly kindled, Japanese cities will burn like autumn leaves'.

Approximately as many people died in this, the first great triumph of air power, as did in the Hiroshima and Nagasaki atomic bombings put together. The step to the atomic bomb was only one of technical means – of efficiency.

Air power may not have won World War II – its bad report cards from post-war teams were overlooked by the public – but it won its own war: the Air Force became an independent service and quickly grabbed the lion's share of the budget from Navy carriers and the Army. The cult of air power would grow as strong in the 1940s and 1950s as the cult of the battleship that LeMay and the others had fought against in the 1920s and 1930s.

The dominance of air power was ratified in 1947 by the establishment of the Air Force as a separate branch of the military, equal in status to the Army and Navy. The same year brought the creation of the Central Intelligence Agency, the declaration of the Truman Doctrine and the Marshall Plan. It saw the invention of the transistor and the breaking of the sound barrier, by Chuck Yeager, over the dry lake at Muroc.

But one of the first tasks the new Air Force found itself dealing with was one wholly different from its anticipated role. It was called upon to explain reports of mysterious craft – possibly craft from distant stars. 'They were as shiny as mirrors,' pilot Kenneth Arnold reported of the objects he saw near Mt Rainier, Washington, on the afternoon of 24 June 1947, 'and there were nine of them, in loose formation, shaped like boomerangs or flying wedges, moving at tremendous speed.'

After landing in Pendleton, Oregon, Arnold described his sighting to Nolan Skiff, a columnist for the local newspaper, the *East Oregonian*, and told Skiff how the objects 'flew like a saucer would if you skipped it across the water'. Skiff wrote a story that was soon picked up by the Associated Press. From flying like a saucer, the objects turned, in the Associated Press story, into 'saucer-like' objects, then into 'flying saucers'.

The flying saucer would come to inhabit the dreams of the postwar era, focusing fears and hopes like the lens whose shape it shares, reflecting the wider culture like its mirrored surface.

Nothing says more about the origins of the flying saucer than the birth of its name in the Press. For the image of the saucer was about to become a new kind of mythological figure, a Hermes or Puck, a unicorn or leprechaun, that flourished primarily not in oral tradition but in the mass media. The first folk figure to emerge from the realm of technology, the flying saucer was established as the most flexible sort of cultural icon, with overtones ranging from the cosmic; dark visions of potential invasions – to the comic; a thousand magazine cartoons with stubby saucers piloted by little green men.

What at first seemed a novelty story persisted. In the days after Arnold's sighting, dozens of additional reports flowed in from around the world. In July, the Air Force boldly issued a press release claiming the 'capture' of a flying disc, at Roswell, New Mexico, then decided that the object had in fact been a weather balloon. It would be quickly forgotten, only to be re-examined in the 1980s as the most fascinating of all crash cases, the subject of many books, and a television film. Within two months, polls showed, ninety per cent of Americans had heard of flying saucers.

Arnold at first thought what he had seen were advanced military aircraft. In Roswell, too, one citizen told the *Daily Record* at the time of the ostensible crash there that he suspected the device 'was an experiment by one of the military forces'. Secret programmes, wildly new technologies announced almost daily, and rising tensions, which in the new atomic age threatened the end of the planet – into this environment the flying saucer was delivered.

'Peace is our Profession'

Curtis LeMay had taken command of SAC in October 1948 and declared it a shambles, with untrained crews who couldn't hit their targets. He staged a mock bombing attack on Dayton, Ohio. It was a dismal failure – most crews missed. LeMay called it the darkest day in the history of air power. He proceeded to get SAC in shape.

His premise was: we are at war already. Since the next war would be won or lost before it started, we were in effect already fighting World War III – a war of deterrence.

Some of his planes had to be in the air at all times. All were designed to scramble quickly, with a red button for one touch, start up, Le Mans-style inside the nose wheel wells where you boarded the plane.

To LeMay it was clear that when World War III came – and he almost longed for it – there would be no chance for the big comeback of World War II. A Pearl Harbor would be fatal.

He had no hesitation about striking first if attack seemed imminent. With every passing year, the margin of advantage for the US grew smaller. SAC's advantage, LeMay said, was a 'wasting asset'. It seemed crazy to him to let the other guys strike first. 'Hit 'em with their pants down,' as George C. Scott urges, playing the general in *Dr Strangelove*. He was based on LeMay.

LeMay had an obsession with security and fear of sabotage. He gained national publicity when he staged a surprise visit to an SAC hangar and found the security guy eating lunch. 'I saw a man guarding our planes with ham sandwich,' was his line. He had crack Air Police patrolling SAC bases, like the units in *Dr Strangelove*. He would test security by dispatching trained 'penetrators' to plant notes that said 'This is a bomb'. This obsession shows up in the film *Strategic Air Command*, in which mild-mannered Jimmy Stewart goes back to the Air Force, and is baffled by the rough security checks at the base gate.

Sometimes they would paste a baby or animal picture on the ID badges just to test security guards. Once a general found soldiers entering his office to repair phone lines. It took him several minutes before he realized that the Air Force used outside repair people. He drew his automatic before they had time to deposit the slip of paper that read 'This is a bomb'. The penetrators became a regular nuisance to SAC crews. LeMay even had his own wife checked out with a bogus repairman who tried to penetrate his residence.

'Do you realize how many babies are born in SAC each month?' said Jimmy Stewart, as the B-36 pilot in the film *Strategic Air Command*. I had been one of those babies. I grew up on an SAC base.

Those were the days of great silver bombers keeping us all safe. Growing up in the shadow of the B-36 also meant growing up amid the lore and legend of air power: the belief that wars would now be won or lost by great silver bombers, raining destruction on distant cities, had sent my father and thousands of others from small towns and the outer boroughs, creating those All-American bomber crew mixtures – the kid from Brooklyn, the guy from Texas, the farm boy and the city boy – that would fly from Wichita to Khartoum and Bombay, to China and Guam, and eventually over the Imperial Palace in Tokyo, for General LeMay.

Behind the SAC logo, an armoured fist with the same glint as off the aluminium back of a B-36 holding a fistful of lightning bolts, was the bomber fleet that stayed airborne around the clock, protecting us from the Russians. The B-36s, bombers with wings so big crewmen walked around inside them to work on engines in flight, flew over our house in Florida. And in kindergarten I modelled B-36s from red and green clay. Often I gave them eight or even ten engines rather than the six props and dual jets podded at the end of the wings. The specific number was inconsequential to a four-year-old. The key point was that there sure seemed a lot of engines on that wing.

'Aluminium overcast' they called the big bombers, with the heavy humour of aviation folk.

The B-36 was huge, but the great glass dome and the bulbous nose gave the plane a stupid, brontosaurian look. In flight, the dome atop the bomber was often filled with blue smoke. The smoke was cigar smoke, which its pilots indulged in during long flights. They felt free to do so because their boss was rarely without his own stogie. And the cigar was one of the few indulgences he tolerated. Sometimes a cigar is just a cigar, but in SAC it was a symbol of jaunty *esprit de corps*, an accent of élan on the way to the end of the world.

Trophies given to the winning crew in an SAC competition one year were ashtrays, with a B-36 mounted on their rim, set on a little stalk as if in flight, circling the smoking ashes beneath. The job, of course, was to leave just such a pile of ashes on the ground.

The B-36 was the flagship of SAC during the 1950s but it was something of a turkey, slower and with less range than promised. Originally designed in 1941 to reach Germany from the United States in case Britain fell, it first flew in 1946. The B-36, whose six pusher prop engines were joined in improved models with four jets riding twin pods at the end of the wings was a mechanically ragged plane, saved by its abundance of engines. There was a joke about it: 'Pilot: Feather four. Engineer: Which four?'

The bomber's big, slow propellers emitted a particular WHUP–whump sound. One pilot recalls how it sounded like a street car rumbling toward take off.

SAC was all about great silver planes that crisscrossed the globe. It was about the nuclear nightmare, which its generals dreamed of daily. And the black planes of Dreamland would come sometimes to rival, and sometimes serve, the silver planes.

In the 1950s SAC ruled the Air Force.

SAC's silver planes would form an odd adversarial relationships with the black planes taking shape in Dreamland. SAC would supply crews and eventually own those planes, but it was never happy with them. And those planes would find targets for SAC and – grimly – prepare to evaluate the effectiveness with which SAC would hit them on Doomsday.

The 1954 film *Strategic Air Command* was a virtual Pentagon tract. The star, Jimmy Stewart, reprises earlier roles – Lindbergh grown up and Mr Smith gone to Armageddon, or at least Omaha, site of SAC headquarters. Even under the threat of the bomb, it's a wonderful life. A good family man, out there defending 'our way of life', he's loyal to his pregnant wife, played by June Allyson, until SAC calls. Fifteen hundred babies, every month, justified their tyranny: SAC's big boom was somehow tied to the Baby Boom and Levittown's sprawl.

The message is clear: constant vigilance was the price of the Eisenhower prosperity – aluminium overcast was a shield. After the B-36 came the jet B-47, chosen instead of the flying wing, the dream of John Northrop later to be realized in the shape of the B-2 stealth bomber, and only that aircraft can steal Jimmy Stewart's heart from his wife. 'She's the most beautiful thing I've ever seen,' he gushes – when he first sees the B-47.

Curtis LeMay needed targets. He had a thousand of those shiny beautiful B-47s on order. What would they hit? He had always counted on targets. When he was commanding the 20th Air Force B-29 group bombing Japan in 1945, he was once asked when the war would end. He motioned an aide over and asked him for a list. 'How many targets do we have left?' LeMay asked. The war would be over, he said, when he ran out of targets.

SAC's Cold War was a new kind of war, but LeMay still needed targets. He needed them to etch into three dimensional Lucite templates for the radar bomb sights of his planes. He needed them to flesh out his Strategic Library Bombing Index. He needed them to shape the SIOP, the sinister acronym for 'single integrated operations plan' – the blueprint for nuclear war.

LeMay needed targets because he alone controlled them. Neither the joint chiefs nor the President knew the targets in case of nuclear war. LeMay kept the information to himself until the early Sixties. And since there were no locks, no Presidential codes for the weapons his bombers – and later missiles – carried until the Sixties, he could have launched a nuclear war on his own authority against the targets.

LeMay feared dilly-dallying politicians: he wanted to 'hit 'em with everything we've got', as quickly as possible at the first signs of any massing of the bombers he was sure the Soviets were rapidly building.

But he had very little information. SAC was still using German maps of the country from World War II. The Soviet Union was a great black empty space as far as LeMay was concerned.

Human agents had little success. They might manage to pass for ordinary Soviet citizens, but ordinary Soviet citizens had virtually no access to the areas and targets desired.

Reconnaissance versions of the B-29 had skirted the perimeter of the Soviet Union since the end of World War II. A variety of electronic listening and air sample programmes had been in continuous operation.

There were other ideas floating around. In the early Fifties a forward-looking officer at Wright Pat had taken a look at new engines and wings and realized it might be possible to fly above radar. Major John Seaberg created Project Bald Eagle, developed to produce a high flying spy plane. Specs were issued, proposals advanced, but nothing came of it.

Several balloon programmes had been used to spy; one was Mogul, the secret programme later asserted to have been the source of the Roswell 'saucer' wreckage, aimed at sampling potential fallout from Soviet atomic weapons.

The most ambitious balloon programme carried cameras: Project Genetrix, aka Weapons System 119L, launched polyethylene balloons high into the jetstreams. It operated under the weather cover story and the name 'Moby Dick'. It was an ambitious effort, involving five launch sites and ten locations for tracking, and the Russians protested as soon as the first flight was made, in January 1956. Almost five hundred balloons were launched, some shot down, many lost, and only forty produced any useful photos. The programme ended with the humiliating spectacle of captured balloons being displayed derisively in Moscow's Gorky Park as evidence of imperialist treachery.

LeMay also enlisted the help of the British for a less confrontational approach and supplied them with planes, Canberra bombers adapted for reconnaissance. They fared poorly. Historian Richard Rhodes records that one pilot from those missions, looking out of the cockpit, realized what a difficult task it would be to find anything in the vast landmass. It looked, he said 'like one large black hole'. Some of the Canberras returned full of bullet holes.

When President Dwight Eisenhower, in his Open Skies proposal, suggested that the US and the USSR should allow each other free reconnaissance overflights, the Soviets were suspicious. They rejected the proposal immediately; it was a confession of the United States' lack of success.

In September 1956, LeMay sent a fleet of RB-47s over Vladivostok at high noon, brushing off the few MiGs that rose to intercept them. He did this without approval from his commanders. LeMay operated alone: he could easily have started a war with such a flight.

In fact, there is much evidence he regretted not doing so. He saw the SAC lead as a wasted asset – use it before you lose it, he thought. When he called in another RB-47 crew who had taken MiG damage on another mission, he joked about 'maybe getting World War III started'.

8

'Paradise Ranch'

FOR CURTIS LEMAY, 1954 WAS NOT THE YEAR OF OPEN SKIES
or Giant Rock, it was 'the year of maximum danger', the year
when the Soviets would have enough bombs and bombers to
hit us and he wouldn't yet have enough of the silver bombers
he wanted to strike back. For the country at large, it was a year
of fear – the height or depth of Cold War paranoia, the high
water mark of McCarthyism.

The greatest fear of the time was of surprise attack, another
Pearl Harbor, a nuclear Sunday punch. Ike feared a surprise
attack too, a lack of intelligence like the one that had nearly
cost him his reputation at the Battle of the Bulge.

Seaberg's proposal was brought out of the files and contractors quietly contacted. Among the proposals offered were
one for a Mach 4 plane launched from the back of a fast B-58
bomber. Another called for a ramjet aircraft to be carried to
high altitude by a huge balloon, then released. Kelly Johnson
of the Lockheed Skunk Works proposed putting long wings on
the fuselage of his F-104 Starfighter – and he could do it quickly,
he promised.

To Edwin 'Din' Land of Polaroid, head of the subcommittee
looking at the issue, the Skunk Works proposal called the CL-
282, seemed the most practical and potentially the fastest way
to put cameras over the Soviet Union. He was impressed. On 5
November 1954, Land wrote a memo to CIA Director Allen
Dulles called 'A Unique Opportunity for Comprehensive Intelligence', pushing the Lockheed idea. 'No proposal or program
that we have seen in intelligence planning can so quickly bring
so much vital information at so little risk and at so little cost.'

Land noted that, 'We have been forced to imagine what the
[Soviet's] program is, and it could well be argued that peace is
always in danger when one great power is essentially ignorant

of the major economic, military, and political activities ... of another great power ... We cannot fulfill our responsibility for maintaining the peace if we are left in ignorant of Russian activities.'

Land made another key point: such a programme was also vital to avoid 'over-estimation' of the enemy – as dangerous as its opposite.

Land was persuasive and the full committee obtained Eisenhower's approval. By December 1954, Kelly Johnson had in his hand a contract to produce twenty of the planes for $22 million – within nine months. The CIA would foot the tab from discretionary, and very much unaccounted for, funds. And it – not the Air Force – would take charge of the project, called 'Aquatone'.

Soon a strange figure began to be seen in the shops and offices of the Skunk Works. A tall, stooped man, he walked in a way that inevitably reminded observers of a stork. Ben Rich thought that in his striped pants and sports jacket wandering around the Skunk Works he looked more fit for the races. No one introduced him, this odd Easterner – anyone at Lockheed could recognize that he was from back East – so out of place inside the yellow hangars in Burbank, except occasionally he was referred to simply as 'Mr B'. He would look even more out of place later on the caliche runway at the base at Groom Lake.

Mr B. was Richard Bissell, a former Yale economics professor who now headed the CIA programme codenamed Aquatone.

He had grown up in comparative privilege, travelling by ocean liner to Europe. Once he tossed his teddy bear off the fantail of the *Queen Mary* and ordered his nanny to retrieve it. As a teenager, he looked out on the Coliseum and the ruins of the Forum in Rome and meditated on the nature of empire building.

It was a mode of thinking that would be amenable to the big picture views current in Washington in the late Forties and early Fifties. Dean Acheson had compared the stand-off in the late Forties between the US and the USSR to that between Rome and Carthage.

A prep school education at Groton, where even he was far from the wealthiest student, imbued him with further ideals.

But in the preppy world, he stood out as a comparative rebel, with a daring that belied his academic success.

But at Yale, he was an America Firster, dedicated to keeping the country out of the mounting European conflict.

He graduated in 1932, and went on to graduate school, standing out in academia and turning to government. He was just in time to become a key figure in one of the unsung but vital logistics battles of World War II. While U-boats roamed in wolfpacks preying on Allied shipping and the codebreakers back in England kept trying to defeat them without tipping their hands, Bissell apportioned the precious commodity that cargo tonnage had become. Bissell almost single-handedly had run the allied merchant shipping programme using a complex system of filecards, figuring out how to turn ships around fast, and whether to fill their limited holds with bombs or oil or coal, how to get fruit and tea to London. The academic-turned-technocrat went on to draft the initial proposal for the Marshall Plan.

In Washington, his connections quickly made him part of the Georgetown cocktail party set which saw the gathering over martinis of the Rostows and the Alsops, the Grahams (Kate and Phil of the *Washington Post*) and the Dulles, John Foster, Ike's Secretary of State and Eleanor, a state department expert in Asian affairs – and Allen, the head of the CIA.

When life at the Ford Foundation grew dull, Bissell gently dropped a hint that he might consider work at the agency.

He was one of the new generation of logistics and technology experts, the technocrats, who came out of the war effort – for World War II had been a war of logistics. He became one of the Ivy League educated cadre that ran the early CIA. While Henry Stimson, Republican Secretary of State and the very rootbranch of WASP privilege had shut down the famed Black Chamber in 1929, saying 'Gentlemen do not read each other's mail', the coming of World War II had made it necessary for gentlemen to spy, and to fight dirty. The same crisis that could supersede gentility persisted into the Cold War. The Ivy League, especially Yale, became a prime recruiting ground for the intelligence agencies, first the OSS and then the new CIA.

The OSS had first brought Ivy Leaguers into espionage. The schemes to get rid of Castro that would shock a nation when they were revealed at the Church hearing in 1973 were like others: the OSS and CIA had come up with wacky schemes before, such as the idea of dropping pornographic literature on Berchtesgarden – Hitler's retreat – to drive him mad with lust.

After World War II, the Yale crew coach Skip Waltz was the chief recruiter for the CIA. A few measured words at the boathouse to a team player, a suggestion in confidence, brought dozens of oarsmen into the CIA.

But while many of the Ivy League recruits had been athletes, men of action, Bissell was unusual – an academic, who came out of a foundation to the agency. Bissell liked systems, flow, tables. He would take little interest in the actual content of the pictures the U-2 or SR-71 would take. He was the champion of the coming thing in intelligence – technology, photint, elint – and it would sometimes put him in conflict with the traditionalists – the humint people.

But Bissell was most interested in the psychology of CIA operations, the manipulation of public opinion, the creation of illusory forces rather than the use of actual weapons.

The U-2, for instance, he would argue in his memoirs, was a kind of psychological weapon as well, showing that the United States could overfly the Soviet Union with impunity. It was for this reason – the humiliation the military felt at having been so brazenly overflown – that the Soviets would insist on their claim to have shot down the U-2 at 70,000 feet with a single anti-aircraft missile. In fact, they probably fired a huge salvo, knocking one of their own fighters out of the sky.

Bissell's first success had come with the overthrow of the dictator Jacobo Arbenz in Guatemala in 1954, which along with the overthrow of Mossadegh in Iran and his replacement by the Shah, was the CIA's proudest achievement since its founding in 1947.

Accomplished at the behest not just of the President but of the United Fruit Company, the Guatemala operation set the CIA on the course of exotic 'covert', 'destabilizing' operations.

The mode of the operation was significant for Bissell's thinking: it turned, not on military force, but on illusion: bogus radio transmissions, telling of gathering rebel forces – the old idea of a few soldiers walking back and forth along a wall to suggest a large army. The rebel air force was a couple of old P51s that Bissell arranged to have Antonio Somoza – the Nicaraguan dictator we would 'turn on' much later – buy and lease out for cover. When real bombs ran out, the planes dropped Coke bottles that emitted a sinister whistle that replicated the bomb noise of cliché and newsreel soundtracks. This was the perfect symbol of American intervention circa 1954: the Coca-Cola bottle as bomb, bringing fear and intimidation – the norte-americano gods must be crazy. This revolution went better with Coke.

Success in Guatemala would lend the CIA a sense of false confidence that would lead to the Bay of Pigs.

In the fall of 1955 Allen Dulles called Bissell in and out of the blue gave him the job of running the programme called Aquatone.

Dulles, cat-like with his whiskery moustache, tweedy and academic, puffing on his pipe, looked his role. But he was a master bureaucrat. Dulles got the Air Force to cover his ass with a letter saying that indeed the absurdly optimistic schedule Kelly Johnson proposed was realistic.

While Johnson was building the plane, special cameras were developed by the best minds in the American photographic industry under the direction of Harvard astronomer James Baker. They would carry 10,000 feet of film on each flight and be able to photograph a swathe of territory 125 miles wide and 3000 miles long.

Bissell would go on to develop the first spy satellite Corona, a project begun in 1958. They all knew it was only a matter of time before Soviet anti-aircraft missiles could reach 70,000 feet or so and make the U-2 vulnerable. And he planned the Blackbird to fly higher and faster.

The first flight of the Blackbird coincided almost exactly with the maiden flight of the Russians' first spy satellite. From now on, aircraft at Groom would have to be kept in hangars or covered with camouflage when Soviet satellites came overhead, as they surely would. They already knew about Dreamland in the Kremlin.

But by the time the Blackbird flew, Richard Bissell was a private citizen. He had been eased out of the CIA, pinned with a medal by JFK and issued with his walking papers, in February

1962 – a dismissal occasioned by the Bay of Pigs fiasco and delayed only for the sake of appearances. He attended the first flight as a guest of Kelly Johnson and only because of Johnson's loyalty was he standing on the white surface at Groom when the long bird took off, with Lou Schalk at the controls.

Work went on building the new plane in Lockheed's hangar at the Burbank Airport. The first flight was scheduled for August, 1955. Soon the Skunk Works engineers would need somewhere to test fly it.

They had the whole West to choose from. First, World War II and then the Cold War had made the great deserts a vast canvas on which the Pentagon daubed bases, depots and ranges. Most recently, in 1950, the military had taken a huge tract northwest of Las Vegas for the Nuclear Test Site, fearing a loss of access to South Pacific test sites in the wake of the Korean War.

But Kelly Johnson knew they could not test the U2 at Edwards. By 1954, that base had become too public. This was a project so secret that its treasury was Johnson's own home mailbox, in Encino and its cover firm C&J (after Clarence Johnson) Inc.

Johnson knew who he wanted to fly it first – Tony LeVier, his top test pilot. But first he had to find a place to fly it from.

One day in the spring of 1955, Johnson, LeVier and Dorsey Krammerer of the Skunk Works, set out east to look for a test site. On several flights, they checked out a variety of airstrips and disused bases. Then finally Osmond Ritland, the CIA's military aide to the programme, remembered a strip in the gunnery range where he had been stationed for a time during World War II. It was in the desert north of Nellis Air Force Base, in Nevada. With the map spread over Johnson's lap, they aimed for the little X, north of the vast Nuclear Test Site. 'Man alive,' Ritland would later recall. 'We looked at that lake, and we all looked at each other. It was another Edwards, so we wheeled around, landed on that lake, taxied up to one end of it and Kelly Johnson said, 'We'll put the runway right there.'

The lake was still littered with .50 calibre machine gun shells from its days as a gunnery range. The lake bed itself was white caliche – ka lee chay, they pronounced it – soil, calcium carbonate, natural concrete, self-mending when the rare rains came, melting its surface and smoothing it flat.

Soon, there would be 75 people working here, paving the runway, building hangars and setting up mobile homes bought from the Navy as barracks. By the time training started, the number jumped to 250. The U-2s were flown in cargo planes, their wings removed. An official CIA history rather prissily explains, 'the site at first afforded few of the necessities and none of the amenities of life.'

They flew Richard Bissell out to the site.

'This will do nicely,' Mr B. commented.

He even liked Johnson's proposed name for the place: 'Paradise Ranch'.

Johnson and Bissell worked out for the Nevada Test Site to take official ownership of the strip. In August construction of the runway began and a Press release was even issued, tying the work to the test site. The job was done by REECO, Reynolds Electric, the subsidiary of EG&G that ran the nuclear test site. It was referred to now as 'Watertown Strip' – perhaps an ironic reference to the dryness of the place – and not Groom Lake, part of the cover story emerging that described the aircraft as a weather balloon.

Meanwhile, a continent away, the office for the programme, the command post for the new desert test strip, was set up in the E ring of the Pentagon. For his part, Bissell moved out of the CIA headquarters on the Mall and into a special programme management office with a staff of 225. It set up headquarters in an old office on L street – one of the temporary wartime buildings that had never been removed, an apt metaphor for the survival of the war mentality into the uneasy peace, that continuing expediency occasioned by continuing crisis. The place was named 'Bissell Center' and some in the Agency began talking of the RBAF as 'Richard Bissell Air Force'.

The photo processing centre was set up in a seedy part of town at K and Fifth St, NW, on four floors above offices of the Steuart Motor Car Company, an auto repair shop. It was codenamed Automat.

'Watertown'

Aircraft ferried workers and materials from the Skunk Works in Burbank and the factory, set up in Oildale near Bakersfield, a scruffy little cotton and oil town where country singer Merle Haggard had grown up in an old box car. The pilots flying to the new secret base were not told exactly where it was. They were simply told to fly to a set of co-ordinates in the middle of the desert and then await instructions from a mysterious air control centre called Sage Control. They were there to listen for instructions from 'Delta'. At a certain point, when the radar picked them up, the crews were ordered to descend into the dark desert, and lower their gears and flaps. Only then did the runway lights of the remote strip flicker on beneath them.

Between those flights, those working at the base were isolated. They lived four to a trailer and could contact families only in an emergency. The phone for this purpose was called the 'hello' phone, because that was the only way it was to be answered. The number was given out for use only in emergencies. A message was left and the worker or engineer would call back. This became a fixture of black projects.

On 17 November 1955, a C-54 making the run from Burbank misestimated its altitude and struck Mount Charleston, northwest of Las Vegas, just thirty feet short of its top. It took three days for a rescue party to reach the crash; one of its members was an Air Force colonel who picked through the wreckage removing briefcases with classified documents from among the bodies. The Skunk Works was lucky; some of its key people had missed the flight due to overindulgence at a beer bash the night before.

Curtis LeMay didn't like the idea of a bunch of civilians running an aircraft programme. But, equally insistent was Eisenhower's conviction that he needed a less biased source of intelligence than the Air Force. Protecting himself and the American taxpayer from the military was as important a function of the U-2 as protecting us from the Soviet Union. LeMay's deputy, Tommy Powers, was flown to the Watertown camp in 1955 and briefed. In the deal that was worked out, SAC would train and 'sheep dip' the pilots – moving them from military to civilian status and training them. And while Herb Miller of Bissell's office helped set the place up, the base now got co-Air Force and CIA commanders.

LeMay carefully planned to let the agency build the U-2 and then take it away on behalf of SAC. But the Skunk Works and Agency worked to build their own credibility over LeMay's head. In December 1955, Secretary of Defense Charles 'Engine Charlie' Wilson was flown to the site to bolster his enthusiasm for the programme. He talked from the tower to a U-2 pilot high above. Later, Allen Dulles himself, pipe and all, dropped in to chat with the pilots in training.

The AEC covered the construction work with a brief statement about the building of the airstrip, suggesting it was for nuclear testing activities, and later the familiar weather research cover story was put to work again. On 7 May 1956, a Press release was issued signed by NACA director Hugh Dryden announcing that the new weather research plane had been developed and flown. 'The first data, covering conditions in the Rocky Mountain area, are being obtained from flights from Watertown Strip, Nevada.' This fooled few people; the Soviets had a copy when they shot down Francis Gary Powers.

At the same time, a long-planned Press visit to the X-15 rocket plane at Edwards was hastily expanded to include a look at a 'NACA' U-2, which had to be moved from the secret North Base section of the flight test complex and painted up. It was given a bogus tail number; the paint wasn't even dry when the reporters entered the hangar – the ground crew was terrified one of the reporters would get close enough to touch it. Photos of the weather U-2 look as if they were retouched, with the NACA initials on the tail.

At 4:30 on the morning of 14 July 1955, 'the Article', as the first U-2 was simply known, was loaded on a C-124 and flown to the new base, with Kelly Johnson and others following in a C-47. By 4 August, it had been assembled and was ready to fly. The first test was to be a simple taxi-ing. There was no question as to who would pilot the first flight. Kelly Johnson chose Tony LeVier, his top test pilot.

LeVier, who had chosen 'Anthony Evans' as his requisite code name for the project was 42 then, with a career wringing out the P-38 for Lockheed and then test piloting the first Skunk Works plane, the XP-80 jet. He was 14 when Charles Lindbergh flew the Atlantic and he immediately began earning money collecting old tyres and other junk in his neighbourhood of Whittier, California, to earn five bucks to pay for his first plane ride. Beginning with the Waco 10 in which he first soloed three years later, LeVier would fly more than 250 different aircraft.

By the time he came to Lockheed in 1941, he was already well-known as a stunt and aerobatics pilot. He flew such exotic craft as the Mendenhall Special from Muroc Dry Lake in 1936 and won major trophy races in 1938 in the Schoenfeldt Firecracker.

At Lockheed, he immediately became involved in helping to figure out the weird compression problems of the P-38 – precursors of the sound barrier – and would put in more hours in its cockpit than any other test pilot. In June 1944 he made the first flight in the jet XP-80a, and flew its successor, the Gray Ghost, the plane he said that came the closest to killing him. In March, 1945, LeVier pushed the jet past 550 mph when a turbine blade let go and he found himself embarrassed by the sudden lack of a tail. The plane began to tumble and with the Gs he could barely reach the canopy release handle. When he did, it came off in his hand. Reaching behind the seat he grabbed the raw cable – it worked, and at 4000 feet he finally managed to bail out. Tony LeVier also had to get out of the next jet, the P-80A, when a turbine wheel departed its mounting and set off like a buzz saw, or flying saucer through the fuselage, the ribs and skin, as if they were nothing sturdier than clouds, and the plane lost its tail. Finally it just turned over and dumped him out and he pulled himself up in a little ball, waiting for it to strike him, but then all of a sudden found himself and what was left of the plane dropping toward the desert at the same steady rate. Once again, however, he survived.

But for all the near escapes and the flamboyance with which his career began, LeVier developed into the most scientific and cautious of test pilots. He was not the wild-eyed Yeager type, but obsessed with safety. He had seen too many guys killed. In his retirement he would establish an organization to teach better, safer flying practices and was constantly frustrated with the lack of support from government and industry. He developed such practical and basic safety devices as the master warning light system, the trim switch on the control stick and the afterburner igniter.

With the U-2, he would take no more risks than necessary. It was hard to see from the cockpit and get a sense of horizon; he wanted the landing strip painted with markings. Finally LeVier himself put strips of black electrical tape on the canopy to indicate the true horizon.

U-2 – 'Utility 2' – was the innocuous and noncommittal name of the plane. But there was another story about how the name came to be.

The plane's long wings gave it so much lift that it was hard to land. It was hard to see out of the cockpit too, and before he went up for the first flight. LeVier planned just to taxi.

'It went up like a homesick angel,' LeVier said, more for quotation than anything else, 'it flies like a baby buggy.' The only problem was it didn't want to come down. In the C-47 chase plane, Johnson kept after LeVier to land nose down, but the plane kept porpoising – it would go groundwards and begin a forward and aft wiggle, the 'porpoise'. After five or six tries, and mounting temper on both sides, LeVier came in and did it the way he wanted to begin with – he stalled the plane to get it on the ground.

Once they were both down, Johnson and LeVier continued to argue. 'What the hell were you trying to do, kill me?' LeVier said. He gave Johnson the finger.

'Well, fuck you.'

'And fuck you too,' Johnson replied in kind.

The 'you too' attached itself to the aircraft.

Or so the tale goes.

Within minutes after the landing a heavy rain began – the first in months, the equivalent of the lake's total annual rainfall.

'You did a great job,' Kelly told LeVier at last. Then that night there was a big beer bash and the armwrestling that Kelly, proud of the strength he had acquired during his youth, always fostered. When they armwrestled, Johnson took LeVier down right away.

The next morning LeVier appeared with a bandage on his arm, wanting to make the point that Johnson had injured the arm of his chief test pilot. But Johnson remembered nothing of the night before.

The project was variously called 'Aquatone' and 'Idealist', but the plane itself, for a long time, was just referred to as 'the Article', as in the mil spec phrase, 'test article'. Soon some at the Skunk Works were referring to it as 'Kelly's Angel'.

After a character in Milton Caniff's comic strip 'Terry and the Pirates', it was later nicknamed 'Dragon Lady'. Terry and the Dragon Lady were erstwhile enemies, became tenuous friends as the Cold War brought hostility between Taiwan and Mainland China. It symbolized the uneasy relationship between pilot and the tricky plane that was the triumph of Kelly Johnson's Skunk Works – and a symbol of the new kinds of weapons that the Cold War demanded.

To take off, the U-2 wore long, drop-off wheels on its wing tips – 'pogo sticks' they were called – and one pilot said they made the aircraft look like a vulture on crutches. That was the right image: the U-2 was delicate and dangerous to fly. It would kill several men at the Ranch before it ever went overseas.

The plane was fragile, with a skin just 2/100ths of an inch thick: its aerodynamics left only a tiny window between over-speeding and stalling. Its fuel could shift suddenly and throw it off balance, its engines were prone to flaming out and its wings were so long they could snap with sudden manoeuvres.

After the training operation was moved from the Ranch to Laughlin Air Force Base in Del Rio, Texas, in June 1957 one eager young pilot decided to fly his plane over his house to show off. He banked, dipped his wings, then stalled and crashed.

In early 1956, Richard Bissell organized an emergency landing. A pilot suffered a flame-out over Tennessee and radioed back. Using a procedure set in place, where sealed envelopes had been left at selected SAC bases for just this eventuality, Bissell had the pilot directed to Kirtland AFB in Albuquerque. Then Bissell phoned the base commander at

Kirtland and told him that in about forty-five minutes a secret plane would be landing at his field and he should immediately remove it from view, cover it and phone for further instructions. Just half an hour later Bissell got the word that all had gone as planned. The U-2 had that much glide range.

What Frank Powers remembered about Watertown, as he knew the airstrip at Dreamland, was the food. The pilots lived in trailers, four men to each. There wasn't much to do – a movie at night, a couple of pool tables, no bar, nor club. Lots of poker. He looked forward to the plane back to Burbank on the weekends and his return from his other identity 'Francis G. Palmer', to 'Francis Gary Powers'.

But the food – it was better food than in Turkey, where Powers was to be stationed, better food than in Lubyanka or Vladimir prisons, that was for sure, where he was faced with fish soup and endless rations of potatoes – and once a week, the highlight of the fare, a cube of meat the size, he recalled, of a thumbnail.

After his U-2 was shot down on 1 May 1960, precipitating a Cold War nightmare for the US, Powers thought back to the food at the Ranch, as he called it, just as he had learned to refer to the CIA as 'the company' or 'the government'. Good food was a theme that would be sounded again and again in the few stories that came out of Dreamland.

Before his release, he would lie on his bunk, dreaming of a good old American martini. Sometimes he would wake with visions of ice cream sodas in his head, food he could clearly feel and smell, but never before he woke, taste. He dreamed almost nightly of banana splits and coconut cream pies, hamburgers and green salads – it shocked him that he could miss a green salad so much. Once, he argued with his cellmates about whether we dream in colour or only black and white. He resolved the argument that night. In his prison cell he had a dream he remembered was clearly in colour – a banquet of food and wine. But before he could taste any of it he woke up.

Powers came to the Ranch in the spring of 1956, in the second class of pilots to be trained to fly the U-2. The week before Powers' class arrived another pilot had bought it, the first U-2 to crash. In September 1956, Howard Carey, a friend from the

Ranch, was killed in Europe after a couple of curious Canadian interceptors zoomed by his U-2 for a closer look. The wake of the fighters tore the spy plane apart.

But Powers had been excited about the boldness and daring of the U-2 scheme from the moment he heard of it. Like many he felt that the US had stalled the Cold War after 'the stalemate and compromise in Korea'. Pulled from his F-84 unit in Georgia, he already had a Top Secret clearance: at Sandia Air Base in New Mexico, in 1953, he had gone through training for delivering nuclear weapons. He was part of the war plan: in case of war, he knew where to go to get his fighter to deliver a nuclear bomb, and what target he would be assigned.

At the Ranch, he noted the miles of uninhabited land surrounding the little strip and in the plane – which fairly soared into the sky, needing only a thousand feet or so of runway – he enjoyed feeling a special aloneness.

The Skunk Works would cite the numbers for ever after: it had taken just eighty-eight days to produce a prototype, eight months to fly the first plane and now eighteen months to provide an operational spy craft. Overflights of the Soviet Union began in July, 1956. The first go-ahead was for just ten days of flying. Ike was leery, knowing from experience that subordinates often exaggerated their ability to deliver. The CIA's Richard Bissell argued for ten days of good weather. Andy Goodpaster, Ike's national security advisor, gave him ten at the most.

But soon it was clear that the whole thing had paid off. They looked for bombers and missiles, tracked nuclear tests with filter paper that recorded the results of the explosions, even flew through clouds of fallout. They monitored and recorded radar and telemetry frequencies. They actually learned a lot about the weather over the Soviet Union, their cover story.

When the first pictures came back to the Automat, thence to the White House, Ike and Allen Dulles gleefully spread the photos on the floor of the Oval Office. They discovered untold intelligence riches. In July 1955, a month before the U-2 first flew, the Russians had showed off a mass of new bombers at their annual Aviation Day parade, and the bomber gap was born. Now, one U-2 pilot found a base that had thirty Bison bombers on the tarmac – was this evidence of a major build up? More detailed surveying showed that this was not only the base where the Bison bombers were stationed; it was the entire fleet. Such information closed the bomber gap; it enabled Eisenhower to keep Curt LeMay's budget demands – he wanted even more B-52s and the B-70 – in check. Richard Bissell's friend the columnist Joe Alsop would leak the word later.

Another pilot discovered quite by accident the space facility at Tyurturam, the Cape Canaveral of Russia; it became a regular target of the flights. The Soviets, who liked to move towns and other features around on their official maps subtly, would name it the Baikonur Cosmodrome after a small town some 200 miles away, but photo-interpreter Dino Bruioni decided to name it after the nearest town.

A third flight located a tower that looked like a nuclear test base. The CIA scoffed, but two days later an explosion was recorded at the previously unknown facility. And the U-2 found new kinds of radar that made it – and later planes – even more vulnerable to detection.

But the most secret flights were the ones the Russians didn't even imagine asking him about, because they were not over Russian airspace. They were the ones that spied on the English, French and Israelis, beginning with the Suez crisis in 1956. From these, Eisenhower learned that the French and the Israelis had lied to him – they had many more Mirage fighters than they had admitted. And after the fighting began, one U-2 did two passes over Cairo West airport in a couple of hours, capturing the before and after effects of a bombing attack.

Officials had figured on getting two years out of the U-2. By 1960, they had four. But the Soviets were tracking the flights on radar, as they had almost from the beginning. They sent MiGs up in a vain effort to catch the U-2. Their SAMs were getting closer. And Ike was getting testier and testier. Often he changed the flight plans or had the flights delayed. It drove the agency and the Skunk Works people crazy. They called Ike 'Speedy Gonzales'.

The last flight was approved for late April.

The best pilot, Powers, was chosen for the last flight, called 'grand slam' because it would fly all the way across the Soviet

Union, south to north, and look at the crown jewels – nuclear test sites, ICBM bases, the works.

Weather delayed the flight. The unit shipped from Turkey to Pakistan, where the flights operated from temporary bases.

Powers was scheduled for the best plane, but it turned out to be due for maintenance. Instead he got number 360, a known 'dog'. The planes built by the Skunk Works – basically by hand – tended to have individual differences, eccentricity, personality. Some were sturdy performers, others plagued with gremlins. Such was 360, which – flying out of Atsugi, the Japanese U-2 base – had made an embarrassingly public crash-landing on a muddy airstrip, where armed guards chased off a crowd of camera-toting Japanese. It was constantly developing new and different technical maladies. Right then, it had a bolshie fuel tank.

During Powers' flight, the autopilot quickly began to go on the blink, adding to his work load. Through the big porthole on his cockpit, he saw the distant farms slipping by.

The Soviet military had been desperate to shoot down one of the planes they had been tracking for a long time. They launched a salvo of SAMs. Nine miles above the Earth, Powers was writing in his log book when he saw an orange flash.

His first thought was 'I'm done for'. Then the wings went and the fuselage began spinning. Powers' legs were pinned against the panel by the force. He couldn't eject – his legs would be taken off above the knee. He decided to scramble out of the cockpit. He blew the canopy, then found himself held half in the cockpit by his oxygen lines. He reached back, trying to reach the destruct button, but he could only get within six inches of it. Then he decided he had to try to save himself.

He remembered a map in his pocket, showing alternative routes back to Pakistan and Turkey. First taking off his gloves, he pulled out the map and carefully ripped it into little pieces and scattered them.

Then he thought of the silver dollar and the poison pin inside. It was the pilot's choice whether or not to carry the silver dollar; this was the first time he had done so. When he decided to fly with it he was thinking of it vaguely as a potential weapon, not a means of self destruction.

Then a realization of the absurdity of the device replaced his previous admiration of its cleverness. What better token of a capitalist spy pilot than a silver dollar?

It was just the sort of James Bond gadget that people expected the CIA to come up with – and the agency tried to meet their expectations. Who in 1960 used silver dollars any more, except on ceremonial occasions?

Powers pulled the pin from the coin, hid it in a pocket of his flight suit, then let the silver dollar sail to Earth. He saw a second parachute blossom above him, which was confusing. But it appeared a Soviet pilot had had to bail out too, whether in a kamikaze fighter or one that had been accidentally knocked out of the sky by other SAMs. Eventually Kelly Johnson and Ben Rich would conclude that as many as fourteen SAMs had been fired to create a great shock wave that could make the U-2 break up.

On the ground, he was surrounded by townspeople. Someone handed him a filter cigarette – Laika brand, named after the dog that rode into orbit on Sputnik II.

Twice, the pin from the silver dollar escaped discovery in body searches. When they took his flight suit he realized it was still there and warned them about the pin. They tested it on a dog. The dog's tongue turned blue, and the dog collapsed. Within ninety seconds it stopped breathing; in three minutes it was dead.

He found his interrogators frequently incompetent. There was none of the torture or Korean-War style brainwashing he had worried about. There was much danger, he thought, in overestimating your enemy.

He told the Russians plainly where he had trained, at the Ranch, Watertown strip. He knew there had been a Press release about it, saying that pilots were being trained for NACA – the predecessor of NASA.

Then, later, his captors came in bearing a map and asked him to point out the Ranch, 'to see if he was telling the truth'. He pointed to a spot on the map. He did not mention that it was a map of Arizona, not Nevada.

The regret in Washington was that the man they had carefully and expensively trained in Dreamland had had the temerity to survive. Khruschev fooled Ike with incomplete statements. He hid the fact Powers was alive until Ike had come out with the cover story about a weather flight.

The Russians displayed the wreckage of what they said was the U-2 – but that was an illusion too. Kelly Johnson took one look at it and knew it was just another game, although he never understood why the Soviets had done it. The real wreckage was later displayed in Gorky Park.

It was a classic Cold War mind game: the US kept insisting that Powers had had a flameout and descended to a lower altitude to restart his engine, while Powers himself insisted he had been shot down at 68,000 feet – the maximum ceiling for the plane. The idea from the government standpoint was to keep the maximum height from the Soviets; the idea from Powers' standpoint was to signal to his employers not to send over any other pilots, that the Soviets had indeed figured out how to reach the U-2's operating altitude with SAMs. In citing 68,000 feet as the maximum altitude, which was not true, he was also subtly showing that he had not told the Russians the real figure.

The Pentagon, for its part, wanted to hide the U-2's true operating ceiling to preserve public trust in the strength of its nuclear deterrent: how long would it take the Press to tell the public that if missiles could reach spy planes above 60,000 feet, they could also reach Curtis LeMay's bombers, which flew at lower altitudes?

So a man had risked his life for his country, only to find that the prevailing emotion of the public and his superiors was dismay that he had failed to hit the destruct button on the aircraft – and disappointment that he had survived the crash.

He had never been told the cover story. As if that would fool anyone. As if the plane had not been stamped all over with the names of its manufacturers. As if Powers hadn't landed equipped with gold coins and rubles and a handgun and two hundred rounds of ammunition in his seat pack. (Khrushev would hold up photos of the gold Swiss coins for the world to see, but he didn't know about the American silver dollar.)

Forced to chose between admitting he didn't know what was happening in his own administration and admitting responsibility for the intrusion, Ike chose the latter, justifying the need for overflights because the Soviets had rejected his Open Skies proposal, to allow international verification flights, and explicitly citing the danger of 'another Pearl Harbor'.

Powers was freed in 1962, traded for Rudolph Abel, who the CIA had described as a 'master spy' but who later said he got ninety per cent of his intelligence from the *New York Times* and *Scientific American*.

The exchange took place on a green bridge between Potsdam and Berlin, a scene out of John Le Carré, like the coda to a spy movie, a lasting image of the Cold War, the two men passing on the bridge – the film, shot through a long lens from far away, became a Cold War classic. In a heavy coat and Russian-style fur hat Powers came into view flanked by a pair of goons, then walked past the thin-faced Abel without acknowledging him.

On the plane home – one of Kelly Johnson's Super-constellations – Powers ate a fine meal of steak and potatoes as good as anything back at the Ranch.

Immediately after being debriefed in a safe house in the Maryland countryside, Powers met Kelly Johnson again.

'What happened to my plane?' Johnson asked him.

He believed Powers' story and, after the grilling and the Congressional hearings, Powers was hired again as a test pilot at the Skunk Works, flying U-2s. Apparently, he never knew his salary was paid by the CIA, not Lockheed.

His book, *Operation Overflight*, came out in 1970, about the time of the tenth anniversary of the flight, and around the same time Lockheed let him go. He became one of the first commercial helicopter pilots, in Los Angeles.

The great national and political coming to terms with the shootdown followed. The Summit collapsed, and Ike went out of office diminished in prestige. The whole incident became surrounded with controversy, a dreamwork of suspicion. The mission had been delayed, waiting for a go-ahead from the Oval Office. When it finally came, there were problems with the radio, so the word had been transmitted by open telephone land line – beyond the pale in security terms. Then there was the 'Granger', the radar spoofer that the Skunk Works had come up with to fool Soviet radar. If the working of the Granger was known, it could itself be used as a tracking device. Later, three Taiwanese U-2s would be knocked down over the People's Republic in a single day by this method.

There was one other dark possibility that Powers himself wondered about much later. A young marine assigned to the radar facilities of the Japanese U-2 had later defected to the Soviets. He had visited the American embassy in Moscow threatening to give the Russians information about radar systems. On three occasions, a formal US government investigation discovered, he had spoken of the vital importance of the information he could provide.

That investigation was the Warren Commission Report, and the young Marine was Lee Harvey Oswald.

Powers had suspicions until the day he died, in August 1977, when his traffic helicopter crashed, just three miles from the Skunk Works. He had run out of fuel, but even that crash made some suspicious.

Weapons of Cold War

Within months after Powers was shot down, Richard Bissell had the temerity to suggest that the programme continue over the Soviet Union. But Ike had ruled it out. Never again, the country collectively seemed to resolve, would manned spy planes make the pilot – and the country – vulnerable.

But in August 1960, the very day Frank Powers stood in the dock in Moscow, being sentenced, another of Bissell's secret projects had finally begun to pay off. After more than a dozen failures, the engineers running the spy satellite programme called Corona – successfully recovered a film pod ejected from the satellite whose public identity was Discoverer XIV. The recovery was announced; the public would not learn of its true mission for another thirty years or so.

Historian William Burrows later noted the brilliance of the satellite's public name: part DIS information, part COVER identity, the name was a device as clever as any to come out of the CIA's contractor labs.

Snatched from the air by a C-119 Flying Boxcar at 8500 feet, the capsule contained film of a million square miles of the

Soviet Union – more than all the U-2 flights together had produced.

This was the future: no human at risk, no violation of air-space. To celebrate, the engineers got drunk and threw each other into a swimming pool in Palo Alto.

But the most important days of the spy plane, especially the U-2, were still ahead of it. The U-2 continued in service, keeping an eye on trouble spots, looking for vital clues of the secrets of allies and enemies alike.

In October 1960, Dwight Eisenhower got to see the plane that had caused him so much trouble for the first time. He stopped in Texas after a trip to meet the President of Mexico. And the same month, he approved U-2 flights over Cuba, where the new government of Fidel Castro was showing increasing belligerence toward the United States.

In August 1962, U-2 photos showed a shape that photo-interpreters recognized from the thousands of images they had of the Soviet Union: it showed the star-shaped emplacements of Soviet SAM sites. In the next few weeks, comparing the new pictures with an extensive database of older ones of the Cuban landscape, they saw more and more sites under construction. By October they had matched equipment, carefully measured by computer, with shapes and sizes known from Soviet weapons displayed in Red Square parades: MiG 21s, and Sandal missiles. The agency's top 'crateologists' – experts in all sorts of weapons and equipment packaging, were consulted. It was soon clear that the medium range missiles that normally carried nuclear warheads were being installed in Cuba.

On Saturday, 12 October 1962, Major Richard Heyster took off from Edwards North Base in a U-2. He reached the coast of Cuba early the next morning and returned with the key photos showing the six-sided star of SAM sites protecting the medium range missiles that NATO codenamed Sandal, at San Cristobal.

Art Lundahl, the head of the photo-interpretation office that handled the U-2 photos, got along with President Kennedy from the first time he met him. Kennedy seemed to enjoy the regular briefings. When Lundahl arrived in the Oval Office, the President would pull up his rocking chair as Lundahl carefully removed the silver humidor that held JFK's cigars from a round coffee table, then spread photographs out across the table top.

When Heyster provided unmistakeable evidence of the presence of Soviet missiles, Lundahl hurried to the White House. By noon on Tuesday, Lundahl was displaying the photos to the President and his top advisors; a week later, Kennedy sat in front of the television cameras, declaring the quarantine (the term was carefully chosen instead of blockade, an act of war in international law).

While the President was speaking, fifty-four of LeMay's SAC bombers joined the dozen that were constantly orbiting on alert. Before the crisis was over SAC would go from the normal Defense Condition Five to DefCon Two – the highest ever reached. Three days later, Adlai Stevenson, accompanied by staff from the National Photo Interpretation Center, was displaying the wares of the U-2 at the UN.

Kennedy ordered more thorough photography of the island, requiring low-level, high-speed RF 101 Voodoos: their snouted shadows show up in the most famous treetop close-ups of the shrouded missiles and launchers.

On 27 October Major Rudolph Anderson was shot down in his U-2. LeMay was all set to devastate the SAM sites. Anderson, who died after losing consciousness when shell fragments passed through his pressure suit, was the sole casualty of the Cuban missile crisis, save for several crews of military aircraft that crashed during the mobilization. Anderson's death came just as the crisis had apparently eased and the Russians agreed to remove their missiles; it was the act, the Soviets said years later, of a trigger-happy local SAM commander.

But even more dangerous was the U-2 that went off course and strayed into Soviet airspace near Sakhalin Island. 'There's always some poor son of a bitch who doesn't get the message,' Kennedy sighed, using a favourite phrase. But Krushchev protested, rightly, that in the current state of tension no one could be sure the spy plane had not been a bomber, the first shot of a nuclear war.

After it was all over, LeMay, the commander of the reconnaissance group and Major Heyster, the pilot who took the first, historic photos were called to the Oval Office for commendation. A photo shows Heyster squeezed on a couch between the big officers. 'Let me do the talking,' LeMay said.

And what LeMay talked about later was how we had lost. He harangued JFK about how he could have forced out, not only the Soviet missiles, but the Soviets and Castro as well with the threat of the nuclear club that was SAC. We had the Russian bear in a trap, he said, and 'we should have taken his whole leg off. Hell, we should have taken his testicles off, too.'

For decades, the U-2 would continue to provide a vital source of the most important political intelligence, the sort of geopolitical gossip on which alliances rise or fall. In the early Seventies, Taiwanese U-2s flew over China as part of Operation Senior Spear, an electronic eavesdropping programme. On 12 and 13 September 1971, one such flight picked up a nationwide air defence alert. It was the first indication of Lin Piao's abortive coup attempt; he was attempting to flee to the Soviet Union when his aircraft was shot down over Mongolia.

Knowing that Lin Piao, who favoured stronger ties to the Soviet Union, was out of the way and his ideas in bad odour, gave Henry Kissinger a key card to play when he visited China shortly afterwards, seeking an opening.

The U-2 was 'Kelly's Angel', but even before it had flown over the Soviet Union, it was clear that the CIA needed an 'Archangel'. Radars and missiles were improving. From the very first flight, the CIA operatives and the Skunk Works had been surprised how quickly the Soviets were able to track the U-2 on radar. They quietly protested about the overflights; to go public would have humiliated the Russians, for they could not shoot down the plane. And the pressure to shoot down a U-2 grew with each overflight.

So after the first flurry of successful overflights, caution set in. After his initial excitement, 'Speedy Gonzales' Eisenhower became tentative, and insisted on personally approving each flight plan, agonizing over his decision for days.

It was clear that the U-2 would have to be replaced with something else. Richard Bissell had the Skunk Works look into the best ways to escape detection by radar – was it speed, height, reduced radar profile, 'cross section', or some combination of the three?

The Skunk Works plunged into an extensive study of a super-plane powered by hydrogen. Project Suntan, as it was called, cost taxpayers the equivalent of two billion of today's dollars before the realization struck that creating a whole system of refrigerated tanks and pipes for liquid hydrogen at bases around the world would cost billions more. The programme would remain secret for nearly twenty years.

The agency finally settled on a Skunk Works plan for a conventionally-powered craft, flying so high and fast – three times the speed of sound – that it could elude missiles and fighters. But it would be built of titanium, the first time for an aircraft.

The programme was called Oxcart. Eisenhower, increasingly nervous about the U-2, just called it 'the big one'.

Secrecy was even more intense, if that was possible, than with the U-2. Cheques were made out to the dummy C&J corporation. Drawn on the CIA's reserve funds, free from over-zealous Congressional or executive auditing, they and the paperwork were sent to anonymous post office boxes scattered throughout the LA area. Once, a supplier grew suspicious of the dummy company and tried to track down the box; he was intercepted by security agents.

The Ranch, Watertown, or 'home plate', as some were now calling it – was prepared for a much larger effort than the U-2 required. A longer runway and larger support staff would be needed by the new plane, called the A-12.

Construction began in earnest in September 1960, and continued on a double-shift schedule until mid-1964. The 5,000-foot asphalt runway was supplanted by a larger, concrete one able to support the weight of the A-12. In time, it would be known as the Blackbird.

Built between early September and the middle of November, the new runway was 8500 feet long and required pouring over 25,000 yards of concrete. Kelly Johnson was concerned that high take-off speeds would cause dangerous vibrations so the Blackbird would need many expansion joints. So the runway was built of offset slabs, layered like tile patterns, each 150 feet long.

The Blackbird would also need about 500,000 gallons of PF-1 aircraft fuel per month. After considering airlift or a pipeline it was decided to rely on trucks, but that requiring paving eighteen miles of highway leading into the base.

SAC was again providing support. In late 1961, an Air Force Colonel called Robert J. Holbury became Commander of the base, with a CIA manager as his deputy. Support aircraft began arriving in the spring of 1962 – trainers, eight F-101s, two T-33s, a C-130 for cargo transport, a U-3A for administration purposes, a helicopter for search and rescue, a Cessna-180 and a Lockheed F-104 for chasing.

The Blackbirds were too big to be loaded on planes and flown in from Burbank like the U-2s, so they were to be carted in by truck. Scouting the best highways, a pilot truck went ahead, measuring the width of the road and checking obstacles – roadsigns, branches, etc. – with bamboo outriggers the size of the finished aircraft, thirty-five feet wide. Then the obstacles had to be removed through negotiation with local authorities.

Between the high technology complexities of working with titanium and lower tech ones – they tested the ejection seat by towing it from the back of a '61 Thunderbird convertible, hired from Hertz, the fastest car they could rent – the Skunk Works fell behind schedule on the Blackbird's first flight and there were stern warnings from Dick Bissell.

Almost all the basics were ready in time for the planned delivery date of Aircraft number 1 in August 1961. But the aircraft would not be coming. For the first time, the Skunk Works had fallen behind. The maiden flight was originally planned for the end of May 1961, but it slipped to August, largely because of Lockheed's difficulties in procuring and fabricating titanium. The raw metal had to be procured in roundabout ways – much of it from the Soviet Union itself.

The manufacturer of the engines, Pratt & Whitney, not surprisingly, found it difficult to turn out a powerplant to drive the big aircraft to three and a half times the speed of sound. It took longer than expected to bring the J-58 engine up to requirements.

In March 1961, Kelly Johnson notified the programme headquarters: 'Schedules are in jeopardy on two fronts. One is the assembly of the wing and the other is in satisfactory development of the engine. Our evaluation shows that each of these

...e to four months behind the current

...k Works way. It must have galled
...e admission and galled him more
... from Richard Bissell. Taking time
...er, the imminent invasion of Cuba, he
...rned of your expected additional delay in
...m 30 August to 1 December 1961. This news is
...y shocking on top of our previous slippage from May
...August and my understanding as of our meeting 19
December that the titanium extrusion problems were essentially overcome. I trust this is the last of such disappointments short of a severe earthquake in Burbank.'

But delays should have come as no surprise, since the Skunk Works was singlehandedly pioneering the use of titanium, learning that the metal had to be carefully protected against contact with chlorine fluoride and cadmium, making half their tools unusable. The engineers discovered that the Burbank water supply was fluoridated, and from then on used distilled water.

A whole new family of lubricants and seals had to be invented, and even so, the plane literally seeped fuel when it sat on the ground with full tanks. For its whole flying life, the Blackbird had to be 'topped off' by inflight refuelling once it was in the air, when expansion had tightened the tanks.

The whole aircraft was compounded of future technology; Kelly Johnson predicted that the aircraft would not be matched for forty years, for the rest of the century.

In January 1962, an agreement was reached with the Federal Aviation Administration that extended the restricted airspace around the test area. It was at this time that a new name was applied to the airspace and its control tower: Dreamland.

A number of FAA air traffic controllers were cleared for the project and NORAD – the North American Air Defense Command – the watchers of the national skies, established procedures to prevent their radar stations from reporting the appearance of the Blackbirds on their radar screens. But at Tonopah on the high radar range, operators would soon be seeing things moving much faster than they could explain.

On 17 February, construction of the first aircraft wa
and in the next few days underwent its final tests. It w
apart and stowed on the special trucks designed to mo
Groom Lake.

A famous clip of film shows Kelly Johnson planning
movement of the first A-12 to the base. On the blackboa
behind him is this list:

    17 Feb – Aircraft Complete
    18 Feb – Aircraft put down on its gear
    19 Feb – 22 Feb – Engineering Final Tests
    23 Feb – 25 Feb – Disassemble and load on trucks
    26 Feb – 4:00 AM – Move out to Area 51

On 26 February 1962, at 2:30 in the morning and under cover
of darkness, the convoy bearing the first plane left Burbank.
After removing and replacing signs along the way that had
been carefully measured and hacksawed in advance, the convoy
arrived by the back road to Groom Lake at about one in the
afternoon on 28 February. When in turn it was moved, the
second aircraft struck a Greyhound bus en route and the
company was quickly and quietly compensated some 4800
bucks to settle the damage.

Not until April was the plane ready to fly. On 25 April 1962,
Johnson flew to the base and stayed overnight. The next day,
pilot Lou Schalk took the plane up and flew it for about a mile
and a half, just twenty feet off the ground. To Schalk the plane
felt like it was wallowing and he decided to set it back down.

From the ground, the crew saw the plane begin a series of
lateral oscillations, jerking to one side, and it terrified Johnson,
who later recorded, 'it was a horrible sight'.

The controllers could no longer hear Schalk, but they could
see the Blackbird disappear in a great cloud of dust. It was
enveloped for minutes, then Schalk made a turn and finally re-
emerged. They were relieved he hadn't run into the mountains.

The first 'official' flight took place a year behind schedule,
and the second on 4 May, when the plane went supersonic for
the first time.

Bill Park soon joined the team as a test pilot, along with Jim
Eastham: the pressure to become operational increased during
that autumn. In October, the Cuban missile crisis erupted and,

at the point of maximum tension on 27 October, U-2 pilot Rudolph Anderson was shot down over Cuba. In January 1963, Bob Gilliland arrived at the test location, ready to fly the Air Force fighter version of the plane. On 24 May, came the first crash, when the pilot's tube iced up and left Ken Collins with no accurate speed indication. He bailed out over Wendover, Utah. A farmer in a pickup truck found him. When Collins announced, 'I've just crashed an F-105 with a nuclear weapon on board. Let's get out of here and find a phone,' the farmer quickly complied.

Park and Eastham went up the next day to replicate the conditions and fix the problem.

On 7 August 1962, the AF-12, the fighter version of the Blackbird, first flew. A whole family of Blackbirds was hatching in the desert, and they could not be hidden much longer.

Shortly after he became President, Lyndon Johnson was briefed about the Blackbirds. He ordered that preparations be made to reveal their existence. It was an election year and being tough on defence would be important for an as yet unproven incumbent. Already Barry Goldwater, the leading Republican candidate, had begun to criticize the current administration's defence policy.

At a Press conference on 24 February, Johnson read a statement which described the new 'A-11'.

There was no mention of the first Blackbird, the A-12, the CIA spy version. And in fact, of course, there were no 'A-11s' – the Lockheed design number for the fighter version of the Blackbird – at Edwards and so some were quickly flown from Dreamland to the base. As the *Oxcart Story*, the official CIA history, reported, 'So rushed was this operation, so speedily were the aircraft put into hangars upon arrival, that heat from them activated the hangar sprinkler system, dousing the reception team which awaited them.'

In July 1964, Bill Park nearly lost his life when his plane rolled to the left just 500 feet above the runway. In December of the next year, pilot Mele Vojvodich ejected safely at an altitude of 150 feet on take-off: an electrician had reversed the yaw and pitch gyros – flipped the controls, in effect – and the result was another fireball on the lakebed.

In November 1964, the aircraft was pronounced ready for

use. There was a certain degree of pressure. As early as October 1962, the agency had been eager to offer the still adolescent Blackbird to spy on Cuba, where the U-2s were vulnerable to SAMs. And in autumn 1964, Krushchev threatened to shoot down U-2s over Cuba after the Presidential election. At Dreamland, hasty preparations were made to make ready A-12s for the job if the Soviet premier carried out his threat.

The Blackbirds were not black at first, but metallic, except in front of the canopy and on edges where the dark paint, like the greasepaint on a football player's cheekbones cut the glare. Now Ben Rich had the idea of painting them black, the better to deal with the heat of high speed flight.

To showcase the new plane's abilities, on 21 December 1966, pilot Bill Park flew 10,198 miles in six hours. Taking off from Dreamland, he turned north over Yellowstone National Park, then eastward to Bismarck, North Dakota, and on to Duluth, Minnesota. Turning south, Park passed Atlanta en route to Tampa, Florida, northwest to Portland, Oregon, then southwest to Nevada. Again the flight turned eastward, passing Denver and St Louis. Turning around at Knoxville, Tennessee, he slipped by Bob Gilliland's home town of Memphis in the home stretch back to Nevada. This flight established a record unapproachable by any other aircraft.

The guys on the start carts – the big twin Buick and Chevy V-8s they would roll up to 'crank' the engines on the Blackbirds – really liked Bill Park. So it was especially tough for them to watch, from the south end of the Groom runway, as the long black plane, just five hundred feet above the lake, went careering to one side, rolling relentlessly, until they could only see the bottom of the aircraft plunging down. The lake filled with an ugly orange balloon of flame, blackening already at its edges. A shame it had to be Bill Park.

They got on the phone and were talking to the guys back at the hangar trying to figure out what the hell had happened, when Park walked up, the picture of calm.

Inside the Blackbird, numbered 133, Park hadn't had hell of a lot of time to think. Try as he would, he couldn't get the plane to respond. It wouldn't stop rolling. It was down to an altitude of two hundred feet when he flicked the arm switch for the seat, then leaned forward and grabbed the big D-ring between his legs – like some big luggage handle – and leaned back with all his weight. Suddenly the top was gone, the air rushing cleanly through the cockpit and in another fraction of a second he was sailing up with the rangey mountains around Dreamland.

Kicking Park himself up the pole was the rocket engine under his butt. As soon as it quit, he got another kick, as the seat ejector threw him out, the way it was supposed to, but he could see he was pretty close to the ground and it must have seemed forever before the chute finally opened. Two things, it seemed to him, happened at the same time. The first was, he was grabbed by the chest and the legs as the chute went taut, drawing him upright. And the second was, that his feet hit the ground. Then he just gathered the chute together and headed up towards the end of the runway, where the cart guys were posted, on the other side of the big blast.

It was July 1964 and not the last time Park would eject at the Ranch.

For the test pilots, Dreamland was just the office. But as Bob Gilliland said, the difference between a test pilot and a regular pilot is that we have emergencies every day.

Understand, however, that the basic mode of life on the ranch was always the mind-numbing tedium of military installations the world over, routine and regimen, paperwork and limited privacy, the composite of irritations known as chicken shit and Mickey Mouse.

One ground support man tried to liven things up – and, it must be speculated, supplement his salary – by showing pornographic movies. Blue movies for the blue sky boys! But Kelly Johnson got wind of it and put his foot down, albeit softly. 'Whatever you've got up there, I just want it out,' he told the man.

Gilliland came into the programme through his friend Lou Schalk, who had made the first flight in the A-12. It came about because of a problem with Bob's Mercedes. Bob had to drop it off at an auto shop on Sunset Boulevarde and he got Schalk, an old friend and fellow test pilot, to pick him up. Schalk had a little red Austin Healey and on the way back the two pilots, jammed together in the little British sports car began talking. Schalk was flying a new aircraft Kelly Johnson was developing and he needed help – another test pilot.

Gilliland was having fun flying the F-104, a real hotrod of a fighter, and he was afraid the new plane was some weird settle-on-its-butt thing like the vertical take-off and landing craft the Skunk Works had dreamed up and Herb Salmon had flown. But he agreed to talk to Kelly Johnson.

Johnson told him that the new plane 'will be faster and go higher and further than the 104'. That got Gilliland interested.

'Now, let's go take a look,' Johnson said. He led Gilliland back into the hangar where the next Blackbird still lay in long, sharp pieces. Gilliland could sense an excitement in the very shapes, as Johnson knew he would. He signed on.

Johnson hated the military test pilots. He always wanted his own to try out the new planes thoroughly before the military boys could get their hands on them.

It all went back to 1939, when Ben Kelsey, the army test pilot, lost the prototype of the P-38. He, or a general, decided to fly it across the country from California to Washington and set a new record. It would impress the top brass, Congress and the public. But he came in too low, an engine gulped and hesitated and he ended up in a bank on a golf course.

It set the programme back two years. Tony LeVier went so far as to say that particular piece of grandstanding prolonged the war. From then on, Kelly Johnson always feared losing one of his prototypes, because each of them represented the capital investment, the research and design kernel of the whole programme.

So Johnson picked his test pilots carefully and their succession is as legendary in the aviation world as that of Yankee centre fielders: Milo Burcham on the P-38, Tony LeVier on the P-80 jet and F-104 Starfighter, Lou Schalk, Jim Eastham, Bob Gilliland, Bill Park.

Security was intense. Lockheed even airbrushed the mountains out of the background to help disguise the location. It was much changed from the early days of the U-2, the surplus Navy structures supplemented with brand new modern hangars, and a work force that had grown by five or six times, to 1100 or so by 1962.

As the CIA plane was succeeded by the interceptor model Blackbird and then the SR-71, schedules routinely seemed impossible. When the SR-71 was nearing completion a few years later Gilliland saw the parts of the SR strewn about the floor of the hangar in Palmdale and he couldn't believe they would be pulled together into a plane that would fly before the end of the year, as promised. There was significant money in making that date, and more if the plane went supersonic.

He voiced doubt to Johnson, and Johnson became angry, saying that if he had listened to all the doubters in his career he would never have got anything off the ground.

Life at Groom was dull, but Bob Gilliland would go jogging and lift weights sometimes to shed stress. You could play tennis and there was a softball team, but not much else. Lou Schalk found other diversions: he brought the red Austin Healey to the base and raced it across the lake bed against Jim Eastham's blue one.

But it was exciting, learning how to carefully move the big missile nose cones that were the key to the engine performance, the inlet spikes, to make the plane go higher and faster, every evening because that was the end of another day, Gilliland always felt, when he had been able to fly faster than any pilot in history. Only no one knew.

Living in that kind of environment, doing that kind of work, could make a man hard. By the autumn of 1963 they were flying the aircraft well beyond Mach 3, at 110,000 feet. There was no television, only radio, and one day Gilliland was flying 'the CIA bird', the A-12, and came back to find that everyone in the hangar was gathered around the radio. 'What's going on?' he asked. 'JFK has been shot, LBJ has been shot, Connally has been shot,' someone told him. Bill Park was there and he said, 'Well, hell, I don't know what all the excitement's about. It's just another Texas shoot out.' The pilots by then were as dry and hard as the Groom lake bed. They seemed to have absorbed the desert itself.

Park was the driest. Ben Rich called him 'an outstanding stick man, cool and calm,' but there was more. When there was discussion of basing U-2s on aircraft carriers, it was Park who was called on to see if it would work. He landed one on the pitching deck of a carrier. Using a special technique he devised himself, in 1958 he had pushed the F-104 to the world record altitude of 91,985 feet – a record the Skunk Works had to keep secret.

When Kelly Johnson strapped the D-21 drone onto the back of the Blackbird, in the programme called Tagboard, he picked Park to fly the dangerous release missions. The idea was to send an unmanned craft over China to take a look at the far western Lop Nor nuclear test area.

After take-off from Groom Lake, the launch run would begin over Dahlhart, Texas, aiming for a release point around Point Mugu, California. The Blackbird took a half a continent's width just to get warmed up to the Mach 3 plus speed necessary for the D-21's ramjet to function.

The backseat man in the SR, now called the M-21 for the drone programme, Ray Torick, was charged with launching the drone when Park put the mothership into a slight forward angle. On the very first time they got the mother plane up to speed, the D-21 let go all right, but it stuck close to the big aircraft. It just seemed to hang, as if reluctant to venture off on its own. Then all of a sudden it veered and dropped – the engine had gulped and faltered – and hit the tail of the Blackbird, pitching the big plane forward. It snapped in the middle and, still travelling at Mach 3, began to tumble down, as both Park and Ray Torick flipped the levers to arm the ejection seats and pulled the rings. In the Pacific off Point Mugu, Park was picked up by rescue helicopters, but Torick's pressure suit filled with water and dragged him to his death.

Kelly Johnson immediately cancelled the D-21 test programme.

Park would become the longest serving of the pilots at Dreamland. He went on to fly Have Blue, the first Stealth prototype.

When he had first seen it, Park didn't see how the thing could ever fly. But he had been up in it dozens of times now, the first Stealth aircraft in the world. It was 4 May 1976, and he was flying the Have Blue prototype. It was the first Stealth plane to fly and a lot of flying qualities had been sacrificed to get the right radar cross sections. Thinner and more dartlike than the Stealth fighter to come, it was painted up in a desert camou, a broken pattern of greys and browns. It also had what was known as an 'an excessive sink rate', a tendency to fall like a stone at low speed. Its wings were too small. This could be fixed in a production fighter, but it was something the test pilots had to live with.

While coming in one day in 1976, the plane began to dip and Park hit hard on the right gear, pulling up and around but when he started to lower the gear again, the right would not go down. He even came down on the left and tried to shake the other gear loose – without success. Park decided he had better take the plane up to 10,000 feet and burn off most of his remaining fuel. 'Unless anyone has a better idea,' he radioed, 'I'm bailing out.' That morning, the commander had asked him about letting the paramedic have the day off. There hadn't been any problems on earlier flights, and the test series was nearing its end. But Park demurred. He always went by the book.

Now he had to pull the ring again, and at comparative leisure, considered and composed. But he struck his head on the head rest, cracked a vertebra and was knocked out. Amazingly, the seat lifted him free of the plane at 10,000 feet; he separated from the seat and the chute opened as designed. But still unconscious, he crashed hard. He broke a leg and his head was dragged to the caliche, where his mouth filled with the dry sand. By the time the paramedics got there his heart had stopped. He would spend six weeks in intensive care and six months in a cast.

Park was the driest of them all, quiet but perhaps smouldering inside. The quintessential Park story is not of any of his bailouts, but of an earlier close call with death.

He was flying a U-2 out of Burbank when it developed fuel problems. The engine quit and he had to dead-stick it home.

He barely made it back to base, clearing a chain link fence by six inches. Ben Rich came out to the plane.

'What happened?' Rich asked.

'I don't know,' Park said. 'I just got here myself.'

The secret black planes would challenge SAC, and LeMay. Dreamland was, indirectly, an offspring too of the blue-sky, high-noon vision that was SAC. While Dreamland would give birth to black planes, they would serve SAC's silver bombers. They would find the targets for the bombers to strike. And they would, the day after doomsday, fly back to see how well the silver planes had done.

One day in 1962 Richard Bissell came to the White House to brief JFK on the new and still very secret Blackbird – the CIA's A-12. The President was puzzled. He looked at the documents, and listened to Bissell telling him how far and fast the agency's new plane could fly. He pondered what he had been told.

'Could Kelly Johnson convert your airplane into a bomber?' the President asked.

'That question is more properly addressed to General LeMay,' Bissell answered diplomatically.

But it got Johnson in hot water: he was not pleased with Bissell. Johnson had carefully not spoken to the Air Force about the bomber version of the Blackbird. He knew LeMay wouldn't like a black challenge to his silver planes. But now he hurried to Washington to make his proposal and try to work his charm on the bypassed generals. It failed. Later in 1962 when the B-70 was cut back from ten planned planes to four, LeMay blamed Johnson.

Finally, the two men met at the Skunk Works in Burbank. The meeting appeared to go well. Their aides drew back as Johnson and LeMay walked and conferred, cigar smoke trailing behind them.

By the end of the day, it appeared Johnson's charm had worked. LeMay seemed all set to order bombers and Blackbirds – a whole fleet, a whole black air force. But by the end of the year, only the SR-71 – the reconnaissance version – had been ordered.

*

With the SR-71, SAC got its own Blackbirds and while it used them to spy on distant countries – the Soviet Union and China excepted – their ostensible job was something called 'post strike reconnaissance'.

They came in handy in 1973, when the United States eased tensions in the Middle East by offering the Soviets photographic proof of Israeli positions; the Soviets had threatened intervention, now they backed off.

But primarily the SR-71s were supposed to be part of SAC's main 'deterrent' mission – fighting nuclear wars. The SR-71's job would be to fly over the Soviet Union in the event of nuclear war, after the bombs and missiles had fallen, and 'assess battle damage' to see how well the bombs had done their job.

In fact, what they did was simple intelligence gathering, flying as needed over the trouble spots of the world, and after the A-12s were phased out in 1968 in favour of the SAC model, the SR-71, they did it for the Agency as well as the Air Force.

But to keep up the original premise, SR pilots had to go through the monthly ritual of refresher courses in post nuclear battle damage assessment, learning to distinguish which cities needed additional strikes and on which targets another nuke would simply, in the famous phrase of the over-kill era, 'bounce the rubble'. It was an exercise that struck the pilots as not only pointless, but also grim and surreal.

Robert McNamara – 'Mack the Knife', the contractors called him – was pushing the THX, one plane, with swing wings, for both the Air Force and the Navy.

The Air Force and the Navy both hated it – if only because it forced them to share. And McNamara in the process not only killed the Blackbird, but ended up by destroying the means of creating it. The Skunk Works buffs all knew the dark day: on 5 May 1970, Kelly Johnson was ordered to sell as scrap the dies and the jigs for the fastest, highest flying plane in history, for just a few cents a pound.

9

'Low Observables'

IN THE 1860s AND '70s, IN QUIET LABS OFF THE COURTYARDS of King's College, London, and the quadrangles of Cambridge, the Scottish-born physicist James Clark Maxwell laid the foundations for understanding the whole of the electromagnetic spectrum.

Light, electricity, magnetism and what would later be called radio and micro waves are all related, and obey the same rules of behaviour, he theorized in his 1873 *Treatise on Electricity and Magnetism*. They are all waves, sharing the properties of reflection and refraction, diffraction and polarization. In this tome lay the origins of radar.

Other scientists, including Heinrich Hertz and Arnold Sommerfeldt, had taken Clark Maxwell's ideas further, refining the maths by the time the theories were ready to move from the lab to the halls of government.

One day in 1932, with Fascism taking hold across Europe, former Prime Minister Stanley Baldwin stood up in the House of Commons to deliver a warning that there was no longer any question of protecting the man in the street from bombing. During World War I, Zeppelins had bombed London, and the British understood that no fleet could provided full defence in the future. The next war, it was declared, would turn on the fact that Britain 'was no longer an island'. 'The bomber will always get through' was Baldwin's famous phrase, to be repeated down the decades as the debate over air power rumbled on.

'The only defence is in offence,' he continued, 'which means that you will have to kill more women and children more quickly than the enemy . . .' It was an endorsement of the beliefs of the air power enthusiasts and a foretaste of the doctrines of massive retaliation and assured deterrence.

But not everyone could accept this idea. Just as Ronald Reagan, half a century later would look to exotic weapons to break the logjam of mutual destruction (with the dream of Star Wars), the British Air Ministry sought in desperation for new ways to shoot down the bombers. They even looked at such exotic ideas as radio wave weapons – ray guns.

How much radio energy would it take to make a man's blood boil? the scientists were asked. How much to blow an aircraft out of the sky?

The results were not promising, but something else interesting came out of them: the idea that you could locate, if not destroy, an aircraft by beaming radio waves at it, and capturing and measuring the reflection.

Clark Maxwell had postulated – and Heinrich Hertz had demonstrated – that microwaves would behave like light waves. The early radar scientists worked on just how this was so.

They had invented a new way of seeing things in the sky.

It took an odd character, met with some disdain by more proper British types in the London gentlemen's clubs where the planning took place to turn the idea into reality.

Robert Watt Watson, a pudgy and loquacious character in the Ministry of Defence, pushed the idea of radio detection and ranging. (The British provided the idea but it was the Americans who would provide the acronym: RADAR.) He tracked a Dutch airliner crossing the Channel in 1937 and by the time of the Battle of Britain he had organized a network of stations that fed into the underground war room, familiar to us from dozens of movies.

Watt Watson created the terms 'angel' and 'bandit' for friendly and unfriendly radar blips, and devised the system of representing them by little counters moved about on a map board by efficient young women with croupier rakes.

And by the narrowest of margins, radar, combined with Hitler's and Goering's failure to strike first at airbases rather than civilians, would win the war in the air for the British in 1940. 'Britain,' Watt Watson declared, triumphantly – but prematurely, 'is an island once more'.

But not for long. And neither would America be a continent for very much longer, protected as it was from attack by even greater extents of water. In *Victory Through Air Power*, Alexander De Seversky warned Americans that, no more than the British, could they rely on oceans for safety. Even Kansas City and Chicago must learn that the 'bomber will always get through'. With the coming of the atomic bomb, the consequences of bombers crossing the ocean became even more frightening.

The same impetus that created radar in the 1930s saw it spread in the 1950s across the North American continent as the DEW line and NORAD, and across the Soviet Union in a mirroring system of air defence.

But knowledge of electronics was advancing more rapidly than jet engines or airframes. By the 1960s, the big bomber was an endangered species. And by the 1970s, radar had such a lead over even aircraft equipped with their own jamming and spoofing electronics that it seemed increasingly unlikely that 'the bomber will always get through'. This became especially clear to the US Air Force in the 1973 Middle Eastern war, when some 30 of the top line fighters it had sold to Israel were shot down by improved radar and SAMs. The Pentagon had been right to kill LeMay's B-70 – new SAMs would have made it obsolete – but smaller, faster planes were vulnerable too.

Stealth

In 1975, the Pentagon began convening special conclaves of scientists, engineers and contractors to consider a response. DARPA – the acronym as sinister as THRUSH or SMERSH – the defence advanced research projects agency, was put in charge. Founded in the wake of Sputnik, DARPA was designed as the Pentagon's version of Bell Labs, a free-thinking outfit dedicated to investigating the frontiers of technology, liberated from bureaucracy and interservice rivalries.

It planned the first ICBMs and designed sensors for McNamara's line, the high-tech barrier planned for Vietnam's Demilitarized Zone. It developed the autonomous land vehicle, a huge walking tank, like something out of the Imperial Army in *The Empire Strikes Back*. DARPA created improved integrated circuits, sensors, and actuators, the sinews and joints of modern weaponry. But most important, DARPA's funds had built up the computer history in the 1960s and, as a spin off, gave us the computer mouse and the Internet – at first called DARPANET.

To come up with a means of eluding the new, powerful radars, DARPA created a project called Harvey – after Jimmy Stewart's invisible bunny pal in the movie – to look into making an aircraft invisible to radar, or at least harder to see. It signed up four of the leading aircraft builders and gave them four million dollars apiece to solve the problem. Lockheed was not among the four.

The irony was that the Skunk Works' achievements in reducing radar cross section on the Blackbirds, including the stealthy D-21 drone, had been so secret that no one in the Pentagon knew – and when the discussion turned to stealth, no one thought of Lockheed. So to get Lockheed included in DARPA's stealth studies, along with established contractors Boeing, McDonnell Douglas, and Northrop, Rich had to do a fast-talking job on DARPA's George Heilmeier.

The Skunk Works was not in good odour. Kelly Johnson was seen as arrogant and difficult, living in the days of its past glories.

Rich had to remind the DARPA scientists of the work the Skunk Works had done nearly a decade ago. Shape provided two thirds of the radar stealth; it would be combined with the iron ferrite paints and other materials which would provide a third of the stealth. Rich had to persuade the CIA to release information on the stealthy technology of the A-12 and the D-21, and with that information in hand he persuaded DARPA to let Lockheed participate.

One day in April 1975, just as he had settled down to a cup of instant decaffeinated coffee, Ben Rich had a visitor. He had taken over as boss of the Skunk Works in January and was looking for work for the place. Now a young man named Denys Overholser sat down and began to tell Rich about a footnote. It was a footnote, moreover, in a nine-year-old Russian technical paper that had only recently been translated by the Air Force Foreign Technology Division. It bore the engaging title 'Method of Edge Waves in the Physical Theory of Diffraction' and was authored by Pyotr Ufimtsev, chief scientist of the Moscow Institute of Radio Engineering.

The principle, Overholser explained, was that using Ufimtsev's updating of the Hertz and Helmholtz equations, you could calculate the radar reflection of a shape, such as that of a plane, as long as you could measure it in two dimensions. That meant you could design a shape that would reflect radar waves off into space, instead of back to the receiver. And you could do this independently of the size of the shape: a huge shape could be made to look small, almost invisible, on radar.

Overholser, a chunky mountain biker and outdoors type who had an unaccountable fascination with radar, was the man who shaped radomes for the Skunk Works, but now Rich assigned him to turn the equations into a computer program and the program into the shape of a new aircraft.

In five weeks, working with Bill Schroeder – the Skunk Works' longtime radar and maths whiz – who in his eighties had come out of retirement, Overholser wrote a program called Echo to do the calculations of an optimum shape, one that would scatter radar beams away from the craft and the receiving antenna. They took the results to a junior designer, Dick Sherrer, and by 5 May were back in Rich's office with the results: drawings of an aircraft shaped like an arrow, which they called Hopeless Diamond.

Radar signatures are always given in rough terms of aircraft or bird types – 'So would this one,' Rich asked, 'be the size of a Cessna or what, a condor, an eagle?'

'Ben,' Overholser said, 'an eagle's eyeball.'

Thereafter, Rich took a number of ball bearings – the approximate size of an eagle's eyeball – to the Pentagon, rolled them across generals' desks and said, 'There's your airplane!'

Some months later, someone on Rich's staff gave him a bowling ball painted 'Top Secret': they told him it was the radar signature of the whole Pentagon after it had been subjected to the Skunks Works' stealth treatment.

When Johnson had seen the sketch of the Hopeless Diamond, he literally kicked Ben Rich in the ass. 'It'll never get off the ground,' he predicted. Johnson had always said that if an aircraft looks beautiful it will fly well. But this plane was ugly.

Rich would write, 'No one would dare to claim that the

Hopeless Diamond would be a beautiful airplane. As a flying machine it looked alien.'

Johnson also loathed electronics, and this was an aircraft designed for its electronics, by electronics. 'If Kelly could find a hydraulic radio, he would use that,' went an old chestnut around the Skunk Works.

Kelly Johnson was famous for his quarter bets on this or that technical point, but over the years few had ever won quarters from him. Those quarters were tokens of his hand-to-mouth upbringing, and also of his penny-pinching ways at the Skunk Works.

But now Rich bet that the Hopeless Diamond would have a lower radar cross section than the fifteen-year-old D-21. (In fact the calculations suggested it would be a thousand times less visible on radar.) On 14 September 1975, they took the wooden models of the two aircraft into an electromagnetic chamber. The results were clear: Johnson handed over the quarter, only mumbling, 'Don't spend it until you see the thing fly.'

Next, in October, they took the model to Gray Butte, the radar cross section facility that belonged to McDonnell Douglas, since Lockheed had not yet build its own RCS test site at Helendale.

On one occasion when the model was on the test pole, there was a sudden blossom of reflection. *Uh-oh*, the guys in the test centre thought, was there some angle they had not considered? Then someone looked out at the model, there on its pole in the middle of the concrete, and saw that a large blackbird had landed on it. Even bird droppings could add to the radar reflection – a decibel and a half, as these things were measured, to a total reflection of three decibels.

And in March 1976, they trucked the black-painted wooden model all the way to the Ratscat – 'radar scatter' facility at White Sands New Mexico – for a 'fly-off' with Northrop's stealth model. Models at RCS tests sit on poles, but the signatures of these craft were so low that the pole itself interfered with the reading. The two companies had to get together to design and build a new pole.

The results were overwhelmingly in favour of the Lockheed model, and Northrop radar expert John Cashen was dismayed.

His model was a clear failure. The Hopeless Diamond was revolutionary – if it could actually fly.

Nor was it clear that Kelly Johnson would be wrong about that: to make this shape fly took a whole new range of controls, dependent on computers. The plane was too unstable simply for a mere human pilot.

Although Kelly Johnson was appalled by it, the Stealth's shape provided the very embodiment of the Skunk Works' simplicity of method, and Johnson's whole philosophy. It was radically different – 'it looked totally alien,' Ben Rich said – because it was radically simple: it was a sculpture on the theme of the cutting away of excess, an airframe compounded of cut corners. An aircraft that was no better than it had to be at flying, so it could not be seen.

Born inside a computer, it was drawn by the simplest of means – a 'wire-frame' drawing – making the most of limited processing power, like the angular tanks, and flying saucers in the early video game called *Battlezone*.

Or as if the polyhedrons that marked those mountains on the radar screen at Nellis's Red Flag war games had taken to the air. And the shapes as if out of a computer game would eventually show up in a new kind of aerial combat that itself resembled a computer game.

With the machinists' union on strike, Skunk Works managers themselves did much of the work on the prototype. It was tested at night, beside the plant, in a rigged-up barrier composed of two tractor trailers.

But on 1 December 1977, Bill Park, having demanded and received a $25,000 bonus to fly the ugliest aircraft he had ever seen – especially ugly, he thought, in the cockpit area which offered very little space from which to escape – lifted off the runway at Groom. He flew what was now called the XST – experimental stealth testbed – or Have Blue.

Now the Skunk Works had to prove the real aircraft was as stealthy as the wooden model on the pole. Parks and other pilots began testing it against real radars, the bad guy radars, surreptitiously obtained, like the Red Hat squadron's MiGs, and as carefully hidden, at a site called Site Four – S-4 or S-IV –

in the remote corners of the Tonopah Test Range adjoining Dreamland.

During one test, Have Blue showed up as bright blip on the screen. The engineers couldn't understand what was wrong. Then it was noticed that three screws had not been driven flat. The heads sticking up just a fraction of an inch triggered a huge radar return.

It was soon clear to William Perry, Stealth's godfather in the Five Sided Funny House, that his scientists were looking at something as revolutionary for warfare as the jet engine, as the machine gun, perhaps even as historic as gunpowder, as the crossbow.

Keeping this shape hidden was vital. More than any aircraft before, perhaps, the form signalled function. You got the idea just by seeing it.

In the late Seventies, most of the world thought stealth meant paints of some kind, or panels that absorbed radar, not the faceting on the body of the craft. So keeping Have Blue invisible became a top priority and the whole programme was the most closely-guarded secret since the Manhattan Project, with only a handful of generals, and fewer congressmen, aware of its very existence.

By day, the strange shape, only three-fifths the size of the 'real' plane, with a cramped cockpit and crude systems, could attract attention. At first the model was painted up in a mottled camou, browns, greys and light blue, to disguise it, but this did not work very well, so it was repainted a light grey. It was never brought outside unless uncleared personnel had been exiled to the windowless mess hall or to their quarters. And when Soviet satellites were scheduled overhead it was put in the hangar or under the shelters, called 'scoot and hide', beside the taxiway.

In June 1977, a small, unmarked passenger plane landed on the runway at Groom Lake and from it emerged Jimmy Carter's national security advisor, Zbigniew Brzezinski. He met Rich there and walked around Have Blue in its hangar, learning how it would fly and elude the purloined Soviet radars up on the range. He was briefed in a secure room about the aircraft and stealth in general. By the end of the month, Carter had cancelled the B-1 bomber and put his faith in the 'Advanced Technology Bomber', the B-2 flying wing.

By autumn, 1978, Have Blue had proven itself well enough that the Pentagon gave Lockheed a contract to build a fighter version. It was to be ready to fly by July 1980.

That fighter, despite Kelly Johnson's revulsion, would in the end come to possess a kind of beauty that seemed at first so far from conventional standards. It was a model of Dreamland itself: hard, angular, unabsorbing, unforgiving.

In reality, of course, the shape of the stealth fighter reflected the state of computer art at the time it was designed: the calculation of radar reflectance from curves was a more complicated task and showed up in the B-2 bomber and the TR3A black Manta or 'baby B-2'.

By 1980 the word 'stealth' had begun to creep into media reports. CBS television correspondent David Martin filed one pointed piece. It was unclear whether leaks in this election year were a matter of politics but in August, 1980, with candidate Ronald Reagan hitting Jimmy Carter hard on defence issues, Secretary of Defense Harold Brown with Bill Perry standing beside him, talked about stealth as a breakthrough. Most people thought in terms of bombers, then, since the revelation helped cover President Carter's flank, exposed by the cancellation of the B-1. But there was a backlash, too, to the revelations, which the Republicans exploited: Carter should not have revealed such deep secrets, they charged.

The formal first flight came in April, 1982, but it wasn't for another six years that the taxpayer would get a good look at the aircraft. With generals and dignitaries lined up, the plane began to taxi forward with test pilot Bob Riedenauer at the controls. It gathered speed and slowly lifted off. But only a few feet above the runway, it began to veer to one side and the shocked crowd watched as it then flipped completely onto its back and fell onto the lake in a huge dust cloud. The rescue trucks – already poised for action, rushed up and cut Riedenauer out, as he hung upside down. He never flew again.

Mechanics had miswired a new control unit, switching the controls for yaw with those for pitch, so that when Riedenauer had attempted to pull up on the stick he actually sent the plane heeling to the right.

Skunkers noted that it was a near duplicate of the accident in which Mele Vojvodich had almost died in a Blackbird on the same runway. But the crash was also a reminder that for this unnatural shape to fly depended as much on software as on hardware. Its workings were no longer visible, in the manner of mechanical things, but hidden in computer code.

One day in 1984, Colonel Robert 'Burner Bob' Jackson was reading the *Wall Street Journal* when a small advertisement caught his eye. The Chevron petroleum company had second-hand oil patch trailers to sell. And Burner Bob needed them: it was his job to get ready for the movement of the Stealth fighter group from Groom Lake to Tonopah.

Jackson bought the trailers for $10 million, but there was more to do: a whole base to be built in the middle of a test range previously dedicated mostly to radar and electronics. The site was south of the old Tonopah Air Field, well out of view. Mustangs roamed the area and scorpions crept into buildings.

Now fences and searchlights went up along the edge of the new base, along with video cameras and motion sensors. Eventually the Air Force would spent $300 million and fit the place out with a gym and indoor pool.

The activity did not go unnoticed. A-7s were kept parked outside, and Soviet satellites passes overhead increased to up to four a day.

The A-7s were part of a cover story. Remember that stealth was still speculated to be a paint, absorbent material, or electronic device, and the unit deployed a number of A-7s to Japan. These carried old napalm canisters painted black and decorated with flashing red lights and lettering that read 'Reactor cooling Fill Port'. The idea was to spread the disinformation that these were an 'atomic anti-radar system'. Ground crews were forced to lie spread-eagled, not looking at the craft as they passed. The lie must be made as hard to get at as if it were the truth.

In autumn 1988, the Air Force released the first, heavily doctored photograph of the fighter. It was so vague and the angle so misleading that some pilots literally doubled over with laughter when they saw it.

But soon the aircraft buffs found out about Tonopah. Jim

Goodall was among the first to station himself, along with John Andrews, on the fence line at Tonopah.

They would spend hours there and by the winter of 1988 were getting glimpses. The photos they had long dreamed of snapping showing the strange flat shape from the bottom, the angular diamond, faceted and crimped.

A schoolteacher and aircraft buff from Escondido, California named Byron Augenbaugh drove up to Tonopah in the spring of 1989. He stopped at a gas station to fill up and asked where he should go to look for the stealth fighter. 'Just look up,' the attendant told him and sure enough, one flew over. He snapped a picture; eventually, it ran in *Aviation Week*. On 1 May 1989, the magazine ran a cover shot of the fighter that was so fuzzy one of its editors said that 'it looked like a French Impressionist painting'.

There was something lascivious about the process of getting the images. In the first pictures of the stealth fighter the Air Force released, the inlets for the engines were airbrushed out, as in a *Playboy* centrefold of the Fifties. The Air Force Chief of Staff went so far as to testify around the same time that an aircraft, like a beautiful woman, should reveal itself – not completely, but bit by bit.

But the artist's impressions of the Stealth fighter and other suspected aircraft that appeared in magazines such as *Popular Science* had their highlights exaggerated like the women in bomber nose art, their shapes fuller and more magical.

These romantic paintings stood in contrast to the spy shots, blurry and grainy, which were like the telephoto images of sunbathing celebrities in European picture magazines.

Some of the images were about the *idea* of seeing, as much as the actual thing seen, like falling in love with love. The whole experience of snooping for stealth was about the means as well as the ends, I thought. It was about telephoto lenses, or about the big binoculars the stealthies called 'hooters' or about the grainy-green mystery produced by night vision equipment – as much as about any real craft.

Jim Goodall, who had the declared ambition of collecting a picture of every aircraft the US Air Force had ever flown, complete with tail number – more than 100,000 pictures – claimed an almost sexual rush when he first saw the stealth fighter. It was the winter of 1988 on the fence line at Tonopah, and for a travelling salesman who pushed computer equipment, he had a surprisingly sensual side of his own, being a sharp dancer in the Holiday Inn discos he visited on the road.

In the desert, Goodall would lie for hours, concealed in camouflage, and he was rewarded by snapping the first clear picture of the underside of the Stealth fighter, in company with a chase plane. Soon he would be able to reel off the tail numbers of the F-117s, and tell the history of each, just as he could the Blackbirds.

Goodall was often joined by John Andrews, the veteran plastic model designer for the Testors corporation. In 1986, Testors released Andrews' model of the Stealth fighter, which it called the 'F-19', based on his glimpses and reports from the other watchers. It was like putting together a police composite sketch of a wanted man, he said. There were the sightings, the engineering theories, the tips from insiders. In 1983, an airline pilot friend of Andrews glimpsed what he thought was the Stealth while flying near Mono Lake and reported the details to Andrews.

The model set off a small storm in Washington. Congress began asking, how could a model company know what America's most closely guarded secret looked like, when our lawmakers themselves did not know? Of course, everyone in and around the black world knew that the last person to be briefed on a project of such high security was a Congressman.

The model angered and embarrassed Congressmen, who held hearings to find out how the shape of the plane had leaked. By one account, the Air Force had to bring a model of the real fighter to the Congressmen, in a locked box handcuffed to a guard, to show them that Andrews was wrong.

But the Air Force and the Skunk Works could only say it was wrong – not demonstrably prove it unless they broke down the very secrecy that was designed to keep people like Andrews at a distance.

At the same time, the security people came down heavily on the Skunk Works. Ben Rich hastily sent people to haul boxes of documents and blueprints out of Kelly Johnson's garage.

The whole way the Skunk Works operated was to get rid of unneeded paper, but the new security procedures required keeping track of every sheet. If it couldn't be accounted for, there was, by definition, a security lapse.

The Road to Tonopah

I drove up to Tonopah one autumn day from Las Vegas, heading in a great arc to the northwest, around the nuclear test site and range. Las Vegas brags that it is 'the city that never sleeps', but I passed acres of new condos west of the town, bedroom communities for the city that never sleeps. Can a city that never sleeps dream? Or is its whole waking life a dream, like a gambler's? The dream of the long shot?

At the entrance to the Paiute Indian reservation a billboard read 'cheap cigarettes'. Further up the road was Indian Springs, an old World War II air base. But there were strange new inflatable buildings – like little hangars – beside the flight line and everything was surprisingly spruced up as if the base had been restored for a film. In one version of the Roswell story, Indian Springs had been the site of the first secret saucer storage facility – and perhaps the storage of alien bodies as well.

After Indian Springs the four-lane highway ran out. I passed a lot of big older American cars with huge grilles. Near the entrance I waved in gratitude as I slipped by, near Mercury, the entrance to the Nevada Test Site.

'Mercury – No Services,' announced the town that had grown from the base camp of the Nevada Nuclear Test Site. Another sign announced that the fronting stretch of highway had, without apparent irony, been adopted by 'Nevadans for Peace'.

Up the road, I passed through little towns whose signs announced elevation rather than population – the former being a far more impressive figure. Behind were distant stage sets of violently tilted mountain strata.

You could, I thought, get sick of this distance pretty damn quick. At first exhilarating, the distance soon became nauseating, deadening. Fresh from the constricted views of eastern cities, I found the cumulative effect numbing. I would come on many long, limitless valleys ahead that hit me in anticipation almost like a roller-coaster dip. I measured one and found it ten miles from hilltop to hilltop.

At the very moment a sign told me I had driven into Nye County, the rough road surface immediately signalled a different set of government budget priorities. Nye County is one of the centres of the 'sagebrush rebellion' against the government which owns most of its acreage. It is also one of the few places in the United States where prostitution is legal. The road here is lined with enterprises of this sort, called 'ranches': Shady Lady Ranch, a clutch of motor homes, with a red light, literally, out front, only it's a police car-type light on a pole so you can see it from far down the road. The Cottontail Ranch. 'We Never Close', the sign said. 'Service with a smile.' Fran's Ranch, where an old plane stood with both its engines gone, like blind eyes.

'Gateway to Death Valley' a sign said cheerfully at Beatty. 'Est. 1903. Rio Rancho RV park. Burro Inn: Full Hookups.' Another pointed to Parumph, 27 miles away, 'Heart of the Old New West.' And home, I knew, of the Art Bell Dreamland Radio Show, where conspiracy theorists talked to sleepless callers late at night.

As I came into Goldfield – 'elevation 6097' – a scene out of the TV show *McCabe and Mrs Miller*, there came the first touches of snow. Dark clouds lent an even more depressing aspect to the old mining town, with its little grey houses stuck randomly on the hillside, scattered among camper tops and other junk. Not far from the big looming courthouse marked 1907, a sign announced a restaurant and bar for sale: another capitalist who had given up on the future of greater Goldfield.

For much of the day it had been reasonably bright, but as I got closer to the town, and the road began to go upwards, the sky became a solid grey and the mountains grew darker, threatening in shape. About six or seven miles before I reached Tonopah huge black clouds began to appear.

By the time I got near town it was virtual blizzard. A huge American flag driven by the wind was noisily beating its heart out against a pole in front of the forest service office south of the town. A sign said 'Elevation 6030 – Home of the Stealth'. There was also a Masonic lodge and the Silver Cloud Motel. I hoped the name of the motel referred to the lining of the clouds that were grey and heavy above me.

I stopped at the forest service office to get out of the weather and look for maps. A heavy woman behind the counter chatted away. 'My husband works out there at the site,' she told me. 'And sometimes I go to pick him up and he warned me that if I ever broke down to just stay in the car.'

'Don't get out,' he said. 'They don't like people poking around.'

At the local museum I saw exhibits on the history of the town and picked up a book on its history. The museum's exhibits consisted mostly of odd pieces of equipment from the mines, chunks of silver ore and pieces of crashed planes. An aerial photo showed a Stealth fighter flying above the old mines. The word Tonopah meant 'land of little wood and water' in Paiute, the book said. But the very mellifluous syllables of the town's name – toe nah pah – had become magic to the stealthchasers.

Tonopah was built on economic booms, interrupted by busts – the silver boom, followed by the big booms at the nuclear test site and the sonic booms of secret planes.

In 1900 silver was found in the Silver Bow mine. And Tonopah boomed, with saloons, casinos and whorehouses, thrown up overnight. The Mizpah Hotel, still standing on main street – named after the biggest vein of the silver ore that started the rush – opened and in 1922 came the Big Casino which touted itself as 'the Monte Carlo of the desert'.

I was looking for the base, which did not appear on the maps. The old World War II base is the civilian airport now. On the official New Mexico state highway map the whole area was vaguely named 'game range'. Even the test site and Nellis Range were omitted.

As the buildings thinned out and then stopped, the sightline shrank to a few hundred yards. The road was marked 'Grand Army of the Republic Highway'. 'Ely 163 miles,' I read, 'Next gas 112 miles.'

Then I saw it to the south: the old World War II base, now Tonopah Airport, with huge arched hangars and earthen bunkers suffused in the soft light that was seeping in under the black clouds.

I drove along the near-deserted flightline. It seemed dark, almost haunted.

In October 1940 the government turned over some 5000 square miles of public land to the military for training. Government silver certificates replaced the pay cheque of the silver miners. A base was in operation at Tonopah by July 1942, and would-be fighter pilots came to the area to learn to fly BT-13 trainers and the P-39, a fighter so dangerous in its handling that both the American Army Air Corps and the RAF had rejected it.

It had been from the beginning a kind of hard luck base. Trainees, suffering from the cold, wind and dust, named it 'Camp Frosty Balls'. Fighter trainees died at an alarming rate. Later, after the base become the site of a B-24 training programme, the bombers kept crashing, too. Once, a machine gun began firing inside one of the bombers and when the crew finally got it back on the ground, two men were dead in the turrets. By the end of the war they were testing bizarre bat bombs, crude radio-directed cruise missiles that foreshadowed the base's future.

Chuck Yeager was one of the first to train there. He lived in a tarpaper shack heated by an oil stove and recalled that the wind never seemed to stop blowing.

Yeager and his pals with the 363rd fighter squadron still saw Tonopah as 'a wide-open silver-mining town'.

'On paydays,' he would write, 'we crowded around the black-jack tables of the Tonopah Club, drank ourselves blind on fifths of rotgut rye and bourbon, then staggered over to the local cathouse. Miss Taxine, the madam, tried to keep a fresh supply of gals so we wouldn't get bored and become customers of Lucky Strike, a cathouse in Mina, about thirty miles down the road, but we went to Mina anyway, wrecked the place and the sheriff ran us out of town. The next morning, a P-39 strafed Mina's water tower.'

In the Fifties, the opening of the test site to the south brought jobs for the miners and other hands. Miners, by a happy coincidence, were in demand at the test site after 1962, when the Atmospheric Test Ban Treaty was signed and the bombs went underground, where long tunnels had to be built to hold test equipment for the milliseconds they would record radiation and heat and blast.

The big booms at the test site set off a minor boom-time in Tonopah. The town enjoyed a brief flurry of notoriety in 1957 when Howard Hughes bizarrely chose the Mizpah Hotel for his second wedding, to long-time companion Jean Peters. He had stolen her from war hero Audi Murphy, who looked for a way to murder the millionaire.

Hughes chose the wedding site because he had business to transact. He was convinced there was still silver in some of the mines. His father had prospected in the area for a while, and Hughes was betting that the veins were not quite worked out. In a few months, he bought up some 710 claims – covering most of Tonopah – along with some 14,2000 acres of Nye and areas in other counties, for 10.5 million dollars. What is less clear is why he got married at all, since he continued multiple affairs with several women – and men, including long-time lover Cary Grant.

It was just about the same time Hughes got married in the Mizpah that the nuclear weapons designers at Sandia Labs in Albuquerque cast greedy eyes on the empty areas of the Nellis Range south of the old Tonopah base and north of the test site. By 1958, they had set up the Tonopah Test and Training Range, dropping bombs to test fuses, cases and parachutes. Soon rockets and radar would join them.

The place was still run by Sandia Labs, in Albuquerque, the main nuclear weapons contractor for the military. The Interceptors had become intrigued by other sectors inside Tonopah's ranges: the Tolicha Peak Electronic Warfare facility, Base Camp, to the north of Highway Six near Warm Springs, and Site IV, where foreign radars are tested and whose name was an odd shadow of Bob Lazar's claimed S-4 at Papoose Lake.

By the time the Stealth arrived in 1984, the Tonopahans had learned the importance of knowing upon which side their bread was buttered. Their conspiracy of silence about the secret aircraft was like that of a seaside town at the height of the summer season when a shark is sighted. They took no notice of the planes flying overhead.

*

Taking off from Tonopah at night, Stealth pilots, like SAC pilots before them, had practise-bombed America in the dark, targeting boat docks in Minnesota and high rises in Denver. 'We could find Mrs Smith's rooming house and take out the northeast corner guest room above the garage,' one of the pilots boasted.

But even those who had trained with the plane were not sure it would work against real radar. Before the Gulf War began, the general sentiment among US pilots in Saudi Arabia was 'I sure hope this Stealth shit works'. Then they saw the bats, the ones that showed up each morning dead on the floor of the hangars, their sonar fooled by the faceted shapes of the planes just as radar would be, and they believed.

On the night of 17 January 1991, there was a banquet to honour Ben Rich, who was soon to retire as head of the Skunk Works. Halfway around the world, the F-117s were loading up to hit Baghdad.

Soon they would be going after another target – the Press. Peter Arnett of CNN, whose coverage was unbeloved of the Air Force, was using Baghdad's phone centre. The switchboard went on the target list and one night, in the ready rooms at the King Khalid Air Force base in Saudi Arabia, off duty pilots waited expectantly, sets tuned to CNN. They counted down the seconds until, right on schedule, their screen suddenly changed to a roaring grey and a cheer broke out.

By the time the Gulf War was over, the F-117 would become a national hero, and the pictures were no longer distant and grainy. The Stealth was photographed by Annie Liebowitz, photographer of the stars, for *Vanity Fair* in a portfolio together with Schwartzkopf, Powell and Cheney. To see the plane there reminded me of those portraits of American Indian chiefs, hauled across the Atlantic to entertain the court in London, dolled up and dressed for presentation to the king, but surrealistically out of place. Stealth was now seen openly and it had become beautiful, the beauty of the jeep or camouflage. And to the advocates of Stealth, the success of its fighter in the Nintendo air war over Iraq put it up there with the longbow or repeating rifle as a military breakthrough. The same sort of claims that Curt LeMay and the air power advocates liked to make were now made for the F-117, that in just so many sorties the Stealth had done the work of the entire bomber fleet of World War II. It reminded me of Curt LeMay, bragging about the B-47 or the B-58, whose weapons pod, he had marvelled, contained the explosive power of entire centuries of warfare.

One of the weapons they were proudest of testing at Tonopah was the Saddam bomb, or Deep Throat. It happened during Operation Desert Storm; a brochure from the Tonopah Range later told the story with pride.

For all the splendid videos the public was shown of smart bombs slipping down air shafts and puffing up concrete shelters so they subsided into ruins, by 21 January 1991, it was clear that some of the toughest, Yugoslav-built shelters resisted even the biggest bombs in stock. Among the superhard shelters was Taji number 2 bunker, northwest of Baghdad, which had been hit three times by bombs that, as one general put it, 'only dug up the rose garden'. Inside might be Saddam himself, and the Air Force was fairly licking its chops at the thought.

So the boys down at Eglin, the Air Force munitions centre, started dreaming up a new bomb, a bigger bomb, a meaner bomb. To fit on the planes, it couldn't be wider, so it had to be longer. They didn't have time to fabricate a special bomb case, so they took an old stock of 8-inch 203-mm howitzer barrels – that one of them happened to know were sitting around in an Army arsenal in Letterkenny Pennsylvania – sent them to the Watervliet Arsenal in New York, and had them machined into what was soon called Deep Throat: the BLU-113/B 'Super Penetrator'. Hand-packed like a giant ice cream cone with 1200 pounds of high explosive, the whole thing weighed 4700 pounds. It was tested on a rocket sled at Holloman Air Force Base in New Mexico, riding the rails for a mile to be sure the shell would penetrate 22 feet of reinforced concrete, tested again a few days later at a windtunnel in Dallas, then four days later shipped to Nevada. On 24 February, the bomb, sans explosive, was dropped at Tonopah onto a special concrete target. It dug a hole over a hundred feet deep – and it sits there still, too deep to be dug out. On the night of 27 February, two of the real bombs, which the ground crew had scrawled with cartoons and obscenities as thickly as a New York back street wall, were slung from the wings of hulking F-111 Aardvarks, which canted to one side with the weight. A couple of hours later, they were deposited into the airshaft of the shelter, popping six blast doors like soda caps.

Not long afterwards, the bomb was used to strike another command bunker and shelter in Baghdad. The failure of earlier bombs had convinced the Iraqis that they would be safe in the specially hardened shelter. It was packed with people. Most were top Iraqi officials and their families. Dozens of civilians were killed by the collapsing roof but, to the disappointment of the generals, Saddam Hussein was not among them.

It was one of the few activities officials at Tonopah bragged of, only a little while later, after the Gulf War had made the Stealth fighter a hero and the boys out on the test range wanted their due credit.

After the F-117 was made public, in the blurry Air Force photo in 1988, at a major show at Nellis in 1990 and most of all after the Gulf War, the locals could show their pride openly. After the war they held a victory parade with a thousand people marching. I drove past the fire station, whose front bore a bas relief of the fighter. But as soon as the Stealth became a hero, it was gone. The whole wing of the aircraft was transferred in 1992 to Holloman Air Force Base near Alamagordo, New Mexico. The base at Tonopah was too distant and too expensive.

Back on the highway I was surrounded soon by snow as if spun in a cocoon. I wouldn't be able to see a thing for the rest of the day. Grey fingers of distant blizzard seemed to mock my expedition.

Turning up the long road that ended at Tonopah's gate, I already knew I would see nothing. At the gate, a missile dented by the stray bullets of vandals reared up, and the big sign proudly identified Sandia Labs as the proprietor. I drove up to the fence, paused a reflective moment or two, then turned around.

Back in town I stopped for coffee and cherry pie – total bill, $1.50 – a few feet from the fire station that proudly displayed a 'Home of the Stealth' plaque on the wall.

The pie was steaming and superb. I complimented the lady

behind the counter. 'Well, tell the people down the road about it,' she said.

I walked over to the pay phone and noticed a plaque on the wall beside it. The plaque showed the outline of the state of Nevada with that of Iraq overlaid on it. In the centre, roughly where Dreamland stood, was Baghdad neatly superimposed on it and marked by red flashes. 'First to strike, January 1991', it read proudly. I was confused about the scale: was Iraq that small, or Nevada that large, or was there artistic licence at work here?

The women behind the counter said not to worry about the snow. I'd be fine once I hit Goldfield but now it was snowing even harder as I passed back through the town.

Soon it was dark enough for headlights, but they only smeared the snow into a cottonwool-like haze. In minutes, I was locked into a bumper-to-bumper backup of trucks and RVs poking along through the ten-foot visibility. It was slow and frustrating, the end to a frustrating day.

On the fenceline, the guards were usually polite and friendly enough, but later the Interceptors discovered another viewpoint, which for obscure reasons they named Brainwash Butte. From Brainwash Butte you could see the base, whose living quarter area was separated by miles from the main runway. The view was not very exciting: the long row of identical hangars that had been built for the Stealth fighters looked from this distance like the little tin sheds of one of those 'U-Stor-It' rental facilities.

Goodall kept going up there; he was convinced something new was going on at the base. The security was tighter than it had been during the height of the Stealth programme he said, and new construction was underway.

One evening in the summer of 1951, when he was just five years old, Jim Goodall felt his father shaking him awake. 'There's something you've got to see,' his father told him, and he went outside and looked up to see two dozen B-36s, hear their rumble and see their shadows – aluminium overcast.

He was fascinated. And when the family moved to the San Francisco area, he found his way to planes again. He once somehow found himself sitting in the prototype XF 104 Star-fighter in a windtunnel in Sunnyvale and managed to close the canopy. Even as a kid he knew enough to be careful of what lever he pulled – and he knew there was such a thing as an ejection seat. He managed to get out and, another characteristic of his personality already forming, he talked his way out of trouble.

He joined the Air Force in March 1962, and in February 1964, was at Edwards working on a communications system. President Johnson had just made public the existence of the Blackbird and Goodall saw his first, a YF-12. He still remembers the date – 29 February 1964. 'I was about to get on the Northrop shuttle to Hawthorne when I heard this incredible roar and ran down to the flight line area and looked to the south.'

There Goodall saw a black plane that at first he thought was the famous the X-15 rocket aircraft, but from the scale of the people standing beside it he realized it was too large. Then it was time to board the shuttle. He got on – it was a little pusher prop – and took off, flying right over the YF-12 as it was taxiing. The moment he saw the Blackbird framed in the window beneath him, he realizes now, he imprinted on it like some infant animal. He was locked into the fascination of his life. 'I could not believe my eyes,' he remembered later, 'At that point I became obsessed.'

Eventually Goodall would have his 'own' Blackbird. After he left the Air Force, he would split time between selling computer hardware on the road as a travelling salesman, and serving in the Air National Guard in Minnesota. What other way could he get his own Blackbird? This was an A-12, the Agency ship, and his was the most meticulously restored, maintained and preserved Blackbird in the world, probably obtained in his capacity as unit historian. In time, Goodall would be admitted to the Roadrunners' Club, the organization of those who worked on the U-2 or the Blackbirds between 1955 and 1968, at the Ranch.

But by the time he went up to Whitesides to look down on Dreamland for the first time, with John Lear in autumn 1988, his obsession had grown.

Goodall thought Lear would never make it, because he has flat feet. But Lear took the pack – sixty pounds of it, mostly water – and carried it the whole way and Goodall was the one who had the hard time.

He would spend some eighty days on the perimeter, he calculated – twice the time Jesus spent in the desert – on Whitesides and Freedom Ridge, then by the fence line at Tonopah, looking for the Stealth fighter, and later at Brainwash Butte. He would take one of the first clear pictures of the F-117, and when he glimpsed it felt an almost sexual rush.

At some point during the revelation of the Lazar story, and talking to those who had worked at the base, Goodall crossed the ridge – or began to straddle it. He came to believe in the presence of alien craft, as did John Andrews, his frequent companion on these trips. 'There are things out there that would make George Lucas green with envy,' he had been told, and he believed it. Lazar's story seemed to ring true to him. But the key moment in his conversion was a letter from Ben Rich of the Skunk Works, in which Rich said that both he and Kelly Johnson believed in UFOs.

But in the account I had, this was a tweak.

He talked often with Rich: they had a bantering but friendly relationship. Rich had less patience with John Andrews, with his constant inquiries, but he respected Goodall, recognized him as a true buff, a fan, and someone who saw that what the Skunk Works had done was important, history. He even appreciated the efforts of Goodall and the others to get the story out; as he grew older, the whole system of secrecy grew more and more onerous. He felt it had got out of hand, and once he compared the Interceptors to Ross Perot, shrilly crying for a change in a system gone wrong.

But Goodall had come to believe in the saucers. He felt something, he wasn't sure what, had happened at Roswell in 1947. He could believe most of Lazar's story. Perhaps Lear – as always a central figure, the key link, had influenced him, but what for most of the Interceptors was just an intriguing possibility became a certainty for him.

It did not reduce his interest in black craft. He was still into every detail of every possible project. He became the butt of gentle jokes about his constant obsession with 'Something new at Tonopah'. He would hide under camou net for days and come back reporting that security was tighter at Tonopah than in the early days of the Stealth deployment there and some new craft must be flying. But he was not able to find out what.

John Andrews was constantly enraging the people at the Skunk Works. The very mention of his name, and his constant letters of inquiry, set Ben Rich off when I talked to him. He fairly raved. Kelly Johnson, too, had been outraged when he learned in the early 1980s that Andrews had been allowed to photograph and measure the D-21 Blackbird drones in storage at the boneyard in Davis – Monthan – the same strange shapes I was told I did not see.

In 1959 he knew all about the U-2, and contacted Lockheed, but he honoured the company's request not to produce a model. Only in 1962, when the Cuban missile crisis had made the aircraft famous, did his U-2 model come out, for Hawk Models in Chicago.

When Andrews was pursuing the Stealth fighter, an AFOSI officer flew out from Washington to visit. 'Just be patient,' he told Andrews. AFOSI keeps an eye on what Andrews is keeping his eye on. He expects that; it's their job, he says. But today, Andrews feels, 'things have changed. Once it was man to man –' a friendly, almost collegial request for co-operation, 'now they are hiding behind regulations.'

When his model of the Stealth fighter, billed as the 'F-19', appeared in 1986, it became the best-selling plastic aircraft model of all time – a million sold – and it is now highly sought after by collectors. Although Andrews estimates its dimensions were accurate to about two per cent of the real thing, and 75 per cent accurate in shape, in fact it turned out to resemble the Russian stealth fighter, the MiG Ferret, more than the American one. But some of the buffs who had long imagined the plane, would later say it looked more like the *idea* of stealth than the real one, the F-117 itself.

Andrews was unapologetic about the model.

'I love my country,' he said. 'In fact the model helped keep the security of the airplane,' he told me, 'because everybody was looking at it, saying that's what it looks like.'

'But', I interposed, 'what if you had been more accurate?'

He had no answer.

*

Andrews next turned out his model of the long-rumoured 'Aurora' spy plane with its pulser engine. It came directly from his visits to the perimeter. 'I've slept on the top of Whitesides,' he said, 'and heard the pulse. You cannot mistake it. I heard it in December 1992. It has a very low frequency; there's nothing like it.'

But to some of the Interceptors, the appearance of Testor's Lazar model showed that Andrews had crossed the line, gone over the ridge.

'I'm quite comfortable with Lazar,' Andrews said, and he seemed to believe most of his story. He consulted with Lazar, and Jon Farhat, a computer graphic designer who is doing work on a long-gestating, perhaps forthcoming, movie about Lazar.

Andrews' model of the Lazar saucer was skilfully packaged so no one could tell just how seriously it was intended. 'Area S4 UFO Revealed!' ran the copy on the box. 'A scale model kit of the alien craft allegedly hidden in Nevada by the US Government. As described by eyewitness and former government physicist, Bob Lazar. Paint and cement not included. Skill Level Two. Sixteen page full colour book included. Type of vehicle: Anti-matter reaction, gravity amplification, interstellar craft.' Made of 'metallic substance of unknown nature, containing an anti-matter reactor to bend space-time, fueled by element 115'.

Rendered in 1/48 scale, it was made up of twenty-three plastic pieces, including a transparent top to offer a view of the anti-matter reactor.

But on the box Testor also carefully stated 'we can neither confirm nor deny the existence of the craft on which the model is based.' Caveat emptor.

It was the saucer Lazar nicknamed the 'sports model', and it sold out immediately, thanks perhaps to the fact that Larry King displayed the model on his desk during the October 1994 show he did from just outside Area 51.

The Testor's model served to make Lazar's tale tangible. Having seen such detailed plastic parts it was harder not to believe in the existence of the real craft.

And Andrews did believe in it. He seemed to buy into the 'trickle out' theory – those bits and pieces, were what the government wanted us to know, so we would be less shocked when the whole truth comes out.

As Andrews' interest in flying saucers grew, his letters to Ben Rich and others at the Skunk Works irritated them more.

Rich finally sent Andrews that handwritten letter in which he wrote, 'Yes, I believe in UFOs, and so did Kelly Johnson.'

Andrews and Jim Goodall too became very excited – they believe! They know!

'Yes, I call them unfunded opportunities,' Rich's note continued. That was, Lockheed ideas the damn fool Air Force wouldn't pay for.

It was a joke, and not a kind one.

Andrews and Goodall spent lots of time at Tonopah. But they also began to venture to the perimeter of Dreamland itself. In 1988, Goodall hiked with John Lear up Whitesides Mountain. After he finished the Stealth fighter model, Andrews began to visit there as well. Now, he was looking for Aurora, or whatever it was that left 'donut on a rope' contrails.

More and more observers joined them. And after Psychospy moved to Rachel and began to publicize the viewpoints, the numbers grew. From a few watchers there evolved, as in complexity theory, the group who would later informally name themselves the Dreamland Interceptors.

'People are seeing things in the sky, basically,' said John Andrews, who, having watched black planes out on the Perimeter since the days of the U-2 in 1988, was the most veteran of the Interceptors.

'It's like a little CIA out there,' he said. 'We collect bits and pieces and put them together in a mosaic.'

The Interceptors developed their own loose camaraderie and culture over the course of many visits to vantage points from which they gazed into Dreamland.

As their totem the Interceptors adopted the aluminium lawn chair – that icon of backyard American suburbia, furnishing for the dream yard of the dream house – and one of the first spin-offs of the aerospace industry.

It was one thing to say you had seen the base – everyone somehow seemed to feel, doing it, that they were among the first, the proud few – but the real badge of honour was to carry that chair up there.

Other equipment was helpful: scanners and binoculars and telephoto lenses. Russian border patrol night vision – the Soviets had beaten us in that technology. A realistic Pro-2006 scanner, Radio Shack or as the Swiss Mountain Bat favoured, an AOR brand 8000 connected to the Optoelectronics 'Scout'. Serious optics, like the big binoculars called 'hooters' or a Celestron 5000 telescope with camera adaptable eyepiece.

Before the Ridge, the best viewpoint was Whitesides Mountain, and further away, after Freedom Ridge fell victim to the expansion of the perimeter, there was Tikaboo. This became the agreed standard for the measurement of the height of other peaks, the strenuousness of other hikes, in planning expeditions to the viewpoints to observe the base at Tonopah, the nuclear test site, mysterious electronic stations and sites of aircraft wreckage. They speculated on areas they could not reach, like the fabled Cheshire airstrip, which was said to turn invisible like just another strip of desert floor until lights made it appear. Or Base Camp, a mysterious facility with no clear purpose north of Warm Spring and Highway 6 or Site IV, deep in between Tonopah and the restricted area around Groom. This was the home, Agent X reported: 'of terrain-following radar development, covert testing of purloined Soviet, Warsaw Pact and Chinese radars and ECM and making sure that they wouldn't jam fuses on our nuclear weapons and disable our penetrating bombers' electronic navigation and counter-measures. It seems to be integral part of the Nellis Range Complex electronic warfare and evaluation capabilities along with the Tolicha Peak Electronic Combat Range.'

They were mock spies – 'a little CIA' – but also the jesters of Dreamland, watching the reliquary of the Cold War with whimsy and cynicism. They wore the same camou as the camou dudes. They reminded me of Marx's famous statement that history happens twice, the first time as tragedy, the second as farce. Their production was a send-up of the Cold War; their spirit that of the old Firesign Theater album cover bearing the revolutionary banners of Marx (Groucho) and Lennon (John).

Of course they were also just another of those self-directing American groups revealing us as a nation of joiners and near obsessives. Their particular obsession was birdwatching – no, it was 'birding', a more intense and competitive activity, charting the appearances of warblers in the brambles, kestrels by the cove. Only these birds were different – maybe it was 'ultimate birding'.

I recognized myself in them: we had been the kids who put together too many aircraft models and spent time at the library looking at *Av Week* instead of reading the Hardy Boys.

They were journalists and buffs, private researchers and conservationists. There were such characters as Peter Merlin, an aviation archaeologist, who found the crash sites of old planes in the desert and was amazing at ferreting out details and documents. Merlin carried a key ring made of bits of famous planes he'd found.

Tom Mahood, a former Bechel civil engineer from Irvine, spent days assembling careful chronologies and descriptions of secret places like the radar cross section facilities. He collated official brochures about Tonopah and studied old maps.

Agent X, a former coast guard agent and reporter for such magazines as *Gung Ho* and *The Nose*, came from his home in Juneau, Alaska, and spent days driving around the perimeters. Agent X was beloved of the rental car company. He kept coming back, and they were even willing to overlook what he came back with – banged up convertibles used as makeshift off-road vehicles. He wrecked a Buick Le Sabre on a cutoff from Groom Road, sliding into a ditch on the left side of the road, doing 60. His report made it sound like a crash of some exotic secret prototype: 'The Le Sabre rose in a 45-degree left roll before hanging for a moment and falling back to the desert floor.'

The Interceptors had no regular or official membership and only the most general of shared values and beliefs. They were against excess secrecy but without the mystery it produced, they wouldn't have been there on the perimeter.

Some derided the youfers, some were curious and tentative, and for many the saucer stories were a little pilot flame of possibility that kept them going – the Biggest Story in the History of Mankind.

'I'm a hardware guy,' Jim Goodall said, but he was willing to speculate on the existence of extraterrestrial hardware.

The Interceptors had no clubhouse. Their social organization could be described as 'ad hoc'. Communication was by phone and e-mail.

Many of the Interceptors admitted that people with more vital social and personal lives did not end up hanging around the perimeter. Some saw going to look for planes or climbing mountains with views of possible secret saucer bases as just another way to get outdoors, camp, get some fresh air.

Some would fly in light planes around the perimeter, an enterprise that felt daring and exciting but offered very little new perspective or information. They would visit places like Mount Charleston, where the wreckage of a C-54 that crashed on its way to Groom Lake still lay tangled near the top. The circle of the Interceptors widened. In August 1994, some sixty people mustered on the Ridge for what was billed as a 'Groom-stock', which included a former pilot from the Blackbird programme, and UFO buffs.

Once, some of the Interceptors arranged to take a tour of the Nevada test site. Derek was their guide. As lunch time grew near, Bill Sweetman noticed Derek looking at his watch with some nervousness. They were taken to the Command Post, with those Naugahyde chairs, by the big long oval tables, the maps and video screens, and given lunch. He seemed in a hurry to get them into the command post, although there was nothing in particular happening there, no event to get there in time for. They ate packed lunches inside. It was only later that it struck Sweetman that they had been deliberately kept inside; he was sure it was so they would not see something flying overhead.

When Sweetman asked him, 'What kind of pumpkins would we have turned into it if we had been outside at noon?' Derek was sheepish.

After the tour they drove down to LA, arriving exhausted in the wee hours of the morning, collapsing into sleeping bags on the floor – only to be awakened a couple of hours later, tossed about by the earthquake.

Many of the Interceptors were engineers or programmers. This was instructive: there was reverse engineering at work on the ridge, whether or not there was inside the perimeter, and a decoding of software. The demographics of the Interceptors tended to overlap those of engineers, as the test site overlapped Dreamland. The techie connection brought with it an attitude, a special irony reminiscent of the mercurial charge of a semi-conductor. It faded in and out, suspended possibility and speculation in a jaded cynicism, like a force field.

'A little CIA,' John Andrews said, accumulating and com-paring facts like any good intelligence agency. For the Inter-ceptors simply laying out the known and marking where the unknown began – patrolling the perimeter so to speak – was enough. Some compiled elaborate tables of sightings, crashes, types of aircraft – known and suspected – even individual aircraft, sometimes right down to tail numbers. In this they had much in common with other American obsessives, or obsessives anywhere on the planet.

If the Interceptors parodied the CIA's assemblage of infor-mation from bits and pieces, they also parodied its surrogate identities and the cult and camaraderie of secret military units. They took on alter egos, in the manner of spies, blues musicians or gangsters, and names to match, mostly e-mail nicknames. The alter egos both resembled and mocked cover names of the UFO informants such as 'condor' or 'falcon'. They created insignia – pins and patches – as if they were a real military unit.

They developed their own personal subset of the Lore.

'It's about two and a half Tikaboos,' an Interceptor would say. 'But how far is it Le Baronable?' the response would come. The Chrysler rental convertible favoured by Agent X had become the standard of measurement for the dirt roads in the area.

One of Psychospy's sources declared that the aliens had bequeathed technology on humans through Hungarians – atomic physicists Leo Szilard and Edward Teller, aerodynamicist Theodore von Karman, weren't they all Hungarian? And the aliens spoke a language like High Hungarian.

So Agent Zero had special decoder rings rigged up that pur-ported to translate Hungarian characters into English. They were made of titanium, the same metal as the Blackbirds, then dipped in a special secret fluid to lend them a silver blue sheen that seemed to me to reflect the whole happy glitzy fascination with Area 51. The secret fluid was Coca-Cola.

*

It was like putting together a mosaic, John Andrews had said, and mosaic was just what the military feared, and why they justified concealing the smallest detail. But in fact what the Interceptors did was more like assembling a cubist vision, a paste-up of little facets, angles, shards of blue and brown and grey – a pattern like the camou they favoured in their tailoring.

Camou and cubism share the visual implication of dozens of simultaneous viewpoints. They represent a multiplicity of mingled attitudes. So it was with the Interceptors. But mosaic was right in another way: mosaic was the first browser program for the World Wide Web. The information the Interceptors gathered found its most natural home on the Web. The trails they trod to distant viewpoints soon had their counterparts in threads on the Internet, on alt.conspiracy.area51, the Skunk Works digest and later on, in elaborate Web pages.

On-line they were rebuilding Dreamland in HTML and reverse engineering it in data. It was Vannevar Bush, the very man reputed to have been head of the secret MJ12 group, who had first laid out the vision of the personal computer and the new ways of organizing information it would bring. In July 1945, in a famous article in the *Atlantic* called 'As We May Think', he described his vision of the Memex, a personal memory or information device. In the process, he projected something that sounds like CD-ROM and the Internet.

Bush's ideas would inspire those who created the personal computer and the Internet, people like Douglas Engelbart, inventor of the computer mouse, who read the *Atlantic* article in a straw hut in the South Pacific when he was in the military.

Bush believed that the human mind operates less by classification and organization – the traditional view of thought – than by association. 'With one item in its grasp, it snaps instantly to the next that is suggested by the association of thought, in accordance with some intricate web of trails carried by the cells of the brains. Yet the speed of action, the intricacy of the trails, the detail of mental pictures is awe inspiring beyond all else in nature.'

Bush had predicted that 'Wholly new forms of encyclopedias will appear, ready-made with a mesh of associative trails running through them, ready to be dropped into the Memex, and there amplified.' And he predicted the rise of a special profession of innovator to mark such trails and distribute them to individual Memex machines: 'a new profession of trail-blazers, those who find delight in the task of establishing useful trails through the enormous mass of the common record.' This anticipated the strategy of the Interceptors. They were trailblazers, not just to the tops of viewpoints but to documents and information.

The assemblage of extremely detailed and factual studies, Richard Hofstadter noted in the Fifties, is characteristic of conspiracist groups. Then, from these edifices of fact, the great leap of conclusion is made. The information the Interceptors assembled was like nothing so much as the conspiracist assemblages. But not everyone was willing to make the leaps of faith.

The Interceptors knew something was happening when they showed up in the movies. In the film *Broken Arrow* a bomber and a nuke have gone astray and the first official instinct is to cover it all up, keep it secret. But a young aide warns, 'don't forget the guys in lawn chairs,' who watch all the bases, noticing a bomber leave but not return. It just showed how quickly Area 51 had crept into the mainstream of popular culture, and it surprised even the hardiest Interceptors.

Their favoured viewpoints were far from civilization; that was the attraction. What was the old joke? 'It's not the end of the world, but you can see it from there.'

Sometimes I imagined seeing the literal end of the world from the ridge, viewing the apocalypse from a lawn chair. I had a vision of Psychospy on the top, welcoming everyone to their lawn chairs, in camou, his MREs at the ready. 'Come on, everybody, the show is about to begin' – then mushroom clouds rise from the plain below.

It was the kind of fevered vision Dreamland inspired.

Psychospy was lying in the back seat of his car parked along Mailbox Road when he first saw them: strange spaceships, dotted with lights, *Close Encounters* style, hovering. They flew right over the car.

It was only later, after rubbing his eyes, coming awake, and thinking about the vivid memories he had had that he realized he had been lying in a position from which he could not have seen ships overhead. Psychospy used the story as an example of how easily it was to delude yourself into thinking you had seen something you had not, how tricky was the business of seeing things in the sky near the Black Mailbox.

'Psychospy' – the anagrammatic quality of the name, psy and spy, struck me immediately: this guy was different from most of the characters swapping lore on-line. Psychospy, aka the Desert Rat, was Glenn Campbell 'not the singer', the irritating tag followed him around. He had been a computer programmer for a successful software company in Boston's Route 128 belt. He had moved to Rachel in January 1993, fascinated by Lazar's story, having bought himself out of the software company.

He dressed in camou outfits bought at Hahn's Surplus store in Las Vegas and talked a lot about his selection of MREs – 'meals ready to eat', the latterday K-rations. Sometimes the impression he gave was of a grown up version of the kid in your neighbourhood who wanted to play soldiers all the time.

He said that he was not a UFO buff or Stealth fan, but a philosopher and inquirer into the nature of truth. His business card read 'Area 51 Research Center. UFOs – Gov't Secrets – Philosophy – Psychology etc'. He would make himself the chief researcher into Area 51, an advocate against secrecy, an extremely useful talking head for television crews, and a spy. 'I am spying,' he would say, 'on behalf of the American people.'

He had quickly run foul of Joe and Pat Travis at The Inn and been exiled to a trailer at the other end of town. The story going around was that Joe Travis, drunk one night, had burst into the trailer and put a gun to his head.

Before I came to Nevada, Steve Douglass had told me about Psychospy, and I phoned him. In return, he sent me a copy of his *Area 51 Viewer's Guide*. It seemed to compare well with some of the better travel guides to Venice or Florence; the very idea that someone had written a travel guide to a place that did not officially exist was exquisitely appealing.

'Don't believe everything you hear,' he scrawled on the cover. Did I seem naive? Had he marked me out as a sceptic? It was the first sign of his tendency – useful for dealing with the Press – to choose his words carefully to match his audience.

I first met him at the trailhead to Freedom Ridge. He was

standing beside his Renault LeCar, still with Massachusetts plates, covered with dozens of little stickers indicating places he had visited.

We both gave each other a look. I think his was suspicious. I know mine was. I wanted to like him, but from that first moment at the trailhead I had found it difficult to warm to him. The Minister theorized he was another shy person, trying to overcome his basic awkwardness in the diffident way shy people often assume. I could accept that. He often had the air of a hired guide, the park ranger of Dreamland, but in time I came to think of him as a kind of ombudsman. You could also see him as a jester, and that good old American word, gadfly. I identified him with Thoreau, with Dreamland as his Walden Pond.

Campbell had written an essay called 'Lazar as Fictional Character', which I interpreted to mean: if Lazar had not existed, we would have had to invent him. It was the same where he himself was concerned: if Psychospy hadn't existed it would have been necessary to invent him. If you were simplifying the story of Dreamland for a TV movie, you would need to combine all the Interceptors in one character, so there would be plenty of time for ads, and Campbell might be that character. He gave good soundbites to the visiting syndicated TV shows, varying his tone as needed. Imagine all the Interceptors' dreams wrapped up in one guy.

He had established what he called 'The Whitesides Defense Council' to fight the military's takeover of the viewpoints there and on Freedom Ridge, and then the 'Secrecy Oversight Council' – a mock organization whose name referred to his enterprise of setting up an aluminium lawn chair on the ridge above Dreamland.

Campbell skilfully tapped into the scepticism toward the Federal government that was one of the few common bonds between native or long-time Nevadans, between political right and left, and between the youfers and stealthies, who wanted to break down the walls of unnecessary government secrecy. He named the ridge he had discovered Freedom Ridge, of course – after all, everyone was in favour of freedom.

Nevadans have long resented Federal ownership of the vast

majority of their lands. Even though the Feds pump billions of dollars into the state economy through the military, the DOE and other agencies that use the land, it is widely resented. What Mark Twain wrote in *Roughing It* about Nevadans pretty much still holds true today: 'Originally, Nevada was a part of Utah and was called Carson County; and a pretty large county it was too.' And when they finally achieved statehood, 'The people were glad to have a legitimately constituted government, but did not particularly enjoy having strangers from distant states put in authority over them – a sentiment that was natural enough.'

Nevada was one of the centres of the Sagebrush rebellion against the Reagan administration's use of the land. Some areas of the state joined together in a fictional or 'notional' – as the military would call it – county they called Bullfrog, after an old mining district. Bullfrog County wanted to separate itself from existing counties that they charged had given the Feds too much free rein. But the real purpose, it turned out, was to guarantee that the benefits from the Yucca Mountain storage facility that was to be built in the area would flow into a few select private hands.

Soon Campbell – in his persona as Psychospy – began distributing a newsletter called *The Desert Rat* by mail and on the Net. He reported on hearings, arrests of perimeter crossers and Area 51 rumour and lore. He told of strange characters that appeared in Rachel, like Ambassador Merlyn Merlin II from the planet Draconis, who said he was a 'Being of Light', although Psychospy editorialized, 'we touched him and found him to be quite solid. He was on a mission to promote the coming "Golden Age", when the aliens would be integrated into our society and we humans would evolve into a higher form.'

He came up with odd sources from within the test site, such as Jarod, who claimed to have worked on 'flight simulators' for the alien craft hidden at S-4.

Psychospy kept showing up at hearings and working the media, irritating the hell out of the military and the Lincoln County sheriff's department. He fought the BLM's efforts to seize more land above Dreamland by demanding that the Air Force explain why it needed the land, what it was doing in Dreamland.

It was a classic bureaucratic Catch 22 that bent back on itself: the government needed the land to keep secret what it was doing on the base that did not exist, but because what it was doing was secret it could not explain why it needed the land.

Psychospy rightly calculated that the hardest thing for the military which takes itself deadly seriously, was to deal with derision. His best line was his response to the signs on the perimeter, and the whole apparatus of secrecy: 'Use of deadly farce authorized.'

Glenn Campbell and Jim Goodall designed their own version of a uniform patch for the workers at Groom. Perhaps they had a real patch, but they could not display it in public. If they did not, he said, then they deserved one. Every unit in the military has at least one patch, designed for special events, manoeuvres or wars, theatres of combat. The design for the patch, done with Jim Goodall, showed an Aurora-like craft sweeping up from a dry lake, with mountains behind it read 'Dreamland Groom Lake Test Site'. Soon we heard it was for sale at the Pentagon store. And Campbell did not hesitate to print it up on T-shirts and caps and sell it through his catalogue and in 'The Research Center'.

But then some took it seriously and it was reproduced in several magazines as if were the real thing – the patch that those inside the base actually wore.

A year or so later I was in Nevada again and phoned Glenn Campbell from Las Vegas. 'Well,' he said, 'I'll have to be in the research centre all day.' This tone of pressing business was new.

'I've never seen the research centre,' I said, trying to keep the archness out of my voice. The research centre was Glenn's trailer, at the south end of Rachel, and in fact I knew it well.

When I pulled up to the little trailer, I noticed more junk outside – a cow skull, with bits of dried rawhide and hair still clinging to it and some old aircraft parts. This was landscaping, Rachel style. In front of the Inn too there was old plane wreckage, which stood in for that of a saucer crash.

There was a large map on the ceiling of the Dreamland and surrounding airspace and a big new Apple Mac on a table. On the wall was a quotation from anthropologist Margaret Mead, about how a few people with conviction can change the world. And on the floor were old socks.

Secret aircraft interested him barely at all. He had once said that if the legendary Aurora landed in front of him, taxied up and ran over his foot he would pay no attention.

When I talked with him about Steve's sighting of the TR3A, the black manta, he was sceptical. 'That's fine,' Glenn said, 'if he wants to believe in it.'

That day, he handed me an article called 'Effects of UFOs upon human beings'. It dealt with odd electrical effects – radio static, flashing lights – the pickup truck scene in *Close Encounters*. I thought it an odd choice and I wondered if there was any meaning in it. He couldn't figure me out any better than I could figure him, was my guess. Then I noticed the UFO article was by a man named 'McCampbell', and the similarity made me wonder if this guy was not some kind of doppelganger of Glenn's, a version of what he wished he could be – if only he could believe. It was a measured, mostly scientific, report on radio interference, sunburn effects, electrical shorts and other phenomena reported by those who encountered UFOs.

There were those who always thought he was a closet youfer. But he soft-pedalled this belief and increasingly he became sceptical of Lazar. Others of course said he was a government agent of some kind. In Rachel, this was the ultimate insult.

Gene Huff, Lazar's pal, took to calling him 'Goober' on-line. 'He tends to alienate people,' said Huff. 'He's a strange bird, a weird guy. He told me he moved out here because of the Bob Lazar story and now he attacks Bob. I call his operation the UFO division of the Mickey Mouse Club. It may be fine for the shitkickers and dickheads in Rachel, but not for the rest of the world.'

Campbell had alienated Huff, for one, by publishing transcripts of Lazar's statements at the Ultimate UFO Conference in Rachel, when Huff believed he was only one with the right to do that.

But Huff took a kind of pride in defending Lazar. He made Campbell one of his particular targets, hinting darkly of immoral, even criminal, behaviour in his background. The word among the Interceptors was that each of the two had something on the other. Glenn had negative information on

The black mailbox, owned by rancher Steve Medlin, a shrine for Dreamland visitors ever since it was used by Bob Lazar as landmark for flying saucer hunters. Credit: author.

The entrance to Area 51: Groom Road at the perimeter, before the 1995 expansion, with warning signs. 'Photography Prohibited', 'Use of Deadly Force Authorized'. Credit: author.

The Little A'Le'Inn, the focus of tourism in Rachel, Nevada. To some who come here, what Rick's Place was to Casablanca, the Inn was to Dreamland. Credit: author.

Gateway to Dreamland: The terminal at McCarran Airport in Las Vegas, used to transport workers to Area 51 and the Tonopah Test Range. Credit: Meinrad J. Eberle

The view from Tikaboo: the last public vantage point into Dreamland (in haze on extreme horizon) after the seizure of Freedom Ridge and Whitesides Peak. Credit: Meinrad J. Eberle

The white Jeep Cherokees of the Area 51 security guards, known as 'camou dudes' are familiar to visitors to the edge of Dreamland. Credit: Meinrad J. Eberle

Below: The famous hangar at Roswell, New Mexico, where saucer wreckage and alien bodies were reputed to have been collected for shipment to Hangar 18 at Wright Patterson Air Base in Dayton, Ohio. Credit: Author.

The F-117 Stealth fighter. The F-117 was developed under the code name 'Harvey' after Jimmy Stewart's invisible rabbit. Credit: Lockheed Martin Skunk Works.

Northrop B-2 Stealth bomber: 'The most expensive aircraft ever built'. Credit: Meinrad J. Eberle.

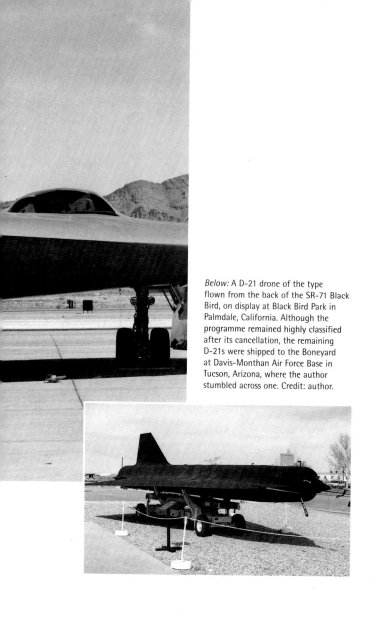

Below: A D-21 drone of the type flown from the back of the SR-71 Black Bird, on display at Black Bird Park in Palmdale, California. Although the programme remained highly classified after its cancellation, the remaining D-21s were shipped to the Boneyard at Davis-Monthan Air Force Base in Tucson, Arizona, where the author stumbled across one. Credit: author.

El Mirage Dry Lake and the General Atomics/CIA facility where the Predator robot aircraft was tested. Credit: author.

Predator Uninhabited Aerial Vehicle in flight – a successor to classified UAVs tested in Dreamland. Credit: General Atomics.

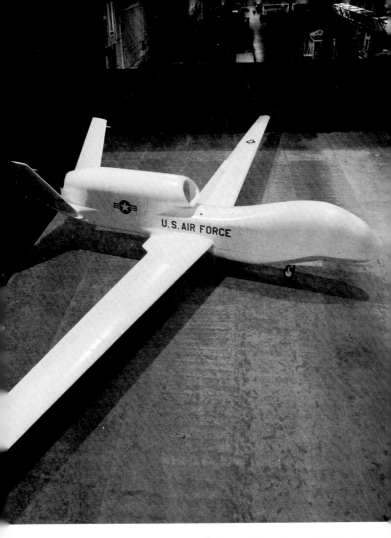

The Global Hawk Tier II plus Uninhabited Aerial Vehicle. With a 116 feet wingspan Global Hawk can loiter at 65,000 feet for 24 hours flying at 400 m.p.h. then return to a base thousands of miles away without refueling. Credit: Teledyne Ryan

The 'Tier III minus' Dark Star UAV. Named for a wacky low budget science fiction film, Dark Star depends on software and other technology developed for earlier black projects, probably including the huge Tier III craft often linked to the legendary Aurora aircraft. Credit: Denny Lombard, Lockheed Martin Skunk Works.

Sikorsky's saucer-like Cypher 'Multi Mission Platform,' a hovering helicopter-like craft. Credit: Sikorsky

Lockheed Martin's proposed 'All Wing Uninhabited Combat Air Vehicle' (UCAV), resembles the 'flying pumpkin seed' shapes spotted by some observers near Dreamland. Credit: Lockheed Martin.

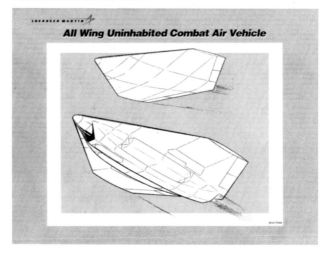

ROSWELL UFO

A scale model kit of the alien craft that allegedly crashed near Roswell, New Mexico in the 1940s.

OP SECRET

estors' 1997 model of the alleged Roswell UFO, very different from the saucer shape of the Lazar model John Andrews designed or Testors earlier. The manta-like shape is based on the account of a man who claimed he took part in the recovery in 1947 of a craft shaped like 'a small B-2 Stealth plane'. Credit: Testors Corporation

State of Nevada road sign erected Spring 1996 to mark the 'Extra-terrestrial Highway', from Ash Springs to Rachel, Nevada. The craft depicted is the quite terrestrial F-117 tested at Dreamland. Credit: author.

Camouflaged military bunker doors in Switzerland. It was doors like these that made Bob Lazar's stories of hangars hidden inside rock walls at S-4 seem believable to the Swiss Mountain Bat. Credit: Meinrad J. Eberle.

Flying saucer diagram 'UFO Art and Science', by artist Ionel Talpazan, 1996. The inscription reads in part 'Special For Senate (in Government USA) ... American Dream...' Credit: American Primitive Gallery, New York

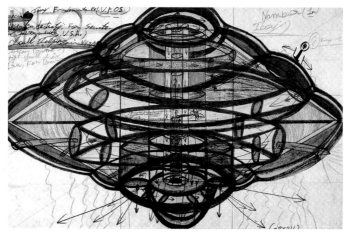

'The Eyeball' as Kathleen Ford calls it, a dreamy image worthy of Odilon Redon or Salvador Dali, or an energy bubble or other emanation, taken along Mail box Road in May of 1993. Credit: Kathleen Ford.

The Black Mailbox turned white: Steve Medlin's new mailbox, of thick steel painted white, as it appeared in the summer of 1996, was a sign that Dreamland had become a tourist destination and Area 51 had been taken over not by aliens but by Hollywood. Credit: Author.

The assembled landscape painters of the CADRE group, April 1997. Organizer Joel Slayton's conceptual 'countersurveillance of Area 51' soon found himself the object of investigation by the FBI and the Internal Revenue Service. Credit: Joel Slayton/CADRE.

Lazar's credibility; Huff had information on Glenn. It was a parody of MAD, mutual assured destruction, so neither could use the stories, even if they were true.

'Well,' Steve remarked wryly when he heard of these rumours, 'I guess we all have our little Groom Lakes.'

Campbell made life difficult for the Air Force by challenging its takeover of additional land, including the Freedom Ridge overlooks. But he sometimes pushed things too far. His whole media act, his pose as 'searcher for the nature of truth', was as pretentious as dressing in camou gear and eating MREs. He could be obnoxious.

On a trip to Tonopah, the north edge of Dreamland where the Stealth fighters had been based, Psychospy hurled himself up against the chain link like an animal trying to get out of a pen. The guard dropped and focused his M16. Usually, you could josh with the guards there but all of sudden the casualness, the joshing relationship that the watchers had traditionally enjoyed with the guards, was gone. Everyone in the party was shocked.

But it was Psychospy who first conceived of the signature rock at the top of Freedom Ridge and the practice of bringing aluminium lawn chairs to the top.

The situation grew more absurd as camera crew after camera crew shot footage of the base from Freedom and broadcast it on national TV, in clear violation of the law. Psychospy was by now well known to the dudes. They referred to him on their radios as 'our friend' or 'the editor'.

Inevitably, he managed to get himself arrested. Accompanying yet another reporter and camera crew to the ridges he had led the dudes on a chase that ended with the group pinned down by a sandblasting chopper, then cut off by one of the dude mobiles. The dudes asked for the film. Glenn locked the doors of his Toyota and they lost patience.

They confiscated his film.

He finally went to court, serving as his own attorney and having bought for the purpose, a $38 suit at the Mormon Thrift Shop in Las Vegas. He took his laptop into court. He argued that by not returning his film, the dudes were in effect concealing evidence of a crime: they had flown the helicopter that sand-blasted him below the 500-foot FAA mandated minimum altitude.

It was all to no avail, of course, as he knew it would be, and he was fined. His community service included working on a history of Rachel and helping at the senior citizen centre.

What they didn't get him for was the removal of a sensor. It may have been on public land, and therefore itself illegal, barring the BLM's permission, but it was government property that he had taken into his own hands. He had a long tortured conversation full of euphemism with deputies who came to inquire about the missing sensor. In fact, it had been sent to another of the Interceptors, who wanted no part of it. He passed it on like the proverbial hot potato.

After Freedom Ridge was closed off in the spring of 1995, and perhaps finding his welcome in Rachel wearing out, and wanting to make contacts with the rest of the world easier, Campbell rented an apartment not far from my favourite hostelry, the Blue Pool Motel. He faced the Janet Terminal and from the front window could see the flights taking off and landing on their way to and from Groom. He called this the Las Vegas Research Center.

But better than anyone, he was able to cut to the key points about the base. Wrapping himself in his cloak of citizen's advocate, he argued that the importance of the Lazar story was not the existence or non existence of UFOs in government hands. That didn't matter: what mattered was there *could* be. Policies of secrecy had made it possible, and those policies were in defiance of all-American moral law and tradition.

Campbell managed to find out that the dudes had been deputized by the Lincoln County sheriff's office, to give them the legal power to operate. The 'oaths of office' were on file at the courthouse. He published a long list of the names.

Psychospy said that the tale that he – only he used the first person plural, the editorial or royal 'we' – had approached aliens at the test site stories 'as folklore'.

'Rather than assuming a story is false until proven true we proceed as though it were true, collecting information about it until we reach an insurmountable roadblock or inconsistency.'

No lie, he was confident, could 'reproduce all the rich inter-connections of reality.

'As long as a story remains interesting in itself, like a well-constructed novel, we are willing to set aside the issue of truth and go along for the ride,' he added, sounding like Jung himself. He also reminded me of someone else: Ernst Mach, after whom the speed of sound numbers are named, but who was also a shrewd theorist of science – and Einstein's teacher.

He supported the as-if notion of science. Mach's idea was to take a premise in physics and ride it out, to its testable con-clusions. That is what he taught Einstein. It is what kids today are taught in elementary school physics: hypothesize, then test. But don't begin by limiting your imagination: begin with creativity, end in facts.

But the real problem was the fact that the military and the government – or whatever higher government conspiracy you wanted to postulate – had been able to keep things just hidden enough to hint at exciting secrets for thousands of citizens. And in the past they had kept things secret, lots of things. At Groom Lake, whole planes had been chopped up, burned, and buried and entire programmes erased from the records. They had kept the first spy satellite secret for more than thirty years and the NRO itself, the agency that ran it, unacknowledged and virtually unknown for even longer. They had managed to hide the stealth building, smack out in the middle of the open strip, mall and spec office landscape of Lee Highway, Chantilly, Virginia – hide it from Congress itself. They had kept secret for years the post nuclear war Presidential redoubt in the basement of the Greenbrier Hotel, West Virginia. Excessive secrecy left the way open – for all kinds of conspiratorial speculations. It even demanded them. If nothing was seen, much would be dreamed.

UFOs had been a big topic on the Internet from the beginning, a place the youfers could gather without fear of the common derision. The gathering of aviation buffs, the wider association of Interceptors on-line, had also been going on for a while. I watched it, lurking on the Internet, as on a high viewpoint, and saw Dreamland, in bits and pieces, taking on a new, shadowy presence in cyberspace – a new blue sky.

At first I browsed through the aviation forums, which were categorized by type of aircraft. There were SR-71 fans and Aurora buffs, but there were also guys reminiscing about their days in the B-36 or C-130.

Sometimes active pilots would appear on-line. There were B-1B crews, chattering and bragging. Then a few days later they suddenly disappeared. I had the very firm impression that a higher up had spotted the postings and been displeased. The B-1 is known to airmen as the 'Bone' and its crews by extension as Bonemen, or Boners, men of camaraderie and enthusiasm, who write poetry 'on beer drinking, cannibalism and such'. Perhaps their colonel was not pleased to read about near-supersonic flight with live ordnance, as in a message headed 'Lots o' Iron': 'yesterday, we were 500AGL, .998 Mach, very very near civilized establishments enroute to the Ft. Sill IP with 84 live eggs on board – that, my friends, is the sound of freedom!'

Soon there were not only newsgroups about Dreamland like alt.conspiracy.area51, but also whole web pages. Psychospy expanded his web page to include a mailing list and here you could follow strange threads and come up with bits of information. This was happening in all kinds of subcultures.

Here's how the web helped in one case. Campbell had previously learned that some mail to Area 51 was directed to 'Pittman Station, Henderson'. Henderson is a town just east of Las Vegas – it was the site of a defunct post office that once received mail for the base. One buff plugged 'Pittman Station' into the Alta Vista web searcher. It came back with a 1990 NASA Press release listing astronaut candidates. Pittman Station was cited as the place of employment of a Captain Carl E. Walz. Another buff then did a search for 'Walz' on the web and came up with a detailed NASA biography. There you could read that Walz's parents lived in South Euclid, Ohio, and that they had graduated from Charles T. Brush High School, Lyndhurst, Ohio. You could also find that: 'In July 1987 he was transferred to Las Vegas, Nevada, where he served as a Flight Test Program Manager at Detachment 3, Air Force Flight Test Center [AFFTC].' The Air Force Flight Test Center is located at Edwards Air Force Base, apparently with a detached unit at Groom Lake, with a Pittman Station mail drop: Walz had apparently worked in Dreamland. Had he flown Aurora? Worked with the STUDs unit? Been a test pilot for some other project? None of that was answered.

Campbell drew it all together. Having previously established that AFFTC 'has a presence at Groom, and now we know that it is Detachment 3 that is housed there. This is consistent with the designation on the cover of the Area 51 Security Manual of "DET 3 SP," with "SP" perhaps referring to "Security Police".'

You could magnify a little detail so it becomes a whole connection. But you could also magnify rumour – and there were frauds and weird entries, although it was not always easy to recognize them, and even when you did, sometimes they were more interesting than the accurate postings.

Stranger and stranger missives were posted on the Internet at such locations as alt.conspiracy.area51.

One man described his 'grandpa' who had worked, he said, at Area 51 or at Tonopah, he wasn't sure which. He would never discuss his work. But when he was dying the report said, and had been 'given Morphone and other asiditives (sic!?)' he finally talked. He had been given a 'metal' for his work, the report went on. After his death, 'an onslaught of Military personal took the Metal, the Bodys and the licke' away.

Another posting offered a chronology of runway expansions at the base that read like a parody of Mahood's painstaking chronologies of events at Groom or the biography of Bob Lazar.

The name of the poster was suspicious to begin with – 'Robert Harry Hover'. Is that 'hover' the way a saucer does?

It's a detailed listing that buzzes with numbers: runway lengths, elevations, magnetic bearings in degrees, minutes and seconds. The startling and suggestive things are slipped in between the numbers so that you almost don't notice their implications: 'Only 70 Base Personnel knew of this place.' '1964 Anti-gravitation device test. Unsuccessful,' and the cryptic '1970 Occurrence Friday, 11 September, at 10 PM for one-half hour'.

Someone had gone to the trouble to fake a photo of the Aurora refuelling behind a tanker in formation with F-111s. A British UFO magazine published it. Steve was suspicious. He checked the date when the photo was reportedly shot: 27 September 1995.

Steve played a couple of hunches and made a couple of phone calls. The first was to the public affairs office at Cannon. 'According to Cannon the only F-111s overseas at the time were EF-111s flying in support of Bosnia and operations in the Middle East. EF-111s have a distinctive bulbous tail and would instantly be recognizable. The aircraft in the photo were not EF-111s.'

There still was the possibility the F-111s could have been in England at the time the photo was taken. The Cannon Public Affairs Office checked their records and confirmed they were not.

A closer look at the photo revealed another inconsistency. The KC-135 refuelling the 'Aurora' was a model powered by four Pratt and Whitney J-57 turbojet engines. In the late 80s all KC-135s were refitted with larger and more powerful JF3D-3B ex-airline turbofan engines. Steve confirmed this by calling public affairs at Altus AFB, Oklahoma.

Such details proved to Steve that the photo was a hoax. Bill Sweetman confirmed Steve's discovery, and Chris Gibson (witness to the North Sea sighting of 1989 on which the picture is based) found out that the photograph was produced by Bill Rose, an astronomer and photographer, for the UK magazine *Astronomy Now*, to illustrate an article on UFO photos and how easily they could be faked.

Another time, Steve received an anonymous letter containing what the sender said were images of two hypersonic aircraft prototypes. The fuzzy Xeroxed photo showed two fighter-sized aircraft said to be code-named 'SANTA'. He was able to discover that the photo was actually of two prototype miniature deep-diving submarines designed and built by an oceanographer named Graham Hawkes.

The more cases like this you read about, the more time you spend on the perimeter, the more belief you acquire in the native human tendency to exaggerate, embroider and outright deceive. There were apparently more nuts that were dreamed of, at least in my philosophy. Dreamland expanded one's sense of the native human tendency to duplicity – and to spite.

Sometimes the exchanges on the Internet moved very quickly from the cosmic to the comic. The Biggest Story in History seemed less interesting than a lot of little stories. Huff called Glenn 'Goober', and pasted a vicious cartoon of him on his web page. He called Agent X 'the queen geek' and slammed Mahood.

'The Most Secret Place in America'

One Friday night a crowd of Interceptors sat around in the Area 51 Research Center – Psychospy's apartment, a few feet from the Janet terminal in Las Vegas – and watched fellow Interceptor, the Minister, appear on TV. It was another of the cable shows dedicated to old aircraft – aeroporn – and the subject was the Blackbird.

The Minister arrived late, just before he appeared on TV. And there he was, sitting in his apartment on the TV screen. I could tell it was his apartment from the pieces of black plane sitting in front of the metal frame windows. Did I glimpse part of his collection of cactuses from secret air bases in the edge of the shot? The Minister on the screen was talking about how they had to make everything for the Blackbirds, that nothing 'from the store' would work, not oil, grease or paint. At the end he did a great impression of Ben Rich of the Skunk Works, a growly voice, the very voice of black planedom.

The next morning we met near Indian Springs. The day's expedition was a hike to the top of Mount Sterling, one of the few places from which you glimpse – albeit from forty or fifty miles away – Papoose Lake and Lazar's 'S-4', the ostensible site of saucer test flights and hangars hidden inside cliffs.

At the base of the trail I met the Swiss Mountain Bat, the most distantly-based on the Interceptors, in his rented Ford Explorer. The Bat had read Timothy Good's book *Above Top Secret* (1987), which told Lazar's and other tales of secret facilities cut into cliffs and deserts in the western United States. The Bat did not find it so hard to believe in hangars inside cliffs at S-4, with door panels disguised and camouflaged as rock, he told me. An American might be dubious, but the Bat had done his three years in the Swiss military and seen all the underground hangars and command centres of Switzerland, a country whose laws require the provision of a bomb shelter beneath every newly-constructed building.

'We've done that all over the country,' he told me, 'Cut into the mountains.

'Like Swiss cheese,' he said with a big smile, as we bounced up the forest service road in his Explorer.

Sure enough, when he got back to Switzerland, the Bat mailed photographs of some of the Swiss installations, rocky cliffs at first glance, but on closer viewing they had perceptible demarcation lines, as if you were looking for a servant's door in the library of a gentleman's mansion. Sheer James Bond stuff.

They had found flying saucers in Switzerland too, over their airbases: some radar plottings had been smuggled out, the Bat told me. He could say no more.

He worked for an insurance company in Switzerland. But the Bat seemed to live from one visit to Dreamland to another. He sold his photos of S-4 and Groom Lake to the UFO magazines. Many of the pictures showed the Bat himself, and they were at least as interesting. He would show up on the cover of UFO magazines with his big camera lens and binoculars, in full camouflage. He regularly e-mailed the Interceptors back in the States.

But he had another agenda, which was to prove that his country, the country of chocolate bars and gold bars, clocks and watches, banks and burghers, had UFOs too, and cover-ups.

'It's no longer about chocolate and cheese in our tiny li'le country now ... Very strange things go bump in deep night over here, too ...' he crowed in his e-mails to the Interceptors, telling of mystery radar blips and lights. His called his home 'Bat HQ'.

The Explorer bounced us up the narrow road, but the hump between tracks was rising with the elevation. Soon we were almost straddling it. When we pulled to a stop the sweet smell of burning sage and pinon came from beneath the vehicle where plants touched the hot exhaust.

This was as far up the rough road as a four-wheel drive would carry us. It was shank's pony the rest of the way, on foot through fir limbs that slapped back on the next person and rough stuff that would scratch your legs. Some of these wounds, I speculated, were worn with pride. The top was 8200 feet, and the going tough.

'If they were serious,' Mahood said on the way up as the vistas began to open occasionally through the trees, 'Lazar and Huff should have come up here before they went public.' They could have brought a video camera and recorded some proof of the flights, taped the rising saucers. Now even Lazar thought the saucers had been moved.

The steepness of the walk kept our eyes on the ground, on droppings of various animals, on red lichens – the same colour as Lazar's element 115. Psychospy, wearing a porkpie hat from K-mart, breathed heavily. Mahood, his eyes deep set beneath an Aussie hat, led the way.

The top came suddenly. A turn and then a sweeping, dramatic statement of a view, a big ambitious landscape, requiring a Tolkienesque description: framed by pine boughs with their beads of sap visible like fresh rain, the lakes slid among the distant overlapping ranges.

'There it is,' Mahood said, 'the most secret place in America.'

At the top, we recovered and ate. I noticed with a start that the bags of food – trail mix, peanuts, and so on, had swollen into little pillows, transparent balloons, at 8000 feet.

Why were they here? No one really believed they would see flying saucers, even hangar doors. Nor were they here to disprove anything. It was possibility that justified the trip – the most outside of chances. Possibility expanded their credulity. The elevated air of speculation expanded their view the way the same altitude expanded the food bags.

'Look out for the cactus,' the Minister warned. 'That one, it looks like my Groomer. I don't know the scientific name, I just call it the Groomer type.' Groomer was his cactus from Freedom Ridge, named after Groom Lake. It was part of the Minister's collection of 'cacti of America's secret bases', which included samples from White Sands and elsewhere.

There was discussion of the comparative virtues of three-colour desert camou versus five-colour. Maps were consulted. Mahood had marked the borders of the test site and range in fluorescent pink and orange and with his engineer's eye, had carefully worked out the sight lines from Mount Sterling to Papoose Lake and other sites. Now, he squatted on a folding canvas and metal stool – and aligned his telescope.

Highway 95 far below showed silver slugs of trucks and black flecks of cars. Near the entrance to the test site, you could see the holding pen where so many demonstrators had been sequestered over the years.

To the right were the Ranger Mountains and a strip of public land. On an earlier trip, the Interceptors had tried to get up to the edge of the Test Site that way, but it was rougher and longer than it looked at first and Zero had nearly collapsed for lack of water. The rule out here was everything was further away than it looked.

You could see the stubs of towers from which blasts had been set off, Yucca Flat, Frenchman Flat, the barely-visible Command Post and assembly buildings. Somewhere out there, I thought, was the nuke site's environmental farm where once the cows had grazed with fistulas in their stomachs.

I imagined what it would have been like to watch the atmospheric tests from up here, to see the mushroom clouds rising from the plains, to feel – half a minute, forty-five seconds later – a wave of heat, a shock wave and sound, there amid the pines.

In the far distance you could even see Bald Mountain with its little dome, the new facility built just a year or so ago and packed with whatever mysterious viewing and scanning equipment the Air Force felt it needed there.

The focus was the light strip that meant Papoose Lake. We should have been looking straight at the wall with sand-coloured sliding doors for secret saucer hangars, pitched at the thirty-degree angle Lazar had talked of.

All that afternoon we sat watching. Various kinds of optics were tried out. As the sun moved lower, the whole landscape seemed to puff up and grow fuller, more sculpted, as if inflating, like the little bags of food. The low light moulded the hills into fuller shapes. The hard hills and the hazy deserts became almost romantic.

'That would be the way to walk in,' Mahood said. 'Up Nye Canyon, across Frenchman Flat.'

To the far right you could see the airfield at Indian Springs with its little x of runways half flattened like a folding chair from the perspective.

We saw a light aircraft pass by. Then someone caught sight of what looked like a building, a blockhouse-like structure, beyond the edge of the test site.

'As the afternoon wore on, they could see more and more,' someone intoned in the voice of a television narrator. The whole experience of Interceptordom was coloured by the way they figured in TV interviews.

The Swiss Mountain Bat jumped. Now with the light shifting he could see the mystery building in the viewfinder. He steadied his huge telephoto lens and delightedly snapped away.

The shadows lengthened. It was cold in the shadows but you could move a couple of feet into the sun and quickly get warm.

It was late when all of a sudden a dark shape came hurtling down from the right of our view: a great bird, concentrating on some mouse or other prey, surprised to find us here. I could see his stunned look – as he banked away down the slope, he lost a single white feather. It was a golden eagle. The little down feather drifted down slowly like a parachute flare, until it landed in the bushes and Mahood scrambled in to retrieve it.

That night, back on the plain beneath Mount Sterling, they camped and built a fire out of the pitiful gatherings of wood – and talked of Jarod and proton cannons and skyquakes.

The campfire and the surrounding darkness for a moment became a surrogate for the black world itself. The fire carved out a cave of light in it, and lore and jokes flew back and forth. This was the closest we got, I figured, to ghost stories or primal folk tales.

Mahood talked of a guy who claimed to have worked on flying saucer simulators, of a man who knew the man who did the ejection seat for the Blackbird and then for the Aurora.

'Most of me,' Mahood said, as if in summary, 'says that what you see is all there is, but part of me wants to believe there is something else.'

In the beginning Mahood was drawn to Lazar's story. For all his 'just the facts, Ma'am,' attitude, he admitted he initially felt that Lazar was telling the truth, that he had been at S-4. Lazar's very presence seemed to have this plausible effect on people, with his sense of self possession, almost diffidence. He continued to feel that way even as more and more information came in that seemed to discredit Lazar's claims about his career, and even when Mahood's head kept telling him that Lazar was a pathological liar. But the emotional link remained. For a time, it gave him restless nights. Like many, he wanted to believe; the wild hopes and cosmic dreams of his heart struggled with his engineer's head.

Now, sitting down beside the fire, he admitted, 'My rational mind says it's just airplanes, but a part of me wants to believe there's something else out there.'

The darkness was profound. I lay on my back in the sleeping bag and saw the Milky Way above, not a collection of stars but a smear. My eye went to Orion, the constellation I learned first at the planetarium in second grade. Zeta Reticuli, putative source of flying saucers, was visible in Cygnus, someone had told me, but only in the southern hemisphere. All at once a single meteorite streaked through the Little Dipper. I wouldn't have believed it if I hadn't seen it myself.

The next morning I woke from a dreamless sleep to a landscape blurred by my myopia. I reached out for my glasses leaning like a flower in a vase against the neck of my left Nike. The focus lengthened suddenly: the huge rich coloured desert erupted into detail.

10

Black Manta

BEAVIS AND BUTTHEAD SNICKERED ON THE SCREEN OF THE TV in the living room of Steve Douglass' ranch-style home in Amarillo, Texas, then Steve popped a tape into the VCR and the boys disappeared into a powdery mix of colours and a roar of static. There was a silence, then solid, grey-blue, then a dot emerged, growing larger, becoming a winged bat, a ray-shaped plane swooping overhead – then the image dissolved into grey grit. Steve flicked the set off.

'Seven seconds,' he said. 'You live for those moments. You listen all those hours for that kind of gold nugget.'

It was, Steve felt sure, the TR3A Black Manta, captured on video for the first time. He also referred to it as Batman's Airplane, The Flying Fuzzy Turd, and the Dorito. But he was proud of it.

Steve had been black plane hunting with Elwood Johnston, his father-in-law and fellow stealthy, near White Sands 1, New Mexico, in May 1993. They were close to Holloman Air Force Base and the adjoining White Sands Missile Range, and the sky was filled with B-1Bs and F-15s. They were there for Roving Sands, the biggest air exercise of the year, which ranges over several states and includes five bases. He packed up his Radio Shack Pro-2006 and other scanners. It was the end of the day.

Elwood saw it first. 'What's that?'

They both saw it on the horizon in the dusk. It was not an F-117 he was sure, it was slower, with a different sound, a different shape. Douglass' radio scanner crackled, the numbers churned on its readout. He raised his video camera – and the battery warning light flashed. He grabbed seven seconds of video before the machine snapped off.

With the help of a frame grabber, Douglass printed an enhanced view of the bat plane after he returned from White

Sands. Then, consulting his wide network of experts in the industry, the aviation Press, and the military, Douglass tweaked the details to create a speculative image of the aircraft. He talked to Bill Sweetman and others.

This sounded like the plane that the Greenpeace intruders had spotted when they ventured across the perimeter at Dreamland in 1986. It had been speculated on before, even speculatively illustrated, as far back as 1990 when the mysterious figure who signed himself 'J. Jones' had asserted its existence. The accepted wisdom among stealth chasers and Interceptors was that the Black Manta operated in tandem with the F-117A Stealth fighter, relaying target information. Evidence suggested it had been used in the Gulf War.

Douglass' frame-grabbed print of the TR3A looks at first glance like a flying saucer.

'Yes,' he would say, of all these planes he chased. 'They are objects. They do fly, and they are unidentified.'

Steve led me into his thickly carpeted retreat, where six scanners work steadily, hopping from channel to channel – short wave, VHF, UHF, sideband – all feeding into a little voice-activated Radio Shack tape recorder that vacuums up every scrap of sound, packing a day's talk into the 90 minutes or so that Douglass listens to late at night. After years of practice, his ear stripped away the static; he listened simultaneously to stereo, television, and multiple scanners. Steve grows restless without a scanner nearby, the bubbling reassurance of its red digits pumping frequencies through its chips and extruding slugs of conversation, important or not, through its speaker. Talk with him on the phone, and you have to get used to sudden soft pauses, as if there was a fault in the line, but which are in fact Steve cocking his other ear toward something or other on one of the radios around him. He might be listening to Air Force One or maybe some drug bust or a mock dogfight somewhere.

Steve had loaded soundbites from his tapes of the White Sands episode onto Soundscan files on his Performa 450 computer. Now he clicked on each little folder on the screen to set them off one by one, so they exploded like tiny firecrackers, with sharp sparks of voice amid the smoke of static.

'You've seen one of these before, haven't you, Steve?' says

the voice of one airman talking to another (the coincidence of the name seems like a taunt). And the pilot complains, 'I've got a couple of screws loose on the heat shield.'

On the radio clips, the maintenance and security people talk about the arrival of a VIP in the morning. Later, Douglass would discover that General Colin Powell, then Chair of the Joint Chiefs of Staff, had been visiting El Paso, Texas, the day before. He suspects Powell might have made an unpublicized side-trip for a glimpse of the Black Manta. The radio traffic referred to the plane as an 'STF'. Did that stand for Stealth or Survivable Tactical Fighter? Another report had it as 'Tactical Survivable Aircraft' and tied its lineage to the Northrop THAP – 'Theater High Altitude Penetrator' of earlier years. But at the history office at Edwards Air Force Base, I would find, they took the TR3A name seriously enough to provide its file among the index of aircraft types, along with the F-15 and the SR-71. The only materials in the file were press clippings, not the flight test reports and other documents included for other aircraft, but the file itself was a hint.

Models of planes hang from Steve's ceiling, pictures of planes line the walls. In one corner lurks a huge oscilloscope – military surplus – and a Hallicrafter's short-wave set, packed with tubes, picked up for $25 at a garage sale. There are maps of military bases and of New Mexico, as well as a Landsat photo of the F-117 base at Tonopah. Red and blue lines on a map show main air routes, and refuelling courses. Amarillo is dead centre of the heart of the country's military flyways.

'Why go to Groom Lake,' he said, 'when the planes seem to come to you?'

Steve has had stealth fighters fly right over the house. 'It's as if they know where you live,' another Interceptor said. Although he rarely ventured to the perimeter of Dreamland, Steve came to be venerated as the Ur-Interceptor, a near legendary figure.

It had been a couple of years since, in one of the coups from which his reputation was made, Steve took the first pictures of the 'donut on a rope' contrail associated with a mystery aircraft. It might have been Aurora, or the 'pulser' jet.

On 23 March 1992, Steve was scanning as usual when he

picked up radio traffic between unidentified craft using the call signs Darkstar November and Darkstar Mike. Then the house began to shake, the windows frames rattled.

He ran out of his house, slapping film into his Canon AE-1. He could hear the sound, like a rocket engine, only intermittent, in regular bursts and even feel it in his chest, but all he saw of the craft itself was 'a silver glint of light, a metallic shape'. Even with a 400-mm telephoto lens he managed to capture only the plane's contrail – a string of roundish puffs, the shape that would become famous among Interceptors as the 'donut on a rope'.

He and other watchers thought it was the spoor of a new kind of engine, a secret aircraft's pulser jet. Within weeks it was published in *Aviation Week*.

Later, he talked by phone with a pulser-jet engine expert he knows at a military contractor's. The engineer played chords on a synthesizer over the phone, striking lower and lower frequencies until Douglass found the one he had heard. 'Damn,' the engineer said, recognizing that his rivals had perfected the advanced jet engine, 'they've done it'.

Steve had grown up in the West, and one of his earliest memories was going up into the mountains to watch a distant nuclear explosion. He recalled how beautiful it was, how it lit up the sky like a rosy sunset.

He was a news photographer for the paper in Amarillo, when he bought his first scanner. It was a simple model for following the police and fire bands, so he could rush to the scene of a car accident or warehouse conflagration to snap pictures for the paper. The more he listened, the more he wondered what else was on the air. 'It was like the old George Carlin bit,' he says, ' "what's on beyond the edge of the dial, after the knob stops? What are they hiding out there?" '

What he discovered was the new world of scanners. Around 1970, solid state electronics had replaced old crystals as the heart of scanners. Before long, you could buy a 200-channel scanner from Radio Shack for about $300. Radio Shack has sold more than 4 million 2006 scanners worldwide, and in theory anyone who knows how to use one can eavesdrop on most military traffic, on Air Force One itself. In practice, Steve figured there were probably no more than about 500 hard-core military monitors in this country, which may mean they belong to those people who have nothing better to do with their time.

Some systems hop from channel to channel to defeat eavesdroppers, but the best of the new equipment can cover thousands of channels a second and listen in on the channel-hoppers too. Encryption is used at high-level bases, but it's expensive and vulnerable to atmospheric shifts. Even at Groom Lake, the camou dudes broadcast in the open most of the time.

He bought more powerful scanners and found all sorts of strange things there beyond the end of the dial. He began picking up the military channels and as a stringer feeding bits of information to the Associated Press. His first scoop came in 1986, when he picked up transmissions from a Soviet nuclear sub with a critical nuclear reactor problem. In an early sign of détente, US Navy ships rushed to the scene to help out. The Pentagon denied the story, but when an AP reporter brought in Douglass' tape – on which a sailor screams: 'It's sinking! It's going down! Radiation counters are going up!' – the military finally admitted what was going on. Television cameras were present when American ships rescued the Soviet crew.

Douglass heard the troops assembling to invade Grenada, then Panama. During the Gulf War, he fed short-wave reports of Scud launchings from troops in Saudi Arabia to network reporters before their Israeli bureaus heard the sirens.

Once, he monitored the radio traffic surrounding the crash of a B-1B bomber. The plane had crashed into a mountainside, and the Air Force blamed the pilot. Investigators went to the father's house, asking him if his son was a homosexual or a drug abuser. Congress was considering further funding for the B-1B and the Air Force wanted nothing said that would pin fault on the aircraft itself. Douglass, after hearing of the crash, checked his scanner tape from the night before. It clearly recorded the pilot complaining of problems with the plane's autopilot. When the news came out, the military brass denied that any 'amateur ham radio operator' could have such information. The father of the dead pilot called him, and Steve – who still had the tape – was able to tell the father the truth.

Steve and his wife Teresa, an artist and computer whiz, began to publish a newsletter for military monitors, called *Intercepts*. It was the first publication that tied together the distant watchers, who were conscious of being non mainstream, and it gave them a sense of the others out there. In the pages of *Intercepts* Douglass ran letters and columns above the codenames of correspondents: Darkstar, November, Big Red, Lone Star, Ghostrider – some of them people with jobs they don't want to jeopardize by using their real names. Douglass soon had subscribers at CIA headquarters in Langley, Virginia and throughout the military.

He established his own dial-up bulletin board, which bubbled away on an old Commodore 128 in his Bat Cave, and then began operating a forum on America On-line called 'Above Top Secret', later 'Project Black'. His book, *The Comprehensive Guide to Military Monitoring*, would become the bible of military monitoring, sharing tricks, frequencies, and some of the wonderful American music of callsigns and radio vocabulary.

On the Net, Steve saw, many stealth chasers were meeting each other for the first time. On-line had become a clearing-house for monitors to share military intelligence: 'a public intelligence network,' he said. Before 'It's true, I saw it on the Internet,' became a joke Steve saw clues and rumours blossom side by side on-line.

One day men in suits began to appear in the windows of the long-vacant house behind Steve and Teresa's home and a bug showed up on his phone. The cellular phone of the local Congressman had been tapped and conversations recorded: Douglass was suspected. The real culprit was later found, but Douglass began to sweep the place monthly for bugs.

We drove out past Amarillo's leading tourist attraction, the Cadillac Ranch; someone had put on a new coat of paint. Military monitoring had been called 'ham radio cubed' or 'super ham' and the scoops monitors provide are often described disdainfully as 'ham radio reports', Steve told me. But it was a whole different culture. 'Hams look down on monitors,' he said. 'Hams say, "you can only *listen*?"' The monitoring culture was actually more closely related to the nation's brief infatuation in the mid '70s with CB Radio. Motorists listened to CB to find out what the police were doing;

many then graduated to police scanners that let them listen to the police directly. Steve, too, played around with CB until 'the idiots all got on'.

Steve had good contacts in the military and defence industry, and he was constantly hanging around bases and watching exercises. He went to air shows and base open houses. Not long before, he told me, he was at an air show chatting with a Stealth fighter pilot. 'How does flying the F-117 compare to the TR-3A?' Steve asked him.

'Well, you see ...' he began. 'Well, I can't talk about that.'

A few months later, Steve spotted what he thought was another craft. He called it 'artichoke', after the pointed-leaf shapes of its trailing edge. He and Teresa caught a glimpse of it in New Mexico: light grey, the size of an F-111. He noticed something else: the military had opened a new MOA near Cannon, the base close to where he had spotted the artichoke. And the local school budget in Clovis was rising – did that mean more kids from the base?

Steve noted other sightings – some halfway around the world. In September 1994, reports surfaced in the UK of a mysterious aircraft crash-landing at Boscombe Down, the UK's own version of Dreamland, the place 'where the boffins play', as one former RAF pilot told me. The British had been testing at least one craft in Dreamland, the evidence suggested, but this was most likely an American plane.

The front landing gear, it seemed, had failed and observers spotted the strange shape, with inward canting tail fins, partly covered by a tarpaulin. A special cargo plane flew in to carry it off. According to one theory it was a spin-off of Northrop's YF-23, which competed unsuccessfully with Lockheed-Boeing's YF-22 to become the Air Force's next generation fighter, replacing the F-15 around the turn of the century. Called ASTRA, for Advanced Stealth Technology Reconnaissance Aircraft, believed to be built by prime contractor Northrop, along with McDonnell Douglas. Others believed the charcoal grey aircraft was the A-17, a replacement for the F-111. Radio intercepts described its being referred to as AV-6 (Air Vehicle Six, its construction number), with USAF serial 90–2414 and the callsign Blackbuck 11. The C-5 that retrieved it was referred to by the call sign Lance 18 with the intended destination code of KPMD – air-controller designation for the airport at Palmdale, California, home of Northrop and Lockheed. Within days, there was another accident, involving a similar plane, in New Mexico. To Steve that suggested some structural problem: had the same part failed after the same length of time and stress?

Once a year, like Camelot, the long-closed base at Roswell came alive again with dozens of aircraft. B-52s now, instead of the old B-29s; F-15s instead of P-15s. It was in April, usually, on the occasion of Roving Sands – the largest aerial military exercise in the country – which took place in airspace that covered five states and several military bases. For Steve and, later, other Interceptors, Roving Sands was the Olympic Games of plane spotting.

Watching the aircraft at Roving Sands, trying to spot something unusual, meant spending hours standing in the back of a pickup truck, listening to scanners and watching the distant horizons. Most of the planes were familiar, but every so often the temptation to toss one of the secret toys into the fray became too great and something strange would appear, usually at dusk. That is what happened the year Steve spotted the Manta.

I headed out one evening at dusk to watch. Across from the base, in front of a neat little house, a tiny Hispanic woman was tenderly washing her husband's highway patrol car.

The landscape on one side of the road was the stuff of sports utility ads or Technicolor Westerns: barbed wire cattle fences with twisted grey posts, the stereotypical decaying windmill for punctuation. On the other side, it was action film, thriller; chain link fence, topped with accordion wire.

While Steve kept his video camera focussed skyward, I found my eyes wandering to the ground. Even when passing directly overhead, fighters did not seem to be moving at astonishing speed, but when you stood back and watched the first appearance of their shadows on the ground far away, then the black wave of that shadow racing toward you across the dry grass, you could sense the speed for the first time.

At night, it is harder. There is a certain phenomenology of

night vision, with its green, teeming imagery grown familiar from crime and war footage, but to the unaided eye, the most mundane craft with their lights could grow surreal. A Navy fighter returning to base: at first far off in the Hollywood western sky it was just a grain of red. But then it defined itself, stronger like a laser, before innocently resolving into two wing-tip lights as it came in to land.

———

Standing on the fence line, waiting for the appearance of flying objects we could identity, Steve and I had time to contemplate the appearances of UFOs.

'Why don't they come as clouds,' I asked, 'so they blend in?'

'Why don't they come disguised as McDonalds Golden Arches,' Steve replied, 'so they can land wherever they want and not be noticed?'

'What,' I speculated, 'if they are unofficial, not authorized? We always assumed they're here doing research but what if they are not part of some ET NASA, but just teenagers out cruising?'

'Joyriders,' Steve said. 'Heck, low riders.'

Sometimes, he told me, he used his scanners to pick up tornado sightings and went off chasing them, as in *Twister*.

'You know,' he said, 'trailer parks cause tornadoes. It's a scientific fact.'

'And maybe deserts cause UFOs,' I replied. 'How come they never land in the car parks of shopping malls in New Jersey?'

One year at Roving Sands, a SEAL unit was apparently assigned to patrol the Roswell base perimeter where the Interceptors were watching the aircraft land and take off. Steve and the others watched a helicopter drop off several shadowy figures. The strange thing wasn't that they were black, but that they were silent. Steve could hear cars on the road a couple of miles away, but no sound at all from the helicopter engines.

The SEALs crept up on the Interceptors, but they were clearly visible on the night vision scopes – the area offered little cover – and clearly audible on the scanners. Every time the SEALs moved up a little bit, the 'ceptors lit them with a searchlight like teenagers hassling couples at the local necking spot. It was Radio Shack versus the Pentagon, and it was no contest.

Finally, the SEALs got disgusted and radioed for a Humm-vee to pick them up. One of the Interceptors had an idea and got on a cell phone: a few minutes later, a Pizza Hut delivery vehicle pulled up to the Humm-Vee parked on the perimeter and delivered two large pepperoni and cheese. The anchovies were the final insult.

We drove past the famous P-3 hangar where wreckage and bodies from the 1947 crash were said to have been loaded in a B-29. It looked much like any other old hangar, and the old base hospital, site of the purported 'alien autopsy' of a disputed film, had been demolished long ago. Beyond the end of the runways were the bunkers where the first atomic bomb unit, the 509th, with its B-29s like my father had flown, had stored bombs. They were overgrown with grass and small saplings.

Heading back into town, we passed the local funeral home, fronted by a Mount Vernon-style porch with white columns. Steve told me that the mortician said he had been consulted about embalming procedures for the dead aliens, and for years afterward he was pointed out around town for this brush with fame.

I had established myself at the town's finest hostelry, El Ranch Palacio, whose big neon sign showed a bullfighter with a red cape – a confused conflation of the red cape of the matador and the red carpet of hospitality. In Roswell, mock Mexicana is big and often jarring. This seemed ultimately appropriate, since Roswell was now into the business of taunting tourists with its legend and luring them for their dollars at the same time.

Two museums dedicated to the crash vie for the Roswell tourists. Walter Haut, the author of the famous Press release (see below), became head of the International UFO Museum and Research Center. Its rival, the Outta Limits UFO Enigma Museum, was closer to the base. Up near Corona, site of the ranch where the wreckage was recovered, a farmer named Hub Corn got tired of chasing away site searchers and began taking them on tours for $15 a head. His crash site was soon rivalled by another – and another. Even nearby Midway, little more than a wide spot in the road, found its own crash site, and established a museum in an edifice composed largely of corrugated tin.

At the International UFO Museum, of which the mortician Glenn Dennis was a board member, Steve showed me the sculpture of a full-size alien in the window. Some years ago, there was a contest to publicize the museum by naming this alien. Steve had won, with his suggestion of RALF – 'Roswell Alien Life Form'. As his prize, he received several hundred dollars-worth of Roswell crash souvenirs.

'Doesn't he have a last name?' I asked.

'Yeah,' Steve said. 'Kramden.'

What made the Roswell story special was that it marked the only time that the United States government ever officially claimed to have captured a flying saucer.

The Press release from Roswell Army Air Field came on 8 July 1947:

> 'The many rumors regarding the flying disc became a reality yesterday when the intelligence office of the 509th Bomb group of the Eighth Air Force, Roswell Army Air Field, was fortunate enough to gain possession of a disc through the cooperation of one of the local ranchers and the sheriff's office of Chaves County.'

'Fortunate', 'cooperation' – the studied casualness made the acquisition sound like a bequest to a museum.

> 'The flying object landed on a ranch near Roswell sometime last week. Not having phone facilities, the rancher stored the wreckage...'

The man who issued the Press release – on orders from his boss, General William 'Butch' Blanchard, head of the 509th Bomb Group, was public information officer Lieutenant Walter Haut.

Haut, interviewed years later, declared he had never seen the wreckage, or visited the crash site, but had been instructed to put the release out by Colonel Blanchard. At first, he didn't really think it was a flying saucer, he would say later – but by the 1980s he did.

This was the special unit that had dropped the first atomic bombs on Hiroshima and Nagasaki in 1945 and, just the year before, the bombs at Eniewetok in the Pacific, called Operation Crossroads. Blanchard himself was a top bombardier who had trained along with others in the secret range near Wendover, Utah. Had his bomb scores been a few points higher, he might have pushed the button himself over Hiroshima.

It was then the only unit in the world with the capability of dropping an atomic weapon, although there were still precious few of them in the US arsenal.

Haut would attribute Blanchard's apparent eagerness to get the word out, via the Press release, to the base commander's long-standing interest in good community relations. Butch Blanchard carefully doled out news from the base even-handedly among the two newspapers and two radio stations. In any case, the local afternoon paper the *Roswell Daily Record* ran the following story on 8 July 1947:

> [Roswell Army Air Field] Captures Flying Saucer On Ranch in Roswell Region
> No Details of Flying Disk Are Revealed
> Roswell Hardware Man and Wife Report Disk Seen
> 'The intelligence office of the 509th Bombardment group at Roswell Army Field announced at noon today, that the field has come into possession of a flying saucer.'
> According to information released by the department, over authority of Maj. J. A. Marcel, intelligence officer, the disk was recovered on a ranch in the Roswell vicinity, after an unidentified rancher had notified Sheriff Geo. Wilcox, here, that he had found the instrument on his premises.
> Major Marcel and a detail from the base went to the ranch and recovered the disk, it was stated: 'After the intelligence officer here had inspected the instrument it was flown to higher headquarters.'

The headlines did not last long. The wreckage was flown to the headquarters of the Eighth Air Force in Fort Worth, where the commanding officer, General Roger Ramey, declared the 'instrument' to be a weather balloon. Only afternoon papers and one edition of the eastern morning papers carried the story before the Press release was 'withdrawn'.

Haut was dispatched to physically retrieve copies of the release from the local newspapers and radio stations. He later denied reports that he had been called directly from the Pentagon. And the careers of neither Haut nor Blanchard seem to have suffered for their embarrassing haste.

The *New York Times* carried the story on the front page of its Wednesday, 9 July 1947 issue – ' "Disc" Near Bomb Test Site Is Just a Weather Balloon' – emphasizing the proximity of the Alamagordo blast location, a hundred miles away. ' "Flying Saucer" Tales Pour in From Round the World.'

Walter Haut's name had become 'Warren Haught' and the story made Irving Newton, the weather man in Ramey's office, a hero for identifying the wreckage as a weather balloon.

But there was enough publicity to keep the phones in Roswell ringing with calls from around the world for a week or so.

A crestfallen *Daily Record* the next day reported, 'Ramey Empties Roswell Saucer' and 'Harassed Rancher Who Located "Saucer" Sorry He Told About It'. The 9 July interview with Brazel was more specific, explaining how little wreckage there really was.

Then, after the affair had faded, the newspaper ran an editorial that implicitly set the whole thing in the context of the wider saucer obsession and the whole mood of the post-war era – atomic weapons and rising international tension. The end of the war was supposed to allow Americans to come home. Instead, the beginning of the Cold War – the Spring had already seen the announcement of the Truman Doctrine of containment and the Marshall Plan – had drawn the country into world tensions seemingly without end. Victory was no longer a goal.

The editorial took a revealing tone: 'The story stands' – an odd choice of words, 'just as all amazing things stand in this day of wondrous feats and curious performances.'

By the early Eighties, Roswell resurfaced. Now it was not just a sighting, it had a plot, a story. Or it *was* a plot, a cover-up. There had been hundreds of flying saucer sightings in that summer of 1947, but Roswell had the elements of a legend: the mysterious wreckage in the desert, the collection and dispersal, the cover up – and then the emergence years later of the apparently true story.

The tale was appealingly simple and dramatic: a couple of

days after a violent thunderstorm, during which he hears another sort of boom amid the thunder, an old sheep rancher comes across mysterious wreckage in one of his fields. It is metal that won't dent, parchment that won't tear, something like balsa wood that won't break, and mysterious writing. He has no phone. He finally makes it to the nearest town, the feed and seed centre of Roswell, and tells the sheriff. The sheriff sends him to the Army Air Force base. Two men come to investigate: an intelligence officer and a counter-intelligence man. They spend the night in a shack, dining on cold beans and crackers, then rise at dawn to recover the wreckage. There is too much to fit in the old Buick, the Jeep Carry-all. Soon, troops appear and the area is cordoned off for full recovery. The rancher goes incommunicado for several days, then returns home taciturn, with a new pickup truck. The Air Corps ships plane and bodies to Wright Patt for analysis, issues a Press release, then, on orders from above, withdraws it. The FBI stops transmission to wire services in mid-sentence. Intimidates witnesses until all publicity vanishes.

The scenario was perfect: the mysterious shiny object in the desert stillness, the grizzled and baffled rancher, the swift deployment of the military, the hush-hush ferrying of wreckage to the secret labs, the cover up. The wreckage bore mysterious symbols, signs or letters – hieroglyphics, they were called, 'like Japanese or Chinese'. It was made for the movies.

Roswell also offered a wonderful cast of characters, from Marcel to Brazel, the stock sheriff, George Wilcox, and among the witnesses who would surface later, such figures as Pappy Henderson, the grizzled old pilot who gave testimony to his friend the dentist. There was Cavitt, the close-mouthed CIC agent and the nurse, who attended the autopsies, then vanished – there were rumours of a fatal plane crash, or that she was in a convent on the outskirts of Roswell. Then there was the teletype operator named Lydia Sleppy, who told of having her dispatch of the Press release interrupted by the FBI.

The world of UFOlogy is as jealous and inbred as any cliquey academic discipline. It has its fads and fashions. UFO researchers, like professors of English Romantic poetry or biochemistry, have to find the hot topics to flourish on the lecture tour and in the world of UFO publishing.

The speciality called 'crash recovery' (C/R), in the 1970s, was a highly unfashionable and suspect realm of the rivalrous and quarrelsome world of the youfers. It had lain in the shadows since the early fifties, when Frank Scully, author of *Behind the Flying Saucers* had been duped by a couple of con men into believing he was in possession of flying saucer wreckage that turned out to profoundly terrestrial – just pot and pan aluminium.

But by the late 1970s, a man named Len Stringfield found his own niche of credibility – gathering hard evidence about crashes, lining up witnesses, and soon he was included on the panels and invited to lecture. He was the first of the new generation to focus on Roswell, and the recovered wreckage.

Sensing Stringfield was onto a good thing, William Moore and Charles Berlitz, whose previous success had included a book about the Bermuda Triangle, joined with UFO researcher Stanton Friedman to publish the book, *The Roswell Incident*, that brought Roswell back to the forefront in 1980.

Several more followed, each adding witnesses and in some cases, new crash sites. In 1989, the Showtime cable network broadcast a film on the case, aptly starring Kyle McLachlan, late of the surreal TV series *Twin Peaks*. Roswell came to be the touchstone of the cover-up theory.

The key witness was intelligence officer Jesse Marcel, who before his death in 1982 told a tale of going out to the crash site, near Corona, about fifty miles north of Roswell itself with a CIC agent named Cavitt and collecting bits of wreckage. The pieces filled a Jeep Carryall and the back of a Buick sedan.

Marcel would later be photographed in the Fort Worth office of General Ramey, commander of the Eighth Air Force, with parts of the wreckage, when it was declared to be that of a weather balloon – but which he knew, he would say years later, was in fact 'not of this world'. He had shown the wreckage to his son, declaring that it was part of a flying saucer.

A key element of the new version was a second crash site, near St Augustin, New Mexico. Did General Blanchard use his 'leave', on 8 July, to visit a second crash site? Why did Air Force

Chief of Staff Twining cancel an important trip on the West Coast on 8 July?

Dark tales of wire service transmissions stopped in mid-flow by the FBI surfaced. In 1992 General Thomas DuBose (in 1947 a colonel and General Ramey's Chief of Staff at Eighth Air Force Headquarters in Forth Worth, Texas) testified shortly before his death that he had personally received a telephone call from General Clements McMullen at Andrews Army Air Field in Washington, D.C., ordering a cover-up. The instructions were for General Ramey to concoct a 'cover story' to 'get the Press off our backs'. In 1990, Retired General Arthur E. Exon, who had been stationed at Wright Field at the time of the crash, described the testing of the Roswell debris which he said included 'everything from chemical analysis, stress tests, compression tests, flexing. It was brought into our material evaluation labs. (Some of it) could be easily ripped or changed ... there were other parts of it that were very thin but awfully strong and couldn't be dented with heavy hammers ... the overall consensus was that the pieces were from space.'

After prodding by a New Mexico Congressman, Steve Schiff, the General Accounting Office was assigned the task of ferreting out the truth about Roswell.

But before its report could be completed, on 8 September 1994, the Air Force issued its first official statement on Roswell in 47 years – a 23-page report stating that the 'most likely' source of the Roswell debris was a balloon from a secret programme known as Project Mogul. The purpose of Project Mogul was to detect Soviet nuclear tests by using sensitive instruments carried aloft by high-altitude balloons.

In July 1995, the General Accounting Office released a report based on its search for any government documents about the Roswell crash. It forthrightly declared that, 'In our search for records concerning the Roswell crash, we learned that some government records covering RAAF (Roswell Army Air Field) activities had been destroyed and others had not.' Which of them had been destroyed and why, was not made clear.

The youfers found it suspicious that the base newspaper the *Atomic Blast* did not mention the incident, and that the official Air Force investigation into UFO sightings, Project Blue Book, did not even mention it. That very absence of information to

13

of
lly
all
the
at I
rce
ent
new
ture
into
dies
very
rida,
ould

every
rned
docu-
ribed
about
dies

with a
ped: it
ooked

saucer
e body
tail, it
raft - a
g of the

11

'Something...

IN 1952, ORFEO
factory in Burba...
man, often in ill
was 'constitution...
born in Italy, was
sure he was going...
California of the e...

He had pretensi...
of the legendary M...
of a thinker. He h...
meaning and for
ambitious philosop...
Entities. Its subject...
and Involution, Ori...

Coming off the la...
1952, Angelucci fel...
he saw a strange re...
'pulsating'. It then s...
degree angle into th...
two smaller orbs like...

He pulled off to th...
green orbs were some...
They moved closer a...
between them; two n...
on the screen and Ar...
be 'friends from ano...
come to earth.

They asked him if h...
1946. He replied that
crystal cup appeared...
from it. The beverage...

The voice told him that distant civilizations were concerned with man's 'spiritual progress', which had not kept pace with its material evolution.

'Weep, Orfeo,' they said. 'For all its apparent beauty Earth is a purgatorial world among the planets evolving intelligent life. Hate, selfishness, and cruelty rise from many parts of it like a dark mist.'

People on Earth, he was told, did not appreciate each other. But the Etherians did. 'Every man, woman and child is recorded in vital statistics by means of our recording crystal disks. Each of you is infinitely more important to us than to your fellow Earthlings ...' They warned of a great cataclysm to strike the Earth in 1986 if changes were not made.

Angelucci would have more such encounters – at the Greyhound bus terminal, and in the dry bed of the Los Angeles River. And in 1955, he published his account of his adventures with the people from space in a book called *The Secret of the Saucers*.

On 23 July 1953, he felt unwell again and stayed home from work. In the evening he took a walk and, in a lonely place, he felt a 'dulling of consciousness'. There, in the bed of the LA River, he saw an 'igloo-shaped' spaceship like a 'huge, misty soap bubble'. A door appeared in the bubble craft. He entered and found himself in a vault about eighteen feet high, lined with some 'etheral mother of pearl stuff'. He saw a chair of the same material and when he sat in it, it seemed to mould itself to his body.

There is a humming noise that puts him into a semi dream state. He is carried off into space, and sees the Earth from a thousand miles away. He passes a UFO a thousand feet long made of a crystalline substance emitting music, visions of harmoniously evolving planets and galaxies. The UFO is equipped with 'vortices of flame' that served both as propellers and some mode of telepathic contact.

He woke to find a mark on his chest, about the size of a quarter: a circle with a dot in the centre that he decided was a symbol 'of the hydrogen atom'.

In September 1953, he would spend a week in a semi-conscious 'somnambulistic state'. Only later does he wake and recall it as if from a dream, that he had been spiritually trans-ported to another planetoid and met Orion and his space-woman friend Lyra. He learned that he had himself been a spaceman in an earlier life, named Neptune.

One avid reader of Angelucci's book was Carl Jung, the great psychoanalyst. Jung had been fascinated with flying saucers since 1949, seeing them as an example of a modern myth being born before his very eyes.

Nowhere was the process clearer than in accounts of 'con-tactees' like Angelucci, as they were being called – people who claimed not only to have seen flying saucers but even to have flown in them and spoken with their crews.

And of these manuscripts thrown up in bottles on the shores of the cultural unconscious, Angelucci's dreamy account fascinated Jung the most. Perhaps it was the naive, almost old-fashioned quality of the experience, as shown even in the design of the saucer itself – with its crystal walls and mother of pearl interior – or perhaps because of the mythological and archetypal overtones of the author's name. Orpheus, the god of the Underworld. Angelucci, angel of light.

To Jung, Angelucci's story was a clear example of the process of UFO sighting emerging from a disturbed spirit. Jung saw Orfeo's visions, as he saw all the saucers, as the expression of a wider cultural unease and disturbance. Orfeo was reaching a solution to a problem through something like the workings of a dream. Jung wrote:

'As our time is characterized by fragmentation, confusion, and perplexity, this fact is also expressed in the psychology of the individual, appearing in spontaneous fantasy images, dreams, and the products of active imagination.'

In 1958, Jung published his own quite strange book about UFOs called *Ein moderner Mythus: Von Dingen, die am Himmel gesehen werden* (*A Modern Myth: Of Things That Are Seen in the Sky*).

When it was translated into English, however, saucers were hot, and the publishers gave it a more marketable title: *Flying Saucers: A Modern Myth of Things Seen in the Sky*.

In the book's Introduction Jung refers to himself as an

'alienist' – the nineteenth-century term (from the French *alieniste*) for a doctor who treats the insane.

For Jung, who analyzed UFOs in their relationship to fantasy and interpreted a number of UFO dreams – taking time to reject Freudian sexual interpretations along the way – UFOs spring from the state of affairs at the time he wrote, the Fifties of the bomb, the Cold War, McCarthyism, fear and confusion.

Jung believed there is a tendency for underlying emotions to 'manifest' themselves in observations of real or imagined things. 'Universal spiritual distress' causes us to see archetypal circles in the sky.

'Something is seen but it is not known what.'

There was no question for Jung that something had been seen: observers had seen something, to change it to the active voice, but whether it was reality or illusion he was not sure – nor did he think the distinction very important.

A round shape in the sky was an archetype, he argued:

'Such an object provokes, like nothing else, conscious and unconscious fantasies, the former given rise to speculative conjectures and pure fabrications, and the latter supplying the mythological background inseparable from these provocative observers. Thus there arose a situation which, with the best will in the world, one often did not know and could not discover where a primary perception was followed by a phantasm or whether, conversely, a primary fantasy originating in the unconscious invaded the conscious mind with illusion and visions.'

Well, in essence, they might be real and they might not.

But where Jung saw the archetypes living in a kind of unconscious symbolic language we all possess, he turned to ancient mythology, religious tracts, astrology, astronomy and alchemy for his primary comparisons.

He overlooked something else: that the message travelled in the media now, that the lore had moved from beyond the old oral and written sources, beyond the campfire, the village square, the learned tome or tract – to the modern news media.

He did not understand when his first statement on UFOs was picked up by the popular Press as a sign he *believed* in flying saucers. He released a clarifying statement to the UPI, and was surprised when it was given far less space than his earlier statements.

Had Jung looked more closely at the history of the flying saucer sightings, he might have noticed the vital role of the Press from the very beginning. Kenneth Arnold's first sighting came on 24 June 1947, when during the search for a lost aircraft near Mount Rainier in the Cascade Mountains, Washington, he saw nine crescent- or boomerang-shaped objects. He calculated that the glinting objects were moving at nearly 1500 miles an hour. They seemed to skip across the clouds 'like a saucer skipped on a pond'. But the phrase that went out on the wire services was 'flying saucer'.

The ensuing wave of saucer sightings seemed as much inspired, as reported, by the Press. Mixing wonder with derision in a formula that was to become standard, a *New York Times* reporter, covering the first sightings in New York City itself in 1947, took the tone of a fashion writer, noting new colours appearing in the reports, bolstering the previous palette of silver and white and described one disc as 'a refugee from an ash tray'.

But while Jung remained undecided about whether the discs were real, he refused to laugh at them. He clung to his for-mulation – couched in that passive voice that is happily native to both UFO lore and the German language. 'Something is seen but it isn't known what.'

'This formulation,' he admits, 'leaves the question of seeing open.'

He was more interested in what *caused* the 'seeing'. It was the world situation, and the feeling of individuals that it was all falling apart, the 'dissolution' of the ego, and disorientation. The round shape, the saucer, is the shape of the centre, located deep in the collective unconscious. It is the mandala, the rotundum, age-old, deep and as powerful as the lenticular shapes of galaxies. God is often described as round, a circle with no edge, no centre – or a watching eyeball. 'The centre is frequently symbolized by an eye,' as in the all-seeing eye of conscience.

When the common centre cannot hold, the round shape appears as a wish. Jung wrote:

'The fears created by an apparently insoluble poetical

situation which might at any moment led to a universal catastrophe. At such times men's eyes turn to heaven for help, and marvellous signs appear from on high.'

And the rationalistic world of science and technology, unable to deal with these things, a world 'of "statistical or average truths"' creates 'an insatiable hunger for anything extra-ordinary'.

And if there really were aliens here? Well, Jung says, we would be in the position of a primitive tribe dominated by a white Western power. The reins of power would be wrenched from our hands, 'as an old witch doctor once told me with tears in his eyes, we would have "no dreams any more" – the lofty flights of our spirit would have been checked and crippled for ever – and the first thing to be consigned to the rubbish heap would be our science and technology. In such a situation, we would just roll up the Iron Curtain and get rid of our weapons.' Jung prefigured Ronald Reagan's oft-cited declaration to Mikhail Gorbachev that should alien invaders appear, our two countries would learn to get along soon enough.

But the question of the reality of the saucers that the wire service literalists insisted on remained. What did it all mean, Herr Doktor Jung? What caused these things to appear in the sky? Were these things 'real'? And there the good moustached avuncular Swiss doctor left a big hole of possibility, a portal to the New Agers who would seize on his ideas years later. It might not be a case of one thing causing another – that was a narrow, rationalistic view, he argued, but of things that happen together, or synchronistic 'acausal, meaningful coincidence'.

In the end, Jung insisted on interpreting the world as a set of symbols, not of realities, of seeing rather than knowing, of 'symbolical rumours' – dreams of the collective unconscious.

But where did the collective unconscious reside? Was it in the absorbed zeitgeist of strange characters like Orfeo? Was it in the newspapers, the tabloids, the magazines, on the wire services, in the movies – hadn't *The Day the Earth Stood Still* (1951) for instance, brought essentially the same message as Orfeo's 'Etherian' visitors? And could not print or film have also perhaps brought that message directly to Orfeo, a couple of years before he saw the red orb pulsating?

In April 1954, when the first of Van Tassel's Spacecraft Conventions was held in Giant Rock, California, Orfeo Angelucci was there, along with most of the other 'contactees'.

The first and best known contactee was George Adamski. He had fought with the cavalry down on the border during the Pancho Villa unpleasantness in 1911, when the first aircraft were being used for war – which must have looked as weird to the peasants then as any UFO ever did later.

In the early Thirties, he established a Tibetan Temple in Laguna Beach, one of whose virtues was that its status as a religious group meant dispensation from the rigours of prohibition.

If repeal had never come, he would later say, in an unguarded moment, he might never have got into 'this saucer crap'. He moved to the slopes of Mount Palomar in California – a locale handy for suggesting some connection to the observatory – and began trying to photograph the saucers. In 1952, he reported, he was taken inside one.

Adamski who, in his 1955 book *Inside the Space Ships* told of being taken on flying saucers by aliens with mythological names, spoke frequently of the 'Space Brothers' who talked to him.

Truman Bethuram, author of the 1954 *Aboard the Flying Saucers*, reported that while laying asphalt in the desert in July, 1952 he saw eight or ten small spacemen. They took him on board their spaceship where he met its captain, a female he described as 'tops in beauty', named Aura Rhanes, from the planet Clarion. Again, the burden of the message was a warning against nuclear weapons and of the need for love.

Daniel Fry's 1954 book *The White Sands Incident*, prefigures elements of the Roswell and Area 51 stories, but with a wholly different tone. Fry worked for Aerojet General at White Sands, the rocket test site. On a remote corner of the base, on 4 July 1950, he saw a flying saucer land. The voice of 'A-lan' invited him for a ride to New York and back. A year later, Fry published *Alan's Message to Men of Earth* which was based, not on a direct encounter, Fry reported, but on 'a voice inside his head'. Like many of the contactees, Fry veered toward mysticism, and tied the saucer tales in with classic pre-war obsessions with the ancient continents of Lemuria and Atlantis. After a great conflict between the two civilizations the survivors had fled to Mars.

George Van Tassel was the founder of the Spacecraft Convention. He had leased an airstrip at Giant Rock, in the desert east of Los Angeles, in 1947. He dug rooms beneath the huge boulder of Giant Rock, fully furnished, complete with a piano. He established a Council of Twelve that provided 'the first mental contact from Ashtar, commandant of a space station'. Under direction, Van Tassel began building the Integratron, a dome-shaped structure that would focus spiritual forces to prolong life and make possible both anti-gravity transportation and time travel. Van Tassel's gathering at Giant Rock in April 1954 drew 5,000 people; the numbers would slowly decline after that.

There was a pattern to the lives of the contactees: almost all had come from the Los Angeles area – and worked on the fringes of the aeronautic industry. Van Tassel was an airline mechanic, and had worked for Hughes, Douglas and Lockheed. Fry worked with Aerojet at White Sands, and Orfeo Angelucci at Lockheed.

The significance of all these accounts is in their tone: these are people who claim to have been taken aboard saucers, not in the menacing, medical experiment way of modern abductees, but in a naive, friendly way. The aliens are 'Space Brothers', who address the contactee as 'pal'.

The ruling spirit here is Klaatu, the alien in *The Day the Earth Stood Still*, here to warn us against our own folly, specifically nuclear folly.

In some of the accounts there is an old-fashioned, almost nineteenth-century feel, as in such theories as that of George Van Tassel, that humans were the result of beautiful Venusians mating with ugly Earth apes.

The world of the contactees in some cases grew from, and sometimes neatly dovetailed with, mystical Californian movements.

Looking back at that early, contactee era, it has a kind of happy naive glow about it. That is because so many other periods of Ufology have followed – most of them darker and considerably less glowing in their implications. Run the film of UFO history backwards and the periods become clearer: for some the aliens are saviours, for others invaders.

The more I read and followed the culture, the more I came to believe that fashions in Ufology marched in neat step with wider issues. The UFO culture offered a shadow version of the wider culture – of fashions in fascinations, mutating mores of mystery.

The first UFOs appeared in the 1890s, just as the fascination with flying machines and balloons was at its height. Look at the famous case of the town of Aurora, Texas. Those first 'airships' came during rapid technical change, urbanization, a wave of immigration and the depression of the 1890s. While the first 'foo fighters' of the 1940s were discounted as mere oddities in the sky, like the false bogies on crude early radar, the ghost rockets of the immediate post war years suggested a fear of attack from the Soviet Union.

The arrival of the term 'flying saucer' and the famous crash at Roswell – both in 1947 – coincided almost exactly with the development of the A-bomb. At Roswell the first US atomic bombers were stationed, and warheads waited in bunkers in the ground. Robert Goddard worked on rockets nearby, and Von Braun's captured V-2s were flying from White Sands, just over the mountains.

The flying saucer craze of the late Forties and early Fifties, culminating perhaps in June and July, 1952, when Washington DC itself was 'buzzed' by multiple saucers, recorded by ground observers, radar watchers and airline pilots, marched along in neat parallel to McCarthyism and the Red Menace. (In Japan, sociologists argued, Godzilla stood for the assault of the B-29s, their incendiary and atomic bombs.) The Fifties of course, with the nuclear threat of the hottest period of the Cold War suggested why the message the aliens brought was of peace among nations – the message the contactees received.

But already a darker theme of cover-up was emerging in the charges of Donald Keyhoe that 'silencers' were at work and the government was keeping the truth secret.

Race sometimes emerged as a theme of UFO stories in the Sixties – the first known abductees of the modern era, Betty and Barrey Hill, were a mixed-race couple. And the theme was struck of government cover-ups – a shadow of the JFK assassination, the Pentagon Papers, and Watergate. Then, later, the humiliations of Vietnam and Iran coincided with the cattle mutilation stories.

Close Encounters of the Third Kind featured François Truffaut playing the thinking man's UFO expert, Jacques Vallée, who echoed Jung's arguments, begging the question of their reality. But in the end real saucers do appear.

Fashions in Ufology changed from the Seventies, when *ET* (1982) stood as a fable for childhood. Children, like aliens, are new to the planet, with innocent assumptions and virtually no knowledge about how life is lived here on Earth. *ET*, one cynical critic said, was not only about childhood, and its sense of wonder – the reference to Disney is made explicit by the insertion in the soundtrack of *When You Wish Upon a Star*, the Jiminy Cricket number from *Pinocchio* – but about Stephen Spielberg's baby, as if left, by the 'mothership' in the earlier *Close Encounters*.

The Eighties' craze for abduction stories was in keeping with the cultural trends of the rest of the decade. Its sexual and personal obsessions – I was taken because I was special, I was abused – tied in with talk show psychology.

Also in the 1980s, Stealth created its own shadow UFO culture in the Lazarites. The F-117 looked like a flying saucer when viewed head-on – and for good technical reasons. Ben Rich would write of the design of the Stealth fighter that: 'Several of our aerodynamics experts, including Dick Cantrell, seriously thought maybe we would do better trying to build an actual flying saucer. The shape itself was the ultimate in low observability. The problem was finding a way to make a saucer fly. Unlike our plane, it would have to be rotated and spun.' This statement was widely quoted by those curious about flying saucers and those convinced of their existence.

The secrecy surrounding Stealth helped to start rumours that it had been created with the assistance of alien technology; one saucer organization noted that when one plane crashed, in the summer of 1986, the whole thing was cordoned off and hushed up in just the same manner as the Roswell crash and other 'recoveries' had been.

*

These eras are like periods in fashion or movements in art. And many of the contactee visions reminded me of something else: what was called outsider or visionary art. In the paintings of these socially marginal and untrained artists, 'kooks' or 'loons' in the later parlance of the Interceptors, flying saucers appeared as frequently and naturally as did angels or Jesus, but so did 727s and locomotives.

'Outsider' or 'self-taught' artists, alienated from the mainstream of the art world in the commercial, critical and academic consensus, often actually paint UFOS – like Alex Maldonado or the Reverend Howard Finster, the Georgia preacher who called himself 'Stranger from Another World'. Like many of the contactees, artists such as Maldonado not only see visions, but hear voices in their heads, inspiring them to paint visions from other planets or construct shrines, even landing pads. That many of the images and sounds may have a connection – as in Finster's case – to childhood blows on the head is beside the point.

Some of these are romantic, soft, vibrant images. They possess a dreamy, swirly quality, like Angelucci's prose, turning Tiny's Cafe in Twenty-Nine Palms into a magic chamber where he sips amber. Others share the detailed alternative engineering and dissident cosmology of the saucer buffs who look to Tesla and Townsend Brown – the technology of conspiracy.

One day in the autumn of 1996, I stopped at the American Primitive Gallery in SoHo, New York, to see a show of 'UFOs and aliens in outsider art'. It reminded me of the alien portrait paintings at the Little A-Le-Inn by the one-armed man.

Its star was himself an alien, a strange Romanian-born man named Ionel Talpazan who draws technically detailed diagrams of flying saucers in coloured pencil. Talpazan was abused as a child and escaped by swimming across the Danube. He lived in a UN refugee camp in Yugoslavia before reaching the US, where he was inspired to draw by a TV documentary on UFOs. He now sees himself as a kind of unpaid consultant to NASA, but what his alien ships reflect most may be his own sense of alienation.

The Giant Rock 'spaceport' had smaller offshoots in many places. I came across a book that documented a whole fringe world of such people who built landing sites for saucers and UFO detectors. They were seen as the vehicles of angels or aliens, or both. Douglas Curran, the author and photographer, recounts that his book's title had come to him in a dream, years before he knew what it would actually contain. That title was *In Advance of the Landing: Folk Concepts of Outer Space*. Curran found what Jung had discovered: when he tried to approach the saucer sighters and cultists as a folklorist, he still kept getting the guys who listened politely but in the end pulled him aside and earnestly asked, but do you *believe*? It was a strong suggestion of just how close these folk cultures were to religion, which helped explain the shrine-like nature of the places Curran photographed. It was as much about other planes of existence as about other planets of residence.

Sightings and imaginings, theories and conspiracies – the cultures of Dreamland – were folklore to take on its own terms: did it matter whether the Aurora aircraft or the 'alien replicated aircraft' actually existed, any more than whether Hermes really had wings on his feet?

Folklore and superstition begin where science and knowledge leave off. And knowing stopped at the perimeter around Dreamland.

After reading Jung, I became more aware that there were patterns to the tales surrounding Dreamland – that the sightings of black planes resembled what he had said of UFOs. Like UFOs, the actual existence of the flying triangles, bats, rays or pumpkin seeds was a matter of debate. And the black plane stories shared a consistency of account and – roughly – of detail, that made up a corpus of experience. I came to think of it collectively as the Lore.

Today a folklore, or the nearest thing we have to it, is constituted or bonded – not by village or family ties – but by technical expertise and collective fascination. It lives in a group's language, assumptions, and outlook, in its prides and prejudices.

Subcultures and sharers of belief in a technology are paralleled by those with a faith in a conspiracy – a hidden order. Could it not be that in an age of technology it takes the unexplained to link us together? That in the age of information, it takes mystery?

About both saucers and mystery planes there is the same compulsive gathering of bits of information, the careful construction of databases of sightings, dimensions, aircraft specifications and numbers. In this regard, both groups resembled Richard Hofstadter's descriptions of conspiracy groups from time immemorial, who built elaborate real structures from which to launch speculations.

John Pike – of the Federation of American Scientists – saw the same sort of dynamic Jung saw at work in the sightings of black aircraft. 'Considered as a sociological and epistemological phenomenon, the parallels between reports of flying saucers and reports of mystery aircraft are striking,' he wrote.

'Belief in the existence of marvelously capable and highly secret aircraft resonates with some of the deeper anxieties of contemporary American society,' Pike went on. 'Aviation has long been one of the distinguishing attributes of American greatness, from Kitty Hawk to Desert Storm.

'It would be reassuring to believe that concealed in the most hidden recesses of the American technostructure were devices of such miraculous capabilities that they will astound the world when at last they are revealed and will restore America to its rightful station of leadership.'

The saucers might save us from the Cold War; the black aircraft might save us from its aftermath.

On Saturday, 20 February 1954, President Dwight D. Eisenhower ('Ike') enjoyed a golfing vacation at Smoke Tree Ranch in Palm Springs, California, rose early at about 6:30, breakfasted, met the Press at 8:30 to announce he had signed 23 bills, and made comments supporting his nominee as Chief Justice of the Supreme Court, Earl Warren.

Eisenhower had made the eight-hour flight out to California on his personal Lockheed Constellation, called the Columbine (after a wildflower he loved from his prairie childhood). He was staying at Smoke Tree Ranch resort as the guest of golf partners Paul G. Hoffman, chairman of the Studebaker Corporation, George Allen, an insurance CEO, and Paul Helms, president of the Helms Baking Company. He played golf with these men daily.

That evening after dinner, Ike disappeared. One can imagine the Press corps, happy for some time out of the Washington winter, happy for a Saturday night off duty, were restless: Ike was late. Could he have had a heart attack? Was a world crisis brewing? James Haggerty, the Press secretary, can have been no happier to have been called out to make an explanatory statement: 'the President was having his teeth fixed'.

But during the hours of Eisenhower's absence, a legend was being born: this, the Lore would record, was when he was secretly flown to Muroc – later Edwards Air Force Base – to meet aliens and view recovered flying saucers. According to one account, 'they keep disappearing, causing him embarrassment'. Eisenhower's toothache, like the crumb of cheese that grows into Scrooge's nightmares, grew into a whole fabric of conspiracy theories that would eventually end up in Dreamland.

'During his evening meal, the porcelain cap on one of his front teeth chipped off,' the *New York Times* reported. 'Mr Helms took him to Dr F.A. Purcell, a dentist, who replaced the cap. When the President goes to church tomorrow morning his grin will look the same as ever.'

And so it did: taking his wife, even his mother-in-law, along to the Palm Springs Community Church, that repaired grin inspired crowds to political rally enthusiasm.

Had Ike made that trip, met those aliens, could the grin have looked the same ever again? It must have been a moment of profound philosophical re-examination for the former general. Could this man have disappeared between dinner and breakfast to view hidden saucers, meet aliens, and then sail off happily to listen to that sermon?

Any mystery four hours, that Saturday night, were under cover of darkness – the idea of a trip to Muroc is hard to buy. It would have had to have been by air, to allow for him to have spent any significant amount of time at the base. Ike would have lost a lot of sleep.

Ike's toothache was established in UFO lore by a letter written in April 1954 by Gerald Light. No one has much idea who Gerald Light was, beyond the fact that he was an adherent of a Spiritualist organization, the Borderlands Foundation, founded in 1945 by a man named Mead Layne to explore 'realms normally beyond the range of basic human perception and physical measurement'. Publishing works by Charles Steinmetz and such volumes as *The Etheric Formative Forces In Cosmos, Earth And Man* by Dr Guenther Wachsmuth, Borderlands was dedicated to investigations of 'ether ships', Vril energy, radionics, and dowsing.

It was a kind of link between the Theosophist groups influential in Los Angeles at the time and today's New Age groups. Layne himself had written about the saucers, which he called 'ether ships' or 'aeroforms', connecting them with the Kabala and other mystical writings.

What the letter does well is convey a certain tone of UFO watchers in the Fifties. It has become a classic of the Lore, a record of suspicion emerging from enthusiasm, excitement mingling with dread.

'My Dear Friend' – Light addresses Layne. 'I have just returned from Muroc. The report is true – devastatingly true!

'I made the journey in company with Franklin Allen of the Hearst Papers and Edwin Nourse of Brookings Institute and Bishop MacIntyre of LA (confidential names, for the present, please).

'When we were allowed to enter the restricted section (after about six hours in which we were checked on every possible item, event, incident, and aspect of our personal and public lives), I had the distinct feeling that the world had come to an end with fantastic realism. For I have never seen so many human beings in a state of complete collapse and confusion as they realized that their own world had indeed ended with such finality as to beggar description. The reality of "otherplane" aeroforms is now and forever removed from the realms of speculation and made a rather painful part of the consciousness of every responsible scientific and political group.'

During his two-day visit, Light went on, he saw five different type of aircraft 'with the assistance and permission of the Etherians'.

The notion that he would have been included with such well-known figures as the Hearst columnist and the bishop is self-flattering.

But there is an unforgettable tone to the combination of sermonly seriousness and offhandedness that sums up that particular era. 'President Eisenhower, as you may already know, was spirited over to Muroc one night during his visit to Palm Springs recently.

'Mental and emotional pandemonium ... is now shattering the consciousness of hundreds of our scientific "authorities"...'

'Pity,' he said, was what he felt watching 'the pathetic bewilderment of rather brilliant brains struggling to make some sort of rational explanation'.

For himself, he said, he had long ago entered 'the metaphysical woods'.

'I had forgotten how commonplace such things as the demateralization of "solid" objects had become to my own mind. The coming and going of an etheric, or spirit, body had been so familiar to me these many years I had just forgotten that such a manifestation could snap the mental balance of a man not so conditioned.'

Light's letter reads like the cleverest sort of propaganda document – one whose real message is oblique. While designed to be read by someone outside, it speaks as an insider: Light would not have to define 'etheric,' for instance, for his pal Meade Layne. The name-dropping of his companions (an unlikely bunch) and the description of the thoroughgoing background check, that only an outsider could imagine, mark it for what it is: an effort to shift the discussion of flying saucers into the territory of the Borderlands and other Spiritualist groups. The flying objects were not from Mars or Zeta Reticuli, but from a 'higher plane', a 'different dimension'.

The assumption of Eisenhower's Muroc trip slips in almost unnoticed.

So uncertainty or secrecy grows into fantasy: if the President catches cold the stock market may get pneumonia. If the President get a chipped tooth, consternation in this year of maximum danger, the year of McCarthy's high watermark, would ensue. From a tiny chip of credibility, from a cavity of dental uncertainty, a crevasse of speculation could grow.

Just a few miles from Ike's Palm Springs vacation site, at Giant

Rock, California, preparations were underway for 'The World's First Interplanetary Spacecraft Convention,' put together by George Van Tassell. It was held on 4 April 1954, and all the important figures from the flying saucer community would be there, including such contactees as Adamski, Truman Bethurum – even Orfeo Angelucci himself. One attendee noted that he was the only one of the contactees she could really imagine on a spaceship, describing him as 'a small, slender, almost fragile man' with 'dark, wavy hair, trusting eyes, and a delicate, semi-ascetic face ... frequently reminiscent of a saint's head by da Vinci. The softness of his voice reflects the quality of quiet perseverance.'

1947 was probably the last time that there was an air of open-mindedness about flying saucers. The lines of opposition had not hardened between private researchers and government. Fear had not overwhelmed curiosity. Theories were still in play, speculation was neither stifled nor rampant. Theories of government cover-up had not yet taken root. In short the question was still open.

On 23 September, General Nathan Twining, commanding General of the Air Materiel Command at Wright Field, wrote a secret memo to Brigadier-General George Schulgen, chief of the Air Intelligence Requirements division at the Pentagon, about the flying saucer question.

Twining's memo offered what seems a reasonable and open-minded listing of possible explanations of the UFOs: they are secret US craft, a secret Soviet system, perhaps developed with the aid of Nazi scientists (shades of future conspiratorial theories). They are an unexplained meteorological or atmospheric phenomenon, or – and this was not ruled out – craft from another star system. Indeed he added, 'It is the considered opinion of some elements that the object may in fact represent an interplanetary craft of some kind.

'The phenomenon is something real and not visionary or fictitious,' Twining's memo concluded, in words that would be cited again and again later. There was a recommendation for further study and a suggestion, later explicitly rejected for reasons of cost, that interceptor fighters be kept on alert to shoot down UFOs.

In December 1947, the Air Force set up Project Sign to track the UFOs and determine their nature. But in 1949 the name of Project Sign was changed to Project Grudge, revealing the change in attitude.

The prevailing reaction of the Air Force quickly turned to irritation. It hated dealing with the UFO problem, the Press, the watchers, the nuts. It was a bit nervous that objects could seemingly fly so easily through its air defences. It was uncomfortable dealing in areas where hard evidence was difficult to get. Most of all, it wanted to be shut of the problem. The Air Force, a joke of the time had it, 'wished [the UFOs] swam so they would become the Navy's problem'.

In 1948, the report of this group, the Estimate, was completed. Neither Chief of Staff General Hoyt Vandenberg, nor Twining, found it acceptable. Concluding that the evidence did not support the conclusions, Vandenberg ordered it destroyed and the Estimate was not made public. Years later when UFO researchers asked for a copy, neither the military nor the civilian agencies could – or were willing to – provide one. And later it would be cited in support of the argument that there was a cover-up. Quotations ostensibly from the unpublished document made reference to descriptions of material that sounded a lot like the Roswell wreckage, which believers saw as proof of a cover-up, that the stuff was indeed part of a saucer, and Air Force units were being asked to be on the alert for similar incidents and objects. The allegations of cover-up would soon begin to be a dominant note in the debate over UFOs. In January 1950, *True* magazine published the famous Donald Keyhoe story that alleged there had been a cover-up – one of the most widely read and noted magazine stories of all time. The Estimate would become legendary; what it left was mostly a legacy of suspicion.

Keyhoe published a book-length version of his argument, *The Flying Saucers Are Real*, in 1950 and soon began to speak of 'silencers', Air Force officers or other government agents who were trying to keep the truth secret by intimidating witnesses. He followed up with *The Flying Saucer Conspiracy*.

The strand of the Lore that belonged to the cover-up conspiracists spun off from that of the happy contactees almost immediately. One part of it was the 'men in black' (MIB) phenomenon, an early and recurrent part of the Lore.

The first MIB story happened in July 1947, when Fred Lee Crisman and Harold A. Dahl from Tacoma Washington – who claimed to be harbour patrolmen – reported that they had seen a group of 'donut-shaped' UFOs near Maury Island and claimed to have gathered scraps of one. There were other mysterious details: their radio was jammed and strange spots appeared on photographs they took. And a mysterious Man In Black had appeared to tell them to keep quiet.

The Air Force dispatched its top flying saucer investigators, Lieutenant Frank Brown and Captain William Davidson from the TID – Technical Intelligence Division. They determined that the whole thing was a hoax, and that Dahl and Crisman were basically wharf rats. But when they returned home, on 1 August, and their B-25 bomber crashed, there were immediate suspicions that someone was hushing things up.

The Tacoma newspaper headlined 'Sabotage suspected'. The MIB legend was established; in the years to come their standard mode of transport, the black Buick, would be upgraded to a black Cadillac.

A book by Gray Barker called *They Knew Too Much about Flying Saucers* was published in the mid-Fifties and established the Men in Black legend firmly in the Lore. In 1952, he claimed, a man named Albert K. Bender organized a UFO organization called the International Flying Saucer Bureau. Within a few months, Barker reported, he was visited by MIBs who said that the government knew the truth and would soon release it and persuaded him to dissolve the outfit.

The Men in Black dressed inappropriately, often too warmly, they walked and talked mechanically, they had vaguely Oriental features. They could have been aliens themselves, even robots. To folklorist Peter M. Rojcewicz they suggested a very ancient archetype: the ominous dark men, the evil tricksters in many folk traditions.

The camou dudes were in some sense imaginative relatives of the Men in Black. Their danger was overestimated; they took on an almost folkloric quality of menace.

Sometimes they inhabited the dreams of watchers, as a sort of modern day version of the Greek Furies. So when Gene Huff talked about his feelings of fear and guilt after visiting the perimeter with Lazar, he talked about 'the Dream Police' – police in his mind. The camou dudes, like the mysteries of Area 51 itself, came at the end of a long tradition.

12

'Majic' or 'Majestic'

IT WAS ONLY A GLIMPSE, A SHAPE SEEN AROUND A CORNER, a name stencilled on shipping crates – 'Redlight' – and dark muttering. But it represented the first important public mention of Area 51. It was the widely-cited account of 'Mike', a worker at the base, who in April 1980 told a representative of MUFON – one of the larger and most powerful UFO organizations – that he had seen a flying saucer at the base when he worked there in 1961–3. The programme was called Project Redlight, he said, and it had gone on until 1962. The story was in part corroborated by radar operators at Tonopah who reported seeing very fast blips on the screen, passing in three sweeps of the antenna from horizon to horizon.

The year 1962 was when the A-12, the original Blackbird, the CIA's version of the plane, had first flown – a revealing correspondence perhaps. Was Mike's report the inevitable result of secrecy, which grew out of compartmentalized information?

But the first time the wider American public ever heard the word 'Dreamland' was on the evening of 14 October 1988, when it was first uttered on national TV, as part of the Fox Network's show *UFO Cover-Up? Live!*

Two 'inside informants', were presented in disguise, code-named Falcon and Condor. Condor described Project Aquarius, and told of Snowbird, another programme begun in 1972 and still being carried out in Nevada at 'an area called Area 51 or Dreamland'. 'The extraterrestrials,' Condor said, 'have complete control of this base.' This was the result of an agreement between the government and the aliens that had gone awry. And in what became the most memorable and derided phrases of the show, Condor went on to describe the aliens here on Earth, saying 'they enjoy music ... especially ancient Tibetan

style music ... their favourite dish or snack is ice cream –
especially strawberry'.

Condor, according to some accounts, was the disguised face
and voice of a man named Richard Doty, a special agent at the
Kirtland AFB unit of AFOSI. In September 1980 he wrote a
report on a series of unidentified lights seen over the Kirtland
range, near Albuquerque, and the Manazano Nuclear Weapons
storage facility there.

He watched a man named Paul Bennewitz, who believed that
aliens were not only actively flying over the range, but had
also implanted human abductees with control devices. He
claimed to have electronically picked up the signals that
activated them and to be in communication with aliens in
spacecraft – and at the base.

Doty was said to have provided him with disinformation,
encouraging his speculations, including a memo analyzing
Bennewitz's sightings, which seemed to lend them credence –
and prove that AFOSI was watching the saucer watchers.

Eventually, Bennewitz, who began as a mild-mannered Albuquerque businessman, would end up chain-smoking and sleepless, with knives and guns around his house, fearing spies and
intruders. Finally, he had to be hospitalized for exhaustion.

One item was a faked memo teletyped from Wright Pat to
Kirtland AFB. In February 1981 the story went, Doty gave this
to William Moore, the author of the Roswell book of 1980,
which began the revival of interest in the case and of the early
'Philadelphia experiment', a 1943 project to make a naval
destroyer invisible, later made into a film.

In February 1981, Moore produced a briefing on 'Project
Aquarius', an effort to make contact with ETs. It mentioned
other projects including one called Snowbird, that since 1972
had been involved in testing a flying saucer 'somewhere in
Nevada'. The Project Aquarius document also referred to restricted access to 'MJ12'. Thus an infamous codename was first
introduced to the world.

In January 1982, Moore met Robert Pratt, a former National
Enquirer reporter, and told him he referred to Doty as a 'Deep
Throat' source. The two planned and wrote a portion of a
novelized version of the story, called The Aquarius Document.
They apparently finished the manuscript, but it was never

published. Whether it was ever submitted to an editor is unclear.

In 1984, the story went on, Doty provided TV producer Linda Moulton Howe, known for her documentaries on cattle mutilation, with a look at what she later said were 'Presidential briefing papers' about flying saucers. It described a meeting between Earthlings and aliens who had landed at Holloman AFB, near Alamagordo, New Mexico, at 6 am on 25 April 1964. There was a similar meeting at Edwards – reminiscent of Ike's legendary trip. Howe claimed that Doty told her there were people who wanted the information to get out. It was time. He promised her that film footage of the meeting and other dramatic evidence of contact would be forthcoming soon.

Actual images of aliens talking with Earthlings! This would be the Biggest Story of All Time!

But the additional material never arrived: Doty explained that there were political problems, a change of heart. He would provide Bill Moore with more information from a whole aviary of bird-codenamed informants; Moore, in return, would report back to him on the activities of UFO researchers. And Moore was collaborating on research with Stanton Friedman, a bearded scientist who had once worked for Aerojet and describes himself as a nuclear physicist. (He has a masters degree in that subject.) He also began to deal with Jaime Shandera, a film producer.

On 11 December 1984, shortly before he was scheduled to lunch with Moore, at a restaurant called the Villa Sunset, Shandera was at his home in Burbank, thumbing through *Variety*, when he heard a rustling and then a thump as something arrived through his letterbox. It was a brown-paper package, with a postmark from Albuquerque New Mexico. (Doty was at Kirtland AFB in Albuquerque.)

The result was a mystery like a manuscript washed up in a bottle: inside the envelope was a roll of undeveloped 35mm film. Moore developed it himself, with Shandera. It was black and white and, as the prints were drying, they could see the words 'TOP SECRET/MAJIC/EYES ONLY' in the red-orange safe light of the darkroom.

It was the beginning of the Majic 12, Majestic 12 or MJ12

story. The group had supposedly been formed by President Truman in September 1947, to investigate UFOs. Among the photographs was one of a document dated 18 November 1952, which was apparently a briefing paper for the then President Elect Eisenhower. It said that the remains of four alien bodies had been recovered two miles from the Roswell wreckage site.

There were references to attached manuals and other information, but they were not included with the photos.

The members of the panel were listed:

Lloyd Berkner, member of the CIA's Robertson panel looking into UFOs and executive secretary of Bush's Joint Research and Development Board.

Detlev Bronk, advisor to Brookhaven lab, physiologist and Chairman of the National Research Council.

James Forrestal, who became first Secretary of Defense in July 1947, under the reorganization of the services, and famously, a suicide at Bethesda Hospital, in May 1949. Under treatment for depression, he leapt from a window to his death.

Gordon Gray, Assistant Secretary of the Army and member of the influential Psychological Strategy Board. Later head of the 5412 committee, Ike's inner circle for national security decisions.

Walter Bedell Smith, CIA director who had discussed the psychological warfare implications of UFOs.

Roscoe Hillenkoetter, who in September 1947, became first director of the new CIA.

Jerome Hunsaker, MIT aeronautical aircraft designer, head of NACA, the predecessor of NASA.

Donald Menzel, director of the Harvard Observatory, later a widely-read UFO debunker, who held a Top Secret clearance.

General Robert Montague, base commander at Kirtland Air Force Base, with adjoining nuclear weapons, test and storage facilities run by Sandia Lab in Albuquerque.

Rear-Admiral Sidney Souers, first Director Central Intelligence Executive secretary of the then National Security Council.

Nathan Twining, commanding general of the Air Materiel Command at Wright Field, who was on record as believing 'the phenomenon is something real'.

Hoyt Vandenberg, the general who had scotched the 'Estimate of the Situation'.

The group's alleged head – called 'MJ1' – was Vannevar Bush himself, the man who had directed science in the service of the military during World War II as head of the National Defense Research Council. He also pushed the Manhattan Project, the Radiation lab at MIT, and such less mythologized – but highly important developments – as the proximity fuse for anti-aircraft fire. Bush, head of the Carnegie Foundation in the late Forties, was exactly the guy anyone would have chosen for the job. He had made the A-bomb happen, and radar and computers. He had a wide and open view of the importance of science: as we have seen, his essay of a couple of years before, called 'As We May Think', would inspire a whole generation of computer scientists. His Memex described a personal computer, in effect, and he projected something very much like the world wide web.

The MJ12 documents were the biggest thing to hit the UFO world in years. Moore, Shandera and Friedman set out to verify their authenticity. Not until 1985 did they make them public – first in the UK, then later in the United States. Critics immediately attacked their authenticity.

All of a sudden, the UFO world sounded as if it had turned into a convention of graphologists.

The critique of the documents, as developed by leading UFO debunker and *Aviation Week* editor, Phil Klass, and others, levelled the following charges: that the TOP SECRET stamp was not custom-made but a changeable type (like old-style library date stamps) that bore a strong resemblance to one Bill Moore used for his own return address. That the presidential directive order number establishing the group was not consistent with the official numbering system used at that time. (Secret directives, Friedman replied, would naturally not be numbered with the standard system.) That the documents bore no Top Secret register number, that the classification Top Secret Restricted Information was not used until years later. That the supposedly Top Secret documents did not have the 'Page — of — pages' indication that is standard. That the document uses the form 'Roswell Army Base' which was not used after

1943. That the text includes the words 'media' and 'impacted' as a verb, years before those locutions were common.

The unusual hyphenation of 'homo sapiens' was also noticeable in the Aquarius briefing paper, with which the MJ12 documents shared a general aversion to the use of commas. That the Truman signature on the 24 September 1947 memo seems to be identical to that on an 1 October 1947 letter to Vannevar Bush, right down to the distinctive skid mark on the H in 'Harry'.

There ensued a dizzying series of debunkings and counter-debunkings turning on watermarks and date formats, bureaucratic procedure, and national security numerical formats.

But the debates that burned up the newsgroups and UFO seminars seemed to turn mostly on the matter of the style of dating: Klass had alleged that the MJ12 documents' use of a zero before a single digit for day of the month (as 01 August or 06 December) had come along only after the advent of computers. It was, he wryly added, also a format used by William Moore since the autumn of 1983 in his personal papers, as well as in the 'retyped' official documents he distributed. In response, Friedman showed several cases where the zero had been used, especially in military documents. The charge and countercharge, assertion and rebuttal seemed to zoom in more and more on that zero, circling it, like a boat in a whirlpool. In the UFO world, that zero was more studied, more debated, than any circle or disc in the sky had ever been.

In March 1985 Moore recounted, he received several postcards from an anonymous sender. They had been mailed to his post office box in the town where he had previously lived, Dewey, Arizona, then forwarded to his new home in LA. One card showed a photo of the African bush credited to the Ethiopian Tourist Commission. The return address read 'Box 189 Addis Ababa, Ethiopia'. But the card had been postmarked in New Zealand. On the back, a single-spaced, typed message read in part: 'To win the war. ... Add zest to your trip to Washington/Try Reese's pieces;/For a stylish look/Try Suit Land.'

Reese's pieces reminded Moore and Shandera of *ET*, of course.

But for Friedman, they were also a reminder of something else.

As part of his effort to validate the authenticity of the MJ12 documents, Friedman had planned to visit the National Archives, where military intelligence records that seem promising sources had been declassified. He and his colleagues were particularly interested in Record Group 341, which their contact, JoAnn Williamson at the military branch of National Archives, had told Friedman had just been declassified.

Friedman called Moore to tell him, and to ask Moore to come to Washington to check the documents out – he, Friedman, was set to go off on one of the lecture tours that are his main source of income. Moore was not excited. He told Friedman about the postcards, and how they baffled him. Then Friedman happened to mention that the records he was planning to review were not at the main Archives in Washington DC, but in suburban Suitland, Maryland, and that they were in the charge of a man named Edward Reese.

There, Moore and Friedman would discover a letter signed by Robert Cutler, Eisenhower's national security advisor, referring to a change in the time of an MJ12 meeting. Later, they realized that the box in which the memo had been found was number 189 – the same as the box on the return address on the postcard.

Who had sent the cards? And if the letter had been planted in the archives, who had done so? Was it a Deep Throat, seeking to let the secret out, or a disinformer, working from inside?

The letter, found loose between two manila folders, was dated 15 July 1954 and referred to 'NSC/MJ12 Special Studies Project'. It was a notification from White House aide James Cutler to Nathan Twining to the effect that: 'the President has decided that the MJ12 SSP briefing should take place during the already scheduled White House meeting of 16 July, rather than following it as previously intended.' A carbon copy on onion skin-type paper, it bore the red slash officially declassifying it. And Friedman and Moore believed this innocuous, procedural note was the smoking gun that verified the existence of the MJ12 group and the authenticity of the earlier MJ12 documents.

But critics attacked what quickly became known as the

'Cutler-Twining memo', noting that it did not bear the standard government eagle watermark, that Ike had no such meeting on 16 July 1954, and that Cutler was not even in the US on the day he was supposed to have signed the letter. (His aide James Lay signed a genuine memo on the same date.) But Richard Bissell, the CIA's man behind the U-2 and the Blackbird, a man who had looked at Top Secret documents all his career, the man who created Paradise Ranch and Dreamland, took a look at the documents and concluded he could find nothing obviously false about them.

MJ12 became a big part of the Lore and its story became more elaborate. The MJ12 tales acquired a forward history: its origins were better known than its subsequent existence. In some accounts it became linked to the Bilderbergers and the Trilateral Commission (whose triangular symbol was said to have been derived from the markings of a crashed flying saucer). In these versions, MJ12 killed JFK, and forced Nixon from power because he wouldn't co-operate.

MJ12 lore continued to grow. After the Lazar stories surfaced, Robert Collins published an elaborate scheduling chart for the organization, dating he said from 1984–5. One prominent branch of the chart was for operations at Area 51 and S-4. His source, he said, was William Moore. John Lear talked of a country club where the MJ12 members held their meetings, playing golf and tennis in between considering the fate of the planet. According to these accounts, Kissinger and Harold Brown had become members, Lear said, along with Lew Allen of Star Wars, and Bobby Ray Inman, former DCIA and NSA boss.

To author and historian Curtis Peebles, the whole thing was very much in keeping with classic American suspicions of secret groups and 'cabals'. Twelve was a neat number – as in the twelve disciples – Peebles noted that the publicly anti-UFO Donald Menzel could figure as Judas. Or, he added, the twelve Jewish elders to whom the notoriously fraudulent *Protocols of the Elders of Zion* had been attributed. (Five of the original MJ12 had 'Jewish sounding names'.)

But the MJ12 group also sounded a lot like real commissions – those formed to deal with vital questions of national security, such as the Killian Commission, with its recommendation of building the U-2 or the later Gaither Commission, formed around the time of Sputnik.

Too good to be true? Or was someone 'inside' working to get the word out? Wasn't there too much in these documents? Reading them, one sometimes gets the sense that they explain too much, like a character in a badly written film trying to fill in the background for the audience.

It was also hard to imagine the social dynamic in the room when Ike was told of all this. He was scheduled for less than an hour of briefings on the day in question, the Pentagon updating the President elect. There were in fact, just 43 minutes for the whole world situation. The briefing schedule implies that somewhere in those 43 minutes, Ike would be informed that, by the way, we have found that flying saucers come from another star system and have four alien bodies and a whole secret committee shrouded in secrecy deeper than that of the Manhattan Project.

Then, in May 1988, Doty denied that he had shown Howe any Presidential briefing paper on Aquarius or anything else, or that he had even heard of MJ12. Early in 1985 he had been transferred from Kirtland to West Germany. It was later charged that he had faked contactee reports there, and that he failed a lie detector test.

In 1989, speaking at the national MUFON convention, Moore admitted that he had been a double agent, spreading disinformation on behalf of AFOSI and spying on UFO believers in order to get closer to the truth behind the cover-up. Desperate not to be left out of the biggest story in history, he had collaborated.

Before long, Moore vanished from the UFO scene. Had he been telling the truth? Was this an AFOSI job? Was Moore really a disinformation agent? Was he a double or a triple agent? Did he simply disinform Bennewitz, or had he by himself, or in collusion with Doty, faked the MJ12 document? And – given that his account seemed to reflect that of Moore and Doty – was Lazar's story a continuation of the same scheme?

To some of the youfers, to be sure, it hardly mattered whether the MJ12 documents were real or not. A number of apologists for the papers worked them into the 'trickle out' theory – they might not be genuine, but they were a preparation, a means of breaking the news gradually. They did not have to be rank disinformation, they could still be part of the Big Plan, from those On the Inside, preparing us with a softer version of the truth.

Linda Howe continued to stick to her story of seeing the briefing papers, but the record was not in her favour.

Was Doty the centre of a disinformation scheme that involved Moore, perhaps John Lear and eventually Lazar? Was he a loose cannon, or a nut? Were the doubts about Doty's veracity evidence of further muddying of the waters by the AFOSI or a recognition that he had got out of hand? Doty left the service and was hired as an investigator in the New Mexico Department of Public Safety. 'I don't do interviews,' he told me when I reached him. 'I can't talk about it. I'm still sworn to secrecy.'

He didn't sound like a nut; he didn't sound like a hard ass military type either. He had a cowboy sort of twang and sounded quite likeable.

'I wouldn't ask you to violate your oath,' I said, and suggested that he might not have been treated fairly in the record of the whole matter.

'I don't worry about it. People can think what they want to think. The truth is known by those that matter.'

'Did you distribute any false documents?' I asked and he repeated that he could not talk about it.

'You feel you acted according to your duty?' Trying one last time.

'Absolutely,' he said.

He suggested he might be able to call me back. I was amazed when he did. He had apparently thought about the subject. 'We did not fabricate any of the papers,' he told me. 'I have been investigated and cleared.'

Howe had brought the alleged briefing paper with her, Doty said. I didn't have to take his word for it. The meeting, he revealed, with Howe had been videotaped; the result backed him up.

He denied having creating any briefing paper, or having delivered it. He did not fabricate the MJ12 papers. Nor did he know who did. AFOSI thought it most likely some private citizen had done so. The implication was Moore, and/or Shandera. Moore, he told me, was 'a low level source'. As for the MJ papers, he was not sure either. The FBI and the OSI tried to determine their authenticity. They failed, running up against classification barriers. 'A lot of time and money was spent trying to determine whether they were genuine,' Doty said. 'The FBI came up with fifty/fifty.'

Doty denied being Falcon or Condor. Falcon was another man, probably now – in the 1990s – in his eighties, if still alive.

I ventured these ideas: that in the past black programmes had always been concealed behind cover stories. The U-2 cover was the weather plane story. The Stealth fighter was covered in part by the phony A-7s with bogus electronic pods. Had AFOSI ever run deception programmes using UFOs as a cover or diversionary story?

'Yes,' he said, 'you're right on the money. We call it legitimate lying. I've never worked on any, but there have been some.'

And, I learned, Doty had been born in Roswell, of all places; his father had worked on the U-2 programme.

In the end, ironically, one of the strongest pieces of evidence against the MJ12 papers was the reference in one of them to Area 51. That designation, bestowed by the Atomic Energy Commission did not, on all the best evidence, exist until 1960 – Peter Merlin traced it to the test site bulletin, and mundane changes in phone numbers. The area had not been used for anything to speak of, until Tony LeVier flew over it in 1955.

But there was incontrovertible proof of the existence of alien craft at Area 51. The military tried to hide their existence, but it was secretly very proud: the alien craft were Soviet aircraft.

13

Red Hats and STUDs

'PRESS BUTTON FOR PLEASURE,' READS THE FORMICA SIGN outside the Shamrock, one of the several legal cat houses of the Armagosa Valley, near Lathrop Wells, most little more than a collection of trailers, linked together and fenced off.

If you had been inside the Shamrock, or in the cafe at Lathrop Wells, where old men linger late, sipping coffee and sopping up their gravy with sourdough biscuits, late on the morning of 26 March 1984, you would have been distracted by the sound of Major General Robert Bond plunging into the ground. He had lost control of his aircraft and smashed into a mountainside.

Secret planes become unsecret when they fall out of the sky. The news of a mysterious plane crash near Dreamland and the fact that a general was in the cockpit meant the story could not be contained. There was immediate Press speculation that Bond had been flying a 'super secret new stealth airplane'. And among UFO watchers, the speculation went further; had Bond been test-flying one of the recovered saucers? As recently as 1991, in his book *Cosmic Top Secret*, William Hamilton declared that 'The Air Force refused to say what type of plane Bond was flying at Area 51, but it seems highly irregular for the Air Force to use a three-star general as a test pilot. Is it possible that the general was test flying a recovered alien spacecraft?' In fact, Bond had been flying a MiG-23.

Bobby Bond was known around the Skunk Works as a stickler and worrier. A hard-driving TAC type, he was also cleared on Stealth and other secret programmes.

Bond's crash brought the foreign technology programme to light. It was run by what was at one time called the Foreign Technology Division out of Wright Patterson – exactly the place in fact where the saucers were supposed to be hidden – alien tech indeed.

The Lore also held that there was other alien technology, buried in the legendary Hangar 18, deep below ground. Alien bodies – some said dead, some said living – in tanks of liquid and cryogenic coolers, the infamous 'Blue Room'. Where but the Foreign Technology Division, believers ask, would the Roswell bodies have been stored? But there is no Hangar 18.

The only piece of alien flying technology ever photographed and positively identified at Dreamland was not from Zeta Reticuli or any other star system. It was a MiG 21 captured by John Lear's camera from the lake edge in September, 1978. That image confirmed what had long been suspected: that there existed a programme for testing aircraft captured, stolen, bribed or otherwise purloined from the Soviet bloc. Like a real world shadow of the UFO testing programmes of the Lore, this 'Red Hat' squadron programme was highly secret, in order not to compromise the sources of the planes – and of the spare parts, engines and tyres needed to keep them flying. The important secrets had to do, not with enemies, but with allies, as Frank Power was given to understand that the U-2 flights to be protected at all cost were not those over the Soviet Union, but those over Israel and Egypt that were aimed at the UK and France.

It began in 1953, in Ohio, when the Air Force's Foreign Technology Division (now the Foreign Aerospace Technology Center) at Wright-Patterson Air Force Base first flew a Yak 23, smuggling it out of eastern Europe, but testing it from the Dayton base as a US 'X-5' painted with American insignia. When the testing was finished, the plane was then smuggled back inside the Iron Curtain.

The 'Black Yak' was followed only years later by a series of test of MiGs, called by the codenames Have Drill and Have Doughnut.

This was the work of the 4477th Test and Evaluation squadron, the Red Hats, who wore red stars on their patches, and the Air Technology Intelligence Center.

When Kelly Johnson had pushed for the Blackbird as a high altitude interceptor, he was thinking of war against the Soviet

Union, of fleets of incoming bombers, to be dispatched by
look-down-shoot-down radar, and missiles. Fighter combat was
largely envisioned by the Air Force in much the same terms: in
the future, the fighter bosses thought, encounters would take
place without the two opposing fighters ever seeing each other.
They would lock on by radar at long distance.

But with the war in Vietnam, dogfighting returned, with US
fighters facing North Vietnamese MiGs. The F-4 Phantom was
losing fights with MiGs at a disturbing rate – a Phantom
downed for every two MiGs.

After the Six Day War, the Israelis ended with a number of
the Soviet planes – captured by rapidly advancing troops, taken
from defectors or, in one case, captured after Libyan pilots
landed at a Sinai base they did not know had already been
taken by the Israelis. They are the probable source of the first
MiG to fly in Dreamland, a MiG 17 obtained by the Defense
Intelligence Agency in 1967. Later, the US would acquire – just
how remains mysterious – a MiG 21, Su-22s, 23s and MiG 23s –
even by the Nineties somehow an Su-27 Flanker, the most
advanced of all Russian aircraft.

After France cut off sales of Mirage fighters to Israel, placating
the Arab nations that provided its oil, the US made getting its
hands on some of the captured MiGs part of a deal that sent
US aircraft instead.

Soon there were enough rumours of the Soviet planes to
spark speculation in the ranks at Nellis and the men began
jokingly referring to the box of restricted air space around the
secret base as 'Red Square'. In time, the lessons learned from
the Soviet planes would be incorporated into the tactics of the
'Red' aggressor forces who took on each new class of Red Flag
pilots – and usually beat them first time.

In the project called Have Drill, the Red Hats flew the MiG-
17 over the desert from Groom Lake to figure out its strengths
and weaknesses. After dozens of simulated dogfights in the
Nevada skies, they learned the secret. The MiG, it turned out,
performed better than the Phantom at low speeds – it could
turn inside the F-4 every time – but if the F-4 pilot kept speeds
up, staying outside and behind, he could win. Using the tactics
developed at Groom, the Navy produced a film called *Throw A
Nickel on the Grass* (a line from an old Navy flier's song) and

brought in classes of pilots for reindoctrination.

By the end of the war the kill ratio had shifted to eight to one.

At the 1969 Tailhook convention in Las Vegas, the talk among the pilots turned to the MiGs. A number of admirals were flown up to Groom and put through their paces in the captured MiGs.

The whole Vietnam experience had made the assumptions of the Cold War nuclear stand-off irrelevant. Part of the war's wider exposure of the US' powerlessness was the failure of fighters that had been designed to shoot down Bison and Bear bombers.

In the Eighties, with more aircraft acquired through Afghanistan, a new programme called Constant Peg was set up at Tonopah. The Red Eagles, as they were called, were part of the same 4477th Test and Evaluation Squadron. They trained Navy as well as Air Force pilots and, after carrier-based fighters shot down two Libyan MiGs in 1989, a Pentagon spokesman bragged that the successful pilots had been trained to anticipate the enemy's tactics.

With the beginning of the collapse of the Warsaw Pact and the Soviet Union, the foreign technology boys could set their sights even higher. It was the military sale of all time, the Army and Navy surplus boom once in a lifetime. By 1993 the American taxpayer was spending half a billion dollars each year for 'foreign material acquisitions'.

Trader tracked down the cost of running one evaluation programme – he could rattle off the number by heart – 207248F. The programme behind the number was called STUDS, for 'special tactical unit detachments'. It is hard to believe than any overtones of this acronym are other than intentional. In the fiscal year 1993 to 1994, this programme went from $885,000 to $20 million, then to $118 million for 1995.

Many of the aircraft have probably come into the country by surreptitious sale or bribery and may even include advanced prototypes purchased from a renegade enemy general or engineer.

But there was a limit to the process – a classic Catch 22. All military systems are supposed to involve fair competition among different contractors or suppliers, with proper estimates.

But since the 'source' of the MiGs was not only 'sole', but secret and clandestine, the Pentagon could hardly hold competitions among corrupt Warsaw bloc colonies or Third World defectors.

14

Darkstar and El Mirage

'TUMBLEWEEDS CLEARED' READ THE ROADSIDE SIGN, A FAIR
indication of the nature of local enterprise. It was the desert east
of Palmdale, California, centre of the US high-tech aerospace
industry.

I had passed Plant 42 in Palmdale, where the B-2 bomber
was hatched. The new Skunk Works was nearby, its huge
hangars crisply painted in a grey worthy of the sharpest vessel
in the Navy.

The road ran east from 'Aerospace Valley', formally known
as the Antelope Valley, although no such animal has been seen
there for years. Instead, you saw still-wet new malls, K-marts
and fast food franchises, giving way to acres of turf and fruit
trees. The map showed a huge expanse of lettered avenues and
numbered streets, the projection of a vast city, dreamed of by
some wildly optimistic planners. It centred around a super
airport that had never been built; the map even showed its
runways and terminal sites.

It was like one of the Nazca earth markers that the von
Daniken people thought represented a landing strip for the
gods. It was a dream airport, as if they were ghost runways
for the phantom craft spotters saw there – the mothership,
the giant triangles, the bats and whales. An airport of the
imagination, I thought, like the airbase of the imagination
at Dreamland.

Then I caught in the corner of my eye the same evil-looking
shape I had seen at the boneyard many years ago. The spot was
Blackbird Park, a strip of grass near the Lockheed Skunk Works
where examples of its proudest works are parked: A-12 and SR-
71 Blackbird aircraft. Beside them sat the little craft I now knew
was a D-21 drone, an unmanned Blackbird, the last of the

Blackbirds, kept secret for years, which had flown from the back of an SR-71, then from beneath the wing of a B-52, to spy on China's Lop Nor atomic test site.

It was a transitional design between manned spy plane and 'drone' or UAV – unmanned aerial vehicle. The engineers called it a 'parasite', riding on the body of an SR-71. Once released from the back of the Blackbird, the D-21 would fly automatically, out of the control of any ground station, pass over a target – the denied area – and photograph it, then fly to a friendly country and land by parachute.

It weighed several tons, a chunky cylindrical shape with stubby wings and tail that clearly suggested the SR-71. It was like a larval version of the big craft. The whole project was called Tagboard.

The D-21 foreshadowed a new generation of UAVs. I wondered if many of the shapes flying out of Dreamland were not of this type. Unmanned craft could and did take on shapes that were – in the words of many observers of things flying above Groom – 'otherworldly'. Because they did not have cockpits or windows, because they did not need to provide protection for a human pilot, they could be more batlike or more saucer-shaped. They could even be pumpkin seed shaped.

Now those UAVs were emerging into the white world. They were unearthly looking, faceless. And there was evidence that many UAVs, flying secretly, had been seen as UFOs.

I drove past old ranches with corrals jerry-rigged from wire and discarded doors, beneath a sky as wide as the plain, looking for a very different kind of plane. I was heading for El Mirage. The dry lake there had long been a favoured spot for hot rodders and motorcyclists, who cut patterns into its surface. Like Groom and Muroc, it provided an excellent smooth surface for dune buggies and light aircraft. And for artists, it was a useful canvas. In the late Sixties and early Seventies earth artists had created temporary sculptures there. Inspired in part by the vast canvas of the desert, one had poured strips of asphalt on El Mirage in an X shape that looked from the air like the little x of the airstrips at Dreamland looked when Kelly Johnson and Tony LeVier had first flown over them. Another artist had sliced long trenches into the lake bed to define 'negative space' and what they called 'nonsite'. They, like the Air Force, were into non-sites.

I had just pulled up to the edge of the field and parked next to an old aircraft boneyard, when I caught sight of it: a tiny fleck that came closer, turning into what looked like a giant white paper plane, with wing tabs turned down, wheeling over the small airfield set amid greenery and desert. But the strangest thing was its nose: it had no cockpit, no windows – it looked blind.

There were no windows because there was no pilot. This was Predator, the most recent US UAV, flying for the CIA and the military, being tested at the desert airstrip of General Atomics, Inc., Predator's builder.

For a long time, we didn't even have a good name for these things. Once, they were dismissively called 'drones' then 'remotely piloted vehicles'. By the mid-Nineties, the term of choice is UAVs. A new generation of UAVs were arriving, relying on advances in electronics and computing, miniaturized sensors, cameras and relay systems. Today's UAVs are spy planes; tomorrow's may be fighters.

UAVs were a whole world of their own, a shadow of a shadow. Overlooked, ignored, they never attracted the attention of black planes.

But before they became fashionable, for how long had they been flying out of Dreamland?

No one knew, but somehow Lockheed had managed to develop Darkstar in a matter of months – and that name by interesting coincidence was the callsign Steve had heard in Roswell when Colin Powell inspected the Manta. Tier 3 – TR3. Was there a secret meaning here? Or just a general confusion?

And even the most famous of imagined Dreamland projects may have been a UAV: 'Glossary of Aerospace Terms and Abbreviations' in the September 1994 issue of *Air International*, claimed Aurora is an acronym for Automatic Retrieval Of Remotely-piloted Aircraft. And the builder of the huge Perseus UAV for NASA was a company called – Aurora. Was I becoming a conspiracist?

Hovering high above unfriendly countries, their proponents say, UAVs can relay video, radar or infrared images via satellite to distant ground stations, watching for anything that moves. 'Lingering' is the favourite term. The Predator, for instance, can fly 300 miles and spend up to two days in the air, where it is virtually invisible to the human eye and hard for radar to spot. (Despite a fifty-foot wing span, it shows up only as a square-metre radar 'signature'.)

The proponents of UAVs have proclaimed the dawn of a new era of aviation and a new kind of pilot – a new 'right stuff' of the future. The joystick in the cockpit may be replaced by one on the desktop and Top Gun may be replaced by Captain Nolo – traditional Air Force lingo for 'no live operator'.

Like robots of any sort, UAVs have the advantage of requiring no room and board, no training or food. They can pull more Gs than human pilots: already, fighter aircraft are limited in acceleration and deceleration, not by the strength of their air frames, but by the G-tolerance of the human body. Cases of 'temporary interruption of consciousness' – the old 'blackout' – have been suspected in several fighter crashes over the last few years. UAVs can't be held hostage, or suffer torture. Politically, they benefit from the new post-Cold War, post-Gulf War emphasis on inexpensive high-tech weapons that avoid putting human lives at risk.

The makers of the Predator, began as a company called Leading Edge, founded in a garage, like a Silicon Valley startup.

Pentagon infighting and Congressional dillydallying brought it to the edge of ruin. It was nearly broke when it was bought by the wonderfully-named General Atomics, a company whose primary business lies in the area of nuclear energy, from reactors to fusion research.

A few weeks before I saw my first UAV, Predators had shown off as part of Roving Sands, in a practice effort to spot 'Scuds', flying 25 flights in 26 days, high above the simulated 'battle-field' and almost invisible to ground observers. The Predator beams its information to a chase aircraft or ground station and will eventually be able to relay signals via satellites.

And a couple of days after I saw it in the air, it was reported that four Predators were on their way to the former Yugoslavia in order to conduct round-the-clock observation of forces on the ground. Predator, a so-called Tier II UAV, follows the Tier I 'Gnat 750' which was less successful when tried out by the CIA

from Bosnian and Albanian bases in 1996. Pilots have been
learning to fly the $1.6 million Predator by joystick and ground
control at Fort Huachuca, Arizona.

That afternoon I drove back west, straight up to the grey and
blue buildings of the Lockheed Martin Skunk Works – it was
the post-Cold War Skunk Works now, the new Skunk Works as
neatly groomed and carefully patrolled as any Hollywood set,
properly outfitted as the high holy of American aviation. I had
come to watch the unveiling of Darkstar, the newest UAV.

Inside the hangar called Building 602 – part of the legendary
Skunk Works – representatives were there to brief us. We had
been given Press packs in neat black folders. It was very efficient;
very commercial.

What I was about to look at, I was told, was Top Secret – for
a few more minutes. We were told that until 2:28 or whenever
the curtain is pulled back, 'the configuration is sight sensitive' –
it is officially classified. Not until then will we get pictures.

Lockheed, Boeing, DARPA and DARO are all partners in the
project and the craft, they tell us, will go from drawing board
to first flight in an unprecedently short twelve months.

'How,' I asked later, 'was such rapid development possible?
Were there other programmes that helped?'

'They were,' a spokesman said, 'able to rely on experience
from other programmes.'

'Could you tell what those programmes were?'

'I could,' he said, 'but I won't.' General laughter ensued.

The room was darkened. Then there was a great rumbling
sound from above. I looked up and saw that the yellow roof
crane that spanned the whole hangar was sliding slowly in the
dark, a cluster of orange lights on its centre, pulling the black
curtain back. As stirring music played, dry ice spread a soft and
ghostly fog around the craft: a white object that looked like
nothing so much as a flying saucer with a large porthole. It
took a few seconds to see that narrow wings grew from the
saucer. It was just like the roll-outs I had seen for new cars in
Detroit – music, stage effects, lights: technology as theatre.

Darkstar was the new so-called Tier-3 minus UAV. The 'Tier'
designations are ARPA 'procurement' project names, bestowed

by a law that gave DARPA special powers under new 'Section 845 – Other Agreements Authority', granted to ARPA by Congress, for prototype development outside the normal channels of Pentagon procurement procedures. The Tier designation delineated the pecking order of UAVs.

Predator is Tier I; Tier 2 plus was being constructed by Teledyne Ryan in San Diego. Tier 2 plus should be able to fly at 65,000 feet for 24 hours or more. Tier 3 was a mystery.

The Darkstar was to cruise at 180 miles per hour using a single jet engine buried inside what looks like the porthole. It could fly as high as 45,000 feet, where it surveys a huge area – some 1,600 square miles with Synthetic Aperture Radar or Electro-optical cameras. But its UFO-like shape makes it more stealthy than the Tier 2 plus. It had been, the briefers said, 'optimized for low observables' – made to look like a saucer to avoid radar detection.

From talking to Interceptors and the network, I had an idea what the other programmes might be. One was the stealthy cruise missile that had been tested at Dreamland. Another was Tier III itself, which the lore had it was also called 'Q'. According to various accounts it was a successor to the Aurora debacle, an offspring of Lockheed's unsuccessful, alternative design for what became the B-2 bomber. It had an 150- or 220-foot wingspan. Some said it was itself a debacle, with huge amounts of money wasted. Two had been constructed and flown, manned from the Groom Lake runway. It had been cancelled because the cost of each aircraft had risen to nearly a billion dollars.

After the smoke had faded, and the oohs and aahs reduced to silence, I talked to Major-General Ken Israel, the head of DARO the Defense Airborne Reconnaissance Office which, along with ARPA – the Advanced Research Projects Agency, which gave us the original stealth fighter – had developed Darkstar.

General Israel used to fly in an EB-66 probing Soviet electronics defences – an electronic spy plane. Now he quotes Shakespeare and touts the future of UAVs as a revolution in aviation, couched in the economic terms of today's cost-conscious Pentagon. Israel's leading arguments for UAVs are humanitarian: 'In the next century, we will definitely rely more on pilotless aircraft to place people out of harm's way.' But they are also couched in the terms of the new Pentagon fashion – 'infowar'.

'We need to know what's on the battlefield before we get on the battlefield,' said General Israel. With its ability to linger over a specific area, Israel says, a UAV can 'view the battlefield with impunity'. With this 'lingering' ability, UAVs can give the generals *real time* desktop infowar.

Look, too, Israel argues, at the 'cost of ownership'. The SR-71 Blackbird costs $38,000 an hour to fly, a U2 $6,000 an hour, but a UAV only $2,000 an hour.

The logic for UAVs had been obvious to some for years. Kelly Johnson himself, twenty years ago, predicted that the future of military aviation would belong to UAVs. They can outperform manned craft, pointed out the man who designed some of the best manned aircraft in history, because they can tolerate more Gs. And they cost less because they do not put a man at risk and do not have to carry systems to protect and nurture him.

'UAVs are part of the great American tradition of substituting technology for human beings,' says Randy Harrison of Boeing Aircraft, part of the Darkstar team. Boeing had built other UAVs, notably the huge Condor and Compass Cope craft. They even had a secret lake testing facility – their own mini Dreamland – at Moses Lake, Washington.

The Gulf War, and especially the difficulty of locating SCUDS on the ground, gave added impetus to UAV proponents.

While for most American TV viewers the Gulf War seemed a model of information efficiency and intelligence gathering, General Norman Schwartzkopf and other generals complained about their lack of 'real time' information. The cool images we saw of smart bombs riding lasers down air vents were actually gunsight films, carried back to base and developed. Real time information about enemy targets was much harder for the generals to get from space or the air. By the time satellite and other images reached the field from Washington, the tanks had often moved, and the Scuds been shifted.

This may be a classic case of fighting the last war, but it also offers an insight into the information war of the future.

Warmaking today is wrapped in the same clichés as private business – they talk at the Pentagon about information and re-engineering, downsizing and empowerment.

But still the image of the piloted plane is central to the Air Force. Which makes General Israel and his cohorts' strategy for achieving acceptance all the cleverer.

'We are like Billy Mitchell,' Israel told me, referring to the hero of the film *The Mitchell Story* – the prophet of air power – played by Gary Cooper, who was court martialled and became a martyr to the futuristic idea of dropping bombs on people in distant cities. Mitchell embarrassed the Navy by sinking ships with bombers. In the process, he laid the foundation for the firebombing of Europe and Japan and the atomic bomb and 'Bombs Away' Curt LeMay's Strategic Air Command. Now, those one-time rebels are saints in the Air Force pantheon and General Israel delights in identifying with them.

Israel and his friends imagine a future war in which batlike robot planes swoop and dive in the sky. The aspirations of UAVs to be real fighting aircraft is hinted at by their names: Hunter, Raptor, Talon, and Predator. Pretty aggressive for mere reconnaissance craft. There is no reason at all, Israel says, that UAVs could not take over the job of the manned interceptor – that Captain Nolo could not supplant Chuck Yeager. It is only a matter of time before unmanned interceptors – fighter planes without fighter jocks – joust with each other in some robot battle in the sky.

But before that, the next step will be to use UAVs as target designators: eyes in the sky that will 'paint' targets with lasers for smart bombs to ride down.

The incentive for the UAV to replace the fighter, for all our affection for the chivalry and heroism of the dogfight, also comes from the Gulf War, where it was made clear how sensitive we have become to any loss of human life. The Vietnam syndrome has been replaced by the Gulf War syndrome: total intolerance of casualties. And we are especially intolerant of the national humiliation occasioned by shot-down pilots who become prisoners, even hostages, to be displayed for the TV cameras.

Cases in point go back as far as the shooting down of Francis Gary Powers in 1960. But another conveniently popped up the very day after the Darkstar unveiling, when an F-16 was shot down over Bosnia carrying pilot Scott McGrady. With UAVs, it might be speculated, there would be less need to send aircraft over such areas, and considerably less chance of pilots becoming hostages or pawns.

Within a couple of days after McGrady was shot down, then rescued, the decision had been made to send the Predator over Bosnia.

Had they been used earlier, they might also have warned of the existence and location of SAMs on the ground ready to menace pilots.

The army had been testing the Predator and training pilots for it at Fort Huachuca, south of Tucson, near the Mexican border – not far, in fact, from where the plane itself was first used in war, in the excursion against Pancho Villa in 1911. This was for reconnaissance, but at that time few ever anticipated it would be useful for more.

Teledyne Ryan's Tier 2 plus, yet to fly, is a semi rival of Darkstar, with a less stealthy shape. There are civilian UAVs too, for research purposes; high altitude, long duration, experimenters such as NASA's Perseus, 'the poor man's satellite'. And if the Pentagon goes to war the next time with UAVs won't the TV networks need them too? They will be the high-tech equivalent of the news chopper, filming the fire, riots or skirmishes.

Studying the Darkstar closely was a man in a blue fatigue cap and pilot's leather A-2 jacket. Lt Col. Jim Greenwood was the RSO – the observer or backseat man in an SR-71 from 1986–90.

Now that the US dearth of aerial reconnaissance tools had led the Pentagon to pull the Blackbird out of mothballs, he was getting ready to fly again.

But in the meantime Colonel Greenwood had become a proponent of UAVs – one of the few within the Air Combat Command, the fighter pilot's command.

'It's a pilot's air force,' Greenwood admits. Some pilots will resist UAVs to their last breath. But as for computers replacing the 'human element' at the controls, Greenwood notes, that began long ago.

Computers fly planes much more often than pilots like to

admit. Many aircraft, such as the F-117 Stealth fighter, are unstable without controlling computers that interpret the movements of joystick and pedals. And airliners full of hundreds of human souls are more readily trusted to computer systems than to human pilots for bad weather landings at the world's major airports.

The first controllers for Darkstar, Greenwood told me, will be trained pilots.

'But in the future,' he adds, 'you might take people straight off the street and give them pilot training, and instrument rating and then have them stop flying real planes and go to UAV school.'

The prospect did not seem to faze the Colonel: video game stars taking over from Top Gun. All those kids – a great national resource. Safely on the ground, our boys will run robots – mechanical mercenaries.

'Gotta go,' he said. 'I've got a date with a T-38.' Not half an hour later, he was arcing skyward at a steep angle, in the sort of plane that may one day seem as quaint as a Sopwith Camel.

No one is quite sure yet whether the operator of a UAV is still a pilot. For Pioneer and Hunter, two simpler short range UAVs, there are two pilots. An 'external' pilot stands beside the runway like a model aircraft handler and gets the plane airborne and on its way. Then the 'internal' pilot, with a game-like joystick, pedals and video screen tied to the nose camera in the UAV takes over for the mission and returns the craft to the general area of the recovery zone. (Some UAVs are retrieved in nets rather than by landing on runways.)

He will plot the mission in advance or respond to video images from hundreds of miles away.

Captain Nolo – 'no live operator' – flew the drones of the past. Today's UAVs, however, don't necessarily need any pilot at all. Darkstar is programmed to roll out of the hangar, take off, fly its mission, land and return to the hangar without human intervention. The Predator, by contrast, is directed by a type of joystick. Darkstar's flight can be changed in mid course, but its interface is much less direct: a series of maps and graphs, a software system modified by mouse and keyboard.

*

The first official squadron of Air Force UAVs was taking shape in the Nevada desert, at Indian Springs, a disused World War II base on the edge of the Nuclear Test Site and the Nellis Air Force base test range: the 11 Reconnaissance Squadron, commanded by Colonel Steven L. Hampton. This, by happy chance, was also where Bob Lazar was debriefed. It was one of the places where legends had saucer wreckage stored.

After driving through the desert for miles, just south of Indian Springs I saw spots far off to the right. They grew from dots into armoured vehicles out on the dry lake named Dogbone. Air Force special operations people – commandos – trained here. There was even a mocked-up Third World village to practise door-to-door combat, like a movie set in the same grey and brown as the desert itself.

The little town of Indian Springs appeared a few miles further up the road, a welcoming string of trees, an oasis. From the distance as I pulled up I saw a dark helicopter heading one way, almost vanishing against the darkening mountain side, while a grey F-16 simultaneously came in for a touch and go.

I pulled up to where access roads parallel the main stream of Highway 95 whose traffic was rare, but high speed.

There, a row of signs for fraternal orders implied a population larger than the structures would suggest. To the left, on closer observation, sat a pitiful strip of houses and trailers, some with old cars in front, one with a mad garden junkyard, overgrown with vines. There's a school and not much else.

On the other side was the old base, used for bombers in World War II, sometime training spot for the Thunderbirds, and right beside it an RV park, a restaurant, a gas station and convenience store, and the inevitable Nevada casino.

I drove up to the base entrance. I remembered that this is where Lazar had said he was interrogated after coming under suspicion. I looked around for the sort of building where that might have taken place, and saw none. It was also where B-29s and B-50s had departed carrying A-bombs to drop over the test site, and some of the buildings seemed little changed since the early Fifties. It was a desolate, somewhat seedy, place. Standard wooden barracks and offices: few people in evidence at all. Groom Lake might have looked like this in the first half of the Sixties.

But there was a new temporary hangar, with a kind of inflated structure behind. The base was to become the home of the new 11th Reconnaissance group, flying Predator UAVs and eventually, it was planned, Darkstar.

A few months later, I ventured back to Indian Springs: the Air Force had agreed to let me meet the pilots of the Predator UAV.

The base had now come alive, like a summer house opened up after long winter. The Eleventh Recon was operating, flying Predator UAVs.

On the road up, by happy chance, there was a demonstration of our aerial military might in the desert. The officers escorting me agreed to stop so we could watch and admire.

The Air Force calls these demonstrations 'Capstone': they take place every few months. VIPs from other services, Congressional aides and others are bussed to a viewing area in the desert. There they sit decked out in hats and sunglasses, as if at a high school football game, while the desert targets are attacked – once more, your tax dollars at work.

First the stealth fighters came in, then the Warthogs, finally F-16s and B-1s, their sticks of bombs falling like a liquid. Brown clouds, edged with ominous grey, slowly blossomed on the desert and six or seven seconds after each blast the shock wave would reach us there by the side of the road. As passing drivers saw the planes out in the distance, more and more of them would stop until soon there was a whole crowd parked along the highway.

It was a fine show, with targets no bloodier than a 'smokey SAM' flare on the desert floor. But if the UAV proponents were right, I thought, that robot attack planes would soon join robot spy planes in the Air Force, then this demonstration could be seen as a kind of elegy for a passing mode of aerial warfare.

'Some good smash,' said one of the military men standing beside me. He was enjoying it greatly. It occurred to me that many of the military types were so stolid that they only reacted to the really big stuff, the huge sky, the big war, the end of civilization as we know it. These were weapons to kill, after all.

In the very facility where Bob Lazar says he was interrogated by the security folks from S-4, in the place where the lore had saucer wreckage stored, there were trailers full of spanking new Pentium computers, desks and filing cabinets. Only one Top Secret sign.

I got the tour of the refurbished hangar and was even invited into the mess – just called 'the dining hall' in the new Air Force. The pork loin with apples was not bad at all. I sat with UAV pilots just back from Bosnia and they explained how much flying an aircraft from a desk was like flying it from the cockpit. A pilot just back from Hungary, where the Predators flying over Bosnia were based, told me that sometimes he finds himself leaning left or right, as if still in a real cockpit, in a real plane.

They tracked tanks and artillery to insure compliance with the complex agreements worked out by UFOR. Directed by the pilots, who live in tents in Hungary, they rode shotgun over the shoulders of the patrols of HummVees that head up into the hills, lingering above for hours, looking for ambushes ahead.

They fly the Predators in two-hour shifts, a tall, boyish captain told me. 'There's still a lot of stick and rudder work.

'It's the unexpected that makes this job interesting.'

Sometimes the weird white bird would ice up in the cold wet air. Sometimes things go wrong mechanically. A couple of days after I spoke to the pilots, one of their fellows had to land a Predator after it developed mechanical problems in a field in the former Yugoslavia. Unfortunately the field was a mine field. The captain avowed, somewhat wistfully, that he knew the 'next generation' would make him obsolete.

15

'The Remote Location'

'LONG AGO,' THE GENERAL'S SPEECH BEGAN, 'IN A GALAXY FAR
far away . . .' – a reference to the movie *Star Wars* that may or
may not have been freighted with implicit criticism of the $40
billion weapons programme of the same name.

This was outside the Air Force Museum in Dayton, where the
plane that would later be nicknamed Shamu would reside from
now on. It had travelled from suspicion to memory by the
shortest possible route. It was going from one museum – at
Groom Lake, open to only the handful of officers with all the
needed clearances – into another. As a result this ceremony was
an odd proceeding, half confession, half celebration. A black
plane was coming into the light. A plane that had flown only
at Dreamland was awakening to curiosity.

On the back of the chair in front of me were stencilled a
collection of numbers and letters and the words 'USAF chair
folding'.

Like Darkstar, like the Stealth prototype, Have Blue, this was
a DARPA project: Tacit Blue, a Northrop stealth demonstrator,
had first flown in 1982, and it had tested some of the round
stealthy shapes that showed up later on the B-2 bomber. Steve
had let me know in advance something like this was coming:
he had hoped it would be the TR-3A.

Interceptors were there in number. A man with a name I
knew only from the Internet, where he provided the most
detailed of specifications of aircraft present and past, wore a
Lockheed Skunk Works T-shirt, a bit tactless considering this
was a Northrop project. He took pictures of everything that
moved, including one of the cargo planes that flew overhead,
then looked around a little sheepishly.

When the curtain was drawn back, it was clear this was the

ugliest aircraft most of the audience had seen. It looked like someone's effort to build a big fibreglass boat from magazine plans, abandoned halfway through.

From the rear, it was shaped like some sort of modern architectural model, something out of Brasilia say, the exhaust vent a rising curve, like a concrete amphitheatre.

It was long with stubby wings, hard to put the shapes together in your head to make a whole you could imagine flying.

It looked like Shamu – the star whale of Ocean World – and the nickname stuck. The men who built it called themselves whalers, for that reason, and even wore little lapel pins in the shape of a whale. That way, they could go out into the soft liberal world full of save-the-whale types and blend right in.

They had worked in a hangar beside the Stealth prototype called Have Blue. For a long time, each of the two groups was forced to stay inside while the other was outside with its plane: special access, need to know. It was the other team, getting a glimpse, that called it the Whale.

And whale was right: for the Interceptors this was a kind of Moby Dick, a great white whale of a genuine mysteriously flying object, long-sought, long-denied, long legendary and mythical as are all mystery planes, now finally admitted. But reality had replaced mystery here with a thud: the physical object was rough and ugly.

It was also weird. And the first thing I thought after seeing it was: who describing such a thing floating over his head would have been believed? Who seeing it could not have had his certainty that all flying objects were of terrestrial origin at least shaken? I wondered if many more strange objects might not be flying somewhere. With revelations as surprising as this, were we to believe that there was indeed no Hangar 18, here at Wright Patt or elsewhere, where bodies, creatures, parts, wreckage might be? Who seeing this craft might not read a little less sceptically such accounts as that of 'UFO researcher' Robert Collins, picked up off the Net, with their elaborate maps and descriptions of multiple underground levels at Wright-Patt, with alien material, inside sources and infrared photography?

'There was a remarkable *esprit*' to the project, the speeches all agreed. It was an esprit born of the isolation of 'the remote location', the silence of the black world, the camaraderie of the initiate. 'We even did our phenomenology work in remote locations,' said Steve Smith, who was one of the top managers for Shamu.

Patriotism drove the project even though it was not actually war time. Steve Smith recalled 'a strong sense of patriotic urgency with respect to Warsaw Pact nations at that time'. In other words, the fear of a big offensive in Europe that would overwhelm the Allied ground forces and force the US to go nuclear.

'There's a reception inside under the B-36,' the Museum chief said, and the Whalers headed inside to stand under the wing of the huge plane – the B-36 I had grown up with – the huge brontosaurus of a bomber. This one, I noted from a sign, was the last ever to fly, when it was ferried on 30 April 1959, from the Boneyard at Davis-Monthan to Dayton.

At the reception, Steve Smith explained how when he was in Iran in the 1970s helping the Shah's Air Force with its new F-20s, a call came from his boss. He was being sent back for a special project, but could know nothing else until he was 'brought in'.

He was briefed on the third floor of a dark garage in a hotel in the San Fernando Valley, he recalled, 'like Deep Throat. It was real cloak and dagger stuff.'

The man in charge was named Jack Twigg, an Air Force colonel, detached to DARPA. Twigg is perfect for the part, looking as if he is laughing at some private joke, an enthusiast. Twigg never wore anything but a sports coat, shirt and tie, Smith recalled. 'Everyone thought he worked for us, for Northrop.'

But when the aircraft emerged, he emerged with it, having changed now into his uniform. There was a huge American flag on the wall, Smith recalled, and the applause was huge, 'the patriotic fever was tremendous'.

Most of the wives and many children were at the ceremony. And that illuminated something it was easy to pass over lightly: that working in secrecy diminished the lives of the workers and often put them in sticky situations. It's not just that they couldn't answer the question, 'Daddy, what did you do at work today?' but that their whole family lives could be jeopardized by the black hole of non disclosure, which could fill like an abscess with suspicion.

The question could never be avoided: was it really the job or something else? A guy could be making it all up because he had a bimbo in Burbank, a floozy in Floral Park – hell, a whole second family someplace, a bad gambling habit or an unsavoury job with organized crime. And there were cases of con artists who pretended to be working in Dreamland, or some other secret facility, or for the Skunk Works. It could be an especially convenient scam when divorce impended.

Was there any sharper symbol of the isolation of the black world than the 'hello' phone, the one-way dead-end telephone number that families of those working at secret facilities like Dreamland are given? They are to call in case of emergency and leave a message. Then they will be called back. But no one is ever to answer the phone with anything other than hello.

In *Blue Sky Days*, his memoir of growing up with a father who worked in SAR programmes, David Beers gives a child's viewpoint of it. His father worked for Lockheed's missile division, near the mysterious Blue Cube, the spy satellite control centre, in Sunnyvale. During the 1980s, the father worked on Star Wars projects in a place that may very well have been Dreamland.

> ... he was gone for days and weeks to a place the mysterious people on the phone called The Ranch.
>
> 'Hal there?' an extremely serious male voice would ask whoever picked up the receiver at my parents' house.
>
> 'No. Can I tell him who called?'
>
> 'Tell him Gunner called. From The Ranch. He'll know.' Click.
>
> What was this Ranch where Ronald Reagan had created new work for my father and for 'Gunner' and for how many more? My mother and her children were curious, of course, but we had only the slimmest of details with which to construct a mental picture. We knew a man would find himself in some very high and precarious places at The Ranch, because one time my father returned wearing a

strange pair of glasses, clunky plastic frames bought off a drugstore rack. He had lost his, he said, 'while stepping onto a catwalk. I bumped my head and off came my glasses. I heard them hit the floor, about, oh, eight to ten seconds later.' My father smiled as he said this, smiling as he tended to smile when he had just told you something that was very intriguing but just shy of violating his security oath.

We knew The Ranch was a place that could be very dark, because another time my father came back with a scabbed cut in his forehead. All he would tell us is that he had been driving across some dim landscape in the middle of the night in a rental car with the lights off and he had run into something and his head had been thrown forward into the steering wheel. 'Why were you driving in the dark with no lights?' his wife and children wanted to know. But his answer was a smile.

That was the cost of working in Dreamland. Divorce rates were very high among engineers and managers in black programmes, and at first for a pilot to join the Stealth fighter programme, where all the flying was at night and weeks ended in weekend exhaustion, almost guaranteed the end of his marriage.

Indeed this seemed to be the key reason for the whole ceremony and the whole revelation of the plane. At last the wives and the children, now grown, could be told. It was not easy. In the Seventies, after Watergate and Vietnam, doing secret things for the government was very far from implying noble and patriotic endeavour. 'All normal methods of communication are avoided, all identities and relationships are denied,' Smith said. 'Total isolation is the goal, and this caused hardship.'

The human effects of the black world were perfectly symbolized by the Air Force's efforts to repeal the laws of the circadian cycle when it first began operating the Stealth fighter at Tonopah.

To keep its shape unseen and secret, it flew only at night. As a result the pilots slept during the day. When they returned home at weekends, they would either continue to sleep all day, ignoring their families, or try, usually in vain, to switch the sleeping schedules, leaving them groggy and irritable. They felt like vampires, some said. Most married pilots in the programme ended up divorced. And their flying suffered as well. Some pilots complained of a nagging exhaustion that would not go away. One of them was Ross Mulhare, who died in a July 1986 Stealth fighter crash near Bakersfield. He had apparently flown into a hillside with no indication of mechanical problems. Mulhare's family were not, of course, aware of what he was doing during the days he disappeared into the desert south of Tonopah, but they did know that he had to take a lie detector test every three months.

Need to know. Special Access Required. Specially Compartmentalized Intelligence – the rules of the black world are designed so that those inside Dreamland are kept there as strictly as we outside are kept out.

To spy you must agree to be spied on. To create a spy plane, you must agree to have your phone tapped, take lie detector tests, have your background and clearance reviewed every five years.

Those who work on black projects must sign an agreement to respect the secrecy of information protected within Special Access Programs called Sensitive Compartmented Information. These agreements, which for earlier programmes were carried out under the Reagan era Executive order 12356, involve an explanation of the system and 'indoctrination'. Those inside understand they can be punished – fined and sent to prison for years – under sections 793, 794, 798, and 952 of Title 18 of the US Criminal Code.

Second-hand accounts of the black world abound with tales of persuasive briefings punctuated by the near proximity of the muzzle of an M-16 rifle and shouting into the subject's face. You will disappear, they are told – the conspiracists infer death threats. Even one former Red Hat flyer simply took it for granted, as he had been told, that people who talked about the programme would disappear.

But the real teeth of the system, the tools for ensuring secrecy are much more mundane: the threat of the end of career, of loss of pension, the regular administration of polygraph tests, the monitoring of phone calls and mail, the careful registration and tracing of the disposition of controlled documents and computer files. The Office of Special Investigations or FBI may also tap phones and watch the movements of employees and even family members.

With these, it is much easier to keep secrets than one would think.

At first the black world was one of intelligence – information. But beginning with the Manhattan Project, black methods were applied to the development of hardware – not just knowing things, but building them. The Western Development Division of Air Research and Development in 1951, the first US effort to develop an ICBM, was another early black programme. Funding for these comes from budgets with codenames or vague headings. Some like the U-2, were paid for by various CIA funds, but the CIA is only one of some 38 US intelligence agencies, departments and divisions, and its \$2 billion budget is dwarfed by that, say, of the National Security Agency.

Today, whole categories of operations are black as well: the SIOP (single integrated operating plan) for fighting a nuclear war, 'continuity of government' plans for post-nuclear war plans, or anti-terrorist operations, for instance.

The biggest misunderstanding about secrecy is that it is a matter of levels – higher clearance gives access to more stuff. In fact, the key is not vertical but horizontal – in compartmentalization. The engineers building a stealth fighter are separated from those building a laser weapon: being cleared for one highly secret project does not mean access to another.

For this reason, the black system was developed with almost scholastic rigidity. Beyond such commonly known stamps as Top Secret or Classified, are code warnings like WINTEL: Warning Notice – intelligence sources and methods involved; ORCON – originator controls access and distribution; NORFORM – meant not to be seen by foreign nationals; NO CONTRACT – not to be seen by contractors.

Categories of information had names different from the sources of that information – it was part of the compartmentalization process. Such names were almost a parody of themselves. Readers of John Le Carré will be familiar with the use of separate codenames for a body of intelligence information and for its source. For example, material called 'Witchcraft' is produced from a source called 'Merlin'.

In the fully developed Cold War system, categories of intelligence had names like Umbra and Spoke. Gamma was the name for intercepts of various Soviet communications. (It was also applied in 1969 to the programme of spying on high-profile American protestors against the Vietnam War.) A whole host of 'G' words – Gant, Gabe, Gyro, Gut, Gult, Goat – some real words, some made up, were used for specific categories of these intercepts. Gamma Gupy, for instance, was the name for tapped telephone conversations of Soviet leaders being driven around Moscow in their limos. It seemed to consist largely of gossip about their various mistresses.

Secret hardware programmes got special names, like the Byeman names for spy satellites. The U-2 was Aquatone and Idealist. Discoverer covered Corona, the first spy satellite.

But it was in the naming of research programmes by the services and by such agencies as DARPA that the new tone of the black world emerged: in names such as Teal Rain and Have Blue.

There is something else, however, that works to protect secrecy: a sense of fraternity, the qualities of a secret society. A sense of belonging to something special. ('Special' is a key word in the Pentagon. Special weapons are nukes, Special operations are commandos.) To define a group, a cult, a religion, not only are certain key words used, but certain words are NOT used. In the black world, there are terms not to be spoken, like the name of God. You never say Groom Lake, you say, the Ranch, or 'the Remote Location'. And rarely do you even say black.

There were also active efforts to penetrate security – like LeMay's old security testers in SAC – and others listening to family phone calls and watching employees to see that the penetrators were not succeeding.

'There were many efforts to do this,' one of the Whalers told me and he added proudly, 'To my knowledge, none of them were successful.'

'Were there also,' I asked 'active disinformation efforts or cover stories?'

'You'd have to ask the professionals about that,' he answered.

Besides the little lapel whale badge, many of the whalers wore another pin, a diamond arrowhead-like shape, icon of the

Pioneers of Stealth, the loose organization of black world engineers who had worked on stealth and now met for occasional reunions, the competition of working for different contractors now put aside in a wave of nostalgia.

To the Interceptors, all this lent the hope that there were more craft that the Air Force and contractors had been denying and hiding, that might emerge soon. Like the Manta or Aurora – other unidentified flying craft. Like Q or the Tier III, perhaps.

I hung around several of the pioneers, and eavesdropped as they talked about their next reunion. Two of them were talking about the conclave. I gathered an invitation for myself would not be forthcoming. I did not speak up but listened. They discussed who might be attending. Several names were mentioned. Then one asked the other. 'And who should we invite from Q?'

Before the ceremony I had walked around the base and the museum, trying to understand how Tacit Blue fitted in to the aviation history laid out there like a diagram.

Today the base is huge – it is three airfields in all – and is the centre of the Air Force Systems command, the MIT and Cal Tech of aviation high tech. It is also the home of the Foreign Technology section – perfect for investigating captured MiGs and, the youfers believed, wreckage from Roswell or other saucer crashes.

I was surprised by how open and green it felt. I had not realized that the base had been built around Huffman Prairie, the Wright Brothers' flying field.

Even if there is no Hangar 18, no 'level 5' where the Roswell bodies are supposed to be kept on ice, there were plenty of buildings that looked right for the part: odd tanks and pipes, cubes and spheres, weird shaped windtunnels, all decorated with wisps of mysterious vapour.

The Air Force Museum – 'where eagles rest' – trades on sentiment, but lovingly and thoughtfully. It felt almost cosy, dark and full of parked aircraft. A shrine to Billy Mitchell, including his gloves and binoculars; leather hats of World War I fliers, jet age helmets and ejection seats – all of it being poked over by grizzled veterans.

Above the larger planes – in the flies, so to speak, of the opera – almost unnoticed, hang uncelebrated little cruise missiles and early UAVs like Tacit Rainbow. These are mammals beside the dinosaurs, the up and coming species. But these do not scamper underfoot. They fly above.

Outside in the grounds is a strange park-like area set with monuments to various units of the Air Force and individuals. Among these, almost unnoticed, is a plaque dedicated to Alexander de Seversky, the pioneer of 'air power'. The ideologue of it all was marked by a lonely stone, hidden among the others.

16
The Anthill

THE MYTH OF HANGAR 18 IN DAYTON HAD CONTINUED TO grow. No report of it has failed to mention Senator Barry Goldwater's inability to gain access to the building, even with his top clearance. He famously tried to get Curtis LeMay himself to let him in. On the Internet, Robert Collins had recently posted an elaborate report on 'underground vaults at WPAFB', based on inside sources and infrared photography.

At Wright-Patt they find all this exasperating. They receive inquiries daily. When Frank Kuznik, reporter for *Air & Space*, visited the base for a story, he found irritated scientists, tired of dealing with the inquiries. No, there was no Hangar 18 or any vaults full of bodies. But if there was, 'do you think we'd tell you? Don't you think we'd be able to hide it?' Certainly, there was enough well hidden material – captured weaponry and electronics, some of it on the base, some hidden elsewhere. Another scientist declared that he wished they did have something alien to put on display, because at just a dollar a head they would make enough money to solve his budget problems.

Long before Area 51 meant anything, Hangar 18 had seeped into popular consciousness. Now Area 51 was becoming a larger version of Hangar 18.

But around Dreamland, deeper darker vaults were suspected.

John Lear held that the Skunk Works had moved from Burbank, not to Palmdale, but to Tejon Canyon, the Northrop RCS range west of Palmdale, the better to hide sinister projects. To him and to others that facility was the 'Anthill', where aliens ruled, incubating hybrid humans, gathering abductees for their vital enzymes. Deep in the night, these watchers say, the portals open to emit flying saucers from structures beneath that extend five, ten, even fifty storeys below the ground.

According to the erstwhile self-appointed expert on Area 51, the leader of expeditions to the perimeter, Gary Schultz, of Secret Saucer Base Expeditions; 'we have found out with incontrovertible proof' that the RCS is only a cover, that the Anthill has forty-two levels underground. There were reports of mysterious blue beams and 'surveillance orbs the size of basketballs'.

Schultz had flown over it in September, 1991. He had seen evidence of concrete being poured twenty-four hours a day for weeks – a million cubic yards of concrete.

But the sceptic asks, where were all the cement mixers lined up? And where was all the dirt?

Those who believed in the underground bases suspected not only the Anthill, but all the RCS facilities. These strange installations look like Dreamland should look, but doesn't: they have mysterious tilting concrete walls, diamond-shaped pads and panels, shadowed overhangs, James Bond-like facilities of the sort that leap to the imagination at the very utterance of the phrase Area 51. They are the radar cross section facilities of the western deserts, the local chapels of stealth, landmarks of the Greater Dreamland: Gray Butte, Tejon Canyon, Helendale, China Lake, White Sands. Hey kids, collect 'em all! And the Interceptors did – they would make trips to the facilities. Tom Mahood even tracked down their ownership in real estate registers and public records.

From the air, they are especially sinister, with runways painted with the words, 'Restricted Runway Do Not Land.'

There is a similar facility – perhaps the largest – inside Dreamland, behind the base itself.

What RCS facilities do is test how hard new aircraft are for radars to see. Each major aerospace contractor has one. In such facilities, models of new aircraft or missiles are set on pylons and test radars are beamed at them. Other aircraft might fly overhead, testing their onboard radars. The tilted walls contain and control the deployment of the radar waves. Engineers measure the way aircraft reflect radar beams, how much and in what direction.

To protect against overflights by nosy satellites, some of the models can be quickly moved inside walls with sliding doors or covers placed over them.

Such is the most practical and banal explanation of the

facilities. But to those less trusting, the RCS sites are actually openings to underground bases, portals to an underworld of secret treaties and alien takeovers.

To Richard Sauders and William Hamilton, the two leading underground theorists, even Plant 42 in Palmdale had secret floors beneath it. In Hamilton's book *Cosmic Top Secret* and video *Underground Bases*, he claims that the first saucer wreckage came to Area 51 in the late Forties and the first underground labs were built at that time. They have expanded ever since. He describes whole baseball diamonds and swimming pools beneath the surface.

In manner, Hamilton is disarmingly non-fanatical. As seen in the video, he could be lecturing the class on post-Keynesian developments in macro-economics. But Hamilton has his sources. They tell of things beneath the surface. 'Thomas C.' describes not only a whole network of tunnels, but also a virtual underground interstate system in the West.

For proof, Sauders and Hamilton offer plans for underground command posts, living quarters and diagrams of tunnel-boring machines from a 1959 report from RAND or the Army Corps of Engineers, organizations which at the height of the Cold War were ordered to figure out how to put practically everything underground. It was the era of the Gaither commission, when concern with civil defence was running high: the fallout shelter fad was about to begin. Living underground was once not considered so far-fetched – or so sinister.

The Collins report on 'underground vaults at WPAFB' begins with unconscious humour: 'As a preamble note I wish to emphasize to the reader that this "Vault Report" is just the tip of a greater iceberg that contains truths from many sources.'

The iceberg analogy was as clichéd as the principle that the underground represented the unconscious. But in the world of those who believe in the underground bases, the analogy is more detailed and specific. To them, physical levels are indications of levels of information and security; but also perhaps of psychic levels: the deeper the facility is dug, the deeper the conspiracy.

Underground is as heavily metaphorical as you could wish. The place of the unseen, it's the realm of death. It's the place of Christians in the catacombs, giant ants in tunnels, like those in the classic Fifties science fiction film, *Them!* The idea of the underground base as hive or anthill is common – areas are 'honeycombed' with tunnels. *Them!*, a parable of the red menace, was echoed in the more recent TV show *Dark Skies* with its designation of the alien origination as The Hive. (In the film's best, and in a sense only, genuinely human moment the little girl who has been terrified by the giant ants – the offspring of radiation, of course – is examined by doctors, nurses and scientists. When she accidentally gets a sniff of formic acid, the stuff of ant stings, she begins screaming uncontrollably: 'Them! Them! Them!')

Thinking of *Them!* I drove west from Edwards toward the Anthill, which was one of the places that was supposed to be teeming with aliens. From the Trader I learned how to get there.

At last when the odometer showed I was close, I stopped and parked, then scrambled up a hill. I could see over the horizon all that was to be seen: a couple of buildings, a radio antenna or two, a watertank. No signs of underground structures. No air vents, no strange doors. All I saw were signs of new water management facilities – canals and culverts. Nothing suspicious. But that was the whole point: the underground was a version of that oldest of menaces, the unseen.

If the depth of the underground systems corresponded to the depth of the projected conspiracy they housed, connections among them represented the extent of hidden links. Tunnels, the theorists argued, linked the sites together – the sinister hidden connections made physical. The accounts included stories of workers who had ridden the rails from the beach in Los Angeles to Area 51, with connections available for Los Alamos and Sandia. Were Amtrak so well run it would put the Japanese bullet train and the French TGV to shame.

So Area 51 connects with Edwards and Sandia and Los Alamos – even with the most terrifying of the projected underground facilities, Dulce, on the Archuleta Mesa, in New Mexico. There the multiple levels include one, Level 4, which is concerned with telepathy and dream control. Level Six or Seven holds the vats with the embryos of half-breed alien humans and grotesque genetic experiments. It is known in the Lore as Nightmare Hall.

The underground conspiracy buffs tend to equate security with physical levels. Twenty-four or 38 levels of underground installations correspond to the same number of levels of 'clearance'. This is, of course, a strong suggestion of the metaphorical nature of their assumptions. Their accounts of insider reports of secret facilities always seem to talk about levels of clearance corresponding to floors of the installation. But in the real black world, it's not just a matter of higher or lower clearance from sensitive to secret to Top Secret to 'Q', but of separation on the same level: of different rooms on the same floor – compartmentalization, need to know. In reality, not only is there distinctions on levels, but distinction in rooms, so to speak, on the same level.

In their descriptions, the lorists seem especially concerned with doors. They minutely describe access panels, as if they were film designers. Sliding cards, retinal readers, weight-triggered access doors – there's a lot of detail on this sort of thing. Many door controllers or speakers are in the shape of an inverted triangle. The inverted triangle is linked in other parts of the tales to the trilateralists and implicitly to the existence of layers below the surface: the inversion of the pyramid on the dollar bill, and the great Seal.

The ultimate end of underground theories is to see the whole Earth as hollow, to imagine not just a hell beneath our feet but the Earth itself as a mere shell. This, the ultimate version of conspiracist theory, has Nazis flying the saucers they developed into the centre of the Earth through hidden portals at the poles. 'Commander X', a former 'Military Intelligence Operative' and author of *Underground Alien Bases* has the Nazis colonizing the centre of the Earth in co-operation with the 'Serpent People' – aliens. The 'Thule Society' was the spiritual arm of the Nazi party. Commander X believes that: 'In reality, many of the craft seen over Area 51 in Nevada are not constructed by aliens. They are instead experimental vehicles derived from the secret plans of Nazi scientists, many of whom were brought to the US and given political asylum, even though they may have taken part in vicious war crimes'. The Nazis perfected anti-gravity and time-warp transportation, and landed on the Moon before 1945.

Hollow Earth theories are as old as the Egyptians of course, but as recently as the nineteenth century they were taken with some seriousness in the United States. The hollow Earthers populated the centre of the Earth with all the features and creatures later theorists and science fiction would move to the planets. Before there was an expectation of space travel, the interior of this planet was the most distant region imaginable. So a *Journey to the Centre of the Earth* would give way to *A Trip to the Moon*.

In 1819 John Cleves Symmes propounded his theory that the Hollow Earth contains five concentric lands. James McBride explained it all in the 1820s in *The Symmes Theory of Concentric Spheres*, demonstrating that the Earth is hollow, habitable, with openings around the poles. One writer of the time imagined the place inside as 'a white land', full of the whitest of humans. In the 1830s an odd character named Jeremiah Reynolds began promoting a South Pole expedition to prove Symmes' theory. Amazingly, he prevailed upon the government to fund – not one, but two – such expeditions. One result was the production of very useful marine charts of the southern waters. Another was to inspire Edgar Alan Poe to write such stories of possibly hollow worlds as *Manuscript Found in a Bottle*, *Descent into the Maelstrom* and *The Narrative of A. Gordon Pym*.

To see the Earth as 'hollow' was ultimately a vision of profound despair. It meant we literally could not trust the ground on which we stood. It meant life itself was empty. Edward Shils wrote of 'the torment of secrecy', the pain of those who believed that all history took place behind a veil of some kind of conspiracy, that the real motive forces in the world are unseen, perhaps undiscoverable. This is a hard philosophy to live with.

Helendale, the largest of the RCS facilities, was built the most recently. It was huge, with its own runway, near which Aurora was thought to have been spotted, and its main radar area, with the sinister name of the Upper Chamber, seemed to cover acres of concrete.

To reach it, I cut through from the highway that ran east of Edwards, then drove over the white sandy bed of the erstwhile

Mojave river, past trailers and little houses. From the road, I could see the distant hangar – Lockheed yellow – and turning up the road came to the fence and gate that barred the way.

But shoved up practically against that fence, I caught sight of a place called Exotic World, a museum of burlesque, the home of an old stripper who has collected the G strings of the great strippers of the past.

Months later, I came across one of those offbeat local colour features TV news loves so much. It showed a beat-up little trailer and fence I thought I recognized. It was Exotic World! There was a nice soundbite from the former stripper who owns it: 'Striptease was not invented,' she was saying. It just happened, when someone caught a glimpse of a dancer pushed out on to stage too soon.

'Striptease', she said, 'is a phenomenon and phenomenons are not made, they just happen.'

I thought of the Air Force general, explaining how a secret aircraft should reveal itself only gradually and seductively. Striptease was about imagination, more than revelation, and so were the RCS sites. Phenomena just happened there. I wondered if a visit to Exotic World didn't say more about the workings of secret aircraft than would standing on the concrete of Helendale's Upper Chamber itself.

17

The Decentral Intelligence Agency

JOHN LEAR DROVE TO DREAMLAND IN A DETROIT DREAM machine. In September, 1978, he got behind the wheel of his Lincoln Mark IV, and drove to the edge of Groom Lake. At that time, the perimeter still ran along the lake edge and the mountains and road were public land.

Lear had long known about the base, about the U-2 and the Blackbird and now he had heard rumours that something else was flying. Ahead of him, the rank of hangars that once held the Blackbirds was visible along with a couple of aircraft – a MiG on the flight line, and a transport plane.

He had brought a camera and quickly snapped off a few shots and watched. 'Then a half hour later this klaxon goes off and we see a little trail of dust.' Two vehicles, heading his way.

Lear quickly finished the film and took it out of the camera. 'I rolled the film up and put it in the ashtray of the Mark IV and put another roll in the camera and shot the same thing again.

'A black guy in a red car came up shouting. "What in the hell do you think you are doing?"

'I decided to play it as cool as possible.

' "So we're not supposed to be here, right?"

'Then I went into a whole line of BS. "My Dad did the autopilot for the U-2, and I've got a lot of good friends in the SR 71 and so on.

' "I used to live near the airport in Burbank and we would always see those three Constellations that went up here."

'The guard calmed down.

' "Do you have film?" he asked.'

Lear pulled the film out of the camera and gave it to him.

He promised not to intrude again and was allowed to leave. Then he promptly drove to Los Angeles, had the real film developed and made big 18 by 20 prints. The image that resulted – a black and white panorama of the base from across the dry lake, which was actually covered with a thin layer of water at the time, would become famous, although so many buildings have been added at Groom that today the picture makes the place seem as crude and primitive as a town from the old West.

John Lear once wrote. 'I can't tell you what the truth is ... I'm not sure such a thing exists. If it does exist, the truth is hidden in an incredibly complex, labyrinthine hall of mirrors with floors of quicksand leading to truly frightening bizarre and awesome events which have been going on for billions of years, if not eternity.' John Lear's writings are apocalyptic, almost hysterical, but in person or on the phone he is charming and reasonable.

He is the son of Bill Lear, who lent his name to the Lear Jet. Growing up he had a very difficult relationship with his father, the aviation pioneer who created some 150 major innovations in radio and control systems, along with the eight-track audio tape, as well as the jet that bears his name.

John Lear's telephone answering machine does not give his name or number. But in his voice, it offers the following recording 'To leave a message for Area 51 push one, to leave one for S-4 push two. The Tonopah Test Range is temporarily unavailable.'

Lear comes on the line, fumbling. He is a top flight pilot, he has flown more than 160 types of aircraft in fifty countries, but he can't figure out the goddam machine and he jokes about it. More often these days he is to be found in the Holiday Inns of distant airports, when he is not in the air, in the pilot's seat. He has had a hard time keeping a job since he became one of the most visible viewers of Dreamland and proponent of UFO theories.

Born in 1942, before war work made his father rich, he was alternately spoiled and abused. From the age of 12, he could barely manage to speak to his father and family meals terrified him. John's father would begin by speaking tenderly but quickly rise to a harangue over some failure of his.

The Lears spent a lot of time in Switzerland. His father

nicknamed their estate there Le Ranch – an ironic name, as if a foreshadowing of Lear's later fascination with the Ranch.

In his teens he was frightened and humiliated. Once his father, dismayed with his son's ducktail haircut, slapped him. He was rarely in any school for more than a year and was eventually sent to Le Rosey, the posh Swiss academy for the rich and famous known as 'the school of kings'.

John Lear was obsessed with flying – perhaps because his father, for all he had contributed to aviation, held the lowest possible regard for those who actually flew planes for a living. He made his first flight at fourteen, in 1956, and got his licence, soloing at sixteen. He immediately declared his intention to become a commercial pilot.

He added twin engine, instrument and aerobatics ratings. In December, 1960, his father's company, Lear International, hired him as a public relations representative and pilot.

Then, on 24 June 1961, trying to get to Berne on an errand, John Lear rented a small yellow single-engine bi-plane, from a club in Geneva. He had often made low wing-wagging passes over the dorm at Le Rosey school in his Cessna and now on his way home he came across again, ready to put on a show of aerobatics.

Screaming like a rodeo cowboy to the students below, he began a three-turn spin at well under a thousand feet, intending to pull up just feet from the ground. After the second turn, with his nose pointed to the ground, he realized he was too low. He saw a barn out of the corner of his vision. He began to pull back the stick, but the plane was still heading down at a thirty-degree angle when it ploughed into a wheat field, smashing him into the instrument panel.

Students pulled him from the wreck. In the ambulance on the way to a nearby clinic doctors performed an emergency tracheotomy. His larynx had been crushed by the edge of the instrument panel. Both sides of his jaw were broken, four front teeth were gone, his heel bones and ankles were crushed and each leg was snapped in three places.

Moved to a hospital in Geneva, he spent five hours in surgery and several days in intensive care. His father, angry and humiliated, came to the hospital immediately, but never returned during John's long convalescence.

In 1962, Lear agreed to attend the Art Center College in Pasadena but then took the $5,000 his father gave him for tuition and lost it on a stock tip. In 1964 he was part of a crew taking a Lear Jet on a publicity-creating round-the-world flight. They went east, violating Indian airspace, making their longest leg – into Singapore – with only enough fuel left in the tanks for three minutes in the air.

A MiG 17 shadowed them near the Kuril Islands, then flew off when one of the crew raised a camera with a telephoto lens and began shooting through the Plexiglas window.

Bill warmed to John after that flight, but the breach was never really healed. Bill Lear's will was generous to John's children – they got 15 per cent of his fortune – though John himself was left out. But at the funeral, he cried uncontrollably.

He eventually became a pilot for Air America – the CIA's clandestine airline in South-east Asia, and for domestic carriers. He lost his job at one airline after a reporter used his name in a UFO story.

During the years he spent in California growing up Lear was aware of black programmes; his father's company supported some of them. He knew about planes that flew workers and equipment from Lockheed in Burbank to the Ranch.

In the mid Seventies Lear heard rumours from a reporter friend that more interesting things were going on at Groom Lake. He decided to go up there one night. In those days there was practically no security. He was almost able to drive down to the dry lake itself.

'That's when I took that famous picture of the lakebed.'

After 1978 he became increasingly fascinated with UFOs. He would eventually drop out of MUFON because the organization wasn't hardcore enough for him. He grew close to those who searched for black aircraft, but also the UFO believers.

In 1987 Lear published his *Darkside* thesis, the most extreme view of the dark dangers of aliens, full of tales of our secret treaties with them and their need for human and cattle bodies.

Lear came to believe it all – the underground bases, the tanks with aliens and alien-human hybrids, the bases on the Moon and Mars, MJ12 and the secret treaties. He even went on record as believing George Adamski, the early contactee.

The aliens needed a special enzyme; that was why they

mutilated cattle. He claims: 'The secretions obtained are then mixed with hydrogen peroxide and applied on the skin by spreading or dipping parts of their bodies in the solution. The body absorbs the solution, then excretes the waste back through the skin. The cattle mutilations ... were for the collection of these tissues by the aliens.'

At the Ultimate UFO Conference in Rachel in 1993 Lear declared that 'In 1979, our alliance with the aliens became a disaster ... 44 US scientists and approximately 66 members of Delta Force security personnel were killed by the aliens in an altercation at a jointly occupied US–alien base north of Los Alamos, New Mexico ... the exact cause of the altercation is not known, but the cause of death was listed as external head wounds. This effectively terminated the alien alliance for an indefinite time.'

The greys of legend were simply robots working for a race of aliens that resembled praying mantises. The government had tried to prepare the public for the release of information on the secret treaties by sponsoring such films as *ET* and *Close Encounters*, but then relations went bad and the whole process stopped. MJ12 was in disarray and confusion. It was time for truth to come out, Lear cried.

Lear's role must be suspicious: he worked for the CIA in Southeast Asia. He knows the Interceptors and he is the one who introduced Bob Lazar to the newsman George Knapp, who publicized his story. John Lear knows everyone. But John Lear also believes everything.

The first time I spoke to him he was looking at photographs of Mars. He subscribed to Richard Hoagland's theory of the face on Mars: the famous space probe photo in which many think they can discern some apparent structure in the shape of a human face. In other pictures, if you look more closely, they say, there are towers, bases and cities.

But today he no longer wants to get the story out. He doesn't think the public is ready. Those who are keeping it all secret known what they are doing. John Lear, who once challenged the government to come clean, now thinks they may be right.

Yes, he says, there may be disinformation. There may be

government influence in the media. Look at all the films on UFOs.

But what shocks me most is this: John Lear doesn't even trust supermarket tabloids. Somehow, he says, they get information early. They manage to take the kernel of truth and distort it just enough to make it look ridiculous. I went away shaking my head. I had never thought to suspect that the government might control the *Weekly World News*.

Suspecting everything might be a clever disguise, driving the highways around Dreamland, staring at the mirages off the blacktop, I also found myself becoming suspicious. Was Lear a spy in disguise, an investigator cloaked in his mock gullibility, a disinformation agent? All I could be sure of, in this refractive world was that, as one of the first to probe Dreamland, he was a key operative in another organization: the loose combination of the curious who followed Lear to the perimeter, the group of mock spies who made up a kind of Decentral Intelligence Agency. For them, as for more and more people in America in the Nineties, the line between suspicion and paranoia was growing hazy.

18

'Space Aliens from the Pentagon' and Other Conspiracies

ON HIS WAY TO THE OKLAHOMA CITY FEDERAL BUILDING, ITS bomber, Timothy McVeigh, slept at a motel named Dreamland. The information caught my eye, and I took it for a token of something I was noticing: just how closely the whole fascination with a New World Order (NWO), the right-wing view of the world, was taking hold of the views of Dreamland.

The New World Order theorists had rapidly developed their own lore, decrying the influences of the UN and FEMA, the Federal Emergency Management Agency. Black helicopters and white (UN) personnel carriers were making furtive appearances. They were UFOs of the militias.

On the Internet the NWO had reached such a filigreed detail of conspiracy theory that one story even claimed that the NWO would abolish all but a single chain of fast-food restaurants: Taco Bell. Believing this, who would not take up arms against the menace? The Golden Arches themselves threatened, and the whole free enterprise system that had given us Colonel Sanders!

And the NWO lore was now overlapping with UFO lore. On Long Island, an aerospace electrician named Ed Zabo, and John Ford, head of the Long Island UFO Network, were charged with attempting to poison the county Republican chairman by slipping radium into his food. Zabo, a government inspector at the local Northrop Grumman plant, firmly believed that the county government was conspiring to cover up evidence of UFO landings, which among other things, he thought, had resulted in the setting of extensive forest fires on Long Island the previous summer. The district attorney shook his head and opined that, 'this all convinces me that there is a side to humanity that defies definition.'

The New World Order was a cipher, a linguistic Groom Lake

waiting to be filled with speculations. I took it as a sign of the absence of the Cold War, much missed. The end of the Cold War had left a yawning vacuum of uncertainty. And I regarded its most fervent adherents as victims of a kind of Cold War post traumatic stress syndrome. It's not easy to take away an enemy you've lived with for nearly half a century. How much easier to deal with an invented enemy, than with none at all. How important for the conspiracist for the world to possess an order, even if that order is a dark and hidden one. Although never very clear on the vision thing, George Bush could hardly have foreseen that the glib phrase his speechwriters had coined would come to be the title of such a malignant mythology.

My friend, the Minister, held it as a sign of economic distress. 'The uneducated shitkicker class in this country is dead,' he argued. Whatever the reason, some of the early believers in the UFO cover-up were converting to an even darker view: that there was an even more sinister conspiracy, using the flying saucers to drive us into the arms of the New World Order.

In the summer of 1996 I visited the national convention of MUFON – the Mutual UFO Network. It was held at a North Carolina Holiday Inn, in the same rooms and with the same tone of seriousness and internal self fascination as a regional gathering of insurance salesmen or social workers. I noticed that no one smiled.

In one room, on seeming acres of tables, every shade of UFO thinking was laid out in the form of books and videos. I felt compelled to read *From Elsewhere; Being ET in America*, about the experiences of a man who felt he was an alien on Earth. You could also buy mugs and T-shirts, glow-in-the-dark alien sculptures. But my eye was caught by a book with a strange pentagon and star device on its cover and the title *Space Aliens from the Pentagon*. It bore the subtitle *Flying Saucers are Man-made Electrical Machines*. I found the 'Revised and expanded' Second Edition of Creatopia Productions (TM) by William R. Lyne. Cover lines: 'Does the CIA write Movie and TV scripts about "aliens"? Have you been brainwashed? Does the CIA control Hollywood and TV? Did you know the flying saucer is the best kept energy secret on earth?'

Lyne argues that the saucers are faked by the Pentagon or

some secret group beyond and behind the Pentagon.

He wrote that 'My "Space Aliens" are actually people, whose philosophy and bizarre masquerade are alien to the American way of life, since they believe in government by anti-democratic hoax, to maintain the secret power of the Trilateral Commission elite, to whom our lives are very cheap. I am striking back against an "alien system" which has attached itself to the nation, which our ancestors strove to create, which would be invulnerable to the "aliens" ... I have concluded that a Secret Government has watched me, attempted to control me ...'

Lyne turned the Cosmic Watergate on its head. Far from being a cover-up, the saucer stories were all a put-on – a Hollywood production to frighten us into the arms of the NWO, to create Reagan's unifying alien threat. The saucers came – not from other galaxies – but from Earth. The Nazis had taken the technology of Nikolai Tesla and developed flying saucers from it. These they used to fly to exile in South America – perhaps even Antarctica. Von Braun flew the flying saucers out of White Sands after the war.

Lyne rolled all the myths together, the saucers and the Nazis and Tesla – the near-mad scientist who is the darling of the fringe – and government cover-ups. You have Hitler escaping and strange artefacts floating around in the hands of old Indians in the southwest – Hollywood stuff. No topic was too large to bring into the web. And none was too small – the powers in Detroit conspired to squash the small inexpensive Crosley automobile of the late Forties.

It reminded me of the line 'a strange alien civilization, the Pentagon'. It was that joke taken seriously. Cynical military types call the Pentagon 'the five-sided funny house', and on the cover of the book the Pentagon is shown as a maze. Embedded in the maze is a swastika and an eye like that on the seal of the United States, an all-seeing eye, the Jungian eyeball in the sky.

Lyne's biography said that he was born in Kermit, Texas, where he saw his first UFO as a child. He had received an MFA in 'studio arts' from Sam Houston State University. He certainly had real artistic talent: his book is illustrated with obsessive and skilful drawings, part engineering diagram, part R. Crumb.

He believed the National Security Act of 1947, that divided the armed services, was treasonable and the Roswell incident was a hoax involving fake aliens which were in fact dead monkeys, crudely disguised, from the rocket tests at White Sands. He had seen photos of the monkeys, but they were stolen by a former girlfriend. In their place, Lyne produces drawings, from memory, in his skilful but jittery style.

According to Lyne, Hitler escaped from the Fuehrer bunker and visited San Antonio, Texas, in 1967 as a guest of LBJ. But when he – and he alone apparently – recognized Adolf and Eva Braun, they were quickly hustled away.

Lyne was a key player in the drama he described. He told how he had quarrelled with Sargent Shriver over his dismissal from the Peace Corps and was offered – but rejected – a high position in the CIA by George Bush in 1975.

Lyne was most fascinated by a box he had seen, but not bought, at a flea market. This phantom box, of which he provides a detailed drawing, was a box remembered, not even possessed. It held the secrets of the saucers. Those saucers were all over, Lyne said. 'I've seen them land in Eldorado,' he said, meaning New Mexico.

While the 'Space Aliens from the Pentagon' account was singular in possessing one clear viewpoint – all information had somehow happened to come to Lyne and him alone – another view of Dreamland was a dizzying collage of clippings and reports.

In his two video tapes entitled *Secrets of Dreamland*, Norio Hayakawa had produced a carefully, not to say obsessively, documented depiction of a vast conspiracy swirling about Dreamland like a dust devil. In its wake, that conspiracy carried a flutter of clippings and references.

The tapes were made up mostly of footage of a lecture Hayakawa had given to a religious group called the Prophecy Network, illustrated with slides of the press clippings. The lecture made token gestures to an apocalyptic sort of Christianity – probably for the benefit of the audience. It was the sort of Christianity whose favourite book of the Bible is the infinitely interpretable, not to say downright wacko, Revelations. The lecture was followed by home video footage of flying saucers along Mailbox

Road: lights jumping in the sky, and turning on the proverbial dime.

UFOs, Hayakawa had concluded, were part of a created threat designed to stampede the populace into accepting the New World Order. 'DREAMLAND is said' – 'is said', that passive tense phrase again – 'to be an acronym for Data Repository Establishment and Management Land. It will be the center for a future satellite linkage system that will centralise all global computer data network system.

'A device known as Battle Engagement Area Simulator and Tracker (B.E.A.S.T.) developed by the US Naval Research Laboratory and which will be launched into orbit under the auspices of DARPA, will link all global data network systems in the air.

'The BEAST' – yes, the famed Beast of Revelations – 'will be some type of a super computer-linking station launched into orbit in a few more years. It may link stations emitting hologramic images into the atmosphere to control the "thinking" patterns of the populace.'

Norio's lecture was generously illustrated with clips about alleged military programmes for mind control, electromagnetic warfare, lasers, and exotic aircraft from such sources as the *Washington Post*, *Wall Street Journal*, and *Aviation Week*. In the last few years, his thinking had taken a turn toward the conspiratorial – specifically toward the New World Order suspicions of the hard Right, the 'new Right'.

The Rockefeller Foundation in North America and the Rothschild Financial Conglomerate in Europe are an integral part of the entity known as the Bilderbergers, he argues, and together they have a plan to establish the New World Order by the year 2002.

In the hours I had spent watching Norio's *Secrets of Dreamland* video tapes I had noticed this shift toward the conspiratorial. There were two tapes, released a couple of years apart, and between them, there was a subtle shift in emphasis that extended to the packaging, an apparent shift in target audience from the youfers to New World Order conspiracists. It was not only good marketing, reflecting a changing world, but it also indicated a change in Norio's own thinking.

'The Lord,' he says on the tape, 'is literally coming to catch his believers in the air. A mass confusion will take over the world.' I wondered at that moment whether he has ever heard of the Louvins' Great Atomic Power, with the victims of the A-bomb rising to meet their saviour in the air.

He makes his argument, drawing equally on scripture and *Aviation Week*. In essence, it goes like this:

The New World Order, a secret government, is using UFOs to frighten us into accepting their tyranny. Strange new technologies are controlling us, including holographic projection and other forms of mind control.

'It is my opinion that an elite group of globalists has always believed that the ultimate way to create some type of global unity was to create an artificial threat from elsewhere. It could be war, disasters, worldwide calamity, etc., to create an artificial "crisis". But the ultimate one is to create an external threat from "outside" and the most convincing one will be an "alien" threat from beyond earth.

'To this end,' he intoned, 'I believe that we have slowly been brainwashed and manipulated to believe in the existence of "extraterrestrial" entities. Look at the proliferation of "alien"-related films and TV documentaries and semi-documentaries. I think that this is all a part of the conditioning process that is preparing us psychologically to accept the "alien" presence and sensitise us to the "alien threat" in the very near future.'

The talk is illustrated with dozens of slides of newspaper and magazine clippings about Star Wars programmes, black helicopters, mind control experiments, hypersonic aircraft, robot planes and the like.

He talks of all sorts of devices to control minds. 'Some of these devices cause maybe temporary memory loss. Certain chemicals are used, and equipment.' There is reference to a Dr Igor Smirnoff – very much his real name – who developed an acoustic device for mind control. Work is going on at Wright Patterson Air Force Base to create brain actuated aircraft controls.

Hayakawa delves into some Joseph Campbell-like interpretations as well. The legendary Majic, Majestic or MJ12 from UFO lore is traced back to symbolic codewords, occult terms from ancient days, linked to magi, fraternities of wise men.

The secret government is sensitizing us, he says, preparing

us for the takeover. The clips from the popular Press prove this. 'When the *Washington Post* says so, it is already done.'

The lecture is followed, as if by an appendix in a book, by clips of Norio's saucer-chasing expeditions. 'The intensity of sound stunned us', he says in the voice-over to one of the video clips. 'You could physically feel the noise from eighteen miles away.' There are shots from Freedom Ridge, a bouncy smeary film of the base at night, and a red glow. Is it a plane? 'It might just be a car,' says a voice on the sound track. 'No,' another voice, overflowing with excitement, counters, 'that's a ship. See, there are trucks around it? . . . They're getting ready to send it up.'

Because of the video tapes, I ended up one August day in Little Tokyo in Los Angeles. From the heat I stepped into a cool dark lobby of a Japanese-American funeral home. It stood near a toy warehouse in an area not so much ethnically colourful as ethnically triumphant: architecture as slick and corporate as Tokyo's: a Buddhist temple in its own little park, a series of looming brutalist apartment buildings with a shopping mall. At one edge of Little Tokyo, however, stood a replica of a building from the internment camps, a tattered barrack-like building, as if it had been pulled from the wreckage of an abandoned training base – the old Tonopah, say, or Indian Springs.

I waited in front of a sign that read 'Slumber Room Viewing'. A sweet odour filled the air and sombre Japanese Muzak drifted by. Then, a friendly man emerged: Norio Hayakawa, UFO buff, Area 51 researcher and full-time funeral director.

I had e-mailed Norio asking to talk to him, and he agreed. He delicately warned me not to mention UFOs if I called on him at the funeral home. 'You know how it goes,' was the phrase he used, the tired phrase of many saucer buffs trying to get by in the more mundane world.

When I realized from the tape that the Book of Revelations was involved, I worried. In my experience, Revelations is a dangerously heady elixir for preachers and prophets of many shades. It's a fevered, obscure vision that can set off a David Koresh or an Oral Roberts with equal ease into prophetic riffs like jazz solos. The vaguer the phrases and images in

Revelations, the surer the interpretations they inspire.

So I worried about how Hayakawa would tie Dreamland into Revelations. It turned out to be a little more complicated: Norio went easy on the specific Biblical references, hailing a more general 'spirituality' which, along with the unification of the various militias, he sees as our best hope of salvation.

After the teeming conspiracy tales of the tape I hardly knew what to expect of Norio in person. Gracious and friendly, he was disarming. We drove to a restaurant on the edge of little Tokyo. Norio seemed weary. He was honoured by my visit and interest he had told me. But he seemed tired of it all.

'My main thesis,' he pronounced, almost as if by rote, 'is the highly developed technology could be utilized to stage fake aliens to desensitize us' – he likes that word – 'to intrusive authority and shocking revelations.

'I think it's always going to be a mystery. It will never be solved. Or by the time we find out what is there it will be too late. We won't find out until all hell breaks loose.'

In his lecture, Hayakawa stated that 1947 was when all these strange things began to happen. He often pointed out important things that happened during 1947: the founding of the Air Force and the CIA, the Roswell crash and Churchill's speech at Fulton, Missouri, coining the term Iron Curtain. He did not mention the death of Bugsy Siegel and the bankruptcy of the Flamingo. Or that it was the year of the Truman doctrine and Chuck Yeager's first flight through the sound barrier.

When I asked, he explained that his own fascination with what he called 'the UFO phenomenon' could be traced back to 1947, perhaps, because that is the year when his father, a fisherman, looked up from his boat off the coast of Japan and saw a strange light in the sky.

He first joined Japanese UFO groups in 1963 and graduated from high school in Yokahama. He attended college in New Mexico and joined other UFO watchers in the state. By 1976 he was teaching at a school in suburban Phoenix. He did not hear of Area 51 until 1988, when the Fox Network, already working its reputation as the tabloid of TV, broadcast a show called *UFO Cover-up? Live!* It included the soon-to-be-famous testimony of 'Falcon', who explained that the aliens showed a weakness for strawberry ice cream and Tibetan music. He also used the term Area 51, the first time Norio had heard it.

It was nearly a year later that Norio heard Bob Lazar for the first time, on the Billy Goodman radio show, broadcast from Las Vegas. His imagination was fired: Norio had long served as a kind of UFO scout or consultant for Japanese television, Nippon TV, and he let them know about Lazar. By February, NTV sent a correspondent and crew to Las Vegas.

With the crew, Norio drove up to meet Lazar at his house in Las Vegas. It was on this trip that he noticed the strange man who accompanied Lazar.

'Lazar showed us the documents. Later we found out that his Social Security number' – on the famed W-2 that showed Lazar being paid $977.11 by the Naval Intelligence – 'belongs to a person in New York'.

On Lazar's advice, Norio and the crew headed up to Mailbox Road. Lazar suggested the times they should look.

The video tape indicates what they saw. 'We were looking toward S-4, over the Jumbled Hills when this strange light came up, went up and down. It was one of the most amazing things I've experienced.

'What we are witnessing right now,' the voice says excitedly, 'this was just unexpected.' The images are jumpy and you can hear a hissing, flickering sound – the desert wind smearing the signal in the microphones, threatening to obscure it completely.

That spring Lazar agreed to fly to Japan to appear live on TV and answer questions. He had even accepted tickets for himself and Gene Huff.

But he never showed. Norio waited impatiently at the JAL terminal at LAX. When Norio telephoned, Lazar told him that he could not come; his life was in danger.

To save face, the network set up a telephone link so Lazar could answer phone-in questions live during the show.

Hayakawa had made many trips back to Mailbox Road, sometimes with Gary Schultz. He had seen the saucers, he thought, and on his tapes there are many lights moving erratically in the sky. He also believed he had seen UAVs flying up there. But he had come to wonder also if some of the things flying had not been illusory images, projected somehow, perhaps holographically, high-tech illusions.

Today, Norio says, 'mystification' has taken over Area 51. He sees patterns and connections everywhere; he links the BEAST computer to Revelations. He is fascinated by numbers – did I realize, he asked, that 1998 will be a critical year, 666 times three? Something big should happen. Is it part of the symbolism for the diabolical trinity? he wonders.

He believes that Lazar's claims are so far beyond any verification that he feels he has been a witting or unwitting tool of disinformation – and quite likely mind control. 'I believe he was used unwittingly to spread disinformation.' He seemed to feel betrayed.

'High strangeness,' he said, as if in conclusion, 'high strangeness.'

I sensed he was a bit weary of the contention, even weary of his own theories, jarred by infighting perhaps. Perhaps he was the outsider par excellence – alienated in the way that only a Japanese-American running a funeral home could be.

Only at the end of our conversation did country and western somehow come up. Norio came alive. He smiled. It was amazing to finally see him smile. He brightened all over.

He was wild about country and western music, he told me. He had a portable keyboard system, simulating many instruments, and he had even played it at the Little A-Le-Inn. I suspected that Norio wanted above all to be a real American.

I felt a wave of affection for Norio, sympathy for his fragmented roles, for his disappointment in Lazar, in the dead ends. He had in a sense been left at the altar by the UFO world – embarrassed by Gary Schultz, with his Waco ravings, and stood up at the airport by Bob Lazar.

Later, Norio mailed me his demonstration tape. Its cover showed him in front of a pick-up truck in the middle of the desert – a classic C&W cover. In the desert, I thought, everyone is a country star, everyone is an American – and in the desert, everyone is an alien.

The songs were classic, *Branded Man*, *Why Me Lord*, *I'll Fly Away*. I would never have expected to hear anything, however, like Norio singing *Sensuous Woman*.

Norio's tape became a key part of my personal soundtrack for the desert, at least in combination with the occasional playings of ZZ Top's version of *Viva, Las Vegas*, as necessary to keep one awake on the long desert drives around the vast perimeter of Dreamland as cups of trucker coffee.

After I talked to Norio, I headed up the road from Los Angeles to Las Vegas. The huge pylons beside the highway seemed to be walking robots, feeling their way along the high tension wires like men on a rope bridge.

The link between the two cities, it always struck me, was like that between the cartoon sleeper and dream bubble above his head. Vegas was LA distillate, a step further into fantasy than even Hollywood could go.

I let Norio's vision of the world shape how I saw everything – I donned his worldview like a pair of polarizing sun glasses. I listened to the radio news with suspicion. I noticed a weird symmetry in the way the sun was going down to one side and the moon was rising – two circles the same height, the same size. As if for a reason.

It struck me, trying to go with his flow, that Norio was a Jungian! He saw as many archetypal meanings in the world as old Carl and Joe Campbell together. Norio's was a world teeming with meanings – too full of meanings, perhaps. Conspiratorial, 'mystified,' meanings. 'Mystified' was what he had said about Dreamland – 'they've mystified it,' and now they were using our fascination with it to delude us.

A little later in the day, when another song by Willie Nelson came on, a verse stuck in my mind:

> Like all the little children
> You'll dream a dream or two.
> But be careful what you're dreaming
> Soon your dreams start dreaming you.

Norio was an admitted 'conspiratorologist' – he used the word himself, and seemed resigned to living in the world such a role created. Living that way, I thought, meant that you encountered Dreamland everywhere you looked. In return for understanding the secret order, you had to accept the impossibility of escaping that order – it grew to take dominion everywhere. 'The place has no edges' – hadn't the Minister warned me?

Stopping for gas at a truck stop in Barstow, I came across the

Area 51 video game. It had turned into a big hit in the arcades, I learned, and I would keep running across it in the oddest spots – in diner lobbies, in mall arcades, outside movie theatres.

The game's opening screen perfectly summed up the new pop mystique the phrase Area 51 had taken on: 'Area' in military crate stencils, '51' in big bank vault metallic letters and numbers, dented with bullets. That was the vague popular understanding of the folk site called Area 51 – that aliens have literally possessed military bodies. 'The fate of humanity hangs in the balance,' the instructions explain, at the same time promising a 'detailed recreation of the most secretive airbase in the world'. And if you read the fine print, you learned that Area 51 had been trademarked. The premise of the game is this: a saucer or other craft has been recovered – somehow the occupants have taken over the base. It is the player's task to get inside as part of a special SWAT team.

Such was the state of the legend: the player battles 'alien-infected personnel', a handy means of conflating evil, non-human expendable aliens with traditional images of bad guys wearing berets and overalls – the folk who die by the dozens in Hollywood action films. Boxes and barrels surround the place; there are hot fighters and tough Hum-vees scattered about. A panel truck bears the designing firm's name: Mesa Logic.

The premise will come as no surprise: shoot 'em as fast as you can, as they pop out from behind boxes and vehicles, dash along catwalks. Hangars make fine settings for shootouts.

The ultimate goal of the game was to 'penetrate' far enough to set off a special nuclear destruction device to rid the planet of the invading scourge. I couldn't help noticing, a little wistfully, that winning the game of Area 51 meant destroying Area 51.

A big success in the video arcade, the game would soon come home and dance across the screens of Sony Gamestations.

Back on the highway, I approached Boron, a town dedicated to the product of its local mines, where huge industrial complexes appear suddenly in the desert. Francis G. 'Borax' Smith had been the colourful entrepreneur behind the material, building railroads and whole towns in his quest to mine and promote it. His legacy was this huge factory on the horizon and a huge hole in the ground.

Boron is used in borax but it can also be used as to fuel jets, even rocket engines.

It was a theme in some UFO lore that aliens often landed near areas rich in boron, which served as fuel for their craft. But at the Skunk Works there had been quite serious investigations into using boron as fuel for high speed aircraft. Ground into a 'slurry', Kelly Johnson thought, a liquid of ground-up bits, might make a kind of milkshake to feed new engines.

Overhead, a huge helicopter, probably running some sort of exercise – had something electronic hung from the big boom that stuck out forward from its chin. It was dark blue or green, but under grey skies, it struck me with the insight that under many conditions, all helicopters are black – at night for instance, or in low light against dark skies, in silhouette.

The black helicopter occupies a kind of missing link position in Ufology. It first cropped up in the days when 'mutes' – cattle and horse mutilations – were the hot theme in youfer lore. Black helos were often seen near mute locations. And sometimes black helos were reported to fly near, or even in, formation with UFOs. And of course the helos around Dreamland that 'sandblasted' intruders, and generally patrolled the perimeter, were reported as being black.

But with the coming of the New World Order watchers, the black helo became a fully-fledged phenomenon of its own.

In early 1995, mentions of sightings of black helicopters started showing up more and more on the Net. Black helos connected the iconography of black planes with the old cattle mutilation tales of the early Seventies and continued it right up to the mid-Nineties: they figured large in the imagery of the paranoid Right. They are the new silhouette of the recent techlore, a conspiracist's icon: a paranoid darkening of vision. The black plane cultures suddenly seemed to connect with those of the militias.

Conspiracy theorists, I was beginning to believe, ultimately had so much in common that their fascinations would grow into each other, especially as the media – high and low – took them up, like watercolours soaking into newsprint.

At first, as is common with such tales, the references were specific and most casual, with the implications behind them seeping only indirectly into the accounts.

It was a simple story: they appear mysteriously from the sky, pieces of the night come down to Earth. Black helicopters, the UFOs of the new Right. In *The Spotlight*, the journal of the 'populist Right', black helos figure as the avant garde of the New World Order, an unholy combine of the UN, the Russians, the ATF and FEMA. They are tied to a shadowy 'Multi Jurisdictional Task Force' coming to take our guns away, destroy our national independence and open our borders to hordes of foreigners.

I got hold of a book that recorded it all, a volume by one Jim Keith, former UFO buff, called *Black Helicopters over America*, subtitled *Strike Force for the New World Order*. The sources cited include Michigan militia chief Mark Koernke; the book is full of dark talk of 'underground detention centers' and of sightings of white UN armoured personnel carriers massing in railyards.

The geometric shadows of blacks helos echo the relentless triganometric logic that sees danger from the Trilaterists and Bilderbergers. Black helo sightings tend to be couched in the passive voice: in an item from *The Spotlight*, warning of an imminent conspiracy to confiscate guns in Mississippi: 'fourteen unmarked black helicopters belonging to the Drug Enforcement Agency (DEA) have been located at Hawkins Field in Jackson.'

Other sightings are recorded on the Internet: at the cafeteria of a small airport in Texas, one tale goes, pilots walk in from the just-landed black helos. Their flight suits are unfamiliar; among themselves they speak only Russian.

Black helo lore is as old as the Seventies, when it appeared in conjunction with the animal multilation craze. A typical account runs like this:

In the early autumn of 1976, a hunter from Bozeman, Montana, was out alone around 3:00pm one day in the Red Mountain area near Norris. He watched as a black helicopter without markings flew overhead and disappeared below a small hill. The curious hunter climbed to the top of the hill. There was the black chopper (a Bell

Jet Ranger, he thought) on the ground, the engine still running. Seven men had apparently exited from the craft and were walking up the hill toward the observer. As the hunter advanced toward the seven, he waved and shouted congenial greetings. It was then that he realized there was something about the men – they were all Oriental. They had slanted eyes and olive skin and were jabbering among themselves in some indecipherable language. They wore 'everyday' clothes, not uniforms. Suddenly they began to return to the helicopter. The hunter, still waving and shouting friendly greetings, started after them. The Orientals quickened their pace. When the hunter approached within five or six feet, they broke into a dead run, crowded into the chopper and took off.

In the magazine *Stigmata*, in 1978, a writer named Tom Adams was already connecting black helos to saucers. He outlined the most prominent speculations for the mutilation/helicopter link, including the following:

'The helicopters are themselves UFOs, disguised to appear as terrestrial craft.

'The choppers originate from with the US government/military and are directly involved in conducting the actual mutilations.

'The helicopters are government/military and are not involved in the mutilations but are investigating them.

'The helicopters are government/military, and they know about the identity and motives of the mutilators and by their presence, they are trying to divert attention to the possibility of involvement by the military.'

This was the familiar magic of possibility flipped inside out to reveal the opposite – a common trait of the conspiracist dreamwork.

But it is the 'new world order' conspiracy that has brought black helos to the level of UFO sightings.

Black helos fit into the national iconography beside the shadows on the grassy knoll of assassination theorists and the Men in Black of UFO lore, who pay housecalls to intimidate witnesses into silence. A folklorist would note their literary kinship to the choppers above Waco, filming the fire, and the dark helos of the failed rescue attempts on Tehran and the song 'My POW Camp'. They are offspring of such imagined film choppers as those in *Apocalypse Now* or the super 'copter Roy Scheider pilots in *Blue Thunder*.

But the real irony is that now they have been imagined, we've had to invent them: black helos actually exist. During Roving Sands '95, the military's largest field exercise, held annually in the Southwest, Steve and the others had spotted the real thing: not exactly black but dark, matte-painted UH-60s, the noise of their engines suppressed, dropping in SEALs and other special ops forces for insurgency practice. Steve saw them; you could hear cars down the road, but not the choppers, even when they are visible.

A few months later Cap Weinberger referred to such noise-suppressing technology in his book on future war scenarios.

'The very strange part ...' one eyewitness reports, was that 'they made NO noise! The air was dead still and calm.' Black – and silent, too.

Steve had confirmed the story: it was a weird turn of events where mythological creatures on the Net had suddenly turned up in reality. It was like falling asleep one night reading about mermaids and waking up the next morning to find a manatee in your swimming pool.

I wanted to get a sense of the place where Lazar was said to have 'pandered'.

I stopped by Lazar's old house – where his first wife had committed suicide – carbon monoxide, in the garage. It was not far, by happy chance, from the BLM office where I went to look for maps. It was empty now. It was a nice, quiet street, exactly the kind that when someone is hauled away on a stretcher the neighbours are interviewed on TV saying they would never have dreamed of it in a thousand years. The phrase 'safe house' leaped to mind.

You can tell a lot about a man from the place where he gets married. So I stopped in at the Imperial Hotel, Las Vegas's take off of the famous Frank Lloyd Wright hotel in Tokyo that survived an earthquake. Here, the only connection is the use of Japanese names and decor where convenient. From the dank garage, I emerged into a courtyard with a pool, with the concrete room slabs towering up around it. The pool had a swim-up bar and even before noon people were swimming up to it.

I passed through the dark noisy casino floor, by conference rooms with Japanese names, made a turn at the Shear Madness hair salons, his and hers, on my way to the chapel called We've Only Just Begun.

The floor was windowless. The proprietor, or preacher or whatever you call someone who runs a wedding chapel in a casino, was out to lunch. I peaked through stained glass windows on the door. The potted palms made it look like a TV studio, or a funeral home.

Signs around the place referred to WOJB, which for a time I took to be a radio or television station, with studios in the hotel. Then I realized the initials stood for 'We've Only Just Begun'.

Standing in front of that dreary chapel, the windowless fluorescent-lit hall, I had one clear impression: this guy was a big time loser.

As I went down in the elevator and out through the noisy lobby, with its clatter and clang of slot machines, I noticed a small game arcade off to the side and I walked toward it. As the sound of the slots receded in favour of the bang and clank of pinball and video, I noticed that in the arcade, sure enough, one of the machines was playing the Area 51 video game.

I continued east, and realized that from the hotel to the apartment I was running almost on a straight line. It led past the Janet terminal on the edge of McCarran airport. This was Dreamland's navel, so to speak, the umbilicus connecting it to the real world.

Following the line further south, I came to the edge of the Hughes Industrial Park, on the other side of the airport. There, in neat slick glass boxes of low buildings like stereo components arranged in a store, Lockheed sat across the street – on its own little loop, Kelly Johnson Drive! – from EG&G Special Projects. SAIC was out here too, in the same building as Bechtel, not far away, and Wackenhut. Here, the contractors who served Dreamland were clustered together in a map that would double for an organizational chart.

'EG&G Special Projects' – a gardener was working around the sign. That word 'special' again – as in special forces, special weapons, special operations. Having run most of the Nuclear Test Site's operations, directly or through its REECO subsidiary, having hired guards and come to own aircraft, and now operating most of Dreamland, EG&G had come a long way from its origins, which were about vision and photography – as far in location from EG&G's Route 128-style headquarters back near Boston, and yet as similar in architecture. It was even further from the labs where Harold Edgerton had started out, at MIT.

Old 'Doc' Edgerton was beloved at MIT. The man who had invented stroboscopic photography was great PR. Harold Edgerton's images of bullets passing through apples and footballs indented by the toe of a kicker turned technology into showbiz. They reached a wide public – the *Life* magazine sort of audience, and they showed science, not as equations or test tubes, but as something fun, exciting and amazing. No wonder that MIT president James Killian – who had headed the commission that recommended building the U-2 – would co-author a book with Edgerton on his photographs.

But they also represented a turning point in the way twentieth century man saw the world. In his standard *History of Photography* Beaumont Newhall writes that photography with the strobe has 'gone beyond seeing, and brings us a world of form normally invisible, which fixes forever form never detected by the unaided eye'. They helped reveal what art critic Rosalind Krauss would later call 'the visual unconscious'. Edgerton's photographs captured the dreams of everyday vision, frozen bubbles and bullets, and the magical crown left by a drop of milk falling into a pail.

Born in 1903, Edgerton spent most of his childhood in Aurora, Nebraska, a science whiz kid. In the late Twenties he experimented with argon lamps and developed the stroboscopic method of photography, a bright, extremely short flash of light in sync with the camera shutter.

He was fascinated with aviation, having seen the Wrights fly at Fort Myers, Virginia in 1909, and during World War II his strobes equipped reconnaissance aircraft. Edgerton's flash illuminated crossroads and town squares the night before D-

Day, documenting the placement of German troops. Later, they would dive with Jacques Cousteau, discover the wrecks of the *Titanic* and the *Monitor*, and catch hummingbirds in mid-flight.

By the 1930s it was clear there was too much money to be made with his strobes not to commercialize it. With his key associates, Herbert Grier and Kenneth Germeshausen, Edgerton established a company to exploit the equipment for industrial and other clients.

They could reveal the inner working of machines and, adapted, strobes would pace the party of the Sixties – their dreamy lighting inducing the reveries of dancing to rock'n'roll – and triggering epileptic fits.

But their most important use would be in capturing the milliseconds of atomic explosion, tracking the fireball out from its plutonium kernel, so that *Life* magazine could reveal the unfolding of the nuclear blooms that obsessed its readers.

Edgerton's cameras were at Eniwetok Atoll in 1946 and a few years later at the new Nevada Proving Ground, set up on a seventy-five-foot tower seven miles from ground zero. There, they captured the nuclear explosion in the moment it hung like a leucocyte, a terrifying organism blown from micro to macro size.

It soon became clear that triggering a camera to take a picture of an atomic blast was very much like triggering the blast itself, and EG&G became one of the AEC's chief contractors. Soon it was running all sorts of things at the test site, such as building and operating the blast doors in underground tunnels, which would shut down in a fraction of a fraction of a fraction of a second to 'sort' the radiation of an underground blast into its components – letting through, say, only the x-rays for a bomb test.

As the Cold War wound down, EG&G began to look to civilian work. In 1993 it obtained a new contract to manage the space shuttle launch and landing complexes for NASA, a task that, according to the company's annual report, required a '200 man uniformed security force and SWAT team'. For DOE, it was developing special bacteria to remove radioactive components from the soil and had grown top-purity mercuric iodide crystals on space shuttle flights in 1985 and 1992 to serve as the heart of new types of extremely sensitive radioactivity detectors. It was building laser detonators for Hanford and Savannah Rivers, and ran facilities for separating tritium – the heavy isotope of hydrogen used in nuclear weapons – from helium. It had branches in Langley, Florida and West Virginia.

I picked up the company's 1995 annual report, which listed some $1.4 billion in sales and touted the company's work in sensors for air bag deployment and other automotive uses, its 'Z-scan' airport security system, and other work. There was a down-played mention of 'continuing assignments for US Customs' and 'from a US federal agency to conduct a classified project'. But there was no mention of the Janet airline, or of Groom Lake, or of the decision to let the contract to run the Nevada Test Site go – to Bechtel. And there is no picture of the building that houses 'EG&G Special Projects'.

19
Searchlight

WE WERE HEADING FOR THE CENTRE OF THE WORLD. IN A rented Hyundai Sonata, Trader and his friend and I were driving east from Las Vegas, then south toward Searchlight, Nevada. Trader had read that the Mojave Indians had believed that a certain mountain called Avikwame was the centre of the universe. Based on its description and hand-drawn maps, he said Avikwame appeared to be Spirit Mountain, part of the Newberry Range near Searchlight, Nevada. Trader's friend was a journalist who had once accompanied one of Gary Schultz's 'Secret Saucer Base' expeditions to the perimeter of Dreamland. In the car, she spoke of another writer and said, 'he does apocalyptic doom really well'.

To fortify ourselves, we stopped at a cafe in Searchlight. The biscuits were sourdough, like the prospectors favoured. The bacon was burned.

We pondered the choice of Searchlight. To us, the town's name suggested that of a black programme – Black Light was an actual special access programme name, or Redlight, one of the names in the Lore, of a secret saucer programme inside Dreamland, or a UFO group's project – Spotlight was the name of a project of the CSETI organization.

In fact, I learned from a poster that Searchlight had been named after a box of matches.

Trader called his own researches Neon Azimuth – a parody of the black programme names we both enjoyed. But from then on I thought of his work as 'Searchlight'. His researches were into secret codes and mysterious symbols: into the black budget that financed secret aircraft projects. Trader audited the books of Dreamland. He followed the money.

Trader was red-haired, tall, not what I imagined – he had been for me a stealthy character behind an e-mail name for so long. He spent his working hours creating and debugging software for a firm in Irvine – that glittery futuristic planned city packed with aerospace and high tech companies. He was a 'Code Warrior'. His name was Paul McGinnis.

I had noticed another overlap: between the Interceptors and engineers, investigators and programmers. Those who were trying to figure out how the black box worked – it made sense – tended to be engineers.

It was not by accident that Trader was also fascinated with mythological symbolism – another downright homegrown Joe Campbell – and odd corners of cultures. He was fascinated by bizarre rituals and distant cultures – and I knew this from scanning his extensive home page – Finnish epics, Betty Page pinups, tattoo art and voudoun, or voodoo.

His Internet home page showed a strange cross-like shape. Trader explained that it was a 'vever', a voudoun symbol of the crossroads which was believed to open the gate to other dimensions.

In the budget, Trader looked for the confluences of information that opened up an understanding of what was going on – for little vevers in the bureaucracy. In a sense, all Dreamland was a kind of vever, too, opening on the black world – linking reality and imagination. Now I saw the black budget was a kind of hoodoo book of instructions, for somewhere between hexes and hexadecimals. For Trader, I concluded, it was all about breaking the code, trying to figure out the inputs and outputs of the black box.

It had gradually dawned on me too, that a good many of the people who bought into conspiracy theories, especially those that tied everything so together neatly, were also engineers or computer software programmers, people who worked in a world where things connected, affected each other, had problems that could be solved. They wanted the rest of the world to work that way, indeed saw the world as behaving that way. They wanted to find the code, debug it.

It was the opposite of the sensibility of the poet, who thinks in big, vague and uncertain concepts. Or were they people who didn't want to deal with the big questions, who were happy with the small and immediate ones, or who couldn't get beyond them?

The military types, correspondingly, needed a Big Deal to get through their protective sedateness. I couldn't decide if this meant they were insensitive or over-sensitive. Jargon is usually assumed to be language of the insensitive. I was no longer sure: perhaps it a language to desensitize – not to shelter hardness but a hardened shelter for some remaining sensitivity.

Trader was doing as a hobby what foreign intelligence analysts do for a living. He became fascinated with all those codenames like Senior Trend and Tractor Bat and Have Donut, and all the programmes behind them. He turned himself into a collector, interpreter, collator, and on-line publicizer of the black budget and its associated 'special access programmes'.

The black budget is the government's classified accounting of the amount it spends on activities it doesn't want to make public: secret military research and weapons programmes, intelligence gathering, and covert operations.

The black budget admits of no easy calculation, but Trader guessed it might be as high as $40 billion a year – a figure larger than Federal spending on education or health care.

Trader explained that the black budget is documented in funding requests and authorizations voted on by select Congressional committees, and published with omitted amounts and blacked out passages. It hides all sorts of strange projects, not just from enemies (foreign and domestic), but from the public and their elected officials as well. The Pentagon's black budget is actually composed of two budgets, a Procurement budget and a Research, Development, Test and Evaluation budget; the tab for the toy testers. There are other black budgets, too, covering defence intelligence and research. An internal Pentagon memo from August, 1994 that was accidentally leaked and showed up in *Jane's Defense Weekly* revealed numbers for some of them: the National Security Agency spends $3.5 billion a year, the Defense Intelligence Agency, $621 million, and the Central Imagery Office, $122 million for spy satellite work.

Trader works mostly by analyzing such government documents as the House and Senate versions of the 'National Defense Authorization Acts', scrutinizing both the reports and the supporting testimony to Congress. He consults the Pentagon's own guides to reading the budget, Department of Defense Handbook DoD 7045.7-H. He spends hours with publications with names like *FYDP Program Structure*, Department of the Air Force document *Supporting Data for Fiscal Year 1994 – Budget Estimate Submission – Descriptive Summaries – Research, Development, Test and Evaluation.*

These are not exactly light reading, and the plots are slow. Trader soon learned that the black budget was a tissue of truths, half truths and quite likely outright untruths, a fabric of disinformation as much as information. Huge items can be hidden by breaking them up into smaller items, mislabelling – or simply omitting – them.

Even the names and responsibilities of the agencies involved are often hidden. The National Reconnaissance Office, in charge of spy satellites, was so secret that until a couple of years ago its very name could not legally be spoken. And beyond programmes marked merely 'Secret' are budget items tagged with such wonderful euphemisms as 'selected activities'.

The reorganization of intelligence gathering has given us exotic and almost unknown organs such as the Central Imagery Office (CIO) and the Defense Airborne Reconnaissance Office (DARO).

In years of work, Trader has learned to read between the lines, that the 'Virginia Procurement Office' is the National Security Agency. He can cite chapter and verse of such Pentagon reports as 'Critical Technologies for the Nineties'. And he looks at curious new requests for proposals in the *Commerce Business Daily*, the standard reference for Federal contracts.

He managed to get such juicy documents as the Rand Corporation's 'Route Planning Issues for Low Observable Aircraft and Cruise Missiles' – a manual about the rules for the China Lake air space, R-4. There was also one, he was sure, for the Dreamland airspace itself. He had security manuals from the Nevada test site that told him you had to have an '8' on your badge to get into Area 51.

Trader had his own strong political convictions, to be sure: he supplies politicians advocating reform with inside information, but more than anything I got the sense he was taken with the joy of the hunt, the thrill of the puzzle.

Any delight or pride he takes in the chase is hidden behind

a clipped and efficient tone of voice. He spoke of 'people inside government who are on our side,' implying that most are not, but he was very far from demonizing the Pentagon or the intelligence agencies.

When he did take some time off from his twin jobs, one his vocation, the other his avocation, it is as likely as not to be a hike in the desert, enjoying the flowers and the birds but inevitably ending up near, say, TRW's classified radar site in the hills east of San Clemente, its three white radomes glowing in the sunlight behind the chain link fence.

The black budget is the tip of a huge iceberg of secret government records, dating back to before World War II. Not an iceberg – a glacier of classification, increasingly exposed as the Cold War thawed.

The list of odd numbers and funny words that is the budget itself stands for something more: a huge mountain of real information that belongs to the American taxpayer. Gradually, that information is beginning to filter out.

The black budget had its origins in such top secret World War II research, known only to a handful of high officials, as the Manhattan Project. It took on added strength in 1958 with the creation of DARPA – the Defense Advanced Projects Agency – in the wake of the Sputnik, and the use of CIA 'reserve funds' for the U-2, the Blackbirds and other programmes. It was the slush fund for Ike's famed 'military industrial complex' and the meeting of science and high technology with the Army and Navy.

The Eighties were the golden years of the black budget, with such projects as Stealth aircraft and the Milstar satellite network as well as Star Wars research, which absorbed billions. The Department of Defense portion of the black budget tripled in the Reagan years.

But even after the stand-off with the former Soviet Union ended, the black budget remained huge. One reason is the Gulf War, which gave high tech weapons an enhanced prestige and strengthened a vision of a video game war in which few human beings – at least those on our side – are actually killed or wounded, and information gathering is vital. We fell even more deeply in love with high tech 'silver bullet' weapons.

In a strange way, the cuts in the overall defence budget led to a new emphasis on the sort of high tech weapons for which the black budget is best known. Smart bombs are cheaper than stealth bombers, the argument goes.

The black budget may even have increased as a percentage of the overall national budget. By the mid Nineties we were still spending perhaps $20 billion on secret weapons research programmes. Some were the planes flying out of Dreamland, some were satellites, some were exotic energy weapons. 'You know,' Trader said, 'Star Wars never really went away.' Work continues on mounting anti-missile lasers in Boeing 747s.

So Trader, who at work was a proud 'Code Warrior', at home would spend long nights trying to decipher the code, going through the mind-numbingly tedious documents in which the black budget is laid out.

He had discovered the black budget because he was a black aircraft buff. Specifically: he became fascinated by Aurora. What distinguished Trader from other Aurora watchers is that he began filing Freedom of Information Act requests about programmes whose names suggested they might be aircraft. (Black budget watchers know that Senior, for instance, is the designation for Air Force advanced R&D projects – Stealth was Senior Trend, for instance.)

It struck Trader that the US military was still fighting the Cold War. In September, 1993, he filed FOIA cases on what he thought was Aurora: Senior Citizen (Program Element 0401316F) and on Groom Lake. Trader found himself exchanging letters with an Air Force Colonel named Richard Weaver (then the Secretary of the Air Force's Deputy for Security and Investigative Programs and later the author of the report tying the Roswell incident to the Project Mogul balloon).

But what really set him off was doing an FOIA on the FOIAs he had filed: he wanted to understand the process, and the reasons his requests had brought back very little information. Reading the censored case files he received from his FOIA, Trader grew angry. 'I became convinced,' he told me dryly, 'that the Air Force (and other military services) had large numbers of senior officials who held arrogant attitudes towards the average American taxpayer.'

In the files were memos from Weaver with such lines as 'His

appeal "justification" is the standard [blacked-out censored words] provided by almost everyone else who makes similar requests for this information. All have been turned down. Mr McGinnis' [Trader's real name] rationale that he somehow should be allowed to perform those oversight functions of Congress, while novel, is not compelling.'

This response turned a mild-mannered inquirer into a much more fervent muckraker. 'I was merely pointing out the Air Force's violations of US classification policy, contained in Executive Order 12356, and how secret spending violated Article I, Section 9, Clause 7 of the US Constitution,' he argued.

McGinnis was referring to the requirement that Congress approve all federal spending – the black budget, he and others would argue, violates that provision by hiding the purpose of the expenditures.

He took further inspiration from a book called *Blank Check*, by reporter Tim Weiner, who had won a Pulitzer Prize for his exposé of black budget programmes for the *Philadelphia Inquirer*. He called the black budget 'a culture of deception'. It is, he argued, a closed world built on the familiar cosy relationship between Pentagon officials, the military brass and defence contractors. The result was waste: Weiner investigated cost overruns and performance failures of such programmes as Milstar, the military communications and control satellite.

Weiner argued that it was all about preserving empires, adding that keeping such programmes secret is an expression of institutional power, part of the closed world of the military and its contractors.

But McGinnis wanted to go further: into the projects whose very existence was hidden. He began assembling his own rendition of the black budget using Congressional and DOD documents. It was like a reconstruction of a plane crash from the parts, or a dinosaur skeleton with conjectural plaster bones filling in the missing gaps. He set up an ftp site, for distributing files on the Internet, and established the Neon Azimuth mailing list.

McGinnis, like most critics of the black budget, argued that for all the triumphs of the Skunk Works, most secret programmes hid waste. That revealing the cost of a Stealth fighter tells no more about how to build one than the cost of a Cadillac does. That black budgeting is more about hiding from Congress and the public than from any foreign enemies. Many black programmes, such as the B-2 Stealth bomber and the Milstar satellite system, ended up costing far more than planned. But by the time the public learned of the cost overruns, it was too late to kill the programmes. Enough money had already been spent, enough hardware developed, that proponents were able to argue that ending the programmes would be a waste. Others failed to work as advertised.

The Bush administration killed the Navy's A-12 Stealth carrier aircraft before it was ever unveiled to the public. Two billion had been spent – the budget, one journalist noted, of the whole National Park Service. I thought of that every time I saw a photo of the A-12, thought of the lodge at Yellowstone, and of rangers in little Smoky-the-bear hats.

Trader's work impressed some of the people in Washington who had been looking for years at the black budget – public interest muckrakers, if you will. One of Trader's admirers was John Pike's colleague at the Federation of American Scientists, Steve Aftergood. Aftergood wrote the FAS's 'Secrecy and Government Bulletin', which tracked the progress of those battling excessive secrecy and in the process, the follies of accidental declassification and the contradictory system. It was only a slight exaggeration to say that what Ralph Nader was to Detroit, Aftergood had been to the Pentagon and the intelligence agencies.

He showed me a new perspective: it's just as much tedious work to keep things secret as it is to make them unsecret.

'It's hard to keep things secret. It's work. People have to sit and read boring hearing records and black things out. It's easy to imagine they would miss stuff.'

It is also expensive to keep secrets.

As McGinnis and Aftergood described it, this huge mountain of classified material began to seem like the information equivalent of the national debt. Information we put off releasing is like money we put off paying. Keeping things secret requires all sorts of costs: guards, vaults, background checks. Think of it as servicing the national information debt. A GAO study placed the figure at $2.2 billion, but pointedly noted that its calculations had been hampered by the refusal of the CIA to co-operate. And private industry spends an estimated $13 billion more adhering to government security standards.

'The more secrecy you have,' Aftergood said, 'the thinner your security resources are spread and there is a loss of respect for the system. That promotes leaks.'

Out of incompetence, exhaustion or spite, leaks had been increasing, Aftergood told me. He wrote in the Bulletin that, '"Accidental" disclose has the great advantage that it does not require anyone to exercise leadership or to take responsibility...'

The leaks are a sign of institutional decadence: 'The government has found it easier to let the classification system disintegrate than to establish new standards that command respect and loyalty.

'If current trends are taken to the limit everything may eventually be classified – but nothing will be secret.'

Aftergood described a secrecy structure that might well collapse of its own weight before anything is done to fix it. I got the picture of a crumbling empire, with a capital city too poor to keep its walls repaired. As he described it, the strange distant civilization of the Pentagon appeared to be a decaying fortress – Rome with the Huns outside, and the black marketeers inside trading through gaps in the crumbling walls. In fact, it sounded a lot like the Soviet Union in its last years.

We parked under blue skies and continued toward the centre of the universe on foot. We climbed into a lovely canyon, soaring rock walls neatly decorated with green. A few other visitors clambered up one of the walls, taking off their shirts at the top in triumph. The canyon narrowed and twisted as you walked into it and the plants at its base grew larger and more verdant. There was more water deep in the canyon, and little beds of dirt, so the grass grew almost like a marsh here – a contrast to the wide delta of desert into which it opened.

We stopped at a cave, where painted big horns loped along the wall. These were homes, and I felt almost an intruder. They were comfortable little ledges where earlier peoples had slept and eaten and laughed, their ceilings blackened by campfires. The walls were as liberally covered with drawings as a New York subway station. Zigs and zags, circles and slashes – and animals, mountain goats and deer, romping.

Trader took pictures with his digital camera. He would post them on his web page, where he had created a map of his diverse interests. On his page along with the vever, and such items as a downloadable 'Aurora' simulator for the Macintosh, were links to pages for the Arcosanti project, pinup queen Betty Page, the Finnish rock group Vartina, the Pink Noise politics page – and native Native American petroglyphs in Nevada. I liked the idea that these most ancient of drawings would be burbling across the most modern of media as soon as he got home.

He had recently discovered a programme for rapidly building makeshift runways and hangars – a programme that could turn all kinds of distant spaces into little Dreamlands, on short notice. He was looking at something called Timberwind, a project for building nuclear rockets – an idea that to most people had been scotched long ago. And of the Star Wars programmes – 'directed energy' weapons – there was even less to be found.

The next night we went together to the DOE's hearing, the reason Trader was in Las Vegas. It was formal solicitation of democratic sentiment on what the DOE should do with the test site now that the Cold War was over. Trader had studied the eight lilac-coloured volumes of the DOE's environmental impact statement, which considered the effects of different courses of action. What would happen if the place was closed? What would happen if it was used for other kinds of testing? But Trader wanted to know why Area 51 was not mentioned at all – Area 51 that had some of the worst-known environmental problems of the whole test site.

Trader recalled some of the earlier hearings he had been to – more colourful affairs than this promised to be. It was a way in which the public, in all its wacko diversity touched the bureaucracy. It made me, I will say, proud to be an American.

At one of the more colourful hearings a man stood up, and said, 'In the name of God, my name is Moe. I'm a permanent resident who has been living in Las Vegas for over six years. Believe in your God!' With that, he raised his green Koran in his hand and began to speak. The number of the area where the secret base was located was 51, he said, so he would read chapter 51 of the Koran:

Believe in your god. Promise in the winds which blow in holy directions. Promise in the clouds that carry heavy rains. Promise to the angels who perform the orders of God. Promise to all corners that whatever you say is true . . .

He came to a passage: 'Abraham said, "What is your duty here?" to the aliens, "What is your duty here?" The answer, "we are here to destroy the bad crime!"'

The man pointed at the Bureau of Land Management officers and continued:

'All aliens! All aliens! We want to see the freedom of those captured aliens, because we are here to save the good from the bad one more time.'

Another man had appeared under the name 'Ben Dover'. He stood up and said, 'Ben Dover, Las Vegas'. It was an old vaudeville joke, one that, coincidentally or not, Ben Rich had borrowed as his agency name during the U-2 programme.

But this evening was much calmer.

There were the usual Greenpeace spokespeople and, by counterpoint, a former Air Force officer who said he had eaten plutonium day and night, and was still here to talk about it. He 'pissed plutonium', he bragged. He had worked cleaning up after SAC when the B-52 bumped the tanker over Palomares, Spain, back in the Sixties, scattering plutonium by accident the way the AEC had scattered it on the ground in Area 51 as part of Project 57, back in the 1950s.

Trader got his chance. He read his formal statement and showed a couple of the gem-like documentary artefacts he had picked up, in support. 'Why hadn't they said anything about Area 51 in the Environmental Impact Study?' he asked. To prove that it did indeed exist, he produced two documents, one a press release from 17 October 1955, announcing the construction of the Watertown air strip by REECO, another a letter on Atomic Energy Commission stationery describing the emergency landing of a small plane at the base in 1957. How could they ignore this part of the site completely? How could anyone make a judgment about the real environmental impact of the Nuclear Test Site, he argued, if they didn't know about Area 51 and Project Timberwind (the secret nuclear rocket programme with a classified Environmental Impact Statement)? No one seemed shocked by what Trader was saying. Both the audience and the DOE panel were silent, listening.

The speaker who made the most impact was a representative of the Western Shoshone tribes who pointed out that the tribes had rejected the whole treaty of Ruby Valley of 1863 under which the US government claimed ownership of the test site. The tribes had never taken the payments specified in the Treaty, the tainted silver, the government payoff that would represent their acceptance. Speaker after speaker had made reference to the fact that taxpayers and citizens owned the test site, and I had always thought of myself as much an owner as a watcher. Now I had to consider that Native Americans might own the test site, and Dreamland itself.

20

'Job Knowledge'

DRIVING OFF FROM THE LAS VEGAS HEARING, IT OCCURRED to me that very likely there were petroglyphs similar to those we had seen in the canyon inside Dreamland itself, as I had read there were in other distant reaches of the Nevada Test Site. There was a whole report on the subject – your tax dollars at work again: 'An Archaeological Reconnaissance of the Groom Range' had been conducted in the summer of 1986, as part of the legal requirements of the 1984 seizure of Bald Mountain and other perimeter areas. And the Shoshone, I had read, referred to legends of 'tortured rocks'. Today, one of their spokesmen at the hearing had associated tortured rocks with radioactive ones.

The archaeologists had also found a number of middens – trash heaps – and from the bones and other bits there could determine what the people had eaten and how they had lived. Now, an effort had begun to poke through Dreamland's own midden. In 1994, an ambitious and idealistic lawyer named Jonathan Turley, who ran an organization called the Environmental Crimes Project at George Washington University, filed a suit on behalf of former Area 51 workers against the Air Force and the Environmental Protection Agency. In violation of the law, the suit charged, the facility had burned hazardous wastes, exposing the workers to dangerous chemicals that made them ill and in two cases, led to their deaths. The best known, Robert Frost, was a sheet metal worker who had died in 1989 of cirrhosis of the liver, before the case was brought. His widow joined the plaintiffs; Frost had tried to sue Lockheed before, to no avail. He had worked burning waste in open pits, he reported. His skin turned red and began to peel. After his death, a Rutgers University biochemist, Peter Kahn, found concentrations of dioxins and trichloroethylene in Frost's body tissues. Another worker, Walter Kasza, died at the age of 73 of liver and kidney cancer.

Others in the suit gave accounts of burning in open pits and huge plumes of smoke. These were dangerous corrosive chemicals – solvents and sealants, plastics, paint wasters, by-products of composites and stealth coatings. Their chemical names were frightening even to the layman: dioxins, methyl ethyl ketone, trichloroethylene and dibenzofurans. The workers who burned them were given no protective clothing or masks, they said, even after they asked for them. They were forced to go down in the pits and rifle through the half-burned material to be sure nothing was left. And soon, they said, they came down with all kinds of symptoms: not just the skin rashes but also eye irritations, headaches, blackouts.

Two big Kenworth eighteen-wheelers were always in evidence, one worker reported, and huge 55-gallon drums were brought in with materials from Burbank.

And where did it happen? Some of the pits were on the edge of Papoose Lake, near the legendary 'S-4' of Lazar's tales. Was the Lazar story some bizarre cover for the burning?

Everything was burned – chemicals, papers, even left over prime-rib and lobster from the dining hall, furniture and vehicles.

The workers who had come forward, even shielded by John Doe conventions in the legal documents, were in violation of their oaths and risked their pensions.

It suggested a pattern like that at the test site, the kind of thing Joe Bacco had recounted, where the desperate need born of national urgency and emergency had led to the abuse of workers and the government. Previously, in 1986, workers for the Skunk Works in Burbank had sued over illnesses they said were acquired from exposure to substances used in building the Stealth fighter – the chemicals used in its composites and in its radar absorbing coverings were extremely toxic. And the local citizenry had joined in later. That was why the original Skunk Works was now bare ground, the fenced-off wasteland I had visited. Now workers who had dealt with similar substances at Area 51 itself were stepping forward.

As I read about Turley's suit and talked to him, I began to see the sort of cumulative secrecy Trader had described to me as a great midden – packed with layers of detritus. Or as a Superfund waste site. Secrecy, so useful in crisis situations, was also a dangerous substance. The abuse of secrecy was the means of hiding the abuse of the chemicals, Turley was charging: 'We have compelling evidence that the government and its contractors have used the secrecy of Groom Lake not to protect national security but to shield the illegal disposal of hazardous waste.'

The suits were 'citizen's lawsuits', not torts or damage claims. The workers weren't after money, they were after information: about the nature of the chemicals to which they had been exposed so they could seek treatment. The Air Force's defence against the plaintiffs was that national security considerations protected it against suits for criminal activity. Even to take soil and air samples might reveal the materials used in secret projects and compromise them.

It was a startling and unprecedented claim, far beyond anything Nixon made at the time of Watergate, for instance. The implications were huge: would the same national security defence have placed the officials beyond the reach of prosecution for murder? (Two of the plaintiffs had died, after all.) But no one had ever sued a black facility before.

At first the Air Force lawyers denied the existence of the facility, but Turley came up with three hundred pages of references to Area 51 and Project 51 in Air Force and DOE documents. Finally the officials acknowledged the memorandum of agreement that charged them with running it. Turley and his associates pushed the government hard enough that the President had to sign another order formally stating that to release any information about what went on in Dreamland would endanger the national security of the United States. And they tried to intimidate the workers by demanding they be identified.

By the middle of 1997, it seemed quite possible the suit might go all the way to the Supreme Court.

As part of the case materials, Turley obtained a copy of the Groom security manual, and before long Psychospy had put it on the Internet. The government responded by retroactively classifying the document – a practice as absurd in law as in the real world.

The security manual includes a list of radio code names, procedures, and even maps of the base and inside of some buildings. The thirty-page booklet, of which there were several copies in multiple revisions, bore on its cover the words 'Det 3 SP Job Knowledge'. 'Detachment 3 Special or Security Police' was the assumed meaning of the initials.

It appeared to be the security manual for Dreamland. The maps showed the Scoot-N-Hide sheds – is this an official trademark, I wondered? – for concealing equipment from satellites and the Quik Kill radars and surface-to-air missiles that had long been rumoured. There were radio code words for area and structures. In keeping with the best military tradition, everything had to be renamed: the test site was 'Over the Hill' and Groom Road was the Freeway.

For years, there was talk of high living at Groom Lake and the manual seemed in its maps to confirm the legends of Sam's Place, the long-talked-about casino and bar – as any in Las Vegas. It also offered some confirmation of the tales of fine food at the base, of grapefruits flown in from Israel, of lobsters and other delicacies, of huge spring water bills. It suggested images of a fleet of Auroras bringing back odd delicacies from the antipodes with unprecedented speed – items fresh from the Great Barrier Reef or the Orient, tucked in the corner of a cockpit.

Was it real? First perusal of the manual led to doubts. It was crude and klutzy. It seemed unlikely that the Air Force would put the words, Liberty and Justice for All, on the badges reproduced on the first page of the manual. The quality, the tone, the feel of the codenames was unconvincing. 'Dutch Apple' for the headquarters seemed inappropriately imaginative – unless it reflected some kind of inside joke. Procedures were outlined for moving test articles. When back in the civilian world the 'special police' were instructed to say that they 'worked for EG&G at the test site'.

There was quite detailed and accurate information on the operation of the road sensors, which was known to the outside. But who was the manual for, what was it for? For the deputized guards, working for Wackenhut or EG&G or other contractors?

But as I pondered it more, it seemed just awkwardly enough written and gawky enough in its thinking to be real. It made me wonder again about the MJ12 documents, which shared some of the same crude explanatory quality.

And if it was not real, why would the government have sought to classify it and have it removed from circulation in print and on the Internet?

Except the government had never before tried such a thing, and by definition information already public cannot be made secret. Did the impossibility of such an effort suggest it was merely a ruse to make the document seem genuine? If so, why?

The case came before Federal Judge Philip Pro. But Judge Pro had previously found the government was not liable for damages to some 216 workers who had been exposed to radiation at the NTS between 1951 and 1981 – some of them workers like Joe Bacco who had been exposed to radiation by Baneberry, many of them workers who had been assigned at times to Area 51 itself. And Pro seemed to believe in keeping security. All he wanted was another letter from the President of the United States, swearing they were needed to keep Dreamland in the dark. And he got it. In September, 1995, Bill Clinton signed a letter affirming that to reveal what Turley and his clients wanted to know about Groom Lake 'could reasonably be expected' to damage the national security.

The government pressed for the names of the John Doe clients, and Turley felt it was trying to pressure them. Judge Pro ordered the documents in the case sealed. What that meant became clear all of a sudden. In the summer of 1995, Turley had flown to Chicago to be by the bedside of his sick father. He got a call: OSI agents were on their way over to the University of Georgetown law centre to seal his office. He immediately called the secretary and asked her to alert campus security: he had a vision of the bicycle mounted campus cops involved in hand to hand combat against OSI commandos infiltrating through the ventilation system. In the end, Turley's office was sealed; all material was placed in a safe to which only he and one associate had combinations. It was like a little patch of secrecy, an embassy of Dreamland in Georgetown.

In 1995, the case against the EPA was dismissed, the next

year, the case against the Air Force. Turley appealed. If the case came to trial, he planned to call the Secretary of Defense, the Secretary of the Air Force and the President's National Security Advisor. If none of them were willing to admit to the existence of the base, then he said he would call representatives of the Russian Embassy. The Soviets after all, had photographed the base from their satellites.

Turley had the government caught in a post-Cold War half Nelson: 'While the United States Government refuses to acknowledge the existence of this base to the American public,' he was able to argue, 'the Russian government recently declassified much of its intelligence information as part of a new openness policy following the fall of the Communist regime and the adoption of democratic process.' And since the 1993 signing of the Open Skies treaty, they and all other signatory nations had a right to do so. It was legal for foreigners to photograph the base, but not for the Americans who had paid for it.

21
Rave

IF SINISTER FORCES WERE MANIPULATING THE MEDIA THEY were doing it quite effectively. Area 51 was infiltrating television as stealthily as any Hollywood extraterrestrials had ever invaded the planet. It kept popping up, like the Area 51 video game, in the oddest places.

In Las Vegas, which presented subcultures as casino themes, the Area 51 club opening was marked with big signs in red and white warning stripes and stencil letters visible from the freeway.

A whole range of cable shows dealing with the mysterious came to Rachel and talked to Interceptors. Psychospy could be counted on to give good soundbites. His sentences were ambiguous enough to be useful; he knew where the editing would happen.

There was a familiar pattern to most of the TV shows: some lights over the Jumbled Hills – Janet aircraft or flares typically, the standard photos of the base, sometimes establishing shots of Las Vegas neon, talking heads saying there were 'mysterious things flying'. But the key to all the segments was to leave the question of whether there were real saucers just hanging, hovering like one of those magnesium flares.

After the image of the Manta appeared in magazines, Steve was flooded with calls from television and print reporters, and even Hollywood producers. Within a few days, the major networks had paid calls on him and *Unsolved Mysteries*, the tabloid TV series, dispatched two trucks and camera crews to his quiet Armarillo street.

Robert Stack, the host and erstwhile battery pitchman, didn't like the anti government tendency he saw creeping into the piece, so they added a line to the script to the effect that 'the Air Force denies the planes are theirs. So the question remains, whose are they?' It was important for the general format of *Unsolved Mysteries* that the 'question should remain'. The truth had to stay out there.

In April, ABC TV clumsily bungled into the camou dudes, and the crew had its film confiscated. Perhaps irritated by the fact that CNN had set up a camera atop Freedom Ridge, a violation of stated law, they stopped the network crew.

Someone mailed Steve a videotape shot by two Las Vegas cops who had read about the TR3A and headed north to Dreamland. Perhaps inspired by beer, they caught sight of something in the sky that danced wildly on the tape, a sign of a camera held by uncertain hands. Their voices were audible screaming, 'It's the fuckin' Manta! It's the fuckin' Manta!' In fact, Steve concluded, the craft was probably a B-1.

By May 1994, the Press safaris to Freedom Ridge had become so frequent, the viewing points so crowded, that Psychospy described a fist fight between two reporters encamped above Groom. It amazed the watchers who remembered when few knew the way up at all. And the camou dudes were getting edgy too.

By the late spring of 1994, an unaccustomed quiet had descended over Dreamland. Nothing much seemed to be flying. There were rumours that Aurora had been cancelled. No skyquakes had been heard for months. But the dudes had become more anxious. They confiscated film from an ABC camera crew and a bumbling New York photographer who goaded the camou dudes and the sheriff's department.

In October, Larry King and entourage descended on Rachel. They set up on the side of the road, with the wrong set of hills in the background, but no saucer landed in the desert could have looked stranger than Larry's whole stage – desk, chairs, lights and coffee mugs – glowing there amidst the trampled sage.

We were watching this real physical place turn almost before our glass and cathode-ray eyes into legend.

All of a sudden, it seemed, you found references to Area 51 everywhere. There were scenery files for the popular Microsoft game *Flight Simulator* that one could download from the Internet to 'fly over' Groom Lake. And that video game of a shoot out at Area 51 was in arcades and on home players. Marvel comics latched on to Area 51 and television embraced it.

The NBC show called *Dark Skies*, set in the mid Sixties, complete with a brand new red Ford Mustang, featured aliens digging an underground base beneath Area 51 – and Howard Hughes catching on to their plans. 'We've got to get to Dreamland,' was the most memorable line. A CD-ROM came out with the old cartoon character Jonny Quest delving first into the mysteries of Roswell and then Area 51.

The story of Area 51 had long had its special appeal to technogeeks. One of the Apple Newton software group, for instance, took an interest in Area 51 after a trip to Rachel in 1994. He hid a secret feature in one version of the software – if you knew which place to push you could show Area 51 on the Newton's map.

The Newton's world map included an entry for Area 51 in its correct location. If the user picks Area 51 from the map, the icons in the datebook application take on an alien theme – alien faces, flying saucers, robots and so on.

Then, in August 1995, the story goes – and we are strictly amid the Lore here – a cryptographer at the CIA was one of the beta testers for the new programme. When he saw Area 51 shown, he went to his bosses, who demanded Apple remove the reference. Management 'caved in', the sources say, but the feature was covered over rather than removed and there is a trick for retrieving it.

The notion of overlapping the Generation X demographic and the UFO one had begun to warm the hearts of marketing types. The Gen X files – that was the concept, and in the second episode of the *X-Files*, the show that would twist the weirdness of *Twin Peaks* to dovetail with all sorts of conspiracy lores, Dreamland was translated from Nevada to Utah, where it became Ellens Air Force Base, 'a mecca for UFO buffs'. It, like Groom Lake base, is omitted from USGS maps. In the *X-Files* version of the story, the hills above Dreamland become tall reeds – equally good hiding places.

Ellens is rumoured to be 'one of six sites' to which the Roswell wreckage was shipped. There the round craft built using alien technology of the lore became triangular; the Little A-Le-Inn a diner, with a fat lady who took UFO snapshots from her back porch.

Mulder and Scully see dancing lights, encounter craft that hover. They are menaced by Men In Black with the requisite sunglasses, and a black helicopter comes at them. There is reference to 'the Aurora project', and dabblings with mental reprogramming. 'That's unreal,' they conclude, 'I've never seen anything like that.' Leaving hanging the suggestion of a causal link between the two statements.

Aliens

The redoubtable engine of American marketing, as simultaneously wondrous and horrific as is the military machine, had quickly mobilized to sell the teen alienation of Generation X back to it.

Soon I was noticing alien faces with almond eyes and big heads everywhere – in the malls, in the trendy shops in the East Village of New York. There was alien jewellery, alien T-shirts, alien temporary tattoos. The alien face had become a wry Nineties equivalent of the Seventies smile badge.

The image of the face of the Grey was set in the early Eighties by Budd Hopkins and Whitley Strieber. The big-eyed alien took over from other images of what the aliens look like.

There had always been images of extraterrestrials, of course, but this was a new image for them. If earlier aliens had represented Communist invaders (*Invasion of the Body Snatchers*) or Aids (*Alien*) or friendly, baby-like creatures (*Close Encounters* and *ET*) the new one was different. Its overtones were of a huge foetus or hungry child, with Keene kid big eyes and head larger than body. There were even echoes in the image of Munch's 'The Scream' – the cliché face of modern angst itself.

This alien face – and it was significant that we had begun calling creatures from other planets 'alien' again in the Eighties, after the Seventies had popularized 'extraterrestrial' – had long been familiar, but had never been so graphically standardized before.

It summed up a growing American subculture devoted to ideas of abduction and implantation that paralleled the fascination with recovering childhood experiences – commonly those of abuse – via hypnosis. In 1995, Testors released a plastic model kit of the Grey alien, indicating that it had established itself as the image of the alien the way the flying saucer established itself as the iconic image of the unidentified flying object.

But the new image of the alien was as much ironic as iconic. Much of the new alien material turned on the puns on the term alien – the joke was that the Greys figured as immigrants. And the face had become as much a graphic cliché, an ethnic cartoon, as Sambo or Uncle Tom. Was America's latest favourite ethnic group from Zeta Reticuli? 'Do we call them Astro Americans?' a friend asked.

Tropes of the alien often serve as parable for dealing with issues of immigration, with the differing degrees of irony evidenced in *Coneheads* ('we are ... from France,' Dan Ackroyd says, and his nemesis is an INS agent in the film) and *Alien Nation*, where the aliens exhibit the irritating traits of various earthly minority groups: they are ex slaves with strange music. They threaten to take jobs and resources from earth natives. They eat bizarre food and score intimidatingly high in maths tests.

My favourite T-shirt on this theme showed a cliché alien wearing a sombrero and bandoliers and bore the legend: 'We don't want no stinkin green cards.'

Its iconism was accomplished when it became subject to manipulation of context and ironic reference. Thus T-shirts show the Beatles with alien heads, or the 'see-no-evil-hear-no-evil-speak-no-evil' trio rendered in alien faces and whole host of alien face pop artefacts – earrings, Schwa artefacts, Alien Factory skateboard graphics. (The latter name comes from Dayton, Ohio, home of Wright Patterson Air Force Base, where 'recovered' aliens from saucer crashes were supposed, in the lore, to be 'stored' in the infamous 'Hangar 18'.

The alien theme was strong in music. In rock 'n' roll bands such as the Foo Fighters (on their own 'Roswell Records' label) and on the cover of an album by rock 'n' roll group Spacehog, called *Resident Alien*, which bore a mock 'green card' for an extraterrestrial.

Television could handle the alien with equal facility as drama or as sitcom. 'Aliens are all around us,' intones the narrator at the beginning of *Third Rock from the Sun*, a sitcom in the tradition of *My Favorite Martian, Mork and Mindy*, or *ALF*. In *Dark Skies*, the alien invasion turns out to have been so subtle and surreptitious that it has influenced every major event of the last fifty years of history, from the shooting down of the U-2 to the Kennedy assassination. Conspiracy theorists are alienated from mainstream explanations, of course. Concealment and conspiracy was another theme behind the image – it was the logo of the Big Coverup, the 'Cosmic Watergate'. 'The government is lying', the T-shirts said.

In time, the alien face came to appear to me as the literal face of the X-files' X-generation suspicion of government – and the projection, perhaps, of that generation's own alienation. 'We are not alone' – the slogan that often captions the Grey face, may be more an expression of hope than an assertion of belief.

That, or the skilful marketing of that emotion – one not unknown over history to younger human beings.

Someone once said, 'aliens are alien because we alienate them.' That person was ALF.

By the spring of 1996, Hollywood had latched on to the Lore. It was turning from folk into fodder for commerce. And the Interceptors were at once amused, irked and perhaps a bit sad. Perhaps it was resentment that the rest of the world and the Hollywood dream machine was taking over their base, at the crass political effort to cash in on the Mailbox.

The idea to rename Highway 375 the Extraterrestrial Highway was to bring tourists to the area. When the Nevada legislature held hearings on the proposal the only witnesses to appear – and they were in favour – were Joe and Pat Travis, the most obvious beneficiaries of it, and Ambassador Merlin Merlyn, himself an avowed Extraterrestrial.

Psychospy took a hard line against the naming – more out of an instinct to oppose government, one suspects, than for his stated reason, which was that no thought had been given to the consequences of bringing tourists to the area and possibly into contact with the camou dudes.

If anything, he felt his own bailiwick invaded – he was after all, the first to produce a tourist guide to the area, the first to lead groups to the perimeter, the first to pioneer four-wheel drive to the top of Freedom Ridge. Now it was all about selling souvenirs and T-shirts. But Psychospy had set all this in motion when he printed up his first T-shirt bearing the invented Dreamland patch.

The dedication of the ET Highway and the unveiling of the roadsigns that marked it was a ceremony that was hijacked twice.

The first time was by the producers of the film *Independence Day*, which would dramatically change the lore about Area 51. In the spring of 1996, whetting anticipation for the summer release of the movie, the stars agreed to join the ET Highway dedication and the production donated a 'time capsule' to Rachel. This guaranteed that the politicians would be over-shadowed.

The event was hijacked a second time on the highway. While Psychospy boycotted the event, the Minister and Agent X rode along in the ET Highway convoy, a rolling photo opportunity that began in a car park in Las Vegas and headed up to Rachel for the unveiling of the new, official, copyrighted ET Highway signs along Highway 375. These showed the silhouettes of flying saucers and – nothing ET here – an F-117 in silhouette.

Agent X led the way in a rented red LeBaron; the Minister's Civic was in fifth place. There were about thirty cars and a big charter bus. As they came down from Hancock Summit into the Tikaboo Valley about 30 miles south of Rachel, just at the point where the Groom Road stretched out to the west, looking as always like a pole of dust rising straight into the air, the Minister caught sight of a bright yellow sign stuck into the dirt by the roadside, with an arrow to the left and the official ET Highway logo. The left turn indicator went on in Agent X's LeBaron, and soon the whole convoy was turning down the dirt road.

In his rear view Agent X could see the convoy following, the big bus bouncing along the rough road and clouds of dust enveloping the whole column, departing from Route 375 for the unpaved road heading toward the mountains and the perimeter.

It was a plot by the Interceptors, specific members unknown, codenamed Operation Coyote, after the cartoon character Wile

Coyote, who is constantly posting fake road signs to divert the Roadrunner.

The Minister determined that he would pull off before he got to the guard shack he knew lay a few miles ahead, because he knew the rule, you're under arrest once you get to the shack, which is on the wrong side of the perimeter.

Then a Nevada highway patrolman realized what was happening, came roaring up, siren wailing, lights blazing, and through the dust ahead, the Minister could see the lead car taking a sharp right turn onto a dusty road that doubled back toward Route 375, through the Medlin Ranch.

But clearly the planners had envisioned, hoped, dreamed that it might go all the way, the governor of Nevada and other dignitaries, the whole movie and business motley crowd arriving at the perimeter – hell! at the guardhouse.

Two more Nevada State Police cars barrelled past the convoy at breakneck speed through the dust, as they headed into Rachel.

Of course, the convoy and the whole event had already been abducted – by the promoters of the film *Independence Day*, who had brought out the stars of the film and dedicated a time capsule in the front of the Little A-Le-Inn and so managed to wrap themselves in the new signage of the ET Highway and the authority of the government of Nevada.

In front of the Little A-Le-Inn, the stars of *Independence Day*, Bill Pullman and Jeff Goldblum, moved among a thin crowd and posed in front of the signs as Nevada tourism officials explained that prospective visitors could call an 800 number to be sent an 'ET Highway Experience' package complete with map. The governor joked that perhaps the signs should have been placed so they could be read from above.

A well-known state legislator named Bob Price, an eccentric and colourful character who led 'fact-finding trips' to the cathouses, appeared costumed as Darth Vader. 'You're Bob Price,' shrewdly commented a Rachel youngster, looking right at him.

'The only aliens I've seen are the people who visit here,' a little girl told Mary Manning, the reporter for the *Las Vegas Review-Journal*, and she was more correct than she knew. Those visitors, buffs and reporters, actors and producers, were the really strange ones. They were the aliens the inn welcomed and prospered from.

With the release of the film itself in July 1996, Area 51 was suddenly the star of Hollywood. *Independence Day*, which set all-time records by grossing nearly $150 million in its first two weeks, established Dreamland in the popular mind – with a twist. The film provided a new key link in the lore. It connected Area 51 directly with Roswell, whose legend was also growing daily.

While, of course, the traditional story had tied Roswell to Hangar 18 at Wright-Patt, the legendary repository of recovered saucers and alien bodies, *Independence Day's* story had them ending up at Area 51.

That tale had been floating around, playing in the background like a minor theme – Bill Hamilton had said that the first saucer wreckage came to Area 51 in the late Forties. But so had murmurings about other possible dispersal and storage sites – Edwards, Indian Springs, the labs at Los Alamos and Sandia, even McDill or Eglin Air Force Bases in Florida became part of the accounts. Now, thanks to the power of the big screen, Area 51's claim surged into the foreground.

At one point, the President says disdainfully 'I can assure you, there is no Area 51.'

'Well, Mr President,' the head of the CIA says, 'that's not ... exactly ... true.' Area 51 becomes the headquarters from which Earth resists invasion. And so millions of people heard about Area 51 for the first time. Gene Huff was delighted – ninety per cent of people had never heard of Area 51 before the movie, he said. The message of ID 4, if it had one, was that an alien attack would bring together the technical nerd, the kvetching Jew, the black, the alcoholic poor white, due to a new global patriotism. It recalled Reagan's remark to Gorbachev – if aliens attacked the earth, then we would all get together, wouldn't we?

Dependence Day, the movie should have been called: if there was a message among its promiscuous borrowing of clichés from the films of the past – *War of the Worlds* to *Star Wars* – then the message was that we need each other.

But the real box office appeal came from the scenes of mass

destruction of well known landmarks – the splitting of the Empire State building or the implosion of the White House.

And the President asks the questions we were all asking about Area 51. 'How come I wasn't told about this place?' 'How did they keep this secret?' 'How did they pay for it all?'

But since Area 51's existence ends up saving humanity, the implication is that we should be grateful it was there.

The film conjures up an underground lab at the base with tilted glass walls behind which aliens are stored in giant containers. There is the usual 'reverse engineering' of a saucer – 'So,' the mad scientist in charge says – long-haired of course – fairly rubbing his hands: 'I guess you want to see the big tamale?'

Hollywood's Area 51 looks more like we imagine it than the real one: it is slicker, shinier, more sci fi. It's packed with high tech equipment: all the war rooms and secret labs of a dozen films of the past rolled into one. It looks in fact, something like the Area 51 in the video game.

The Pentagon thought Hollywood would be leading the way in simulations of the future battlefield as well – perhaps in the controls and interfaces for the aircraft of the future, UAVs. But Hollywood was leading the way in defining Area 51 now, painting Dreamland.

At the end of the Cold War, in the early Nineties, Ed McCracken, the CEO of Silicon Graphics, whose workstations are used both to devise new aircraft designs and to produce movie special effects, declared that demands of mass media had supplanted those of the Pentagon as the driver of technological prowess. The Air Force New Vistas report declared that 'entertainment organizations' had the skills and means to produce better simulators than the military.

Was Hollywood supplanting the Pentagon? Would the Dreamworks be the future locale of Dreamland's technology? Once, DARPA had spurred the computer industry. Now Disney did.

'Calling all "Encountered People"!' read the proclamation that appeared in August 1996. An outfit calling itself Zzyzx Productions and 'The Center for the Study of Aerial Phenomenon' announced 'Abduction, live at Area 51', 'An all-night political action rally and UFO watching vigil' and 'rave party'. The fine print coyly declared an intention to 'encourage peace, love and harmony, so leave your ray guns at home'. The tickets, $25 a head, would be available through Ticketmaster.

That seemed reasonable for a pass to Area 51, only the party turned out to be scheduled for a lot behind the trailers in Rachel. The music would be techno – the robotic dance stuff of the new Germany, steeped in the dust of the Wall, now imported, manipulated and cut to street strength. Techno – the music of the post Cold War era.

The idea seemed to be that the fellows at the base might warm to this New Age Woodstock.

The most romantic thing about it was the dust swirling in the big floodlights. The light carved a bright cave out of the darkness. But the promoters had promised 'sunbaked desert dance dirt,' a 'fire-breathing tribal drum circle' and all night dancing in the shadows of the Jumbled Hills. They held open the possibility the boys at the base might be tickled enough to float a saucer up just over the ridge, offering just a hint of the mysteries beyond.

I drove up to see what would come of the event.

On the way up to Rachel I stopped for gas. As I paid and came back to the car I noticed a guy with a sleeveless shirt and a beat-up truck, looking world-weary. 'How are ya?' I asked.

'A little closer to somewhere,' he answered, as if trying to convince himself.

And I almost said, 'But still a hell of a long way from anywhere.'

Beside the Black Mail Box, I spotted a Camry with Arizona plates. I pulled over to talk. A young couple were looking toward the ridge. The man was a stockbroker, he told me. 'They say this is the place,' he commented, dreamily. 'We drove all the way from Tucson, just to see.'

In Rachel, the locals – piqued by the prospect of drugged and drunken youth from as far away as Los Angeles showing up – watched with interest. The sheriff's office required the promoters to post a large bond and the deputies' cars roamed the area showing force as the best deterrent.

Strange vehicles – Woodstock era Microbuses, and Sixties

compacts – with out-of-state plates, began to appear in front of the Quik Pik and the Inn.

At the Research Center, some of the Interceptors gathered to watch. In the little yard by the trailer they dipped crisps and roasted hot dogs and marvelled at the speed with which the media machine was latching on to the mythology of Area 51.

'It's the dominant urban folk legend of the Nineties,' Zero said in the kitchen, unwrapping more crisps. He was referring to all those tales like the Phantom Hitchhiker and the woman with the termites in her bouffant, those 'FOAF' tales (told by a friend-of-a-friend) about his cousin's ex-wife, the tales assembled by Jan Van Brunwand, now compiled on-line by the urban folklore news groups.

Behind the trailer was a little shed, with a platform on its roof: we climbed up to look at the assembling trucks and lights and speakers being set up in a neo-tribal circle. It was a little Freedom Ridge! A mini Tickaboo! Except that it would only bear the weight of three or four people.

They took turns climbing up, returning to the little grill where the hot dogs were roasting, the burgers grilling.

The souvenir vendors had arrived first, in the morning. This was a time to cash in. The latest item was a T-shirt showing a saucer over the lakebed and the legend 'Area 51 Yacht Club'.

One of them was an enormous man in a minivan who told me he used to be with Navy Intelligence. He sat in the mini van at the Quik Pik, wearing a SEAL team T-shirt and an LAPD bomb squad cap. For sale he had brought glow-in-the-dark alien heads, T-shirts and charms.

'Naval Intelligence,' he repeated. 'Ever hear of Richard Marcinko? Seal Team Seven. It's not supposed to exist but it does.'

He had strong opinions on Bob Lazar. 'That W-2 is as real as can be,' he said.

Huge screens surrounded the circle of dance floor, flashing music video images back on themselves, reminding some of old drive-in movie screens. But only a few dozen dancers showed up, dodging the cows who sat on the edges of the ET Highway, almost begging to be mutilated. Groggy after the long drive up, the newcomers wandered onto the dance floor.

A few misguided Hollywood types ended up on the site. At one point a limousine turned into the parking lot and as it slowly curved around in front of me I caught a glimpse of a softly-lit interior, packed with cut crystal decanters glowing like artefacts in an old-fashioned sci fi film. Then the dust rose up and covered it all.

The UFO souvenirs failed to sell well. At the end of the evening, I caught sight of the Naval intelligence man, still sitting in the minivan. There was no evidence he had ever left it.

22

Remote Viewing
or 'Anomalous Cognition'

AT THE RAVE PARTY, THE PROMOTERS HAD LINED UP A SERIES
of real life 'abductees'. They sat at card tables arrayed under
tents, looking ill at ease. But among them was a woman who
did not claim to be an abductee, but she was willing to talk – a
lot, very fast and in run-on sentences, all about black helicopters, Tesla, thought bubbles, interdimensionals and portals
and so on. Her name was Kathleen Ford and around the time I
first climbed the ridges and looked down on the base, Ford
began taking pictures of strange floating or flying objects along
Mail Box Road – Nevada Highway 375 – looking west over the
Jumbled Hills toward Dreamland.

Some of these I had seen on the wall at the Little A-Le-Inn
in Rachel, along with all the other greasy, dusty, spotted images
of lights in the sky. There was even a snapshot of Ford herself,
dressed for photographic action. In the picture, she appeared a
rather frumpy character, but a swollen-up down-filled jacket
will do that to anyone.

Ford's snapshots were all carefully labelled with details about
the camera and film used. In almost every instance, the name
of the camera was misspelled. The captions were typed on
white paper and included as much specificity about the time,
date, and equipment used to take them as there was lack of
specificity about the images, such as: 'Two visible ships taken
by Mail Box Road Cannon with 200 Zoom Kodak Gold 200';
or 'Invisible ship with light beam going below mountain. This
photo was shot facing west at Mail Box Road at 7:50 A.M. Fugi
(sic) Automatic with 80 zoom, Kodak T-Max, 400 B/W.'

It was one word of the last caption that caught my attention:
'invisible'. As in: 'This invisible object appeared after I experimented with music.'

That, and a picture showing what looked like a floating

eyeball or giant martini olive. 'Tesla, Come Here I Need You!' that one was entitled.

I didn't understand what Ford meant by this until months later, when I met her at the Rave party.

'At first I wanted to take pictures of UFOs and sell them to magazines and make money,' she told me. A blackjack dealer in Las Vegas, she would come every few weeks and take photos day and night along Mail Box Road.

She was defensive about these photos – clearly smarting from a long history of encountering scepticism – pointing out that this image, say, couldn't be a flare from a fighter plane, dropped to fool heat-seeking missiles and commonly confused with flying saucers, or that one was surely not the effects of lens or diaphragm. She pointed out that one photo was shot on Easter Sunday, a holiday that even the denizens of Dreamland respected and on which they never flew.

Ford began shooting regularly near the Mailbox. 'I sort of used myself for bait,' she told me. She wrapped herself in a blanket and lay down in the back of a pickup.

'I approached it like a job and went out regularly every couple of weeks and shot ten rolls of film, T-max black and white.'

Then one night other sorts of images began showing up on her film. I understood her to mean that things showed up in the photographs without having been visible when the shutter was snapped.

'That's when I got the eyeball,' she said.

'The what?' I asked, knowing full well what she meant.

'The eyeball – this one. I give them all names and this one I just call the eyeball. It's translucent.'

Indeed it could be an eyeball, floating in front of the flash-lit, out of focus, grassy margin of the highway, the soft LED digits of the dating function visible in the lower right-hand corner. It was Emerson's transcendental eyeball, Jung's eye in the sky – whatever you wanted. And I took it and Ford herself as a token of the fact that you could see just about anything you wanted along Mailbox Road.

'After I got this one I went, "Oh my God!" I cried for three weeks ... They've lied to us, I thought.

'When I saw this everything I had read about UFOs and

dismissed suddenly became feasible and I cried, cried, cried, cried.'

I picked up the book Ford said had inspired her. The paperback of *Silent Invasion* by Ellen Crystal, PhD bore on its cover an image of an alien face, like a film still. Inside were lots of photographs that resembled Ford's.

Ellen Crystal had taken many similar pictures of 'Tesla globes', spaceships and even aliens, near Pine Bush in West-chester County, New York.

Crystal was the clear source of inspiration at least for Ford's captions: the author, with her aptly New Age name, applies the same specificity of camera and film type, time and so on in labelling her photos of what she says are alien craft, aliens and various types of energy sources. Here was a typical Crystal title: 'Large Tesla Field. Taken: June 12, 1988, at Pine Bush, New York. Camera: Nikon 35 mm SLR with 50 mm lens. Film: Kodacolor negative print film (ASA 400). Exposure: 1/60 sec. at f//1.4 with flash.'

Elsewhere, Crystal supplied the name of her developer: Fotomat.

Crystal's globes and ships could also, I thought, have been drops of some kind of staining liquid on film or lens. But Crystal saw them as Tesla bubbles – and beams and ships and even aliens themselves. She might not have seen it unless she believed it. There was a twist: while Ford had photographed UFOs she couldn't see with her eye, on the spot, Crystal claimed to have seen UFOs that didn't appear in her pictures. Some UFOs, she believed, generated shortwave or other radiation that made them invisible.

All this was happening in the otherwise mundane world of Pine Bush, New York – a long way from the desert. The point was that there were dozens of UFOs around if you knew how to photograph them, not just in the famous desert spots, but all over. Crystal had seen triangles in Westchester County that sounded like the black planes seen in Nevada and California. But, she recounted, these were not generally tested in populated areas. So Crystal had a different interpretation: 'there may be forms of stealth aircraft that are "true" UFOs built and operated by human beings.'

But she argues that the B-2 Stealth bomber shown to the public 'is really a decoy to divert attention from where the money and effort are really being placed – namely, on construction of enhanced stealth craft capable of hovering at ground level, cruising at speeds ranging from a slow walk to thousands of miles per hour, and turning invisible to the human eye. In other words American UFOs.' When I read that, I thought of a posting I had seen on the Net that suggested the opposite: that disguising a spy plane as a UFO would be a brilliant strategy to veil it in derision.

Crystal's photographs, like Ford's eyeballs or Tesla globes also reminded me of the strange and sinister balls, like malign bacteria seen through a microscope, of Harold Edgerton's photographs of atomic blasts in their first microseconds at the test site. They even showed the same flash-overexposed Joshua tree silhouettes. These were slices of time and vision thinner than the human eye could grasp. Only the mechanical eye of Edgerton's cameras could do it. No vision of an alien invasion ever conjured up a more sinister looking lifeform than these death forms.

Invisible craft made visible – that was Ford's goal. I was reminded of a chapter in the New Vistas report from the Air Force boldly headed 'Invisible airplanes'. The report talks about all the planes of tomorrow, unmanned, stealthy to radar, to heat seekers, to the human eye.

Stealth makes aircraft almost invisible to radar, but not to light: so they fly only in the dark: 'We rule the night,' Lockheed's ads bragged. But not the day. The next step was to do for vision what stealth did for radar: create high-tech camouflage...

There was pretty good evidence that some of the planes flying in Dreamland were now aimed at making themselves invisible by day as well, the new stories held. They wore electronic skins. They used a technology that was like wrapping the whole plane in liquid crystal or lead or some computer screen, turning that into a fabric that could be bent or built up like tile or mosaic. It was something called Polyaniline Radar Absorbent composite, 'optically transparent' except when charged with a 24-volt current that triggers the camouflage receptors. These read the ambient light – its brightness but also its hue – and adapt to match. They were chameleon planes.

One such programme had been around for a while, called 'Ivy'. Could that come from IV for invisible? I thought – reminding myself again of Norio. I called Steve and asked him about it: did this mean that the reason people hadn't been seeing any planes recently flying above Dreamland was because they couldn't be seen? If you didn't see them, they must be invisible.

'Had there been,' I asked Steve, before thinking of what I was saying, 'any confirmed sightings of these aircraft?'

Ford's photographs were confirmed sightings all right – proof that you had to believe to see. She could feel the creatures she said. And she learned to lure them close, with music, *Close Encounters* style.

'We used something called toning, just making a [soft] sound like ahhh. If you have a group of people where the men are low and the women are high it sounds like angels.'

It apparently also drew the entities, or 'thought balls', she sometimes calls them.

She pushed another image forward, with multiple geometrical shapes on it – diaphragm reflections, I thought. Sometimes, she said, she got blobs like radioactive jelly fish and paramecia and bubbles. 'Tom Dongo gets the bubbles,' she says. 'He lives in Sedona.' Ford has studied in Sedona with Tom Dongo, whose name I had heard before: he was a champion of the vortices of Sedona, centres of magnetic and spiritual power that, when I visited, I found helpfully pointed out on the tourist channel of the hotel cable TV system. Vortices seemed to be as common in the valleys of Sedona as windchimes were in its boutiques.

'When I go out there alone I get into alpha beta,' she says.

I look baffled.

'You know, dream state, alpha beta.

'And these images are very dreamy.'

In other pictures Ford pointed out a different sort of blob. They might signify creatures from other realms of space-time, she was telling me.

'People told me there are interdimensionals. Aliens that can move in and out. John Lear talked about the government having EBEs – "extra biological entities" – and the government is having a hard time with them. They keep them in an electromagnetic field but they just drift in and out.'

At the Inn these days Chuck Clark was talking about interdimensionals too. Far out as it sounded, the idea of interdimensionals struck me as one of the most thoughtful areas of UFO lore. What we had once taken for aliens from another star system, this sort of theory went, might instead be time travellers or venturers from parallel universes.

You didn't have to be a nut or wacko to speculate on some of these things at a time when the new astrophysics was dabbling in the most startling of ideas. Space-time 'wormholes' made time travel a theoretical possibility. String theory projected scenarios where an original universe of 21 or 34 dimensions might have collapsed into the present four.

It all went back to quantum mechanics and Heisenberg's uncertainty principle. Subatomic particles could apparently be in several places at once, in one interpretation. From these bits of quantum doubt, like conspiracy theories from Eisenhower's toothache, whole theories of parallel, alternate, universes had arisen.

A parallel universe might be identical to this one, except that in the second I have brown instead of blue eyes. Or, more to the point, a subatomic particle that is *here* in one universe might be *there* in its neighbour.

There had been quite respectable efforts to solve the quantum uncertainty principle by experimenting with the theory of parallel universes. It began in the late Fifties when the respected physicist Bryce DeWitt proposed parallel universes as a solution to the uncertainty problems of quantum physics. It wouldn't take so many of those universes, DeWitt argued: only about 10 to the hundredth power.

The new physics implied that the universe was full of mysteries. All those little bits of quantum doubt, all that black matter, made the universe a kind of sponge of uncertainty.

A physicist named Fred Alan Wolf, in *The Dreaming Universe*, argued that parallel universes might be the source of schizophrenia, visions, even dreams. UFO sightings, he noted, seemed to many viewers to possess a dreamlike quality. Could UFOs have an existence that was half-in, half-out of this universe? This was taking Jung's idea of manifesting archetypes onto a different, more literal plane. It was awfully close to the borderlands folk or the contactees and their 'ether'. The things that were seen in the sky, to this new way of thinking, might inhabit some realm halfway between the state of a thought and the state of a material. The key question, he said, was how matter gave rise to thought – 'how does meat dream?' But could thought make matter, dreams make meat?

Are then these visions created by psychic disturbances? How literally are we to take the idea of objects in the sky being manifestations of cultural unease? The idea of one universe as the dream of another gave Dreamland a whole new meaning.

This was pretty far afield for my philosophy, Horatio, but no wonder those inclined to such thought, like remote viewers, were coming up with reports of their travels via 'anomalous cognition' that left them with a new sense of the universe. Our world, they would say, is like a single page in a great encyclopedia of worlds, a leaf in infinitely unfolding strata of possibilities, a kind of existential filo dough.

'Now this one I took on the border,' Ford said.

It showed one of the familiar round metal sensors, those strange mirrored spheres that mark the perimeter of Dreamland. But there was something else in one corner. 'See this,' Ford said, pointing to what looked like a boulder.

'I think this is a remote viewing blob.' The camou dudes, she suspected, could carry out remote viewing of the border from their guard houses. Why they bothered to head out in Blazers and Blackhawks if they could do this I did not ask.

But remote viewing at 'the remote location' seemed eminently appropriate. And hadn't the Army taken the technique seriously enough to spend my tax dollars on it?

Remote viewing (RV) – the ability to see at a distance – is a paranormal technique in which the units from the CIA and the Pentagon believed enough to spend at least $20 million to investigate it over a 20-year period. Also known by the wonderful phrase 'anomalous cognition', the idea was developed by Drs Harold Puthoff and Russell Targ at the Stanford Research Institute (SRI) in the 1970s. Their first and prime viewer was an artist named Ingo Swann – Hollywood could never come up with names like these! – who directed the effort to turn remote viewing into a useful military intelligence tool. Fearing that a psi spy gap with the Soviets was emerging, the CIA began funding remote viewing and later handed the research to the Army.

It began with some degree of scientific rigour, with the finding that some people did a better job of 'psi-hitting' – say, picking cards face down on a table several rooms away – than they should have by chance alone. But in Project Grill Flame, later Scannate and Stargate, psychic abilities were applied to such tasks as discovering the locations of Soviet submarines or finding hostages in the Middle East. But results kept turning up that embarrassed the Army. When the viewers were directed to search for secret Soviet aircraft, they came back with reports of UFOs – alien craft.

Viewers were sometimes led through brainwave feedback and meditative techniques to become more sensitive receptors. Two of the early remote viewers were Ed Dames and Joseph McMoneagle. Dames claimed that 'we employed people who used altered states to take a look at the radio station in Tehran, Iran prior to our aborted rescue attempt'. Saddam Hussein's locations were another target. The success of those efforts makes one sceptical about remote viewing.

But I tried to think of remote viewing, perhaps charitably, as equivalent to the police faced with a frustrated investigation, turning to a medium to locate a body. Much of the programme was operated in a series of shed-like buildings at Fort Meade, Maryland. After the official military programme was ended remote viewing moved into the private sector. Ed Dames established a firm called Psi-Tech that did 'business research', or, put less politely, industrial espionage. For an auto company, for instance, he said his viewers, 'go into this library in the sky if you will, what we call the matrix, the collective unconscious, (and) pull out designs that are Japanese and German.' The 'collective unconscious' – had Dames turned into a practising Jungian?

Other alumni of the programme were less positive. Joseph McMoneagle disparaged Dames. Another veteran, David Morehouse, wrote *Psychic Warrior* (1996) declaring that the Feds had recruited him as a remote viewer then made his life miserable. And an associate professor of political science at Emory University named Courtney Brown, was taught RV by Ed Dames. Brown established an outfit he called the Far Sight Foundation, and claimed to be able to view inside the Oval Office and to visit secret bases on the Moon and Mars. He envisioned our Mars probe being destroyed by defending alien craft. And when Brown appeared on Art Bell's Coast-to-Coast radio show, he suggested that the comet Hale Bopp provided cover for an extraterrestrial spaceship that was heading for our planet.

The Heaven's Gate cult latched on to Brown's idea and stuck out their figurative thumbs to hitch a ride. Before their mass suicide, they visited Las Vegas and played the slots; some may have attended a conference on Area 51 there.

Ford's notion that the camou dudes could remote view, however, was a new one on me. So was the idea that the presence of these remote viewers might take the form of glowing balls. But if the camou dudes had remote viewing, why did they need the video cameras and sensors at the perimeter?

'Does it really work?' I asked Ford.

'Sure, I've been taught how to do it. First, you have to give yourself permission to let yourself invent. And when you understand it's okay to make it up then things start to appear and you say to yourself, "Hey, I didn't make that up."'

And so, I ventured gingerly, 'Can you remotely look over the hills here and see what's on the other side?' I meant over THERE, into the base at Groom Lake, into Area 51, into Dreamland.

'Sure,' she said, as if it were the most natural thing in the world. 'I've been there. It's empty.'

Maybe she was right, whatever she meant by 'empty'. Maybe the secret warriors had folded their tents under cover of night and crept away. Maybe the cuts of the post Cold War years had reduced the role of the base, maybe the glare of publicity had made operations untenable. I remembered the statements a Congressman made at the time of the annexation of Whitesides to the restricted area. The watchers, he said, were a tremendous inconvenience to the men at the base. They had to shut things down, he said, when the watchers appeared. 'It's not fair,' he said, almost petulantly.

Bill Sweetman thought that the cost of doing business in

Dreamland had priced it out of the market – in the new, austere Pentagon, all that security and the expense of moving things in and out was too much. He thought the projects were elsewhere.

'Groom is pretty much useless for Stealthwatchers any more,' Steve had told me a while ago.

Even Dale Brown had dismantled the Dreamland of his fiction: in *Shadows of Steel* (1996), he told how a spy had shot down a super secret plane at HAWC – his imagined 'Hightech Aerospace Weapons Center' at Groom Lake, where inspired mavericks create silver bullets, struggling against the bureaucracy and the brass – leading to the closing of the facility and dispersal of people and equipment.

In another sense of course, it had always been empty, and that was its attraction: the emptiness of mystery. Empty meant you could fill it up with whatever you wanted. We needed it empty: its function was as a container for speculation.

Or maybe we had all emptied it, squeezed out every bit of speculation, overtaxed that humble collection of metal buildings, big hangars and military issue dorms, demanded too much meaning of it.

But in another sense there was more and more inside. Perhaps Dreamland was not empty but full now – it could hold no more speculations or fantasies.

On the Internet, you could hear this sentiment expressed: what would the Interceptors and more distant speculators do if the place was opened up? 'I hope we never find out what's in there,' one of the buffs said in a note he posted, rather wistfully. 'I'd just like to observe something about us Area 51 freaks. As much as we talk about wanting to know what goes on in there, I think that's all just posturing. What would happen if the US government opened its doors to us and let us see all that was going on? Depending on what is there, we'd be either vindicated or disappointed, but we would also rapidly lose interest. What would we focus our attentions on? Where would we go next? ... the greatest thing about Area 51 is its mystery, otherwise nobody would care.'

Some hardcore black plane buffs had been saying for a while now that all the attention on Groom had led the Air Force to shift test programmes elsewhere. To push suspicion to the limit, some speculated that Groom had long been a Potemkin village of a base, designed to draw attention away from somewhere else, to hold down the armies of watchers like Fortitude held down Panzer divisions on the coast of France before D-Day.

Maybe the real projects were going on at some long-rumoured 'new Groom', or 'baby Groom', in Utah, in New Mexico, in Alaska, in Australia. 'The new Groom', speculated on around campfires and in e-mails, became nearly as fabled among the Stealthwatchers as the original, or as El Dorado among the Conquistadors. Was it at Eielson Air Force Base, in Alaska, perhaps, where Agent X now kept his look-out, but whose vastness made Groom look like a mere golf course? Or Pine Gap in Australia, perhaps – several Northrop aero-dynamicists, including the legendary John Cashen, had moved to Australia, rumour had it. To Utah, near Dugway and the dreaded storage area for chemical and germ warfare weapons? One top aviation journalist, who told me everything had been moved from Groom, said, 'we've heard the pulser in the Southeast, out in the swamps.'

Or was it, as Steve had heard, to a new secret base, over the hill from White Sands in New Mexico? We went to look.

Steve had scouted the area and kept discovering downright weird things. He found the Air Force's super camera installation in the hills east of Alamagordo, a camera used to look at satellites, outfitted with lenses so powerful it had been used to look for missing tiles on the space shuttle. He drove up boldly – then dashed down the mountain with guards after him.

Once he stopped at Three Rivers Petroglyph Site, part of the jutting escarpment east of White Sands, and walked up the path from the highway into the hills. The ancient spirals, stars and crosses of the petroglyphs seemed burned into the rock. But further up, at the top of a peak, he came upon the shrine of the Penitentes religious group. Near a large cross, silver jewellery covered the creosote bushes. These were valuable, and must have tempted many, but they were sacred, and it was established among the local populace that this fanatical group, which was rumoured to crucify a living human being each Easter, would not take lightly to their removal.

I had driven down from Albuquerque, across the lava plains

north of the White Sands Missile Range, a few miles north of the Trinity site, where the first atomic bomb was detonated. I passed the northern entrance to the range, called Stallion Gate, and saw a white Blazer with official plates fall in behind me. The driver was speaking into a mike with its corkscrew of cord trailing behind. I imagined him checking up on me and grew nervous for no reason.

I passed through the Valley of Fire, a landscape of rough stones that resembled coral, as if a whole beach of lava had been laid bare by the receding tide. There was a rolling quality to the depressions and outcroppings: you could almost imagine the rock itself as still liquid.

Driving across it, I could understand how day after day of looking at the relentless distance could inspire despair – the depression early settlers felt, and tried to treat with patent medicines, mostly alcohol.

The next day we climbed to the top of the ridge and from the solar observatory above Alamagordu saw the whole valley laid out.

Outside Holloman Air Force Base, where the Aquarius briefings said the saucers had landed for treaty negotiations, Stealth fighters, transferred from Tonopah, trained in daylight now. We parked across from the fence at Holloman. Traffic whizzed by. Seen through binoculars, the base was like a movie rendition of an air base, a terrorist's eye view: tower, water tank, palm trees. The F-117s kept taking off over our heads, mingled with black T-38s. Again and again they came over the highway, fat darts. The shadows slid across the pavement, shimmering with cheap mirages.

The next day we stopped by the local BLM office, in a modern sandstone structure. Three empty government issue office chairs held a conference in the lobby. I noticed that they were the same kind of chairs as in the photographs of the Roswell wreckage, in General Roger Ramey's office. I suspected I was overconnecting again.

Inside, we looked through the sample books, flipping over page after page of the big maps until we found the right ones. Steve focussed on the valley west of the mountains that sheltered Holloman.

We stopped at a Dairy Queen to study the maps. A man

with a tattoo unlike any I had ever seen walked in, a Mexican with a black Mephistolean beard, but contradictorily patient and gentle eyes. I tried not to look at the tattoo directly, but it was irresistible. As I stared at it the image seemed to deepen and become solid. The tattoo showed a shapely woman wearing nothing but a gauzy blouse and bandoliers of cartridges. It shimmered like a printed reproduction of a photograph with big dots – stand far enough back and the image comes to life, the dots disappear: depth establishes itself behind surface, signal overwhelms noise.

I wanted the message of the maps to come clean, to tell us openly whether there was a new base, and where behind the mountains it was hidden.

John Lear had been here searching nearby before us. He thought the new base might be hidden somewhere on the Apache reservation, but found nothing. Half a dozen of them scrambled up a fire lookout tower for a better view. When they got to the top they met a sign that said the tower could only support the weight of two people.

Now we focussed our search on the area of the Oscura Mountains. There was a new restricted air space, number R5107, and we first studied the aeronautical charts, the spaces marked mostly purple and brown, like healing bruises.

We trudged across White Sands, aiming for the tower of the old Northrop Strip, now called 'Space Harbor'. The name dated back to the Star Wars era. A few miles from where atomic energy was first made into a weapon, the Star Warriors planned to send it into space.

All we could see were the tops of its antennas and water tower, which barely peeked above the white dunes of a thousand advertisements, a cliché version of the desert that had stood in for the Sahara, and for Mars.

Steve had been here before, at night. Creeping over the brow of the last dune, whiter than white by moonlight, Steve had seen the base unfold, crisscrossed with beams of light – huge lasers – and dotted with multicoloured lights. Word had it they'd put in the most powerful runway lighting system on the planet. The shuttle astronauts could see it from space. They'd landed here once, when bad weather spoiled the usual landing strips at Edwards or the Cape, and TV crews were kept away from the landing for the first time.

Now, we were foolishly doing it in daytime. We crawled across the sand in a comic reprise of all those beer and car ads shot at White Sands. The more we looked at the maps, the more we drove and wandered through the rippled dunes, the more hopeless and foolish we felt. You would have to have up-to-date satellite photos, and a plane with free access to the air space to have a prayer of finding anything.

23

The White Mailbox

'THIS NEW WORLD ORDER IS QUITE FUCKING REAL,' JOE
Travis said from behind the bar, at the Little A-Le-Inn. A few
minutes later he would be doing an informal karaoke version
of *Little Red Riding Hood* by Sam the Sham and the Pharaohs
playing on the radio. It lent a nice air of menace to his
warning.

But Joe's act was wearing thin. There was a new mood around
the Inn. Tourism in Rachel had become a tired joke – 'Area 51'
was a punchline now – and some of the Interceptors were
becoming embarrassed by the whole thing. The Minister had
had enough of the Interceptor gatherings and Mahood issued
a 'final report' decrying Lazar as a liar and went off to study
physics in graduate school.

Much as they might denounce the abuse of government
secrecy, they had been drawn there by the mystery, and it
seemed to me mystery was now in short supply. That was why
so many TV shows and movies worked so hard to provide it.
Just as wilderness feeds and nurtures a society that is over-
civilized, I theorized one day in the car, mystery nurtures a
society that is over-informed. It occurred to me that the
unknown and unpredictable were rarer and rarer qualities in
our world of vast information storage and retrieval systems, of
sophisticated planning, scheduling and prediction. We had a
fundamental need for uncertainty.

But secrecy did not necessarily provide uncertainty or
mystery. In the spring of 1997, a report from a Congressional
committee that brought together such odd bedfellows as Jesse
Helms, Pat Moynihan and Lee Hamilton proposed declassifying
anything older than ten years, with the usual 'special excep-
tions'. The committee estimated that there were some one and
a half billion pages of classified documents more than a quarter

of a century old. It was a huge time capsule, requiring expensive maintenance.

The usual talk of means of 'penetrating' the perimeter continued: a model plane, a balloon, even a radio-controlled model car run along the road. The Air Force's New Vistas report suggested just the thing: it looked to tiny robot craft – 'micro aerial vehicles' a few inches long – mechanical dragon flies.

Norio Hayakawa had his own scheme. He began talking of a 'million-man march' to the perimeter. It would take place, he told me, on 6 June 1998 – with its multiple sixes when something dark and dangerous would probably happen. 1998, he calculated, was 666 multiplied by three and June 6 to Norio was not the anniversary of D-Day but the significant sixth day of the sixth month.

One Saturday in late April, 1997 four SUVs pulled out of Rachel and drove north on Highway 375. About twenty miles north of the town, they turned left on a gravel road, rambled toward Dreamland and pulled up to the new perimeter line of the restricted area.

Some twenty kids emerged and began hauling easels and canvases for painting up the hills. They established themselves in a neat line, close to the perimeter fence and set up their easels, each about six feet away from their neighbour. They spent five hours painting landscape views: deadpan, Sunday painters.

They were young artists and art students directed by a man named Joel Slayton, who taught at San Jose State University, there to collaborate on what Slayton called 'a site-specific conceptual artwork involving landscape painting as counter-surveillance of Area 51.'

The camou dudes trained their binoculars on them, making Slayton feel a little creepy. What they must have made of it one can only imagine. It must have been another case of 'this job just gets weirder every week'.

The painters were members of 'the CADRE Institute (Computers in Art and Design/Research and Education)' who thought deep thoughts about the nature of art and information and how computers figured into art. They were pursuing the dumb old-fashioned technique of landscape painting in oils and acrylics. 'The resulting installation of easels and paintings stood alone as a sculptural manifestation atop the bluff.' Slayton eloquently put it in his write-up of the event.

Now Dreamland drew artists, who drew it.

Slayton's official manifesto declared that, 'The social banality of landscape painting and painters was strategized to be used as a mean of counter-surveillance by the surveyed, serving as a no threat typology of threat. In this context the artists demonstrate a perception of art as safe and innocuous, permissible and lacking in relevant information content. The need to surveil such activity is both necessary and unnecessary simultaneously.'

The camou dudes had been, in effect, drawn into serving as artists themselves, Slayton's argument went, 'serving as a critical agent to assess the significance of the event and resulting information liability.'

The poor dudes.

The whole exercise, he proclaimed, constituted 'critical discourse on the nature of information culture and information systems.' It also seemed a pretty good parody of us serious watchers of the area.

He kept calling the place a simulacrum. 'Area 51 is a simulacrum,' he said. No longer a real place, I guess, but 'a reality constituted from a media folklore, super secrecy and the government's denial of its very existence'. It existed 'only as pure simulation, constructed from the voluminous de-centralized and publicly assessable [I think he meant 'accessible'] information that surrounds what might be there.' It was a 'composited identity formed of electronic networks, e-mail correspondence and media folklore'.

'Area 51's notoriety as a physical and virtual tourist attraction provides a cultural experience as information simulation ripe with conspiracy theory, Hollywood style potentialities and the guarantee of being surveilled.[sic]'

Whew – that struck me as pretty much critical discourse on those who looked at Dreamland as seriously as I did, or the millions for whom it had become a point of reference like the Bermuda Triangle.

The paintings were hauled back down to Psychospy's trailer – the 'Research Center', and put on sale for $51.51, with a 51 per cent commission going to the research centre. Buyers of the paintings were asked to document the location in which the painting was hung and to 'engage in dialog' about the whole experience, via e-mail.

But one frequent visitor to the perimeter who saw the group grew suspicious. He was sure they were some sort of security force themselves. They had short hair, he noted, and looked like camou dudes. If they were painters, he said, then he was a B-1 pilot.

What was it about Dreamland that turned everyone into a philosopher? Dreamland's incorporation into an elevated work of art made me speculate again about just how artful its own deceptions were. One might conclude with Norio that the whole thing was a brilliantly artful deception.

But art was about concealment too. Artists had invented camouflage, created the very stuff the dudes one side of the perimeter wore and the Interceptors on the other side wore – the original 'low observables'.

During World War I, Picasso and Braque stood on the side-walk, watching tanks and other camouflaged vehicles roll through the streets of Paris. 'Look,' Picasso said, '*we* are the ones who did that.'

'Pattern recognition is what you have to be concerned about,' one camouflage expert once told me. 'You don't have to see a whole car to recognize a Cadillac; the tailfin is enough.'

For deception was surely artful.

It was all about suggesting multiple viewpoints. Dis-information could work the same way, by providing the hints of other possibilities. Multiple viewpoints, multiple possibilities – that was all that was needed to create noise, to disguise the real signal.

Physical camouflage offered a perfect model for the larger deception. The principles at work there were the same as the principles of secrecy; breaking up the shape into parts was the equivalent of compartmentalization – the same strategy as 'need to know'. Burying the important in the mundane, and burying black programmes under bureaucratic terminology such as 'advanced research activities' was the equivalent of painting the black programme in grey officialese language, or hiding a black programme among white ones.

At the time I began spending more time on the Net tracking stealth chasers and youfers, one day, on impulse, I did a search – and typed in one word: 'Dreamland'. The Internet, even then, was already well dotted with UFO and black plane links and sites, but only one reference came back: to Edgar Allan Poe's poem, stashed away in a university collection of great works of literature.

> By a route obscure and lonely,
> Haunted by ill angels only,
> Where an Eidolon, named NIGHT,
> On a black throne reigns upright,
> I have reached these lands but newly
> From an ultimate dim Thule
>
> From a wild clime that lieth, sublime,
> Out of SPACE – out of TIME.
>
> Bottomless vales and boundless floods,
> And chasms, and caves, and Titan woods.
> With forms that no man can discover
>
> For the spirit that walks in shadow
> 'Tis-oh, 'tis an Eldorado!
> But the traveller, travelling through it,
> May not – dare not openly view it!
> Never its mysteries are exposed
> To the weak human eye unclosed;
> So wills its King, who hath forbid
> The uplifting of the fringed lid;
> And thus the sad Soul that here passes
> Beholds it but through darkened glasses.

Poe was the patron poet of Dreamland. In *The Power of Blackness*, my old professor Harry Levin had written, 'Poe seemed at home only in Dreamland.' He dreamed, another critic has written – quoting a famous phrase of the poet's – of 'a happier star'. He was one of those 'Southern gothic' writers who W. J. Cash described, in a great phrase, as 'romantics of the appalling'. Romantic and appalling – that fits what had happened in Dreamland, Nevada.

'The weak human eye unclosed' or 'darkened glasses' evoked long camera lenses or night vision devices. 'Haunted by ill angels' – there was the U-2, Kelly's Angel, and whatever other strange winged objects you wished. 'Out of Space – out of Time – ' there was Lazar's description of the saucer propulsion system, just stretching the space-time continuum, warping gravity, like a hammock's net.

There was even the dry lake itself, I began to fantasize, in the 'Lakes that endlessly outspread/Their lone waters, lone and dead.' And – warming now to the job like a conspiracist making connections, I latched on to the 'fringed lid'. A playful look at the security 'lid', to be sure, and the fringe groups who visited there.

There were even stories that the Poe poem had been the inspiration for the tower control name – suggesting that sitting out in an isolated base leads to more reading than might otherwise be expected of military types.

Thinking about Poe, too, carried me back to Freedom Ridge, and what I saw flying in the air space of Dreamland – ravens. Poe's totemic bird. My mind leapt to the raven I had seen in another place I had visited shortly before, another space that was closed off but visible, another black box: Poe's own room, at the University of Virginia, in Charlottesville.

It was the room where young Poe had lived in 1826, while studying at the university, before he was expelled for gambling debts. The wooden door has been replaced with glass doors, floor to ceiling like those in a bank or department store. Visitors push a button and the blackness inside is replaced with a dim light. You see a crude rope bed with Jacquard coverlet, a desk, a pen and – some historical licence – a stuffed raven. A black bird in an almost black room.

The room was set in the mews, the side of the buildings facing away from the Great Lawn, a less desirable part of the university, with a feel of being half buried – very Poe like. And the preservation of that room, as a viewable but unreachable space, part-memorial, part-exhibit, struck me like the Groom Box itself. The room, I thought, was like the whole black world – a special exception, a dark chamber in the white and stately colonnade of American life and polity. Thinking about Poe's room, I thought I understood where this dark vision fits into the idea of American order. Like the secret vaults in the capital where SAR programmes were reviewed – a heart of darkness behind the bright classical facade, like the Black Mailbox itself.

One day, I was heading back up the road toward Rachel in the summer, catching a glimpse from Hancock summit of the same hazy hovering white stick of road that led up the base. As the road curled around and began its long subtle dip – the Mailbox Road stretch – I settled back into the familiar unfolding of the landscape, the range of Jumbled Hills to the west.

Coming down the big dip toward Mailbox Road something caught my eye and I nearly drove off the road: the black mailbox was white now!

It was no longer the standard rural route job approved by the US Postal Service, but a box of heavy steel, locked with a bright brass padlock. Steve Medlin, the rancher, had stencilled his name and the route in black.

I had to pull over, and walked up to it and all around, noticing that someone had stencilled a tiny black skunk on the back – a wry comment, saying this thing is built like the Skunk Works would do it. But it was white, white as the camou dudes' Jeeps, white as Darkstar, white as the famous whale.

At the Little A-Le-Inn I asked about it. 'He got tired of people shooting at it,' Joe Travis said of Medlin. 'Shooting up his mail and all. Made a new one out of quarter inch steel plate. Now it would take a thirty-ought six.' And snorted a little laugh.

The steel might resist, but the white couldn't. Soon after it went up someone came by and spray-painted the new box black. Medlin repainted it. I got the idea this could be going on for quite some time.

There was a black mailbox out in front of the Inn now, but Joe said it was just a replica. A replica! I asked what had happened to the original. A man on the stool beside me said that it had been sent to be auctioned off a while ago, to raise money for town recreation, but that a producer from Hollywood had come in and pre-empted the sale with an offer of fifteen hundred bucks. This seemed appropriate, but, as with so much in Dreamland, it proved impossible to determine conclusively.

Bibliography

ASSEMBLING THESE AUTHORS AND TITLES, I WAS STRUCK WITH A mischievous sense of how the accidents of alphabetization put sworn enemies side by side, pose the conspiracist beside the technologist – a further reminder of how weirdly disparate are the little Dreamlands so many viewers have created. It's as if all were lined up – on Freedom Ridge, say – for a group photo. Many listed here may feel like the school kid, stuck beside the bully who jams an elbow into his ribs at the moment the class picture immortalizes you all. All editions are American except where indicated.

BOOKS

Aftergood, Steven, Pike, John, Preslar, Dorothy and Tyler, Tiffany. *Mystery Aircraft*. Federation of American Scientists, 1992.

Andrews, George C. *Extra-Terrestrials Among Us*. Fate/Llewellyn Publications, 1993.

Bamford, James. *The Puzzle Palace: A Report on America's Most Secret Agency*. Houghton Mifflin, 1982.

Berlitz, Charles and Moore, William L. *The Roswell Incident*. G. P. Putnam's, 1980.

Beschloss, Michael R. *Mayday: Eisenhower, Khrushchev and the U-2 Affair*. Harper & Row, 1986.

Bissell Jr., Richard M. with Lewis, Jonathan E., and Pudlo, Frances T. *Reflections of a Cold Warrior, From Yalta to the Bay of Pigs*. Yale University Press, 1996.

Blum, Howard. *Out There: The Government's Secret Quest for Extraterrestrials*. Simon & Schuster, 1990.

Boyer, Paul. *By the Bomb's Early Light: American Thought and Culture at the Dawn of the Atomic Age*. Pantheon, 1985. 2nd edn, University of North Carolina Press, 1994.

Brown, Courtney. *Cosmic Voyage: A Scientific Discovery of Extraterrestrials Visiting Earth.* E. P. Dutton, 1996.

Brown, Dale, *Sky Masters.* Donald I. Fine/G. P. Putnam's, 1991.

Brugioni, Dino A. *Eyeball to Eyeball: The Inside Story of the Cuban Missile Crisis.* Random House, 1991.

Bryan, C. D. B. *Close Encounters of the Fourth Kind: Alien Abduction, UFOs, and the Conference at M.I.T.* Alfred Knopf, 1995.

Buderi, Robert. *The Invention That Changed the World.* Simon & Schuster, 1996.

Burrows, William. *Deep Black.* Random House, 1986.

Campbell, Glenn. *The Area 51 Viewer's Guide.* Self published, 1993.

Campbell, Glenn. *A Short History of Rachel.* Self published, 1996.

Clark, Chuck. *The Area 51 and S-4 Handbook.* Self published, 1995.

Coolidge, Matthew/The Center for Land Use Interpretation. *The Nuclear Test Site: A Guide to America's Nuclear Proving Ground.* The Center for Land Use Interpretation, 1996.

Cooper, William. *Behold a Pale Horse.* Light Technology Press, 1993.

Crickmore, Paul F. *Lockheed SR-71: The Secret Missions Exposed.* Osprey, London, 1993.

Crystal, Ellen. *Silent Invasion.* St. Martin's, 1991.

Curran, Douglas. *In Advance of the Landing: Folk Concepts of Outer Space.* Abbeville Press, 1985.

DeLanda, Manual. *War in the Age of Intelligent Machines.* Zone/MIT Press, 1991.

Douglass, Steve. *The Complete Guide to Military Monitoring.* Universal Electronics, 1993.

Fawcett, Lawrence and Greenwood, Barry J. *The UFO Cover-up.* Prentice Hall, 1984.

Flammonde, Paris. *The Age of Flying Saucers: Notes on a Projected History of Unidentified Flying Objects.* Hawthorn Books, 1971.

Franklin, H. Bruce. *War Stars: The Superweapon and American Imagination.* Oxford University Press, Oxford, 1988.

Friedman, Stanton T. and Berliner, Don. *Crash at Corona: The Definitive Study of the Roswell Incident.* Marlowe & Company, 1992.

Friedman, Stanton T. *Top Secret/Majic.* Marlowe & Company, 1996.

Fuller, John G. *The Day We Bombed Utah: America's Most Lethal Secret.* New American Library, 1984.

Giangreco, D. M. *Stealth Fighter Pilot.* Motorbooks International, 1993.

Goin, Peter. *Nuclear Landscapes.* Johns Hopkins Press, 1991.

Good, Timothy. *Above Top Secret: The Worldwide UFO Cover-Up.* William Morrow, 1988.

Good, Timothy. *Alien Contact: Top-Secret UFO Files Revealed.* William Morrow, 1993. (First published as *Alien Liaison: The Ultimate Secret.* Random Century Group, London, 1991.)

Goodall, James. *America's Stealth Fighters and Bombers.* Motorbooks International, 1992.

Goodall, James. *SR-71 Blackbird.* Squadron/Signal Publications, 1995.

Graham, Richard H. *SR-71 Revealed: the Inside Story.* Motorbooks International, 1996.

Haines, Richard F., ed. *UFO Phenomena and the Behavioral Scientist.* Scarecrow Press, New Jersey and London, 1979.

Hall, George. *Nellis: the Home of 'Red Flag'.* Osprey, 1988.

Hallion, Richard P. *Test Pilots: The Frontiersmen of Flight.* Smithsonian Institution Press, 1988.

Hamilton III, William F. *Cosmic Top Secret: America's Secret UFO Program.* Inner Light Publications, 1991.

Hesemann, Michael and Mantle, Philip. *Beyond Roswell: The Alien Autopsy Film, Area 51, and the US Government Cover-up of UFOs.* Marlowe & Company, 1997.

Hofstadter, Richard. *The Paranoid Style in American Politics.* Vintage, 1965.

Jacobs, David. *The UFO Controversy in America.* Indiana University Press, 1975.

Johnson, Clarence L. 'Kelly' with Smith, Maggie. *Kelly: More Than My Share of It All.* Smithsonian Institution Press, 1985.

Jones, J. *Stealth Technology: The Art of Black Magic.* Aero Books.

Jung, C. G. *Flying Saucers: A Modern Myth of Things Seen in the Skies.* Trans. R. F. C. Hull. Princeton University Press, 1964.

Keyhoe, Major Donald. *The Flying Saucers Are Real.* Fawcett, 1950.

Keyhoe, Major Donald. *The Flying Saucer Conspiracy.* Henry Holt, 1955.

Klass, Philip J. *UFOs Explained.* Random House, 1974.

LeMay, Curtis with Kantor, McKinley, *Mission With LeMay.* Doubleday, 1965.

Lindemann, Michael, ed. *UFOs and the Alien Presence: Six Viewpoints.* The 2020 Group, Visitors Investigation Project, 1991.

Lynes, William. *Space Aliens from the Pentagon: Flying Saucers are Man-made Electrical Machines.* Creatopia Productions, 1993.

Marrs, Jim. *Alien Agenda.* Harper Collins, 1997.

McCracken, Robert D. *A History of Tonopah Nevada.* Nye County Press, 1990.

Miller, Jay. *Lockheed Martin Skunk Works: The Official History.* Aerofax, 1993. Rev. edn Midland Publishing, Leicester, 1995.

Miller, Jay. *Lockheed's Skunk Works: The First Fifty Years – The Official History.* Aerofax Inc., 1993.

Pace, Steve. *Lockheed Skunk Works.* Motorbooks International, 1992.

Peebles, Curtis. *The Moby Dick Project.* Smithsonian Institution Press, 1991.

Peebles, Curtis. *Watch the Skies! A Chronicle of the Flying Saucer Myth.* Smithsonian Institution Press, 1994.

Peebles, Curtis. *Dark Eagles: A History of Top Secret US Aircraft Programs.* Presidio Press, 1995.

Pocock, Chris. *Dragon Lady: the History of the U-2 Spyplane.* Motorbooks International, 1989.

Powers, Francis Gary with Gentry, Curt. *Operation Overflight.* Holt Rinehart Winston, 1970.

Randle, Kevin D. and Schmitt, Donald R. *UFO Crash at Roswell.* Avon, 1991.

Rashke, Richard. *Stormy Genius: the Life of Aviation's Maverick, Bill Lear.* Houghton Mifflin, 1975.

Rhodes, Richard. *The Making of the Atomic Bomb.* Simon & Schuster, 1986.

Rhodes, Richard. *Dark Sun.* Simon & Schuster, 1995.

Rich, Ben R. with Janos, Leo. *Skunk Works: A Personal Memoir of My Years at Lockheed.* Little, Brown and Company, 1994.

Richelson, Jeffrey. *The US Intelligence Community.* Ballinger, 1985.

Richelson, Jeffrey. *American Espionage and the Soviet Target.* William Morrow, 1987.

Saler, Benson, Ziegler, Charles A. and Moore, Charles B. *UFO Crash at Roswell: The Genesis of a Modern Myth.* Smithsonian Institution Press, 1997.

Saudek, Robert. *Underground Bases and Tunnels: What is the Government Trying to Hide?* Adventures Unlimited Press, 1995.

De Seversky, Alexander P. *Victory Through Air Power.* Simon & Schuster, 1942.

Sherry, Michael. *The Rise of American Air Power: The Creation of Armageddon*. Yale University Press, 1987.

Shils, Edward A. *The Torment of Secrecy: The Background and Consequences of American Security Policies*. Ivan R. Dee, 1996.

Shul, Brian and Watson Jr., Walter. *The Untouchables Mission Accomplished*. Mach I Inc., 1991.

Simonsen, Erik. *This is Stealth: The F-117 and B-2 – in Color*. Greenhill Books, 1992.

Skinner, Michael and Hall, George. *Red Flag Air Combat for the 1990's*. 2nd edn, Motorbooks International, 1993.

Solnit, Rebecca. *Savage Dreams*. Sierra Club Press, 1994.

Steinbeck, John. *Bombs Away: The Story of a Bomber Team*. Viking, 1942.

Strieber, Whitley. *Majestic*. Putnam's, 1989.

Sweetman, Bill. *Stealth Aircraft: Secrets of Future Airpower*. Motorbooks International, 1986.

Sweetman, Bill. *Stealth Bomber, Invisible Warplane, Black Budget*. Motorbooks International, 1989.

Goodall, James and Sweetman, Bill. *Lockheed F-117A: Operation and Development of the Stealth Fighter*. Motorbooks International, 1990.

Sweetman, Bill. *Aurora: The Pentagon's Secret Hypersonic Spyplane*. Motorbooks International, 1993.

Thomas, Evan. *The Very Best Men: Four Who Dared – The Early Years of the CIA*. Simon & Schuster, 1995.

Thomas, Kenn ed. *Popular Alienation: A Steamshovel Press Reader*. IllumiNet Press, 1995.

Thompson, Keith. *Angels and Aliens: UFOs and the Mythic Imagination*. Addison Wesley, 1992.

Titus, A. Costandina. *Bombs in the Backyard: Atomic Testing and American Politics*. University of Nevada Press, 1986.

US Air Force, US Bureau of Land Management. *Draft Environmental Impact Statement, Groom Mountain Range, Lincoln County, Nevada*. October, 1985.

US Department of Energy, Nevada Operations Office, Las Vegas, Nevada. *Draft Environmental Impact Statement for the Nevada Test Site and Off-site Locations in the State of Nevada*. January, 1996.

US Department of the Air Force. *AFP 205–37. Preparing Security Classification Guides*. 1991.

Vesco, Renato and Childress, David Hatcher. *Man Made UFOs 1944–1994: 50 Years of Suppression.* Adventures Unlimited Press, 1994.

Weiner, Tim. *Blank Check.* Warner Books, 1991.

Welch, John F. ed. *36 Days At Rapid City,* Silver Wings Aviation Inc., 1994.

Wheeler, Lt. George M. *Preliminary Report Concerning Explorations and Surveys, Principally in Nevada and Arizona.* US Army Corps of Engineers, 1872.

Wilcox, Robert. *Scream of Eagles.* John Wiley, 1990.

Wilcox, Robert. *Wings of Fury.* Pocket Books, 1996.

Wills, Garry. *Reagan's America: Innocents At Home.* Doubleday, 1985.

Wolf, Fred Alan. *Parallel Universes.* Touchstone/Simon & Schuster, 1988.

PERIODICALS

Basagio, Andrew D., 'Area 51 and the CIA', *MUFON UFO Journal.* July 1992, No. 291, pp 10–12.

Boylan, Richard J., 'Secret "Saucer" Sites', *MUFON UFO Journal.* August 1992, No. 292, pp 14–15.

Broad, William J. 'Wreckage in the Desert was Odd but Not Alien', *New York Times.* 18 September 1994, pp 1, 40.

Brown, Stuart, 'Searching for Groom Lake's Secrets', *Popular Science.* March 1994, pp 52–54, 84–85.

Brown, Stuart and Douglass, Steve, 'Swing Wing Stealth Attack Plane', *Popular Science.* January 1995, pp 54–6, 86.

Castro, Jane, 'Grapevine', *Time.* 25 May 1992.

Dornheim, Michael, 'United 747 Crew Reports Near-Collision With Mysterious Supersonic Aircraft', *Aviation Week and Space Technology.* 24 August 1992, p. 24.

Douglass, Steve, 'Flying Artichoke', *Popular Science.* December 1994, p. 16.

Fialka, John J., 'Clinton to Disclose Tab for Spying, Propose Overhaul', *Wall Street Journal.* 24 April 1996, p. 1.

Fulghum, David A., 'Groom Lake Tests Target Stealth', *Aviation Week and Space Technology.* 5 February 1996, pp 26–27.

Fulghum, David A., 'Payload. Not Airframe Drives UCAV Research Oversight', *Aviation Week and Space Technology.* 2 June 1997, pp 51–53.

Green, Marian, 'Unions Win Representation Elections For Workers At Groom Lake', *Las Vegas Review Journal*. 17 February 1996.

Haines, Gerald, 'A Die Hard Issue: CIA's Role in the Study of UFOs, 1947–90', *Studies in Intelligence*. Central Intelligence Agency, Langley, Virginia.

Humphrey, Fred L., 'Geology of the Groom District Lincoln County Nevada. Nevada State Bureau of Mines', *University of Nevada Bulletin*. June 1945, Vol. XXXIX No. 5.

Jacobs, Margaret A., 'Secret Air Base Broke Hazardous-Waste Act, Worker's Suit Alleges', *The Wall Street Journal*. 8 February 1996, p. 1.

Kuznik, Frank, 'Aliens in the Basement', *Air & Space*. August/September 1992, pp 34–39.

Lear, John, 'The Grand Deception: How the Gray EBE's Tricked MJ-12 into an Agreement'. *CUFORN Bulletin*. March/April 1989.

Matthews, Samuel W., 'Nevada Learns to Live with the Atom', *National Geographic*. August 1953, pp 839–850.

McInnich, Thomas P., 'Studies in Intelligence', Central Intelligence Agency. Winter 1970–71.

McQuiston, John T., 'Plot Against L. I. Leaders is Tied to Fear of UFO's', *New York Times*. 22 June 1996.

Paine, Gary, 'A Mine, the Military and a Dry Lake: National Security and the Groom District, Lincoln County', *Nevada Historical Society Quarterly*. Vol. 39 No. 1 pp 20–42.

Rothenberg, Randall, 'Area 51, Where Are You?' *Esquire*. September 1996, pp 88–97.

Schumach, Murray, 'Disks Soar Over New York, Now Seen Aloft in All Colors', *New York Times*. 8 July 1947, pp 1, 46.

Schumach, Murray, '"Disk" Near Bomb Test Site Is Just a Weather Balloon', *New York Times*. 9 July 1947, pp 1, 10.

Scott, William B., 'Black Projects Must Balance Cost, Time Savings with Public Oversight', *Aviation Week and Space Technology*. 18 December 1989, pp 42–3.

Scott, William B., 'New Evidence Bolsters Reports of Secret, High-speed Aircraft', *Aviation Week and Space Technology*. 11 May 1992, p. 62.

Scott, William B., 'Recent Sightings of XB-70-Like Aircraft Reinforce 1990 Reports from Edwards Area', *Aviation Week and Space Technology*. 24 August 1992, pp 23–4.

Scott, William B., 'Secret Aircraft Encompasses Qualities of High-Speed Launcher for Spacecraft', *Aviation Week and Space Technology.* 24 August 1992, p. 25.

Sweetman, Bill. 'The Invisible Men', *Air and Space.* May 1997, pp 19–27.

Webster, Donovan, 'Area 51', *New York Times Magazine.* 26 June 1994, p. 32.

Weir, Christopher, 'Paint It Black', *Metro.* 9–15 January 1997.

Williams, James A., 'Scanning "Area 51"', *Popular Communications.* April 1995, p. 8.

UNATTRIBUTED PERIODICALS

'Scientists' and engineers' dreams taking to skies as "black" aircraft', *Aviation Week and Space Technology.* 24 December 1990.

'Possible "Black" Aircraft Seen Flying in Formation With F-117s, KC-135s', *Aviation Week and Space Technology.* 9 March 1992, pp 66–7.

'Groom Lake Desert Rat', Glenn Campbell, 1993.

'Tesla at 78 Bares New "Death-Beam"', *New York Times.* 11 July 1934.

'Eisenhower Plays Golf on Vacation', *New York Times.* 20 February 1954.

'The Mystery at Groom Lake', *Newsweek.* 1 November 1993, p. 4.

'America's New Secret Aircraft', *Popular Mechanics.* December 1991.

'Secrecy and Government Bulletin', Federation of American Scientists, 1993.

WEB SITES

Keeping up with new discoveries in Dreamland is best done through sites on the World Wide Web. The following are the most useful and all contain links to other sites of interest:

Glenn Campbell's exhaustive and indispensable Area 51 and UFO site:
   http://www.ufomind.com/area51/

Steve Douglass's Project Black site on black aircraft, plus the Intercepts newsletter:
   http://www.perseods.com/projectblack/

The Federation of American Scientists: http://www.fas.org/

Dan Zinngrabe's site with extensive histories of Aurora, the TR3A, and Tier III:
http://www.macconnect.com/-quellish

Andreas Gehrs-Pahl's extensive aviation site:
http://www.umcc.umich.edu/-schnars/aero.htm

Paul McGinniss ('Trader') and the Freedom Ridge Oversight Council:
http://www.frogi.org/

Index